Agricultural Terracing
in the
Aboriginal New World

VIKING FUND PUBLICATIONS IN ANTHROPOLOGY
Number Fifty-Six   Arthur J. Jelinek, *Editor*

Agricultural Terracing
in the
Aboriginal New World

R. A. DONKIN

Published for The Wenner-Gren Foundation for Anthropological Research, Inc.

The University of Arizona Press   Tucson, Arizona

About the Author . . .

R. A. Donkin, Fellow of Jesus College and University Lecturer in the Geography of Latin America at Cambridge University, has also held teaching appointments at the Universities of Edinburgh, Birmingham, and Toronto and a research fellowship at the University of California at Berkeley. His major research interest outside the field of Latin American geography has been in the work of the Cistercian Order in medieval Europe. In addition to numerous journal articles, Donkin's publications include a *Bibliography of the Cistercian Order* (Documentation Cistercienne, Rochfort, 1969) and two recent monographs: *Spanish Red: an ethnogeographical study of cochineal and the opuntia cactus* (American Philosophical Society, Philadelphia, 1977), and *The Cistercians: studies in the geography of medieval England and Wales* (Pontifical Institute of Mediaeval Studies, Toronto, 1978).

THE UNIVERSITY OF ARIZONA PRESS

Library of Congress Cataloging in Publication Data

Donkin, R   A
    Agricultural terracing in the Aboriginal new world.

    (Viking Fund publications in anthropology; no. 56)
    Bibliography: p.
    Includes index.
    1. Indians — Agriculture.   2. Terracing — America.
I. Wenner-Gren Foundation for Anthropological Research,
New York.   II. Title.   III. Series.
E59.A35D66   333.7'6'097   77-15120
ISBN 0-8165-0453-9 pbk.

CONTENTS

ILLUSTRATIONS

FIGURES

DIAGRAMS

MAPS

PREFACE AND ACKNOWLEDGMENTS

The subject of agricultural terracing has been strangely neglected by students of the cultural landscape. In the New World, terracing is both old and extensive, and it is plainly relevant to current enquiries into the history of water control, plant improvement and, more generally, the intensification of land use in association with the growth of population. In opposite circumstances, large tracts of terraced land have been permanently abandoned.

The present volume is a preliminary study, inviting work at the regional and the local scale. Archaeological investigations are beginning to yield important results. The potentially useful written sources are almost inexhaustible, but, so far as I have been able to discover, agricultural terracing is mentioned all too rarely in early accounts of the New World.

My investigations in Middle and South America occupied the greater part of 1966 and six months in 1969.

Over the former period I was privileged to hold a Leverhulme Research Fellowship. In Mexico, the late Dr. Alfonso Caso generously supplied introductions to the field centres of the Instituto Nacional Indigenista at Tlaxiaco and San Cristóbal de Las Casas. The libraries to which I am indebted include those of the Universities of Cambridge, Texas and Toronto, the British Museum, the Royal Anthropological Institute (London) and the Museo Nacional de Antropología (Mexico).

I owe much to the Wenner-Gren Foundation for Anthropological Research, the sponsors of this volume; also to the care and patience of the present editor of the Viking Fund series and of the publishers, the University of Arizona Press; and, finally, to former colleagues at the University of California, Berkeley, who first turned my interests toward the aboriginal New World.

R. A. D.

PART I: ASPECTS OF INDIAN AGRICULTURE IN THE HIGHLANDS OF MIDDLE AND SOUTH AMERICA

PRE-HISPANIC AGRICULTURE

Some important features of pre-Columbian agriculture are beyond dispute. In the first place, there is the striking contrast between the success of the Indian as a plant breeder and his poor record in the matter of animal domestication. Draft animals were unknown and cultivation involved the use of only hand implements. This limited the scale, the level of organization and, to some extent, the distribution of native agriculture, but not necessarily its variety and quality, which ranged from shifting cultivation of the most extensive kind, through various fallowing procedures, to horticulture and the permanent use of irrigated land. The Spaniards were impressed by the horticultural skills of the Indians of central Mexico.[1] Agricultural labor was also esteemed in Inca Peru.[2]

Highland communities particularly were often in a position to exploit several distinct habitats[3] and to combine intensive with extensive methods of husbandry. The more advanced techniques employed, capable of producing a regular surplus of foodstuffs, included irrigation and terracing and comparatively small areas of swamp farming.[4] Whether such agricultural progress preceded or broadly accompanied the rise of classic urbanism in the first millennium A.D. is not entirely clear;[5] but terracing, with and without irrigation, has been associated with evidence of increasing population, and later comparatively high densities, in northwest Argentina,[6] central Peru,[7] the Sierra Nevada de Santa Marta,[8] southern Guatemala,[9] the Vaca plateau of British Honduras,[10] and several parts of Mexico: Chiapas,[11] the valley of Oaxaca,[12] the Mixteca Alta,[13] and the valley of Mexico.[14]

The maintenance of soil fertility: The need to maintain or to restore soil fertility was met, in different parts of the New World, by manuring, fallowing, systems of rotation, and by mixed cropping.

Regular applications of organic matter are particularly desirable under arid and semi-arid conditions.[15] Very intensive forms of manuring were practiced in the valley oases of coastal Peru. Sixteenth- and seventeenth-century writers refer to the planting of fish *(anchovas, sardinas)* or fish heads with seeds of maize,[16] and guano from the offshore islands was an important source of

1. Cortés (1524), 2, 1908, 201; Anon. (c. 1530), 1917, 16, 37; López de Gómara (1552), 2, 1954, 138; Cervantes de Salazar (1560-75), 2, 1914-36, 24; Sahagún (c. 1570), 10, 1961, 41-42; Pomar (1582), 1891, 53-58; Alva Ixtlilxochitl (c. 1640), 2, 1892, 210. The "botanical gardens" of the Aztec nobility (Gerste, 1909, 57-80; Maldonado-Koerdell, 1941, 79-84, and 1942, 62-74; Langman, 1956, 17-31) are evidence of a special interest in the plant world. At least as early as 1536, Old World fruit trees were being grafted on native stocks (Cline, 1968, 133-35).

2. Prado, 1941, 36-38; Gibson, 1948, 44, 96; Karsten, 1949, 93. Cf. Las Casas (1527-59), I, 1958, 200.

3. Murra (1967, 1968, 1972, 1975) has emphasized "the vertical control of diverse ecologies" by Andean communities in the sixteenth century and earlier. Regional as well as local differences in environment were exploited through dependent colonies *(mitmaqkuna)*. See also Webster, 1971, 55-64; Fioravanti-Molinié, 1975, 35-57.

4. On "advanced" agriculture generally, see Carrasco, 1960, 42; G. Reichel-Dolmatoff, 1961, 84; Willey *et al.,* 1964, 448; Sanders and Price, 1968, 86-94.

5. S. F. Cook, 1947-8, 49; W. C. Bennett, 1946b, 106; Dumond, 1961, 312; Towle, 1961, 143; Borhegyi, 1965a, 30, and 1965b, 65; Jiménez Moreno, 1966, 30; Willey, 1966b, 274.

6. Bennett and Bird, 1949, 88.

7. Collier, 1955, 23.

8. G. Reichel-Dolmatoff, 1950, 96, and 1961, 88.

9. Borhegyi, 1959, 108, and 1965b, 65.

10. Lundell, 1940, 11.

11. L. E. Guzmán, 1962, 400.

12. Paddock, 1966, 235; Flannery *et al.,* 1967, 451-53.

13. Spores, 1969, 560-63.

14. Wolf and Palerm, 1955, 273. H. O. Wagner (1969, 193) associates terracing with high population densities in Mexico generally c. 1500.

15. Kellogg, 1953, 28.

16. Cieza de León (c. 1550), 1864, 255; Cristóbal de Molina (c. 1552), 1968, 67; Las Casas (1527-59), I, 1958, 200; Jiménez de la Espada (ed) (1570), I, 1965, 154; Lizárraga (c. 1600), 1968, 42; Dorantes de Carranza (1604), 1902, 73; Garcilaso de la Vega (1604), 1871, 10-13; Torquemada (1615), 2, 1723, 482; Vázquez de Espinosa (c. 1628), 1942, no. 1332.

nitrate from the Mochica period if not earlier.[17] Under the Incas "each island was . . . set apart for the use of a particular province or, if the island was large, it served two or three provinces."[18] In the middle of the sixteenth century, according to Cieza de León (1518-60), the size of the maize harvest in the *hoyas* depended on the use of guano.[19] Llama trains carried it into the Sierra,[20] where dried and pulverized human waste was also used.[21] Garcilaso de la Vega (1539-1616) associated this with the cultivation of maize, irrigation and terracing *(andenes),*[22] while "throughout the Collao . . . where it was too cold to grow maize, potatoes and pulses [were manured] with the dung of llamas."[23]

In Colombia, neither the Chibcha of the *altiplano* nor the farmers of the sub-Andean chiefdoms are known to have used fertilizer.[24] Diego de Landa (1524-79) observed that the Yucatan Maya did "nothing except collect together refuse and burn it in order to sow afterwards."[25] The peoples of central Mexico used human, animal and green manure, and almost certainly domestic refuse was deliberately scattered over permanently cultivated house gardens and the nearer fields, as is the custom today.[26] The *chinampas* were maintained by adding marsh vegetation and fertile lacustrine silt derived from the adjacent volcanic slopes; and in the eighteenth century, if not earlier, the Indians of Xochimilco also used bat manure from the caves of Ixtapalapa.[27]

Seeds as well as tubers were planted rather than broadcast, and the advantages of mixed cropping appear to have been widely appreciated. The planting together of maize and nitrogen-fixing legumes, particularly in South America,[28] reduced the need to fallow. Chemical analysis of soil taken from abandoned Inca terraces above Chosica suggests that beans were planted on the higher surfaces, thereby ensuring a flow of soluble nitrates through the entire system.[29] It is also possible that legumes were used as green manure. In the high Andes today, quinoa, barley, beans and the staple tubers are rotated to conserve fertility,[30] and this (excepting barley) was probably customary in pre-Hispanic times.

The most elementary method of restoring soil fertility is to cultivate only periodically. Shifting cultivation usually involves bush or forest fallow in a cycle of fifteen to thirty years, while permanent fields may be rested after two or three sowings for anything up to ten years. Garcilaso remarked on the fallowing of "poor land" that was neither irrigated nor planted to maize.[31] There can be little doubt that the practice, in one form or other, is as old as sedentary cultivation itself. Terracing certainly does not imply continuous cultivation.[32] Many terraced fields, particularly in the central Andes, lie fallow for longer periods than they are cultivated, and this too may always have been the case.

Planting surfaces: Agricultural terracing represents an attempt to overcome the problems inherent in cultivating slopes. In areas with a pronounced dry season, which include much the greater part of the terraced lands of

17. Rowe, 1949, 39; Reparaz, 1958, 53; Collier, 1961, 105.

18. Garcilaso de la Vega (1604), 1871, 11; Rivero y Ustariz and Tschudi, 1853, 83.

19. Cieza de León, 1864, 265-66.

20. Vázquez de Espinosa (c. 1628), 1942, nos. 1385, 1418; Paz Soldán, 1862, 464. Cieza de León (1864, 266) states that guano "was considered so valuable as to become an article of trade between natives."

21. Garcilaso de la Vega (1604), 1871, 10.

22. *Ibid.,* 5. For the use of guano on terraces, see Wright, 1962, 99-100, quoting Keller, 1946. Gamarra Dulanto and Maldonado (1945, 54) found no proof of the use of either guano or fish manure on the terraces of the lower Rimac.

23. Garcilaso de la Vega (1604), 1871, 11. Forbes (1870, 263) did not observe the use of manure among the Aymara; similarly Bandelier, 1905a, 450. Concerning the pre-Columbian inhabitants of Chile, Juan Ignacio de Molina (1782)(1809, 15) wrote — "They were acquainted with the use of manure, called by them *vunalti,* though from the great fertility of the soil but little attention was paid to them [*sic*]."

24. Haury, 1953, 78; Reichel-Dolmatoff, 1961, 84.

25. Landa (1566), 1941, 97. On one occasion he also noted ashes being put around the roots of a "useful tree" *(ibid.,* 194). See also Roys, 1943, 39.

26. Stadelman, 1940, 104; Tschopik, 1946a, 517; Beals, 1946, 20; Kaplan, 1960, 202; Wilken, 1969, 231. Stewart and Donnelly (1943, 42-43) provide evidence of the filling of terraces with village refuse (Citadel Ruin, Arizona).

27. Gibson, 1964, 558; Sanders, 1968, 102. Pennington (1963, 51) mentions the former use of bat manure by the Tarahumar Indians of northwest Mexico. Where flood-water farming was practiced, annual increments of sediment served to maintain fertility (Schmieder, 1926, 122-23; Castetter and Bell, 1942, 172, and 1951, 151).

28. Sauer, 1950, 498 *(Lupinus sp.),* 503 *(Phaseolus vulgaris).* See also Rycroft, 1946, 183; Ferdon, 1959, 16; G. Reichel-Dolmatoff, 1961, 84. According to Franke and Watson (1936, 41), the growing together of beans and maize was probably a feature of aboriginal agriculture in parts of the Southwest of the United States.

29. Gamarra Dulanto and Maldonado, 1945, 58.

30. Kuczynski Godard, 1945, 32; Hodgson, 1951, 187; Leonard, 1949, 256.

31. Garcilaso de la Vega (1604), 1871, 5. See also Clavijero (c. 1780), 2, 1945, 268; Forbes, 1870, 263; Schmieder, 1926, 123; La Barre, 1948, 85; Bunzel, 1952, 16; Soria Lens, 1954, 86; Vellard, 1963, 131; Belshaw, 1967, 76.

32. Forbes, 1870, 263; Bandelier, 1910, 5; Latcham, 1923, 37; Bowman, 1924, 321; Schmieder, 1930, 46; Chaves, 1963, 131.

the New World, the soil cover is often thin, easily exhausted and quickly dries out. Deep soils over steep slopes are chiefly confined to certain volcanic regions, as a result of exceptionally rapid weathering or the accumulation of pumiceous ash. In all cases, slopes of any consequence make irrigation difficult if not impossible.

Other artificial planting surfaces found within the New World were also related to the supply or control of water. In the coastal valleys of Peru and northern Chile, fields *(hoyas, mahamaes, pukios, cultivo de fondo)* were excavated to tap underground water.[33] Garcilaso drew an interesting comparison when observing that "in one part [of Peru] they dig these *hoyas*, just as in another they build *andenes* [terraces]."[34] Conversely, within several extensive and seasonally flooded lowlands, mounds and broad ridges were prepared,[35] apparently to ensure adequate drainage. Similar features are found in parts of the highlands, notably around Lake Titicaca[36] and the *sabana* of Bogotá.[37] The *chinampas* of the valley of Mexico[38] and "drained fields" in other parts of Mexico[39] represent essentially the same technique applied to shallow lakes or swamp conditions. Planting ridges on wet hill slopes have also been reported.[40]

The topographical, ethnographical and archaeological literature of the New World contains many references to agricultural terracing. Those that concern particular places are listed in the appendix.[41] Early statements (c. 1540-1675) are discussed in Part II. Modern studies of agricultural terracing are rather rare, but all the main areas are represented — northwest Mexico and the Southwest of the United States,[42] Chiapas,[43] and Mexico generally;[44] central Colombia;[45] Peru;[46] and northern Chile and Argentina.[47] Some regional studies of pre-Columbian agriculture also are useful.[48] There is, however, no published account of terracing in the New World as a whole.[49]

FIELD IMPLEMENTS

Before the arrival of the Spaniards, agricultural operations in all parts of the New World were conducted entirely with hand implements. The spread of the plow in company with draft animals, and the consequences of their introduction into Indian agriculture, while self-evidently questions of great importance, have not attracted

33. Cieza de León (c. 1550), 1864, 236-37, 255; Las Casas (1527-59), I, 1958, 200; Jiménez de la Espada (ed) (1570), I, 1965, 154; José de Acosta (1590), 1880, 267-68; Lizárraga (c. 1600), 1968, 45; Dorantes de Carranza (1604), 1902, 74; Vázquez de Espinosa (c. 1628), 1942, nos. 1332, 1351; Kroeber, 1930, 65; Latcham, 1936a, 286-94; Schmidt, 1951, 247; Collier, 1961, 105; Engel, 1966, 57; J. R. Parsons, 1968, 80-85; Moseley, 1969, 485-87; Regal, 1970, 32-34; Parsons and Psuty, 1975, 259-82. Canals, both surface and underground, also brought water to the *hoyas* (Tschudi, 1847, 495; Rivero y Ustariz and Tschudi, 1853, 250; Rossel Castro, 1942, 196-202; Regal, 1945, 82; Kobori, 1964, 136).

34. Garcilaso de la Vega (1604), 1871, 13.

35. Nordenskiöld, 1913, 205-55; Oramas, 1917, 140-44; Schmidt, 1923, 965-68, and 1951, 246; Schmieder, 1932, 140-41; West, 1935, 184; Sapper, 1936, 39; Métraux, 1942, 136; Rouse, 1956, 171; Denevan, 1962, 91-113, 1963, 540-45, 1964, 17-24, 1966a, 346-51, 1966b, 78, 84; Rouse and Cruxent, 1963, 10; Plafker, 1963, 372-78; Parsons and Bowen, 1966, 317-43; Parsons and Denevan, 1967, 93-100; J. J. Parsons, 1969, 76-80; Lathrap, 1970, 160-63; Siemans and Puleston, 1972, 228-39; Zucchi, 1972, 95-99.

36. Gilson, 1938, 535; Parsons and Denevan, 1967, 100; C. T. Smith *et al.,* 1968, 353-66.

37. Joaquín Acosta, 1848, 204; Eidt, 1959, 386; Broadbent, 1968, 135-47.

38. *Infra,* p. 41.

39. West and Armillas, 1950, 172; Wilken, 1969, 215-41, and 1971, 439 (Guatemala); Matheny, 1976, 639-46.

40. Aguado (1581), 1906, 297 *(camellones);* J. J. Parsons, 1949, 34-35 *(surcos de indios);* West, 1958, 279-82 *(eras);* Eidt, 1959, 386. Cf. Bonavia, 1967-8, 274.

41. Terraces are a characteristic feature of pre-Columbian architecture; they also served as house platforms and for purposes of defense (Maler, 1903, 115; Boman, 2, 1908, 601-606; Rowe, 1946, 278; Lister, 1947-8, 67-77; Bonavia, 1964, 19). Consequently there are some ambiguous references, particularly in the archaeological literature; these are listed in the appendix (with "?") but not plotted on the various maps.

42. Stewart, 1940; Stewart and Donnelly, 1943; McCabe, 1955; Rohn, 1963; L. Herold, 1965 and 1966; Howard and Griffiths, 1966; Griffin, 1966; Dennis, 1967.

43. L. E. Guzmán, 1958 and 1962.

44. Hopkins, 1968; West, 1970.

45. Broadbent, 1963; Donkin, 1968.

46. O. F. Cook, 1916b and 1937; Romero, 1929; Zevallos, 1929; Guillen, 1943; Gamarra Dulanto and Maldonado, 1945; Flores García, 1945; Swanson, 1955; Bonavia, 1967-8, 262-78.

47. Ardissone, 1943, 1944, 1945; Wright, 1963; Field, 1966a, b; Suetta, 1967.

48. Steffen, 1883; Schmidt, 1951; Latcham, 1926 and 1936a (Chile); Parodi, 1935 (Argentina); Soria Lens, 1954 (Bolivia); Ugarte, 1918, Barrientos, 1923, Baudin, 1927, Guimet, 1937, Valcárcel, 1942, Bernedo Málaga, 1949, Horkheimer, 1958 and 1960. Caballero Farfán, 1959 (Peru); Meyer l'Epée, 1943 (Mexico); Wilken, 1971 (Guatemala).

49. Perry (1916), Spencer and Hale (1961), and Wright (1962) refer to the New World in the course of wider discussions. Agricultural terracing in Africa south of the Sahara may be comparable in many respects to that in the Americas. Floyd (1964, 92) has published a small scale map of the distribution of "indigenous terrace agriculture" in tropical Africa. De Young's reference (1958, 49, 52) to terraces for sweet potatoes in Haiti raises the possibility of a connection with Negro Africa.

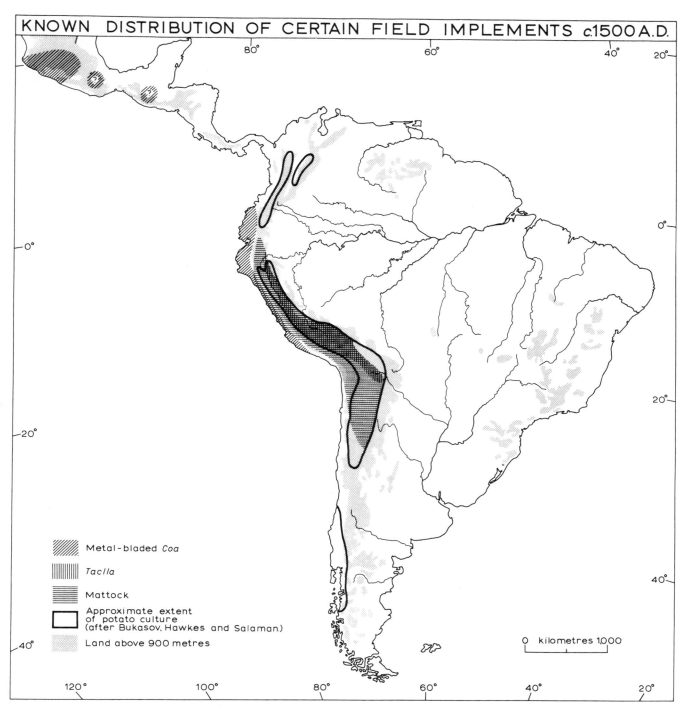

KNOWN DISTRIBUTION OF CERTAIN FIELD IMPLEMENTS *c.*1500 A.D.

Metal-bladed *Coa*

Taclla

Mattock

Approximate extent
of potato culture
(after Bukasov, Hawkes and Salaman.)

Land above 900 metres

0   kilometres 1,000

MAP 1.1

a great deal of attention.[50] We know that the plow began to be adopted during the sixteenth century,[51] and thereafter there are scattered references to its presence along with indigenous field implements.[52] Garcilaso recalled: "The first bullocks I saw at the plow were in the valley of Cuzco in the year 1550 . . . they belonged to a knight named Juan Rodríguez de Villalobos. . . . There were only three. . . . A whole army of Indians took me to see them . . . astonished at a sight so wonderful and novel for them and for me. They said that the Spaniards were too idle to work, and that they forced those great animals to do their work for them."[53] Again, in a request for a *repartimiento* at Sololá, Guatemala, in 1773, the petitioner, Don Juan de Carrascosa, stated that "for plowing with oxen, for threshing and other mechanical tasks, I make out with volunteer workers, for the pueblo Indians do not know how to plow or thresh."[54]

The traction plow was best suited to the cultivation, often for the first time, of broad levels and particularly the grassy floors of intermontane basins with their compact soils developed over old fluvial and lacustrine deposits. In the more tropical areas, such cultivation was pioneered from piedmont-sited *haciendas*. Elsewhere, the levels were left as grazing. Indian fields were small and characteristically located on patches of new alluvium or outwash fans, where soils were easy to work, and, above all, on valley slopes from which woodland could be sufficiently cleared by burning. Today, the cultivation of moderate to steep slopes remains a notable feature of predominantly Indian areas. The plow may be employed on the broader surfaces, but for the innumerable plots on rocky hillsides and over steep slopes generally, hand implements are indispensable. Where irrigable bottom lands are available to a particular community they are usually in the hands of the comparatively wealthy who have plows and oxen, while the slopes are patterned with temporary *milpas* (Náhuatl: *tlacololes*) on which the poor have mainly to rely. The important distinction between plow culture and hoe culture was drawn by Eduard Hahn and Friedrich Ratzel in 1891.[55] It has been examined in a Mexican context by Oscar Lewis.[56]

Hand implements are closely allied to traditional methods of cultivation in the Americas,[57] in particular the practice of mixed cropping and the attention given to individual plants. Indians spend much time on weeding; the hilling of maize is general,[58] and most tubers are either planted in mounds or later ridged. In the words of Bernardino de Sahagún *(Codex Florentino*, c. 1570): "The good farmer . . . is . . . dedicated to separate things; . . . he works the soil, stirs the soil anew, prepares the soil; he weeds, breaks up the clods, hoes, levels the soil, makes furrows, makes separate furrows, breaks up the soil . . . he stirs the soil anew during the summer; he takes up the stones; he digs furrows; he makes holes; he plants, hills, waters, sprinkles; . . . he sows beans, provides holes for them, fills in the holes; he hills [the maize plants] . . . ."[59]

The hand implements in use in the highlands of the New World c. 1500 (map 1.1) were more varied than in the tropical lowlands. Nevertheless, they can be placed in two main categories:[60] (i) digging or planting sticks and spade-like implements, with a blade, if any, in the same plane as the handle; and (ii) hoes or mattocks, with a blade set at an angle to the handle.

Digging or planting stick: The digging stick was the basic agricultural implement, not only in the highlands but throughout the New World. It might be no more than a branchless stick, pointed and fire-hardened at one end, but some were tipped with stone[61] or metal[62] (fig. 1.1); others apparently were weighted.[63] Their most specific use was in planting, and they were often restricted to

50. The consequences are briefly discussed by Palerm, 1967, 45-49.

51. Motolinía (1541), 1950, 270; West, 1948, 36; Faron, 1960, 267-69; Gibson, 1964, 309.

52. For example, Vázquez de Espinosa (c. 1628), 1942, no. 1727; Molina (1782), 1809, 15.

53. Garcilaso de la Vega (1604), 1871, 470.

54. Simpson, 1938, 106.

55. Noted and discussed by Kramer (1967, 81-82), quoting Hahn (1891, 481-87) and Ratzel (1891, 741). See also Braungart, 1881, 4.

56. Lewis, 1949, 116-27.

57. See Meyer l'Epée, 1943, 375-85.

58. Weatherwax (1936, 11) points out that maize "has always been the ideal cereal for hand cultivation."

59. Sahagún, 10, 1961, 41-42.

60. In both cases there are innumerable minor (i.e., nonfunctional) variations, the result of individual manufacture; moreover the very generalized descriptions of implements in many regional accounts lead to difficulties in classification. A further problem concerns finds of blades that could have been hafted in several different ways.

61. Rydén, 1944, 126. Mendieta y Núñez, 1940, xxxix ("una vara resistente con un pedernal engastado en uno de sus extremos"). Briceño Iragorry (1946-47, 17) observed that "barretones de piedra labrada, que llamaban *coas*" were in use until recently in the Venezuelan Andes. See also Chaves, 1963, 223 ("los barretones [chícoras o *coas*] de piedra dura"); Pérez de Barradas, 1951, 21 (in Colombia "los indios encababan los barretones por el mismo sistema que las hachas, pero no perpendicularmente, sino en la dirección del mango").

62. Hutchinson, 1873, 183; Baessler, 1906, figs. 23 *(Brechstange)*, 33-37 *(Feldgerät)*; Verneau and Rivet, 1922, 280 (shaft secured with copper nail); Sapper, 1936, Abb. 19.

63. Nordenskiöld, 1931, 94; Wauchope, 1964, 370. Some "weights" may equally well have been part of clod-breakers.

Fig. 1.1 Socketed copper point (left), probably part of a planting stick, from Zorritos, northwest Peru (? Chimú) (University Museum of Archaeology and Anthropology, Cambridge)

this as other implements became available. Mayan codices depict a long planting stick with a turned handle.[64] Today the Indians of central Chiapas, who have the plow and several kinds of hoe, employ, in sowing maize, a 5- to 7-foot long pole fitted with a wedge-shaped steel point.[65] Where the digging stick was of considerable thickness and sharpened in the manner of a chisel,[66] it might also be used to lift and turn the soil. Such an implement was then close in form and in function to the bladed *coa*.

Coa: The name *coa (cohua, coauacatl)* has been applied at different times to almost all digging tools except the Andean *taclla*. It is, however, best reserved for a one-piece bladed implement that was something between a planting stick and a shovel. According to Jiménez de la Espada, the word *coa* was transferred from the Antilles to Mexico by the Spaniards.[67] The Náhuatl term for the same implement was *huictli (uictli)*.[68] This was generally made of some hard wood such as mesquite *(Prosopis juliflora)* and had a narrow, asymmetrical blade, thickened toward the digging end but terminating in a point. The foot could not be engaged. The *coa* appears in several of the "Mexican" codices, including the pre-Hispanic Fejérváry-Mayer[69] and Borgia.[70] Florentino shows it being used for planting and hilling maize, planting and harvesting *metl* (maguey), transplanting flower seedlings, and directing irrigation water (figs. 1.2 to 1.5).[71] The Codex Osuna (1565) depicts Indians excavating the foundations of the cathedral in Mexico equipped with *coas* (fig. 1.6).[72] Very similar implements were doubtless used elsewhere;[73] one of the early Peruvian digging sticks *(Grabhölzer)*

64. Thomas, 1882, vii, 67, 71, 74, 78; Villacorta Calderón [*Codex Tro-Cortesianus*], 1933, 276, 278, 294, 296; Saravia, 1965, 59, 61, 63 *(estacas)*. Fernández de Oviedo y Valdés (1535) (I, 1959b, 227) refers to the *palo de punta*. Stephens (1843) (I, 1963, 137) remarked upon the use of a "pointed stick" in Yucatan. and upon the absence of the hoe and the plow.

65. Observed in use around Chamula, Aguacatenango and Las Margaritas. A. D. Hill (1964, 38) refers to it at Villa las Rosas *(macana)*. See also Weathers, 1946, 316; Kelly and Palerm, 1952, 108 *(espeque)*; Moriarty, 1968, 472 *(punzón or huitzoctli,* in *chinampa* farming). Fuente (1949, 78) has an illustration of a *coa de sembrar* with a socketed iron point (reproduced here, fig. 1.8 j). An iron-tipped *barretón* is reported from the Venezuelan Andes by Watters (1967, 39).

66. Castetter and Bell, 1951, 94. On the planting stick in the Southwest of the United States, see W. W. Hill, 1938, 32; Dozier, 1961, 102; Ezell, 1961, 38.

67. Footnote to Cobo, 4, 1895, 190. See also Pichardo Moya, 1956, 99 *(coa* or *koyéré).*

68. López de Gómara (1552), 2, 1954, 261; Seler, 3, 1960, 358. Clark (3, 1938, fol. 70) states that *coa* was a Spanish corruption of *quauitl,* a pole. It should also be noted that *coatl* meant a snake, which the wooden *coa* rather resembled (Seler, I, 1960, 422). Orozco y Berra (1950, 372) appears to have regarded the *coa* and the *huictli (o pala)* as different implements.

69. Seler, 1901-2, 29.

70. Seler, 4, 1960, 676. The *coa* is also illustrated in *Codex Vaticanus A* (Loubat, 1900, 83, 91, 93), *Códice Xolotl* (Dibble, 1951, pl. III, 1-3/C), and *Codex Mendoza* (Seler, I, 1960, 210). *Codex Féjerváry-Mayer* and *Codex Borgia* belong to the Mixteca or to Puebla-Tlaxcala; manuscripts from the valley of Mexico are probably all of post-Conquest date (Dark, 1958, 11).

71. Sahagún, 4-5, 1957, figs. 96, 97, and 11, 1963, figs. 739, 750, 854-55, 783. See also Durán (1581), 1880, lám. 6a (13).

72. Robertson, 1959, pl. 36.

73. Salas (1956, 105) states that the Mucus of the Cordillera de Mérida had wooden *coas* (possibly just dibbles). Denevan (1966, 126) draws attention to an eighteenth-century reference to tribes in the Orinoco *llanos* cultivating the savanna with *macanas,* "spades or wide-ended digging sticks." Note also Pérez de Barradas, 1951, 21 ("pala de macana...en forma de espátula"). The weeding or "side-scraper" hoe of the Yuma, Pima and Papago, though shorter than the *coa,* was otherwise similar; among the Pima and Papago it was also used for digging irrigation ditches (Castetter and Bell, 1942, 135-36 and 1951, 95).

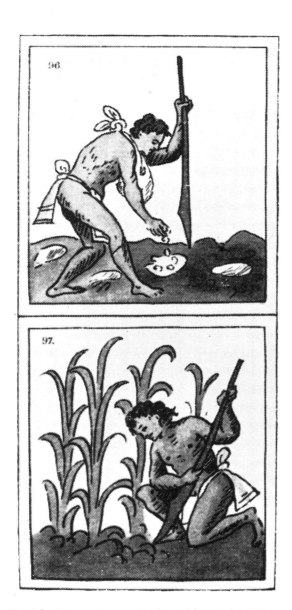

Fig. 1.2 *Coa,* used as a planting stick and for hilling maize (*Codex Florentino,* c. 1570)

Fig. 1.3 Planting and harvesting *metl* with *coas* (*Codex Florentino,* c. 1570)

Fig. 1.4 *Coa* used in transplanting flowers (*Codex Florentino,* c. 1570)

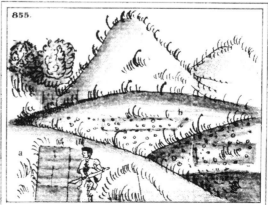

Fig. 1.5 *Coas* used in directing irrigation water and in general cultivation (*Codex Florentino,* c. 1570)

Fig. 1.6 Excavating the foundations of the cathedral in Mexico using *coas* (*Codex Osuna*, 1565)

reported by K. Sapper[74] is indistinguishable from the Mexican *coa*. The Codex Florentino also portrays a farmer using a one-sided wooden spade or spit (fig. 1.7).[75] This was probably a post-conquest development.

The wooden *coa* in its traditional form seems to have all but disappeared from the highlands of the New World,[76] its place being taken by a variety of more specialized implements.[77]

Copper and bronze were used for axes and the blades of agricultural implements in the Andes from northwest Argentina to central Ecuador, in Mexico and Guatemala, and possibly also in Colombia. No early representations of metal-bladed implements of the *coa* type have been found,[78] but Bernabé Cobo (1582-1657) appears to refer to them in Peru,[79] and unhafted blades have been recovered. The latter are either triangular, ending in a point or a cutting edge, or more nearly rectangular (fig. 1.8 b, f, g, h). They were fastened to a long handle by a socket or flanges,[80] or attached by means of a tang and thongs.[81] At the end of the fifteenth century, such metal-bladed *coas* appear to have been restricted mainly, if not entirely, to the north coast of Peru,[82] western Ecuador,[83] and to western and central Mexico,[84] and even in these areas they were probably very uncommon in comparison with the all-wood variety. Modern *coas* with blades of steel are reported from parts of central and southern Mexico[85] where they are used for weeding and the final stages of cultivation (fig. 1.8 i, k).

Fig. 1.7 "The good farmer" (*Codex Florentino,* c. 1570)

74. Sapper, 1936, Abb. 15 (extreme right). See also Schmidt, 1918, 21, Abb. 2; Jijon y Caamaño, 1949, figs, 26, 28, and pl. C 1.

75. Sahagún, 10, 1961, 70, 71.

76. Krickeberg (1956, 40) provides a drawing of "eine moderne Coa aus dem Hochland von Toluca," but the "blade" is more spade-like than in the old form of the *coa*. Palerm (1967, 46) writes: "today, a one-piece *coa* with or without metal edges is a rarity in Mesoamerica."

77. In the valley of Mexico in the eighteenth century only the *indios pobres* still had the *coa,* although its use was known to lead to higher yields (Gibson, 1964, 309).

78. Possibly Boban, 1891, pl. 33. The *coa* shown in lám. III of Gómez de Cervantes (1599), 1944, may have had an (?) iron blade.

79. Cobo (1653), 1895, 190 (*"lampas* que los mexicanos llaman *coas,* y es un instrumento como azada, salvo que el hiero era de cobre, y no corvo, sino llano como pala corta de horno"). The earliest reference discovered for Mexico is in Clavijero (c. 1780), 1945, 267 ("Servíanse de la *coatl* que era una pala fuerte de encino, cuyo extremidad era comúnmente de cobre para aflojar y remover la tierra").

80. Nordenskiöld, 1921, 55, 75; Rivet and Arsandaux, 1946, 206-207.

81. Museo Nacional de Antropología, México (reproduced here, fig. 1.8 h).

82. Sapper, 1936, Abb. 19; Nordenskiöld, 1921, 55, 75; Baessler, 1906, figs. 28-32 (described as "shovels" or "spades," but without well-marked "shoulders"); Hutchinson, 2, 1873, 183; Squier, 1877, 175. Disselhoff (1967, 30) illustrates what appear to be wooden prototypes.

83. Uhle, 1889-90, pl. XXIV, fig. 24 (a fine triangular blade from Cochasqui, Imbabura); Reichlen, 1942, 206-207. G. H. S. Bushnell reports finding a socketed hoe blade, possibly Manteño, near La Libertad, Santa Elena Peninsula (personal communication).

84. Brasseur de Bourbourg, 3, 1857-59, 633 ("cuivre avec un manche en bois" which he distinguishes from the [introduced] hoe); Valentini, 1879, 81, 108 ("blade of an *uictli*" from Monte Albán, but more likely a knife or axe (money blade); Meyer l'Epée, 1943, 378; Palerm, 1951, 29; Krickeberg, 1956, 509 ("kupferne Grabscheitklinge"); Caso, 1965, 917; Gortari, 1963, 111. There are examples of copper or bronze *coa* blades in the Museo Nacional de Antropología, México; the Museo Michoacán, Morelia; and the Museo de las Culturas de Occidente, Colima. Blades of agricultural implements are not mentioned by Pendergast (1962). Stadelman (1940, 107) states that a tin and copper alloy was used in Guatemala for axes and "hoes." For pre-Hispanic metal working in western Mexico, and possible connections with Central and South America, see Pendergast, 1962, 520-45; Rivet and Arsandaux, 1921, 261-80; Brush, 1962, 1336-38; Easby, 1962, 23-24; M. D. Coe, 1962, 180; Caley and Easby, 1964, 507-17; Noguera, 1966, 127-32.

85. Bullock, 1824, 277 ("triangular . . . of wood armed with iron"). In an account of the area around Cholula, Bandelier (1884, 143) mentions "hoes" (which were not particularly common), the "American" spade, and an implement with "a broad blade fastened to a long handle." See also Beals, 1945, 102; Waibel, 1946, 206; S. F. Cook, 1949b, 29; Lewis, 1949, 119; Mendieta y Núñez, 1949, 473; Fuente, 1949, 78 *(tarpala:* reproduced here, fig. 1.8 k); West and Armillas, 1950, 178; Kelly and Palerm, 1952, 108; A. D. Hill, 1964, 39; West and Augelli, 1966, 243. There are fine examples of triangular blades in the Museo Regional de Oaxaca and the Museo Nacional de Antropología, México.

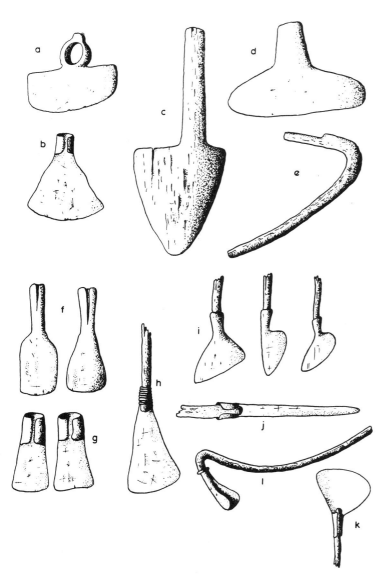

Fig. 1.8 Field Implements

a) Bronze blade of an *azada,* Colonial period, from San Antonio de los Cobres, northwest Argentina (Ambrosetti, 1904)
b) Bronze hoe blade (c. 14 cm wide), from Cochasqui, Imbabura, Ecuador (Uhle, 1889-90)
c) Blade of a wooden spade. Grave equipment, from Morohuasi, northwest Argentina (von Rosen, 1924)
d) Hoe blade of slate, from a dwelling site at Casabindo, northwest Argentina (von Rosen, 1924)
e) Implement handle of wood, from a tomb at Casabindo, northwest Argentina (von Rosen, 1924); probably for a hoe blade of the type shown in *d.* It might, however, have had a narrow blade of the typical *liukana* type (see Ambrosetti, 1904).
f) "Bronze" (in fact, copper) hoe blades from Peru (Squier, 1877; Mead, 1916)
g) Copper hoe blades from Ecuador (Rivet and Arsandaux, 1946)
h) Bronze-bladed *coa* (Museo Nacional de Antropología, México)
i) Metal (? steel) *coa* blades used in Central Mexico (Augelli and West, 1966)
j-l) Hand implements with iron blades in use at Yalalag, Oaxaca, Mexico (Fuente, 1949): *j) coa de sembrar, k) tarpala,* and *l) garabato*

Spade: The *coa* was strictly a hand tool. Only in the Andes is it quite clear that there were implements that also brought the foot of the cultivator into use.[86] The most important of these was the *chaqui-taclla* or foot-plow. In addition, some wooden implements had blades with a sharply defined "shoulder" on one or both sides of the hand piece. They closely resemble true spades and were almost certainly used as such. The best available examples, published by E. Von Rosen (fig. 1.8 c),[87] are from tombs in northwest Argentina, to the south of the *taclla* distribution. In some cases, separate blades were lashed to a long handle. Primitive spades may also have been used on the coast of Peru and in parts of Ecuador[88] (within the area of metal-bladed *coas* and dibbles), but the evidence for this is not wholly satisfactory. E. Nordenskiöld discussed the distribution of the "wooden spade" in South America.[89] His map shows a concentration of evidence between Potosí and the Gran Chaco and a few reports from widely scattered sites within the Andes. An accompanying illustration makes it clear, however, that he included paddle-like implements (without "shoulders") that would have served as shovels but could not have been driven into the ground with the foot.

Chaqui-taclla:[90] The *taclla* or foot-plow *(chaqui,* "foot")* was the most distinctive of pre-Columbian field implements. It is represented in pottery of the Chimú period

---

86. A reference by McBride (1942, 261) to the foot plow in pre-Columbian Guatemala appears to be unsupported. On the other hand, Herrera (1601-15), writing of Honduras, refers to a digging stick with "two projecting hooks or branches . . . so that pressure could be applied by both arm and foot" (Roys, 1943, 121; also Stone, 1957, 107).

87. Rosen, 1924, 74. Parodi, 1935, 127 *(pala de madera);* Casanova, 1946, 621, and 1936, 217; also, for northern Chile, Latcham, 1938, 107, 152-54; Rydén, 1944, 123-26; W. C. Bennett, 1946c, pl. 131.

88. Schmidt, 1918, 21, Abb. 2; Gillin, 1945, 18 (spade-like implements of Mochica-Chimú cultures); Engel, 1965, 60 *(pala* or *llacta);* Meggers, 1966, 129 (Manteño culture). Gillin (1936, 550) remarks on the use of "long wooden spades" in northern Ecuador. Nordenskiöld (1931, 94, fig. 10) reported a short, paddle-like "spade" from Nazca; it was fitted with a counterweight that would have made it more penetrating and also given greater leverage.

89. Nordenskiöld, 1919, 30-31; see also Nordenskiöld, 1920, 23-24.

90. Or *yapuna, yapana* — see Domingo de Santo Tomás, 1560; Goncalez Holguín, 1608; Markham, 1908. In Aymara, *uysu* or *vsu* (Bertonio, 1879 — "el arado o instrumento de palo con que los indios aran la chacara"), *oiso* (Forbes, 1870, 262-63), *uisu* (La Barre, 1948, 80), *uysu* or *wiri* (Soria Lens, 1954, 305).

(A.D. 1300+).[91] The actual implement is described by several sixteenth- and seventeenth-century writers,[92] and Felipe Guamán Poma de Ayala's *Nueva Corónica* (1615) includes a number of valuable illustrations.[93] There are (or were until recently) regional variations in the form of the *taclla*. The main piece was a pointed stave, between 1 and 2 meters long, straight or gently curved[94] and flat in front near the digging end.[95] The foot-rest consisted of one or two pieces of wood[96] lashed securely to the side of the stave.[97] The second handle was similarly fastened somewhere between the foot-rest[98] and more than half way up the stave but always pointing away from the cultivator.[99]

"The *taclla* plow is driven deep into the soil by a thrust of the foot and the pressure of the hands. The long handle is then pressed downwards and, with a hand on the upper handle, the clod of earth is prized up."[100] This lever action explains the curious forward position of the "upper handle."

The *taclla* was a specialized implement, made to penetrate and to tear apart the fibrous sod of the shallow valleys of the *altiplano*; the working of loose earth was a secondary consideration. It was generally employed on open stretches of flat or gently rolling ground, mostly between 3500 and 4500 meters above sea level, rather

Fig. 1.9 Pottery model of a *taclla* (Courtesy of the Trustees of the British Museum)

91. Reported by Vargas, 1936, 16, fig. 2, and Horkheimer, 1960, Tafel 3. The British Museum possesses a similar representation with a pot and a small corn cob attached (fig. 1.9); it is described as being from "an unlocated site, North Coast of Peru" (E. Carmichael, personal communication). There is, however, no reason to believe that the *taclla* was used on the north coast of Peru. The models, in this respect, are comparable to the Mochica "potato pots" of the same region, for both the *taclla* and the potato belong to the highlands. Lanning (1967, 161) states that the *taclla* was an Inca invention but gives no authority for this.

92. Cabello de Balboa (1586), 1838, 240; Murúa (1590), 1946, 189; Garcilaso de la Vega (1604), 1871, 8; Santa Cruz Pachacuti-yamqui Salcamayhua (c. 1613), 1927, 171 *(tachha)*; Vázquez de Espinosa (c. 1628), 1942, no. 1727; Cobo (1653), 1895, 190. The *palas agudas* referred to by Augustín de Zárate (1555) (n.d., 37) were probably *tacllas*.

93. Poma de Ayala, 1936, 22, 48, 250, 1147, 1153, 1156, 1165. Poma associates the *taclla* with Viracocha "primer yndio deste rreyno."

94. Chervin, 1908, 215-16, figs, 118, 120; Means, 1931, fig. 222; Vargas, 1936; Sapper, 1938, 23-27; Troll, 1958, figs. 3, 4; Nachtigall (1966, 94) illustrates a very long-handled *taclla*.

95. It was sometimes shod with copper or bronze (Rowe, 1946, 211; Salaman, 1949, 46). McCown (1945, 306-307) describes metal objects that were probably "shoes" of *tacllas*. Modern *tacllas* are fitted with an iron plate or "shoe" (Núñez del Prado, 1955, 11; O. F. Cook, 1920, 488).

96. Garcilaso de la Vega (1604), 1871; 8; Poma de Ayala (1615), 1936, 1153, 1165; Forbes, 1870, pl. XXI.

97. To left and right in different illustrations in Poma de Ayala. Vázquez de Espinosa (c. 1628) (1942, no. 1727) states that the right foot was used. Fig. 1 in O. F. Cook (1920) shows pressure being applied with the left foot; and the foot-rest is on the left in the Chimú model.

98. Forbes, 1870, 262, fig. 4; Bingham, 1916, 452, and 1948, 42; O. F. Cook, 1920, 488.

99. The similarity, both in form and use, between the *taclla* and the foot-plow of the Celtic lands is discussed by Salaman (1949, 232). Jiménez de la Espada, in a footnote to Cobo (1895, 190), compares the *taclla* to the *laya* of the Basque country (cf. the *loy* of Scotland); also Jiménez de la Espada (ed), 2, 1965, 227 n. 2. In the nineteenth century, the Zuni used lateral stumps on their digging sticks as foot-rests (Henshaw, 1887, 11; Weule, 1912/1924, 64). Such implements were also used as stilts (Culin, 1907, 732). The Yucatan Maya danced on stilts (Landa [1566], 1937, 65; Villacorta Calderón [*Codex Tro-Cortesianus*], 1933, 296; Thomas, 1882, 71), but had no implements with foot-rests.

100. Salaman, 1949, 46.

Fig. 1.10 A *taclla* team, women turning the sod (Poma de Ayala, 1615)

Fig. 1.11 Planting (? irrigated) maize using the *taclla* (Poma de Ayala, 1615)

Fig. 1.12 Planting tubers using the *taclla* (Poma de Ayala, 1615)

Fig. 1.13 Harvesting potatoes using the *taclla* and *liukana* (Poma de Ayala, 1615)

than in the narrow terraced fields of steep rises and of deep valleys on the flanks of the Andes.[101] Men worked in line formation, with women following to turn the sod (fig. 1.10).[102] The crops typical of *taclla* land were tubers, above all the potato, but also oca *(Oxalis tuberosa),* ullucu *(Ullucus tuberosus),* and añu *(Tropaeolum tuberosum).*[103] The small grains quinoa *(Chenopodium quinoa)* and caña-hua *(Chenopodium pallidicaule)* were sometimes sown after potatoes; then the ground was allowed to rest for three to eight years during which the turf reformed. Poma de Ayala shows the *taclla* being used as a planting stick for maize (fig. 1.11).[104] The ridges in which potatoes were planted were prepared by two men working side by side and (with the help of the women) turning the sod to left and right respectively to cover strips of un-broken ground.[105] Today old potato ridges *(huachos)* as well as "ridged fields"[106] are common along the north-western shores of Lake Titicaca and in the lower valley of the Río Lampa. The *taclla* was also used in setting and harvesting tubers (figs. 1.12, 1.13).[107] It was, how-ever, by no means generally associated with potato cul-ture (map 1.1), being absent from Colombia[108] and, apparently, northern Ecuador. The center of maximum distribution (? and origin) of the *taclla* appears to have been the basin of Titicaca and the highlands to the north and the west (Departments of Cuzco, Puno and Apuri-

mac) where it may occasionally be observed today (fig. 1.14). It was probably known throughout the highlands of Peru[109] and neighboring parts of Ecuador.[110] To the south, Vázquez de Espinosa (c. 1628) mentions the *taclla* around Sucre in central Bolivia. R. N. Salaman argued that it was employed in the extreme south of Bolivia[111] and on the island of Chiloé,[112] part of an isolated area of potato culture. On the evidence adduced, this is doubt-ful. A late eighteenth-century account of Chiloé refers to what I take to be a breast plow,[113] and J. J. Von Tschudi (c. 1840) described the use here of digging sticks in pairs, one placed obliquely under the other to provide lever-age,[114] suggesting an approach to the foot-plow. S. Rydén

101. Núñez del Prado (1949, 203), writing of Chinchero, Peru, notes that the *taclla* was then used on wet land *(terreno húmedo),* while drier areas were plowed with oxen.

102. Garcilaso de la Vega (1604), 1871, 8; Poma de Ayala (1615), 1936, 250, 1153; Bingham, 1916, 452; O. F. Cook, 1920, 488.

103. Hodgson, 1951, 187.

104. Poma de Ayala (1615), 1936, 1156. Note also the refer-ence (note 91, *supra*) to the pottery representation of a *taclla* and a corn cob. Certain varieties of maize are suc-cessfully cultivated on the islands of Lake Titicaca where the surrounding body of water has an ameliorating effect on the climate.

105. Salaman, 1949, figs. 43, 44.

106. Smith *et al.,* 1968, 353-67. Land was also cross plowed (Mishkin, 1946, 419).

107. Poma de Ayala (1615), 1936, 1147, 1165. In recent times, potatoes have been planted by hand between the undis-turbed and reversed sods of ridges, or in holes made by the *taclla;* in the latter case, the sod is replaced over the tuber and ridges are formed after sprouting has commenced (Hawkes, 1941, 64-65).

108. West, 1959, 270. *Eras* were apparently dug with a triangular-bladed *coa (pala, chuzo).* Cf. Simón (1626), 2, 1882, 309 *(palas de madera).* Cochrane (1825, 5) remarked on the use of the "[introduced] plow in the cold districts (the *sabana* of Bogotá), and the hoe in the hotter or lower level." There was no Chibcha word for foot-plow (Urico-echea, 1871). Field ridges, prepared with a digging stick or "spade," are known from the middle of the first mil-lennium B.C. in northwest Europe (Steensberg, 1960, 342).

109. Vázquez de Espinosa (c. 1628) (1942, no. 1446) refers to the *taclla* at or near Castrovirreina, about 230 kilometers south-southeast of Lima. The "long pole with a small spade or spike at the end" observed between Huánuco and Cerro de Pasco by Smyth and Lowe in 1834-35 (1836, 57) was probably a *taclla.* See also Means, 1931, fig. 222; Tess-mann, 1930, 90 (Campa Indians); Bonavia, 1964, 54-55; Nachtigall, 1966, 100 (Chavín).

110. Jiménez de la Espada (ed), 2, 1965, 227 (1573) and Jiménez de la Espada (ed), 3, 1965, 152 (1582).

111. Tschiffely (1933, 54), his authority, only mentions "wooden spades, resembling oars" at Tupiza.

112. Salaman, 1949, 72: "[The Araucanian natives] cultivated the potato, even as late as 1830, when Tschudi visited Chiloé, with a foot-plow which seems not only to have been identical with the Peru-Bolivian *taclla,* but to have been used in a similar manner." Cf. note 114 *infra.*

113. Molina, 1809, appendix 1, based on F. Pedro González de Agüeros (1791): "Their substitute for the plow consists of two separate stakes, about seven or eight feet long: one end is sharp, the other inserted in a round ball. These they take one in each hand, fix the point against the ground, and force the ends on with the body, which is protected with a sheepskin during this rude exertion." It appears that the principle of the "breast plow" was also known in similar northern latitudes, among the Clatsop, one of the Chinook tribes (Allen [ed], 1842, 134).

114. Tschudi, 1847, 14: "As to the regular plow, I do not be-lieve such a thing is known in Chiloé. If a field is to be tilled, it is done by two Indians, who are furnished with long poles, pointed at one end. The one thrusts his pole, pretty deeply, and in an oblique direction, into the earth, so that it forms an angle with the surface of the ground. The other Indian sticks his pole in at a little distance, and also obliquely, and he forces it beneath that of his fellow-laborer, so that the first pole lies as it were above the second. The first Indian then presses on his pole, and makes it work on the other, as a lever on its fulcrum, and the earth is thrown up by the point of the pole. Thus they gradually advance, until the whole field is furrowed by this laborious process." Latcham (1936a, 616) mentions the "heavy pointed [digging] sticks" of the Atacameño; see also Latcham, 1926, 359. Long digging sticks were used in the temperate highlands around Tenamaxtlán and Tecolutlán, Mexico, in the second half of the sixteenth century (Sauer, 1948, 81). The heavy digging stick, like the *taclla,* is probably important in relation to the culti-vation of sod grass.

Fig. 1.14 *Tacllas,* Yucay, Peru (P. Atkins and T. Peacock)

Fig. 1.15 The *azada,* Tenancingo, central Mexico

believed that the *taclla* was not known in the valley of the Río Loa (northern Chile) or in northwest Argentina.[115]

To some extent the iron-shod traction plow (rather than the more primitive all-wood variety) has replaced the *taclla,* particularly on large holdings and on land that is now cultivated with only short periods of fallow. But another important reason for the disappearance of the foot-plow has been the widespread abandonment of the heavy bottom lands or their use simply as grazing for cattle, sheep and llamas.

Mattock: The importance of the mattock among field implements in pre-Columbian Middle America has not been clearly established. Today, a hoe *(azada* or *azadón)* (fig. 1.15) of Spanish origin with a large, rectangular blade *(circa* 30 cm x 20 cm*)* socketed at right angles to the handle is the basis of hand cultivation in Middle and Central America and in parts of the Andes.[116] In the

volcanic highlands of western and central Guatemala it is used to make the characteristic contour ridges on steep, ash-covered slopes.[117] The question arises as to whether this hoe replaced something similar, or indeed any implement other than the dibble and *coa.* In some areas it appears likely that it did, although the available evidence is disappointingly small.[118]

---

115. Rydén, 1944, 129.

116. Ambrosetti (1904, 310, fig. 100) has reported a remarkable bronze blade of the colonial period (reproduced here, fig. 1.8a) from San Antonio de los Cobres (Salta province, Argentina).

117. Similar ridges made with the *azada* are common on the slopes of intermontane basins between Otavalo and Riobamba (Ecuador), and they may occasionally be observed in Colombia (Gachancipá) and Venezuela (Apartaderos). A *relación* of 1573 concerning Quito and its neighborhood refers to "el maíz en camellones, habiendo poco más de un pie de uno a otro" (Jiménez de la Espada (ed), 2, 1965, 212).

118. The Museo Nacional de Antropología in Mexico has a "mattock" with a copper blade lashed to a hooked stick. The *Codex Osuna,* c. 1565 (Robertson, 1959, 35), shows an Indian, under the supervision of a Spaniard, cultivating with a twin-bladed pick, but (although the *coa* is depicted in the same scene) this was almost certainly of Spanish origin. For mattocks with iron blades attached to a hooked stick, see Beals, 1945, 102 ("hoe" with flat blade lashed to a handle), and Fuente, 1949, 78 (reproduced here, fig. 1.8 l).

Fig. 1.16 The *liukana,* used in cultivating maize
(Poma de Ayala, 1615)

Fig. 1.17 Steel-bladed *liukanas,* Copacabana, Bolivia;
the crop is oca

On the other hand, the mattock has a long and well authenticated history in the central Andes.[119] There are words to describe it in Quechua and Aymara.[120] Poma de Ayala shows it being used with the *taclla* in the harvesting of potatoes (fig. 1.13)[121] and in cultivating be-

tween maize (fig. 1.16);[122] it is also referred to by Cobo.[123] The *liukana* (to use a variant of the common Aymara name) was roughly equivalent to the Spanish hoe, and it was not in direct competition with the incoming plow on small terraced fields. A less specialized implement than the *tacla,* it has been less affected by the retreat of upland farming. The only significant difference between the modern and prehistoric forms is the use today of a steel blade (fig. 1.17).[124] Copper or bronze blades that are generally assumed to have formed part of *liukanas* have been reported from archaeological sites between southern Ecuador and northwest Argentina/Atacama,[125] that is, throughout the Inca empire. Wood, stone and bone, particularly the scapula of the llama,[126] were al-

---

119. Carneiro (1961, 62-63) and Denevan (1966, 97) remark upon the absence of the "hoe" from the tropical forest and circum-Caribbean lands. When studied by Nordenskiöld (1920, 23-24; also 1919, 31), the Chiriguano and Chané of southern Bolivia and northern Argentina had no primitive hoes, "although we are here on the border of the area of distribution of the genuine American hoe." According to Schmieder (1926, 147), however, the Chiriguano once used a wooden hoe *(Hackbau).* The earliest known use of the word "mattock" in the context of the aboriginal New World is in Schmidtmeyer, 1824, 108 ("the spade and the mattock only were used for agriculture in the New World").

120. Aymara — *liukana* (La Barre, 1948, 80), *ocana* (Weddell, 1853, 113; Forbes, 1870, 263). Quechua — *raurana* (Jiménez de la Espada, in footnote to Cobo, 1895, 190), *racuana* or *raucana* (M. Saenz, 1933, 119; Gade, 1970, 58). *Luk'ana* (Aymara) and *Ruk'ana* (Quechua) mean a "finger" (Middendorf, 1891, 289) which the blade of the mattock resembles. According to Markham (1964), *llaclana* "adze" in Quechua. Vázquez de Espinosa (c. 1628) (1942, no. 1727) refers to the *caucana* or "dibble" for weeding near Sucre, central Bolivia.

121. Poma de Ayala (1615), 1936, 1135, 1147.

122. *Ibid.,* 1132.

123. Cobo (1653), 1895, 190 ("Un palo corvo, que hacía forma de hazuela de carpintero ó de almocafre").

124. Nordenskiöld, 1906, fig. 35, and 1921, 145. A socketed twin-bladed pick is now also employed.

125. Ambrosetti, 1904, 199-202; Nordenskiöld, 1912, 42, fig. 23, and 1921, 38, 39, 53, 82, 86, 92, 96, 98, 103, 115; Krickeberg in Buschan, 1922, 391, Abb. 154 ("Kniehacke mit Kupferblatt," from Pachacamac); Latcham, 1938, fig. 141; Rydén, 1944, 129. Pérez de Barradas (1951, 19 — after Restrepo Tirado, 1917) notes stone blades of *hachuelas* (? adzes) from Colombia.

126. Forbes, 1870, 263, fig. 6; La Barre, 1948, 80. Wedel (1964, 205) states that hoes (not necessarily mattocks) made of the scapula of the bison continued in use in the Great Plains after the introduction of iron.

most certainly also used.[127] The blade was attached to the elbow haft of a hooked stick by means of thongs;[128] in modern examples, a piece of wood is usually placed on top of the blade to make it more secure. The *liukana* is widely used for harvesting tubers, weeding, and for generally working the soil.

In the extreme south of Bolivia and in northwest Argentina "blades" of slate and schist have been found, but unlike that of the *liukana,* they are either roughly square or relatively wide (fig. 1.8 d). A short neck or tang strongly suggests that these blades were attached to a handle, possibly again a hooked stick (fig. 1.8 e),[129] and as such they would have resembled the *azada.* Rosen doubted their efficacy for cultivation and suggested that they were used for "reaping"[130] or for removing the soft

exterior of the pillar cactus.[131] E. Casanova on the other hand describes them as stone hoes *(hoces o azadones),*[132] and R. E. Latcham has reported similarly shaped bronze blades *(cuchillos de bronce)*[133] from the Atacama that could have formed part of mattocks.

Metal-bladed tools were almost certainly becoming more common at the time of the Spanish Conquest (after which many blades were probably refashioned or melted down). The *taclla,* which harnessed man-power most completely, also may have been spreading northward under Inca influence. Nevertheless, the great majority of the farming population of the New World depended upon simple hand implements of wood and stone. The ox-drawn plow promised benefits that were complementary to those realized by the use of hand tools, namely larger scale operations and some expansion in the area that was cultivable. In the event, however, such expansion was more than offset by the abandonment of land holdings as population numbers fell sharply during the sixteenth and seventeenth centuries and the Spanish authorities attempted, with some success, to enforce a policy of *congregación.*

127. The long, pointed blades shown in Poma de Ayala suggest the use of wood; see also Horkheimer, 1960, 19, Abb. 1. Nilles (1942-45, 209, figs. 2, 2a) describes a *liukana*-like implement with a wooden blade from east central New Guinea; similarly Werth, 1954, 138, Abb. 30/4-5, 139, Abb. 31/2 (South East Asia), Abb. 36/4 (Cameroons). The wooden *crocan* of the Scottish Highlands, used for digging potatoes, bore a strong resemblance to the *liukana* (Salaman, 1949, 586, fig. 80).

128. Ambrosetti, 1904, 200, fig. 16 (a hafted blade found in a tomb near Casabindo, Puna de Jujuy).

129. Rosen, 1924, 25, fig. 25, and W. C. Bennett (1946c, 613, pl. 131) reported stone blades with a more pointed cutting edge and lashed to a straight handle to form a spade. See also Latcham, 1936a, 616.

130. Rosen, 1924, 25.

131. Rosen, 1905, 576.

132. Casanova 1936, 450, fig. 24 (found "en los andenes de cultivo"). There are examples in the Museo del Pucará de Tilcara. See Krapovickas, 1958-9, 91-92, and on the use of stone for the blades of hoes, see Sonnenfeld, 1962.

133. Latcham, 1938, fig. 143.

PART II: AGRICULTURAL TERRACING

EARLY EVIDENCE

The student of pre-Columbian America has very few contemporary documents at his disposal. For South America there is nothing, but in the Mexica-Maya area of high culture forms of picture writing had been developed. After the Spanish Conquest, thousands of such manuscripts were destroyed or otherwise lost, and most of the so-called codices, while of Indian or part-Indian workmanship, date from the early colonial period. They are useful for the study of agriculture in general but, so far as is known, in no case do they show terracing.

We are left with four sources of information: (i) archaeological investigations; (ii) local nomenclature and verbal inquiry; (iii) written descriptions from the early colonial period onward; and (iv) what can be observed in the field or from aerial photographs.

ARCHAEOLOGICAL DATING

Very few terrace systems have been independently dated. J. A. Neely's work at Hierve el Agua in the valley of Oaxaca, Mexico, is an important exception. Conclusions regarding periods of construction (fig. 2.1) are generally based on dates assigned to associated settlements. The earliest of these come from the highlands of central and southern Mexico and from the central Andes.

The scientific examination of terrace fill might be expected to yield dateable material, in particular fragments of pottery,[1] and to show how the fill was formed,[2] whether by the accumulation or deposition of material from higher ground or by the introduction of earth from adjacent bottom lands.

Southern Mexico, Guatemala, British Honduras: Work in the valleys of Oaxaca and Tehuacán, and at Monte Negro-Tilantongo in the Mixteca Alta, suggest that terracing for agriculture, with, in places, irrigation, commenced in the pre-classic period, several centuries before the beginning of the Christian era.[3] This may also be true of the highlands of Guatemala,[4] but here, as in Chiapas and the Vaca plateau of British Honduras, the only reasonably firm evidence comes from the classic period (c. A.D. 300-900).

Central Mexico: Agricultural terracing in the valley of Mexico-Teotihuacán is probably as old as in southern Mexico, in other words a feature of the late pre-classic[5] and the classic periods.[6] It has been proved for the close of the post-classic period from the eastern and southern sides of the valley and from the tributary basin of Teotihuacán. In the Texcocan province of Acolhua and around Teotihuacán terracing was accompanied by irrigation. Similarly late dates have been advanced for the terraces of the western Teotlalpan (valley of the Río Tula) and of Tecaxic-Calixtlahuaca (basin of Toluca). R. S. MacNeish has reported very substantial rock-faced "terraces" from the Sierra de Tamaulipas belonging to three successive periods of occupation (c. 600 B.C. to c. A.D. 1000);[7] some connect with "house platforms built at the same elevation along the hills." But in MacNeish's view, the terraces were probably built "for landscaping rather than for agriculture."

Central and Southern Andes: There is reason to believe that terracing also commenced here in pre-classic times, *circa* 500 B.C.,[8] and continued during the classic (Tiahuanaco) period. It is generally accepted that the construction of terraces for agriculture long antedates the Incas,

3. Spores (1967, 47) gives two carbon-14 dates from Tilantongo: BP 2680 (+/− 200) and 2518 (+/− 250), but these do not specifically relate to the agricultural terraces. Terracing in the Nochixtlán valley of the Mixteca Alta appears to date from c. A.D. 300 (Spores, 1969, 560-61). Palerm and Wolf (1957, 34-35) thought that terrace-building in Mesoamerica possibly commenced as early as c. 1000 B.C.

4. Borhegyi, 1965b, 65.

5. Gibson, 1964, 2, 5; Willey, 1966b, 268; Sanders and Marino, 1970, 55; J. R. Parsons, 1971, 31, 185.

6. Hopkins, 1968, 69.

7. MacNeish, 1958, 133, and fig. 44c.

8. Willey, 1966b, 268; Sanders and Marino, 1970, 72. See also Bonavia, 1967-8, 270. The Formative site of Chanapata, near Cuzco, is sometimes said to include agricultural terraces, but this is doubted by Rowe (1946, 198).

1. Sanders, 1965, 61, 152; Field, 1966a, 42.

2. Wright, 1963, 71; Bonavia, 1967-8, 274-76.

Fig. 2.1   Table: Dates or Periods of Time Assigned to Agricultural Terracing in the New World

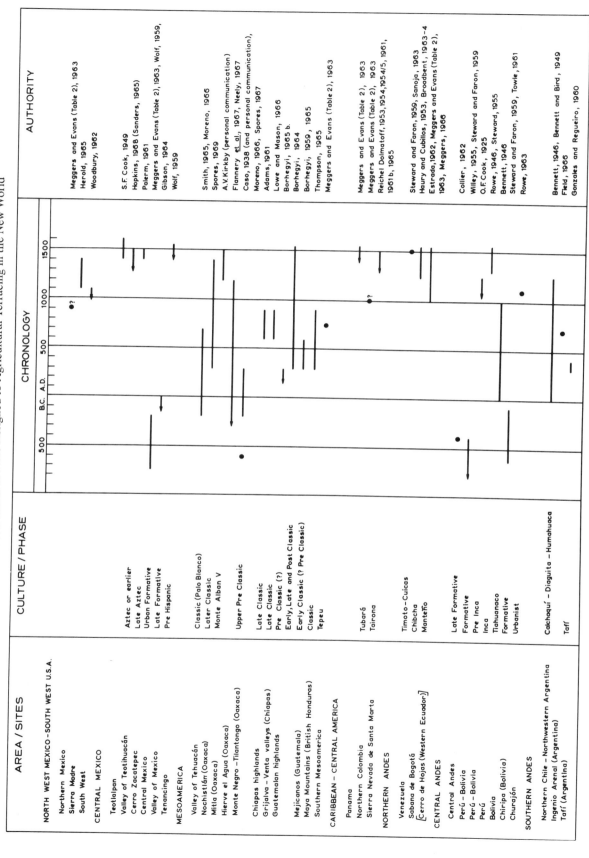

AREA / SITES	CULTURE / PHASE	CHRONOLOGY	AUTHORITY
NORTH WEST MEXICO-SOUTH WEST U.S.A.			
Northern Mexico			Meggers and Evans (Table 2), 1963
Sierra Madre			Herold, 1965
South West			Woodbury, 1962
CENTRAL MEXICO			
Teotlalpan			
Valley of Teotihuacán	Aztec or earlier		S.F. Cook, 1949
Cerro Zacatepec	Late Aztec		Hopkins, 1968 (Sanders, 1965)
Central Mexico	Urban Formative		Palerm, 1961
Valley of Mexico	Late Formative		Meggers and Evans (Table 2), 1963, Wolf, 1959, Gibson, 1964
Tenancingo	Pre Hispanic		Wolf, 1959
MESOAMERICA			
Valley of Tehuacán	Classic (Palo Blanco)		Smith, 1965, Moreno, 1966
Nochistlán (Oaxaca)	Later Classic		Spores, 1969
Mitla (Oaxaca)	Monte Alban V		A.V.Kirkby (personal communication)
Hierve el Agua (Oaxaca)			Flannery et al., 1967, Neely, 1967
Monte Negro – Tilantongo (Oaxaca)	Upper Pre Classic		Caso, 1938 (and personal communication), Moreno, 1966, Spores, 1967
Chiapas highlands	Late Classic		Adams, 1961
Grijalva – Venta valleys (Chiapas)	Late Classic		Lowe and Mason, 1966
Guatemalan highlands	Pre Classic (?)		Borhegyi, 1965 b.
Mejicanos (Guatemala)	Early, Late and Post Classic		Borhegyi, 1964
Maya Mountains (British Honduras)	Early Classic (? Pre Classic)		Borhegyi, 1959, 1965
Southern Mesoamerica	Classic		Thompson, 1965
	Tepeu		Meggers and Evans (Table 2), 1963
CARIBBEAN – CENTRAL AMERICA			
Panama			Meggers and Evans (Table 2), 1963
Northern Colombia	Tubará		Meggers and Evans (Table 2), 1963
Sierra Nevada de Santa Marta	Tairona		Reichel Dolmatoff, 1953,1954,1954/5, 1961, 1961 b, 1965
NORTHERN ANDES			
Venezuela	Timoto-Cuicas		Steward and Faron, 1959, Sanoja, 1963
Sabana de Bogotá	Chibcha		Haury and Cubillos, 1953, Broadbent, 1963-4
[Cerro de Hojas (Western Ecuador)]	Manteño		Estrada,1962, Meggers and Evans (Table 2), 1963, Meggers, 1966
CENTRAL ANDES			
Central Andes	Late Formative		Collier, 1962
Perú – Bolivia	Formative		Willey, 1955, Steward and Faron, 1959
Perú – Bolivia	Pre Inca		O.F.Cook, 1925
Perú	Inca		Rowe, 1946, Steward, 1955
Bolivia	Tiahuanaco		Bennett, 1946
Chiripa (Bolivia)	Formative		Steward and Faron, 1959, Towle, 1961
Churajón	Urbanist		Rowe, 1963
SOUTHERN ANDES			
Northern Chile – Northwestern Argentina	Calchaquí – Diaguita – Humahuaca		Bennett, 1946, Bennett and Bird, 1949
Ingenio Arenal (Argentina)			Field, 1966
Taff (Argentina)	Taff		Gonzales and Regueiro, 1960

Chronology axis: 1500 · 1000 · 500 · B.C. | A.D. · 500

who, however, developed the art to its highest point. M. A. Towle suggests that all the agricultural techniques associated with the prehistoric cultures of the central Andes were known by the end of the classic period (c. A.D. 1000).[9]

Churajón, "the only site of the urbanist period [c. A.D. 1100] that has ever been recognized in the southern Andes" includes agricultural terracing.[10] Formerly irrigated terraces at Tafí del Valle have been provisionally dated A.D. 300 - 400[11] (Tafí culture), the earliest known ceramic and agricultural horizon in northwest Argentina.[12] Here and in northern Chile, as in the central Andes, the Incas were heirs to a thousand-year-old, and probably continuous, tradition of terrace building.

Northern Andes: Terracing in the Cordillera de los Andes of Venezuela is thought to be of late pre-conquest date. Some of it is associated with the Timote (Timoto-Cuica). In western Ecuador, people of Manteño culture (c. A.D. 1000) were apparently responsible for the terraces of the Cerro de Hojas and the Cerro Jaboncillo, south of Manta. Around the *sabana* of Bogotá, unfaced "agricultural terraces" of Chibcha origin have been identified, but it is doubtful whether these were deliberately constructed.[13]

Central America and the Caribbean: G. Reichel-Dolmatoff confidently associates agricultural terracing in the Sierra Nevada de Santa Marta with the Tairona culture which flourished just before the Spanish Conquest. Similar terraces in the hills around Tubará[14] are tentatively dated A.D. 1000 by B. J. Meggars and C. Evans.

Northwest Mexico and the Southwest of the United States: According to L. Herold, the agricultural *trincheras* of northern Mexico belong to the period *circa* A.D. 1100 - 1450. Their constructors shared in the Casas Grandes culture, "a manifestation of Pueblo culture in northern Chihuahua." The eleventh century has been suggested as the period of origin of the terraces of the Southwest of the United States.

Archaeological investigations in the New World might, in due course, indicate several independent centers of origin for the most elementary terracing, followed by the diffusion of more advanced forms in association with stone-working and earth-moving skills and canal irrigation.

NOMENCLATURE

Spanish authors, including the early chroniclers, generally describe terraces as *andenes,* "platforms." Unfortunately, their agricultural use cannot be assumed. Fernando de Montesinos, who was in Peru from 1628 to 1642, recounts the building (under the Incas) of *andenes* in "the high mountains which bear the name of Pucará;"[15] however these, like some of the *trincheras* of northwest Mexico, were for purposes of defense.[16] Bartolomé de Las Casas (1474-1566) mentions *andenes* near Cuzco where defensive considerations were combined with agricultural use.[17]

Other names include *gradas* or *graderías,*[18] *tablones, terraplenes, bancales,* and *llanadas* ("llanos hechos a mano").[19] *Camellones* usually mean raised seed beds, planting ridges arranged against the slope, or simply long, narrow fields,[20] but Francisco de Burgoa (1605-81) used the word to describe agricultural terraces in the Mixteca Alta.[21] *Poyos* or *apoyos*[22] refer to the supporting walls, particularly in the Venezuelan Andes.

The aboriginal nomenclature deserves further investigation.[23] It includes *pata*[24] in Quechua; *pata, suca*

---

9. Towle, 1961, 143. See also Rowe, 1946, 211-12.

10. Rowe, 1963, 16; Ishida, 1960, 467-68. Cf. Bernedo Málaga, 1949, 103-104. Churajón lies about 30 kilometers southeast of Arequipa.

11. González and Regueiro, 1960, 493. But according to Santamarina (1945, 19, 23) and Rohmeder (1955, 251), some of the terraces at Tafí del Valle may have been built or extended under the Jesuits.

12. Field, 1966a, 319.

13. Donkin, 1968, 199-207.

14. G. Reichel-Dolmatoff, 1950, 97-98.

15. Montesinos, 1920, 61.

16. *Pucará* (Quechua, *pukara*) means "fortress."

17. "Por debajo tenía grandes andenes como murallas; pocos hombres podían defendella de mucha gente. En el ancho destos andenes sembraban algunas legumbres" (Las Casas [1527-59], I, 1958, 194).

18. Paso y Troncoso and Vargas Rea (eds), 7, 1944, 24 (Chilchota, 1579); Alva Ixtlilxochitl (c. 1640), 2, 1891-2, 210 (Tetzcutzingo); Debenedetti and Casanova, 1933-5, 17 (Titiconte).

19. Paso y Troncoso (ed), 4, 1905, 141 (Ocelotepec or Ozolotepec, Oaxaca, 1580).

20. Boban, 1891, pl. 33.

21. Burgoa (1674), 1934, 275.

22. Simón (1626), 2, 1882-92, 197; Salas, n.d., 104; Febres Cordero, 1935, 15.

23. Regal, 1945, 81; Bonavia, 1967-8, 265-66.

24. Santo Tomás, 1560 (*pata pata:* "escalera de barro, o de piedra o escalón"); Garcilaso de la Vega (1604), 1871, 237; Poma de Ayala (1615), 1936, 54; Cobo (1653), 1890-95, 188; Jiménez de la Espada (ed), 2, 1965, 24-25; Middendorf, 1890; Markham, 1908; Brundage, 1967, 352 (*palta,* agricultural terrace). Bertonio (1612) translates *pata* as "poyo o grada." Both *andén* and *pata* were also used in the sense of "pathway" (Vázquez de Espinosa [c. 1628], no. 1492; Lira, 1944). *Pata* is a common element in place names in southern and central Peru.

(sucre)[25] and *taka (takha, takhana)*[26] in Aymara; and *catafós*[27] in Timoto-Cuica (Venezuela). The terraces on which coca is grown in the eastern Yungas of Bolivia are sometimes known as *humaċas (humaċanakas)*[28] or *takhanas*. The Náhuatl word *kaláltin* is used to describe the ancient irrigated terraces above Texcoco in the valley of Mexico.[29]

REFERENCES TO AGRICULTURAL TERRACES BEFORE 1675

Four of the known descriptions of agricultural terraces from the first half of the colonial period belong to Mexico. In the *Relaciones geográficas* (1579-81) there are references to terraces at Chilchota, Michoacán,[30] and at Ozolotepec, Oaxaca.[31] Alva Ixtilxochitl (1570-1649) mentions the terraces of Tetzcutzingo (Acolhuacán),[32] and Burgoa (c. 1674) noted flights *(escalones)* of *camellones*, probably both hillside and cross-channel benches, between Achiutla and Tilantonga in the Mixteca Alta.[33]

For Peru, there are more and lengthier observations. Pedro Sancho, secretary to Francisco Pizarro, was perhaps the first to refer to terracing anywhere in the New World. He remarked (1535), with obvious exaggeration, that "between Tumbes and Cuzco all the mountain fields *(montañas agrias)* are made in the guise of stairways of stone" *(escalones de piedra)*.[34]

Cieza de León (c. 1550), describing the marshy valley of *Xaquixaguana* (the basin of Zurite or Anta, 30 kilo-

meters northwest of Cuzco), commented upon "fields . . . divided from each other by broad walls, with crops of maize and roots [and wheat] sown between them, and thus they rose up the sides of the mountains."[35] Around the basin of Cuzco itself there were "broad terraces on which they sow their crops, and they rise one above the other like walls, so that the whole slopes were formed in these *andenes*."[36] Pedro Pizarro (c. 1515-85) also observed *andenes* near Cuzco and at Ollantaitambo in the valley of the Urubamba, and he referred to the characteristic steps that facilitated movement between one level and the next. The terraces at Cuzco "were of cut stone . . . on all of them they sowed maize. And in order that the water might not destroy them they had them thus surrounded by stone [walls] as great as the amount of earth required."[37] At Ollantaitambo they were "high . . . very steep and strong."[38]

The *visita* of Ortiz de Zúñiga (1562) refers to cultivated terraces around villages along the Río Yarumayo and Río Yanahuanca, southwest of Huánuco: "tierras en andenes y laderas buenas y de buen temple donde se dan maís y trigo y papas. . . ."[39]

Pedro Sarmiento de Gamboa (1532-92) relates that the great Pachacuti Inca Yupanqui (fifteenth century) "considering the small extent of land around Cuzco suited for cultivation, supplied by art what was wanting in nature. Along the skirts of the hills near villages, and also in other parts, he constructed very long terraces of 200 paces more or less, and 20 to 30 wide, faced with masonry, and filled with earth, much of it brought from a distance. We call these terraces *andenes*, the native name being *sucres*. He ordered that they should be sown, and in this way he made a vast increase in the cultivated land, and in provision for sustaining the companies and garrisons."[40]

25. Sarmiento de Gamboa (1572), 1907, 98; Bertonio, 1612 (*suca:* "el camellón de las chacaras"): Middendorf, 1891. 299 *(suca, die Furche)*; Latcham, 1936a, 13; Lira, 1944. Possibly the more correct form is *lucre* or *lucri* (Brundage, 1967, 351); c.f. Bonavia, 1967-8, 266 *(rucri)*.

26. Bandelier, 1910, 5; Rydén, 1947, 345; Soria Lens, 1954, 89.

27. Febres Cordero, 1935, 15; Acosta Saignes, 1952, 54; Chaves, 1963, 131.

28. La Barre, 1948, 67-68. Forbes (1870, 265) observed, "when coca is grown on level ground, which is more seldom the case, the plants are placed in furrows *(uachos)* separated from one another by little walls of stone called *umachas*." This follows Weddell (1853, 519) and Gosse (1861, 27), except that the *umachas* are here described as "petits murs de terre bien pétrie."

29. Wolf and Palerm, 1955, 267. Náhuatl *metepantlis* = "semi-terracing" *(bancales)*, that is flattened surfaces between lines of maguey (West, 1970). The element *teopan*, "terraced mound," is incorporated in several place names (Clark [*Codex Mendoza*], 2, 1938, 7, 37, 40, 43, 46, 54).

30. Paso y Troncoso and Vargas Rea (eds), 2(7), 1944, 24.

31. Paso y Troncoso (ed), 4, 1905, 141.

32. Alva Ixtlilxochitl (c. 1640), 2, 1892, 210. See also Pomar (1582), 1891, 53 (irrigated *huertas y jardines)*. The *Codex Xolotl* (c. 1550) shows walled fields, with *coas*, on the outskirts of Texcoco (Dibble, 1951, pl. III, C 1 - 3). Cervantes de Salazar (1554) (1953, 59) perhaps alludes to terraced fields around the basin of Mexico.

33. "Y todos los montes y barrancas están hoy señalados de camellones de arriba abajo, como escalones guarnecidos de piedras, que eran las medidas que daban los señores a los soldados, y plebeyos, para las siembras de sus semillas. . . ." (Burgoa [c. 1674], 1934, 275).

34. Sancho, 1917, 149.

35. Cieza de León, 1864, 321.

36. Cieza de León, 1883, 160. See also Las Casas (1527-59), I, 1958, 194.

37. Pedro Pizarro (1571-2), 2, 1921, 305.

38. *Ibid.*, 332.

39. Ortiz de Zúñiga, I, 1967, 216 (Atcor, Queros, Auche, Guauya); 2, 1972, 30, 43, 58, 83 (Tancor), 88 (Yacán), 117, 120 (Guacor). See also Fonseca Martel, 1972, 321 ("este bolsón, saturado de terrazas artificiales").

40. Sarmiento de Gamboa (1572), 1907, 98. Cf. Santa Cruz Pachacuti-yamqui Salcamayhua (c. 1613), 1873, 98 ("He [Pachacuti Inca Yapanqui] ordered that all the provinces from Quito to Cuzco should make farms and *collcas* or granaries"); also Matienzo (1567), 1910, 12. *Pachacutec* = "reformer of the world."

Viceroy Don Francisco de Toledo (1575) ordered the *alcades* to look to the maintenance of terraced fields *(chacras de andenes)*.[41] The *Relación de la Provincia de Collaguas* (1586) by Juan de Ulloa Mogollón contains a passing reference to unirrigated terraces in broken country, probably the upper Colca valley: here "las chácaras y sementeras que tienen, son hechas a mano en andenes hechos en cada era una pared. . . ."[42] And of the adjacent *provincia de Condesuyo*, Baltasar Ramírez (1597) wrote: "los y(ndi)os poblados en los valles por la major parte tienen sus labores y sementeras e(n) las laderas de los cerros las quales labran con notable artificio haziendo *andenes* en estas laderas que son de poco mas de una bara [vara, about 80 cm.] en ancho y traiendo *acequias de agua para regallos* de muy lexos. . . ."[43]

Garcilaso de la Vega (1604) associated terracing with land reclamation and irrigation under the Incas, and, like Sarmiento de Gamboa, he stated clearly, what in places can be inferred from conditions of site, that the steeply-banked terraces had to be partly filled with soil brought from a distance:

"As soon as the Ynca had conquered any kingdom or province, and established his Government amongst the inhabitants according to his laws and idolatrous customs, he ordered that the cultivated land capable of yielding maize should be extended. For this purpose he caused irrigation channels to be constructed, which were most admirable, as may be seen to this day; both those that have been destroyed, the ruins of which are yet visible, and those still in working order. The engineers led the irrigation channels in directions required by the lands to be watered; for it must be known that the greater part of this land is barren as regards corn-yielding soil . . . and no maize crop was sown without being also supplied with water. . . . Having made the irrigation channels, they levelled the fields and arranged them in squares, so that they might get the full benefit of the water. On the sides of the mountains, where there was good soil, they made terraces so as to get level ground, as may be seen at this day round Cuzco and all over Peru. These terraces or *andenes* consisted of three walls of strong masonry, one in front and two at the sides, slightly inclined inwards, as are all their walls, so as to sustain the weight of the earth, which was filled in until it reached the top of the walls. Over the first *anden* they constructed another narrower one, and above that another still smaller. Thus they gradually covered the whole mountain, levelling the ground after the manner of a flight of stairs. . . . Where there were masses of rock, the rocks were removed and earth was brought from elsewhere to

make terraces. . . . The first terraces were of a size conformable to the position of the site, capable of containing a hundred to two or three hundred *fanegas* more or less; and the second was smaller; and so they went on diminishing in size as they ascended, until the highest only gave room for two or three rows of maize. . . . In many places they led an irrigation channel for fifteen or twenty leagues to irrigate only a few *fanegas* of maize land, that it might not be lost. . . . Most of the *andenes* belong to the Sun and to the Ynca, because the sovereign had ordered them to be made."[44]

Father Bernabé Cobo (1653) also remarked that *andenes* varied in width according to the steepness of the natural slope: "En las laderas muy echadas y de poca cuesta, vemos andenes muy capaces de á cincuenta, á ciento á doscientos y más pies de ancho; y en las muy agrias, tan estrechas y angostas, que parecen escalones, pues algunos no tienen más que tres ó cuatro pies de ancho."[45] He went on to commend the dry stone masonry of the *andenes* around Cuzco.

A reference to agricultural terracing in (? pre-Inca) folklore from the province of Huarochiri (middle and upper Rimac) is recorded by Francisco de Avila (1598-1608): thus "*Coniraya Uiracocha* . . . the Creator of all things . . . by his word of command, caused the terraces and fields to be formed on the steep sides of ravines, and the sustaining walls to rise up and support them. He also made the irrigation channels to flow. . . ."[46] Similarly, Poma de Ayala (1615) preserves the tradition that *chacras andenes* and *acequias de agua* were constructed during the second "era" of Peruvian history (4200-2900 B.C.).[47]

41. Ballesteros (ed), I, 1752, 148; Toledo, 1925, 376.

42. Ulloa Mogollón, 1885, 46 (also in Jiménez de la Espada (ed), I, 1965, 331).

43. Ramírez (1597), 1936, 41.

44. Garcilaso de la Vega, 1871, 3-5 and 324 (Tupac Ynca Yupanqui). Garcilaso (*op. cit.* 470) also recalled witnessing (c. 1550) the plowing of a "very beautiful terrace *(andén)* above the one on which the convent of St. Francis [in Cuzco] is now built." An account of 1549 (Helmer, 1955-6, 40) mentions labor services under the Incas "para hazer paredes." Gregorio García (1607) (1729, 254) drew attention to the presence of *andenes* in Northwest Africa and Peru, thus: "De los Bereberes de Africa se sabe, que en las laderas hacian andenes para sembrar, como refiere Marmol; i los Indios del Perù eran diligentisimos en esta obra, à costa de gran trabajo, por aprovecharse del agua para regar, según Garcilaso. . . ." Murra (1960, 395) has discussed the connection between irrigation and the cultivation of maize in the highlands of Peru.

45. Cobo, 3, 1893, 188.

46. Avila, 1873, 124. See also Avila (? 1598), 1966, 23 ("Con sólo hablar conseguía hacer concluir andenes bien acabados y sostenidos por muros. Y también enseñó a hacer los canales de riego arrojando. . . ."), and 201.

47. Poma de Ayala, 1936, 54 *(chacras andenes* and *pata chacra;* also "rromper tierra virgen y hazer andenes en las quebradas y en penas").

Terraces, elsewhere than in Mexico and Peru, seem generally to have escaped the notice of the early chroniclers and natural historians. The only exception is Father Pedro Simón who observed (1612-13) *poyos* in the Venezuelan Andes.[48]

CONTINENTAL AND REGIONAL CONSIDERATIONS

Territorial distribution: The areas of agricultural terracing shown in map 2.1 are based on the distribution of recorded and observed sites (map 2.2) and on the known absence of terraces in certain adjacent districts. The limits will undoubtedly be revised as further information comes to light, but knowledge of the full distribution may be unattainable. Even aerial photographs sometimes fail to reveal the existence of terraced slopes that are now more or less heavily vegetated. At the same time, the majority of abandoned terraces appear to lie in areas that, whatever their primeval condition, are presently covered with low and/or open vegetation, and in these circumstances aerial photography is the most appropriate means of detailed mapping.[49]

The most northerly zone of old terracing extends from southwest Colorado (36 degrees N) into the Sierra Madre of western Mexico. The actual distribution here is very dispersed and consists mainly of cross-channel fields along narrow *barrancas*. In Middle America, two important zones are effectively separated by the low isthmus of Tehuantepec, and there are few reports of terracing south of the western highlands of Guatemala. The Andean distribution is extensive, but not continuous, from Venezuela to northern Chile and northwest Argentina (32 degrees S). The upper altitudinal limit (about 4700 meters) lies in the highlands to the north of Lake Titicaca. On the eastern slopes of the Andes, terraced sites have been reported down to about 800 meters,[50] well within the zone *(Ceja de Montaña)* of dense broadleaf evergreen forest. There appears to be no close parallel to this in Middle America. Areas of terracing that stand apart from the mountain backbone of the Americas include the Vaca plateau of British Honduras, the Cerros de Hojas and Jaboncillo (western Ecuador), the Sierra Nevada de Santa Marta (Colombia) and the hill country to the south and west of this massif.

Climatic associations: Terracing approached the northern and southern limits of aboriginal agriculture in the Southwest of the United States, in northern and central Mexico, and in Chile-Argentina (map 2.1). In the extreme north and south, the distribution overlaps with that of P. Meigs's

"arid and semi-arid homoclimates" (below −20 evapotranspiration) (map 2.2),[51] and amounts of rainfall are also highly variable. Ninety-five percent of known terracing lies in regions with a "desert" (BW), "steppe" (BS) or "warm temperate/winter dry" (Cw) climate (map 2.1), while the remainder largely falls within the Aw category ("moist tropical/distinct dry season").[52] Approximately 85 percent of the total area experiences a dry season of five months or more and has an average annual rainfall of 900 mm or less. In the New World, terracing seems to be comparatively rare in areas with significant amounts of precipitation at all seasons. (Af, Cf).

Cultural associations: Agricultural terracing was practiced in most if not all of the relatively advanced parts of the highlands of the New World:[53] the Southwest of the United States, central and southern Mexico, Chiapas-Guatemala, the Timoto-Cuica province of Venezuela, the flanks of the Sierra Nevada de Santa Marta (Tairona and related cultures), and the Inca realm from southern Ecuador to northern Chile and Argentina. Terracing in the central Andes has received less attention than canal irrigation, but the former, according to D. W. Lathrap, "may have played a greater part in determining the pattern of population distribution at the time of the first European contacts."[54]

In 1957, A. Palerm and E. R. Wolf endeavored to recognize "key areas" in the prehistory of Middle America. They defined a key area as "an area of massed power, in both economic and demographic terms ... supported by the most efficient systems of soil use, transportation and communication ... the center of an economic network ... a symbiotic region."[55] Although agricultural terracing was not used as a criterion, it is in fact a feature of all the "key areas" of the highlands,[56] some of which maintained their position from pre-classic times to the Spanish Conquest.[57]

---

48. Simón (1626), 2, 1892, 197 ("están todas labradas y hechas poyos á trechos, donde sembraban sus raíces y maíz para su sustento").

49. Kedar, 1958, 585.

50. Isbell, 1968, 114.

51. Meigs, 1953. Based on Thornthwaite's moisture index (precipitation in relation to the needs of plants): O = annual precipitation adequate for maximum evaporation and transpiration.

52. Köppen classification (Köppen and Geiger, 2, Teil G (1930), H (1932), J (1938); Blüthgen, 1964).

53. The territory of the Chibcha—the *altiplano* of Boyacá-Cundinamarca — is a possible exception (Donkin, 1968).

54. Lathrap, 1970, 171.

55. Palerm and Wolf, 1957, 29.

56. In the central highlands — the *valley of Mexico,* the frontier march of southern Hidalgo, the *valley of Cholula-Puebla,* Tlaxcala, and the region around Lake Pátzcuaro; in the southern highlands — Morelos, the *Mixteca Alta,* and the *valley of Oaxaca;* the southeastern highlands (Chiapas); and the *highlands of Guatemala.*

57. Italicized in n. 56 above. Spores (1969, 568), however, maintains that the Mixteca Alta only became a "key area" in post-classic times, "and even this must be qualified."

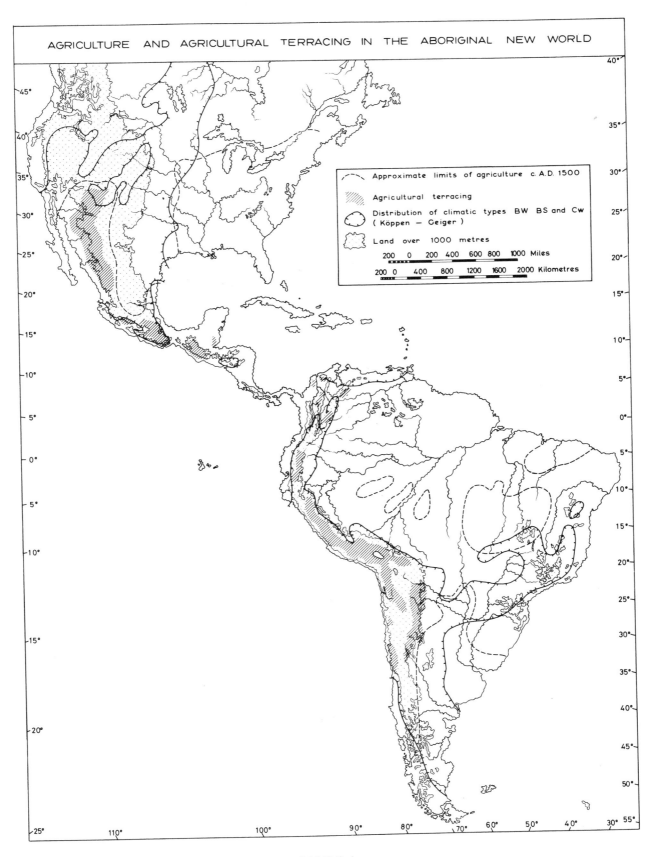

AGRICULTURE AND AGRICULTURAL TERRACING IN THE ABORIGINAL NEW WORLD

Approximate limits of agriculture c. A.D. 1500

Agricultural terracing

Distribution of climatic types BW BS and Cw (Köppen — Geiger)

Land over 1000 metres

200 0 200 400 600 800 1000 Miles

200 0 400 800 1200 1600 2000 Kilometres

MAP 2.1

AGRICULTURAL TERRACING IN THE ABORIGINAL NEW WORLD

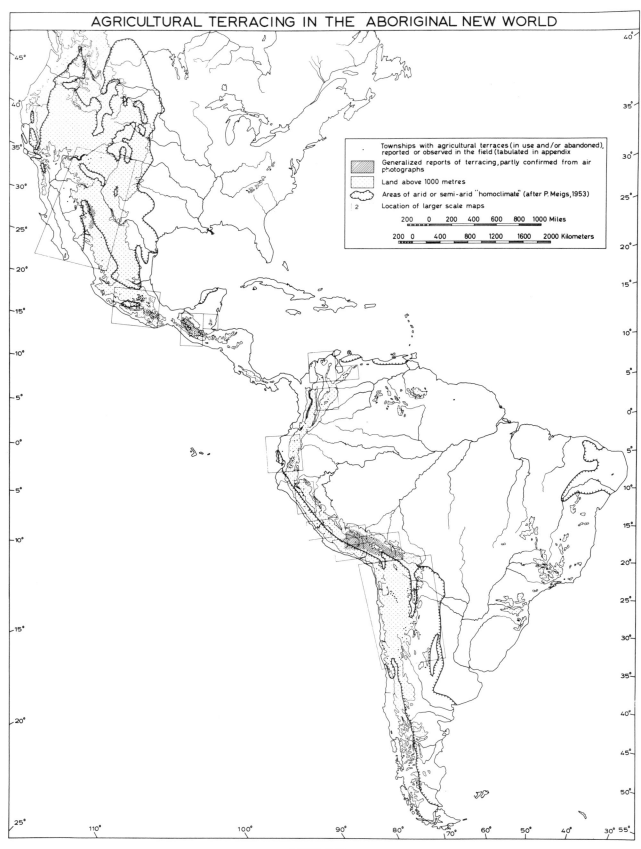

Townships with agricultural terraces (in use and/or abandoned), reported or observed in the field (tabulated in appendix

Generalized reports of terracing, partly confirmed from air photographs

Land above 1000 metres

Areas of arid or semi-arid "homoclimate" (after P. Meigs, 1953)

Location of larger scale maps

200 0 200 400 600 800 1000 Miles

200 0 400 800 1200 1600 2000 Kilometers

MAP 2.2

TERRAIN AND THE DISTRIBUTION OF AGRICULTURE

"The Indians liked hills better than plains." — Francisco Cervantes de Salazar *Dialogues* (1554)

"The season for sowing began in [the eighteenth] month — on slopes and hills.... This feast [in honor of Tláloc and Matlalcueye] was designed to encourage sowing on the hills. This was done early because, as they say, moisture begins on the hills, rainstorms being more common there before they appear on the flatlands." — Diego Durán *The Ancient Calendar* (1579)

"Lack of drainage and lack of relief, with which lack of fertility is associated, have been the main deterrents to aboriginal man in the New World." — Carl O. Sauer (1958)

The early Spaniards found the intermontane basins and valleys of Middle and South America heavily populated. However, our knowledge of the agriculture of these areas is still very incomplete, and certain questions are likely to remain unanswered in view of the nature and rarity of pre-Columbian documents. Habitation sites invite archaeological study, for the information they yield is at least relatively concentrated. Former fields, as extensive features, often poorly defined, and of only economic significance, have attracted much less attention.

The simultaneous introduction after 1492 of a whole range of Old World crops, domesticated animals and implements provided the basis for new and distinctive forms of land use and for certain changes in the distribution of agriculture. In particular, basin levels became more important with the creation of large estates for cattle and grain and, in time, with the spread of the plow among the Indian communities.

SLOPES AND LEVELS

The sub-tropical highlands of the New World have well-marked seasonal climates, wet in "winter" *(invierno)* and dry in "summer" *(verano)*. In northwest South America, there are two wet and two dry periods. The single dry season lasts for from three to ten months, generally increasing away from the equator to between latitudes 30 and 35 degrees north and south. Northern Mexico, northern Chile and northwest Argentina have arid or semi-arid "homoclimates" (map 2.2). Rainfall is relatively low, regardless of latitude, between the flanking ranges of the highlands and particularly within intermontane basins and entrenched valleys where rainshadow conditions often obtain.[58]

North of the neo-volcanic axis of central Mexico, on the high plateau of Chiapas and western Guatemala, and throughout the central Andes above about 2500 meters, frost is an additional seasonal hazard.[59] The basin floors and broader valley bottoms are especially vulnerable following temperature inversion at night; and frost has maximum significance where maize has long been a staple food plant, that is in Middle America[60] and below 3200-3500 meters in the central and northern Andes. According to W. T. Sanders, "in the early occupation of the valley [of Teotihuacán] before humidity conservation techniques were developed, the frost-free hills were selected for cultivation."[61] And R. C. West observed that "prior to the introduction of the plow, the flattish basin plains of the [Tarascan] Sierra apparently were infrequently cultivated. Early accounts of Tarascan farming emphasize the importance of *desmonte* agriculture on the steep slopes. A report of 1599 describing the pueblo of Corundapan (now nonexistent) in the Sierra near Tingambato, states that the natives had no lands in adjacent basin plains, but, as was customary among Tarascan peoples, planted on the slopes in order to obviate frost hazard ("por abrigar sus sementeras de los yelos"). The probable occurrence of a grass sod in the basin plains may also have discouraged their cultivation. A description (1603) of the lands of Capacuaro mentions the large number of *desmontes*, but points out the possibility of cultivating an unused plain nearby, which was relatively free of shrubs and trees. Such areas, though difficult to till with the aboriginal digging stick, were readily adapted to plow culture."[62]

In the higher parts of the Andes, frost-resistant varieties of potato, oca *(Oxalis tuberosa)* and especially ullucu *(Ullucus tuberosus)*, as well as the hardy grains quinoa *(Chenopodium quinoa)* and cañahua *(Chenopodium pallidicaule)*, were available. This, and the invention of the *tacla*, presumably narrowed the advantage of slopes over levels on the *altiplano*. At the same time, maize was widely cultivated in the high valleys of the Cordillera Occidental de la Costa. Juan de Santa Cruz Pachacuti-yamqui (c. 1613) records a tradition of large

58. Portig, 1965, 73; Hastenrath, 1967, 218.

59. For the Puebla-Tlaxcala area, see Jáuregui, 1968, 15, and Fig. 31; for the Andes, Troll, 1943a, 161-71, and 1958, 31-40; Antezana, 1952, 23-24.

60. Sauer, 1950b, 494-95. Gibson (1964, 452-59) tabulates references to "agricultural conditions" (notably drought and frost) and maize prices in the valley of Mexico, during the colonial period.

61. Sanders, 1968, 94.

62. West, 1948, 36. Mendieta y Núñez (1940, xxxi) maintained that the development of *latifundios* in the former Tarascan domain did not fundamentally affect Indian occupancy.

harvests (at a time of general famine) from "farms at *Calla-chaca* and *Lucrioc-chullo* that the dews always descended upon at night and frost never visited."[63] In discussing the agricultural terraces of the Sierra, E. Romero[64] and G. D. Zevallos[65] suggest that good air drainage and the relatively low incidence of frost were among the chief reasons for preferring slopes for cultivation. It is also possible that terracing magnified the effect of air drainage by inducing a certain amount of turbulence.

Slopes possess other important advantages. They are invariably better drained than adjacent levels; in fact, some dry out too quickly for shallow-rooted crop plants. However, the problem of supplying just enough extra water, by hand or canal or by diverting streams, apparently was more easily overcome than that of effective drainage, and irrigation was widely practiced in pre-Columbian times. Another general advantage lies in the normal downslope movement of soil, accompanied by chemical weathering at no great depth, which together ensure the renewal of essential minerals at the surface.[66] In contrast, old lacustrine and alluvial deposits of basin floors are often deficient in plant nutrients.

The preferential use of slopes for agriculture also seems to be directly related to the siting of rural settlements on hill tops and valley spurs. The latter is frequently reported in the archaeological literature, and the use of the Náhuatl word *tepetl* for both "hill" and "community"[67] is very significant. Defense was generally an important consideration in the siting of villages in pre-Columbian times[68] and fields that were immediately adjacent could be most easily protected as well as cultivated.

The juxtaposition of level, grassy surfaces and wooded breaks of slope is common under both tropical and temperate conditions.[69] The physical explanation, so far as the tropics and sub-tropics are concerned, appears to

turn on differences in soil structure and associated drainage. The levels may be permanently waterlogged or, where a clay pan has developed at a little below the surface, waterlogging may alternate with periods of severe desiccation.[70] Both conditions are unfavorable for tree growth. In the Andes, the Quechua-Aymara word *pampa*[71] is used to describe a variety of level, grassy terrains — valley flood plains, basin floors, and the wide surface of the *altiplano*. It is also a fairly common element in place names. Vázquez de Espinosa (c. 1570-1630) generally associates *pampas* with levels, and other words in use in the highlands of Middle and South America have much the same connotation: *vega*,[72] *llano* or *llanura*,[73] *sabana*,[74] *pradería*,[75] *pasto*,[76] and *potrero*.[77] The Spaniards were inclined to note the presence of good pasture as promising cattle country. Pietro Martire d'Anghiera (1457-1526) referred to "tracts of land [around Cholula] admirably adapted for cattle raising."[78] Cortés himself remarked upon "plains, covered with grass," and again "a very level and beautiful country, with no forests, save now and then" in northeast Chiapas.[79]

The Andean ranges, west of the *Ceja de Montaña*, are also generally treeless, a fact upon which many of the chroniclers remarked.[80] This may be largely the result of cultivation quickly followed by the spread of sod

63. Santa Cruz Pachacuti-yamqui Salcamayhua, 1873, 98. Under the Incas, "one hundred brown [llamas] were sacrificed in August-September to ensure the survival of the newly planted maize fields against frost and drought" (Murra, 1965, 208).

64. Romero, 1929, 4-5.

65. Zevallos, 1929, 115-19.

66. Lewis, 1949, 117, 124; Aschmann, 1960, 5.

67. "The stylized *tepetl* figure [was] a universally recognized community symbol in Aztec hieroglyphic codices" (Gibson, 1955, 581). See also E. Guzmán, 1939, 3.

68. J. Miranda, 1962, 186-90. See López de Gómara (1552), 1964, 119.

69. Myres, 1936, 164, 166; Sauer, 1950a, 20; Beard, 1953, 149-215. There are many supporting statements in travelers' accounts: for example, Ruiz (1779), 1940, 49; Smyth and Lowe, 1836, 84 ("The mountains here [to the east of Huánuco, Peru] are partially covered with small, stunted trees, but where the ground is level it produces rich pasture for cattle").

70. Beard, 1953, 149-215; Denevan, 1966b, 5.

71. Middendorf, 1891, 289.

72. Las Casas (1527-59), I, 1958, 28; Krieger, 1929, 473; Howard and Griffiths, 1966, 14.

73. Piñeda (1594), 1908, 436; Joaquín Acosta, 1848, 204; Enock, 1914, 211; Palacios, 1928, 55.

74. Apparently first used by Fernández de Oviedo y Valdés (1535) (1959a, 107), and Las Casas (1527-59) (I, 1958, 13, 16, 20, 52 — *zabanas* in Hispaniola). Ponce (1584-92) (I, 1875, 88) observed "Hay en aquella provincia (México) muchos valles y llanos muy grandes y espaciosos que en esta tierra se llaman *sabanas* y en Castilla *dehesas*, donde hay grandes pastos." Cf. Jiménez de la Espada (ed), 2, 1965, 37; Carvajal (1541-2), 1934, 169. On the origin of the word *sabana*, see Beard, 1953, 150; Sauer, 1957-8, 191.

75. Johannessen, 1963, 19. Cieza de León (c. 1550) (1864, 360) remarked that the "plains [of the Collao] form beautiful and extensive meadows."

76. Johannessen, 1963, 48 (1571-74).

77. Cochrane, 2, 1825, 5; West, 1964, 53.

78. Anghiera (c. 1521), I, 1912, 83. For the Iberian antecedents of cattle ranching, see Bishko, 1952, 491-515.

79. Cortés (1525), 2, 1908, 275-77; Gil-Bermejo García, 1963, 169. See also Fernández de Ovideo y Valdés (1535), 1959a, 11; Las Casas (1527-59), I, 1958, 11, 16, 18; Cervantes de Salazar (1560-75), 1914, 9, 696; Mota y Escobar (1601-3), 1930, 123; Garcilaso de la Vega (1604), 1871, 467, 472.

80. Xérez (1534), 1872, 38; Sancho (1535), 1917, 146, 161; Andagoya (c. 1540), 1865, 59; López de Gómara (1552), 2, 1954, 328; Zárate (1555), 1581, 37, 1853, 468; Matienzo (1567), 1910, 179; López de Velasco (1571-4), 1894, 495; Ramírez (1597), 1936, 42; Murúa (1590), 1946, 277.

grass, continuous cutting for firewood and charcoal, and, since the Spanish Conquest, the grazing of sheep and goats. Polo de Ondegardo (c. 1515-74) reported that "the Ynca made . . . regulations with regard to the forests, in the districts where they were of any importance. They were assigned for the use of the regions where there was a want of fuel, and these forests were called *moyas* of the Ynca, though they were also for the use of the districts in the neighbourhood of which they grew. It was ordained that they should be cut in due order and licence, according to the requirements."[81] The hardy native shrub *queñua (Polylepis tomentilla)* was certainly once more widespread.[82] O. F. Cook observed woodland in ravines "too narrow ever to have been cultivated" and also the colonization of old terrace surfaces by native trees that "sprout readily from stumps and endure repeated cutting."[83] The eucalyptus is similarly endowed and now thrives in a wide variety of situations from valley tracts a few hundred feet above sea level to sheltered sites on the plateau around Lake Titicaca.[84]

Man's part in developing or accentuating important topo-vegetational contrasts is generally difficult to substantiate. It is, however, agreed that his use, or misuse, of fire has been highly significant, and that woodland has suffered and grassland gained by his presence as hunter or farmer. Both slopes and levels have been deliberately burned over long periods of time. Wooded slopes are burned for the purpose of cultivation. The exposed earth, enriched by wood ash,[85] is usually well aereated, friable and easy to work. In the case of temporary *milpas*, charred stumps are simply ignored. The area required for such cultivation is characteristically small, and fire, burning up-slope, can be satisfactorily controlled. When, after two or three years, the land is abandoned, regeneration is not notably hampered by distance from colonizing woodland. Moreover, the results of burning are not uniform over broken ground and woody species tend to survive where accidentally protected.[86] Control is more difficult where level areas

are fired and regeneration may be hindered by the scale at which change occurs.[87] Areas of fast-growing and fire-tolerant grasses will expand as burning continues, if not to permit cultivation, then as an aid to hunting. Increased frequency of burning everywhere gives advantage to grass over trees.

Discussion of the role of fire has centered upon the formation of extensive grasslands, the Venezuelan *llanos,* the *pampas* of Argentina and the prairies of North America. C. L. Johannessen's study of the *praderías* of interior Honduras is an important exception. He shows that when the Spaniards arrived, soon after 1552, grassland covered most of the basin floors and flat valley bottoms. "Agriculture was probably fairly well restricted to the hills"[88] which were, and remain, predominantly wooded.[89] The grasslands were maintained by burning.[90] What purpose this served is not entirely clear, but preparation for cultivation is unlikely according to Johannessen.[91] Fires were probably started to improve the quality of grazing for wild game and to flush animals during hunting, and if this were so, there would be little or no reason to limit the area affected. The spread, in modern times, of scrub and mesophytic woodland into the levels is apparently the result of relatively heavy and selective grazing by cattle, accompanied by less frequent burning.[92]

Whatever the origin of grassland, it is generally less attractive than woodland to cultivators who lack plows and draft animals. Fernández de Oviedo y Valdés (1478-1557) reported that the Indians of Hispaniola burned woodland to plant maize; grassland was considered less fertile.[93] Perhaps more important, it is often difficult

81. Polo de Ondegardo (c. 1560), 1873, 165. Cf. Hernando Pizarro (1533), 1872, 121; and Toledo (1575), 1925, 372.

82. The sixteenth-century *relaciones* of Peru refer to stands of *queñua* (Jiménez de la Espada (ed), I, 1965, 208, 316, 331, 340) as the chief exception to the treelessness of the Andes (*ibid.,* 307, 328). Lizárraga (c. 1600) (1968, 86) and the *relación* for Abancay (Jiménez de la Espada (ed), 2, 1965, 22) mention the use of *queñua* in charcoal burning.

83. O. F. Cook, 1916a, 288-89; 1916b, 500, 512. Concerning the coastal *yungas*, Pedro Pizarro (1571-2) (2, 1921, 377) remarked: "These valleys are very insalubrious for mountain folk; they have many groves of trees and many reedy swamps."

84. Dickinson, 1969, 294-307.

85. Fernández de Oviedo y Valdés (1535), I, 1959b, 226; Ponce (1588), 1932, 311.

86. Beard (1953, 180) writes: "The forests of the slopes (in La Gran Sabana, Venezuela) always give the impression of nestling into some protective cranny in the hills."

87. "Intensive fires may eliminate most species of trees on flatlands, where fires sweep unimpeded" (Johannessen, 1963, 110).

88. Johannessen (1963, 73), writing here with special reference to the valley of the Río Aguán. In the area of San Marcos de Colón, hill slopes are preferred for cultivation "because of the extreme wetness of valley bottoms" in the rainy season (Dozier, 1958, 32).

89. Johannessen, 1963, 5, 99.

90. See also Taylor, 1961, 48; West, 1966, 108-22.

91. "Honduran farmers have traditionally considered flat grasslands unpromising for crops" (Johannessen, 1963, 100).

92. C. L. Dozier (1958, 26) reports burning to maintain pasture for cattle in the Danlí district of Honduras.

93. "Porque la tierra donde nace hierba, y no árboles y canas, no es tan fértil" (Fernández de Oviedo y Valdés (1526), 1942, 55; (1535), I, 1959b, 226). Cf. Rouse, 1939, 37. Denevan (1964, 23), however, refers to "thousands of mound fields" in Hispaniola, presumably in poorly drained savanna. On preference for woodland, see P. L. Wagner, 1962, 265; A. D. Hill, 1964, 60.

to penetrate with ordinary digging sticks on account of heavy root development and a compact clay horizon.[94] These problems were partly overcome in limited areas of the New World by the use of large digging sticks and, in the Andes, of the spade and the *taclla*.

WATER AND MARSH

Most intermontane basins are poorly drained. Many contain residual lakes, and some of the most accomplished agricultural terracing in the New World is to be found around lakes or former lakes in the basins of Mexico, Pátzcuaro, Atitlán and Titicaca.[95] The explanation of this may lie only partly in the scarcity of level land or in the difficulties of using such land. Fishing and the trapping of water-fowl widen the resource base,[96] making the economy as a whole more secure and settlement more permanent, which in turn encourages investment of time and energy in agricultural improvements.

Peru: From the highlands of the New World there are few reports of early drainage works, in contrast to the many references to irrigation. Cieza de León (c. 1550) described the floor of the basin of Zurite as "a large and deep morass" and then remarked upon the terraced fields of the surrounding piedmont.[97] The remains of these *andenes* can be clearly discerned. Some of the bottom land is now cultivated, but most of it is unimproved pasture for cattle. The basin of Oropesa, below

Cuzco, also is flanked by old agricultural terraces.[98] E. G. Squier (1877) commented upon the shallow lake of Muyna (or Oropesa) "with its surrounding marshes, through which the road follows an ancient causeway of stone."[99] According to a tradition preserved by Cieza de León, the site of Cuzco itself had to be drained before building could commence.[100]

The major valleys of northern and central Peru have long, trough-like sections parallel to the folds of the Andes. In places, the floors are poorly drained, with patches of marsh, small lakes and wider levels of lacustrine origin. Abandoned settlements along the middle and upper Río Santa (Callejón de Huailas) include stone-faced terraces for house sites and agriculture.[101] The highest open valley tract is known as the Pampa de Lampa. Again in the Jauja valley (Río Mantaro) former settlement sites are "located for the most part in the foothills."[102] Lake Paca, north of Jauja, is probably a residual feature. Wet lands *(islas)* near Muquiyanyo are under grass,[103] and the rectilinear field boundaries of cultivated fields probably date, like most of the present settlements *(reducciones),* from the Spanish Conquest.[104]

Attempts to protect low-lying cultivated land seem to have been comparatively rare in pre-Columbian times. Soria Lens states that the ancient Aymara built river defenses,[105] and the Incas are credited with similar improvements.[106] A short stretch of the Urubamba near Pisac has clearly been straightened and confined to the western side of the valley. At Ollantaitambo the banks

94. Brand, 1943b, 227; Beals, 1945, 130; West, 1948, 36; J. J. Parsons, 1955, 45; Palerm and Wolf, 1957, 15; Ferdon, 1959, 17; Johannessen, 1963, 75, 101-102; A. D. Hill, 1964, 32; Reina, 1967, 1. Cowgill and Hutchinson (1963b, 277) mention the use today of a "hoe-like stick . . . to break the sod" in the Mayan lowlands.

95. Agricultural terraces have also been reported around lakes Parinacochas, southern Peru (Bingham, 1922, 84), Tuctucocha, northern Peru (Wiener, 1880, 172), and Amatitlán, Guatemala (Borhegyi, 1959, 105).

96. Several scholars have stressed the importance of fish and water-fowl in the economies of the pre-Columbian inhabitants of the basins of central Mexico: see, Clavijero (c. 1780), I, 1917, 387; Linné, 1937, 56-74, and 1948; S. F. Cook, 1947-8, 46; Muller, 1952, 8-16; Deevey, 1957, 220-52; West, 1964a, 47; Tamayo, 1964, 111; West and Augelli, 1966, 242; Bruman, 1967, 17; Flannery, 1968, 83-86. Supporting illustrations include the map of the valley of Mexico by Alonzo de Santa Cruz, 1555-62 (Díaz del Castillo, 3, 1910); Barlow, 1949, pl. XIII; Robertson, 1959, pl. 57. Cervantes de Salazar (1554) (1953, 59), Díaz del Castillo (c. 1568 (2, 1910, 73) and Gage (1648) (1928, 76) refer to the use of aquatic bugs *(oquilín)* as human food in the basin of Mexico. See also López de Gómara (1552) 1964, 162; Anon. *(Códice Ramírez,* 1586-9), 1903, 30; Ealand, 1915, 211; Ancona, 1933a, 51-69, and 1933b, 103-108; Guerra, 1969, 39.

97. Cieza de León, 1864, 321. The village of Zurite lies on the northwestern side of the basin.

98. Bingham, 1922, 135, 141.

99. Squier, 1877, 421-22. Garcilaso de la Vega (1604) (1869, 230) refers to the building of a causeway across a swamp on the orders of Inca Mayta Ccapac.

100. Cieza de León (c. 1550), 1883, 99 (under the second Inca, Sinchi Roca). See also Díez de Betánzos (1551), 1880, 9.

101. W. C. Bennett, 1944a, 12, 14, 62; Dobyns, 1963, 494; Doughty, 1968, 10, 153.

102. Tschopik, 1947, 9. Cf. R. N. Adams, 1966, 3. Ishida (1960, pl. 27) shows agricultural terraces in the valley of the Río Mantaro.

103. R. N. Adams, 1966, 9.

104. R. N. Adams (1966, 3) states that the valley floor was tilled in pre-Columbian times, but provides no evidence for this. Lathrap (1970, 171) suggests that there was a shift from "bottom land farming" to slope farming (with terracing) in the basin of Huánuco after about 100 B.C.

105. Soria Lens, 1954, 91.

106. Sancho (1535), 1917, 154; Díez de Betánzos (1551), 1880, 111; Cobo (1653), 4, 1895, 189 ("En las tomas de los ríos hacían muy fuertes reparos contra sus crecientes y avenidas"); O. F. Cook, 1916b, 484 (Río Pampacahuana); Bingham, 1917, 253-60, 1948, 22; Regal, 1945, 102 (Río Paucartambo); Barrientos, 1923, 16; Comas, 1956, 198; K. Kelly, 1965, 328; Brundage, 1967, 17 (Río Huatanay, below Cuzco).

of the river have been strengthened,[107] most obviously near the site of an Inca bridge, but most of the anciently improved land here lies in broad terraces in a tributary valley behind the town. At Yucay, an outwash fan, magnificently terraced, impedes drainage, and the levels on the upstream side include stretches of undrained *pampa*. Agricultural terracing was a highly developed art in the middle Urubamba. Reclamation of the valley floor was probably a late and relatively minor achievement of the Incas.[108]

Ridging, apparently to form strips of cultivable land above a fluctuating but generally high water table, has been reported from several extensive lowlands and also from the basin of Lake Titicaca. The grassy levels beside the lake, in embayments and along the broad tributary valleys, present several problems for the cultivator. Recent alluvial soils are fertile but need to be drained. The shorelands, although workable, are to a varying extent saline, and salts also accumulate along the tops of ridges, eventually making them unsuitable for cultivation. Heavy clays underlie some of the flat *pampas* further removed from the lake.[109] In all cases, preparing land for cultivation is heavy work, calling for the *taclla* or the ox-drawn plow. In fact, large areas now serve chiefly as pasture for cattle and sheep and for small herds of llamas and alpacas.

The escarpments overlooking Lake Titicaca have been extensively terraced to make benches of deeper soil. Even after several years of fallow the ground is loose and only lightly covered with clumps of *ichu* grass. It can be worked with the aboriginal *liukana* or elbow hoe. J. A. Vellard observed — "les cultures, les *aynokas*, limitées et divisées par des murettes de pierre (i.e., *andenes*), couvrent une partie des versants dominant le Titicaca et le haut-plateau. Une règle traditionelle voulait 'les champs sur les pentes, les pâturages dans les pampas,' les parties basses."[110] In the basin of Titicaca, the lowest levels and the highest flights of terraces are now generally uncultivated.

Colombia: There are also "fossil" ridges and mounds within and around the margins of the *sabana* of Bogotá,[111]

suggesting the beginnings of reclamation, but the known evidence of Chibcha occupation, including "terracing,"[112] largely belongs to the surrounding slopes.[113] The levels of the Colombian *altiplano* were occupied by lakes during the more pluvial phases of the Pleistocene.[114] The chroniclers of the sixteenth and seventeenth centuries mention several lakes and areas of marshland.[115] As late as 1825, C. S. Cochrane commented that "[the plain around Bogotá] is principally divided into *potraras (potreros)* for grazing cattle and horses . . . a large portion of the plain is inundated during the whole year."[116] Ditching and the planting of eucalyptus have produced some improvement; nevertheless much of the *sabana* is used as pasture.

Ecuador: W. C. Bennett refers to high, intermontane flats around Ibarra that have "probably never been cultivated."[117] Some of these swampy *pampas* contain large artificial mounds *(tolas)* which could have been house platforms. In the central highlands between Cajabamba and Chunchi terracing of a rather simple kind is fairly common. Around Lake Colta terraced fields lie above wet lands that are partly under grass and partly reclaimed for agriculture.

Guatemala: Pedro de Alvarado (c. 1485-1541) noted that the basin of Quezaltenango *(Xelahum)* was heavily populated at the time of the Spanish Conquest.[118] How much of the floor was then cultivated is not clear, but Juan de Piñeda (1594) described the piedmont-sited *pueblo* of Quezaltenango as "asentado en un llano junto una ciénaga."[119] Some of the volcanic basins of western and central Guatemala probably once held lakes that dried out in late pre-Columbian times. Both the slopes and the levels are now intensively cultivated. The former are shaped into contour ridges or, in the case of the basin of San Marcos, terraced behind rough stone walls. Some of the higher terraces are now abandoned.[120]

107. Observed by Squier, 1877, 507.

108. Hutchinson (2, 1873, 47) questioned whether the flat floor of the valley of the Rimac was cultivated when the elaborate terraces above Chosica were constructed. Means (1925, 435) and Lanning (1967, 5) assume that bottom land generally was cultivated first.

109. Tschopik, 1951, 154.

110. Vellard, 1963, 68.

111. Joaquín Acosta, 1848, 204 ("Anchos *camellones* que son vestigios de antiguos cultivos de estos pueblos eminentemente agrícolas"); Eidt, 1959, 386; Broadbent, 1968, 135-47.

112. Haury and Cubillos, 1953, 83-86; Broadbent, 1963, 501-504, and 1965, 9; Donkin, 1968, 199-207.

113. Haury, 1953, 77. Fals-Borda (1962, 86-87) refers to hill sites in local legend. Cf. Broadbent, 1966, 7.

114. Van der Hammen and González 1960, 266.

115. Castellanos (1559), 1886, 111, 280; Rodríguez y Freile (1636), 1961, 35, 37; Fernández Piedrahita (1668-88), I, 1942, 47. See also Triano, 1922, 37-44.

116. Cochrane, 2, 1825, 5.

117. W. C. Bennett, 1946a, 5.

118. Alvarado, 1924, 59.

119. Piñeda, 1908, 436; 1925, 338.

120. According to Mayer-Oakes (1960, 170), the chief settlements in the valley of Guatemala at the time of the conquest occupied high ground.

British Honduras: Abandoned agricultural terraces on gentle limestone slopes have been reported from the Vaca plateau, south of El Cayo.[121] Settlement and land use studies of the upper Belize valley[122] indicate that the ancient Maya built house mounds on the better drained alluvial lands and farmed the slopes, as their successors do today. Here, as elsewhere, terracing was an effective means of accumulating cultivable soil.

Chiapas, Mexico: In high Chiapas, around and to the north of San Cristóbal de Las Casas, certain aspects of land use appear not to have changed much since the conquest. The floor of the basin of San Cristóbal itself is wet for much of the year and largely uncultivated. The more northerly basins are essentially small *poljes* with flat grassy bottoms that are sometimes grazed. Cultivation is restricted to the slopes, in the form of temporary *milpas* and terraced fields distributed along short tributary valleys. The *cabecera* of Chamula now occupies the (uncultivated) floor of its basin, but the hamlets of the dependent *parajes* are mostly sited on high ground close to their fields.[123] The larger and less isolated basins to the south of San Cristóbal, such as Aguacatenango and Amatenango-Teopisca, display greater evidence of change. The surrounding terraces[124] are largely abandoned. The wooded interfluves are cleared for temporary cultivation, while the basin floors, arranged in large fields, are regularly plowed and, in the case of Aguacatenango, irrigated.

Prehistoric settlement in the highlands of Chiapas involved, at different times, the occupation of headlands and "valley floor" sites.[125] The regrouping of population along the piedmonts *(despeñolamiento)* under the *pax hispánica* may have reinforced a current trend towards the levels. But re-siting before the conquest, unaccompanied by improvements in technology, was not necessarily followed by changes in the distribution of cultivated land. R. M. Adams writes: "The pre-Hispanic distribution of settlements [in the central highlands of Chiapas] in the main is confined to the interior basins and their immediately surrounding hills, suggesting that cultivation of bottom lands in these basins was a far more important source of local subsistence than it is at present."[126] The inference appears to disregard the wide extent of terracing of a kind still in use in the remoter parts of the highlands.

Central and Northwest Mexico: Several of the basins on the southwestern margin of the Mesa Central contain residual lakes or stretches of marsh, and in parts of the *Bajío* highly weathered soils lie over hard pans "so compact as to present an obstacle to the penetration of water, plant roots and agricultural implements."[127] Grass-covered plains were evidently a feature of this area at the time of the conquest, and it is doubtful whether they were much cultivated.[128] The wet lands of Zacapu, once the property of neighboring Indian tribes, were only reclaimed for *haciendas* at the end of the nineteenth century.[129] The Río Lerma rises in marsh and in numerous small lakes on the eastern side of the high basin of Toluca. Agricultural terraces of late pre-Columbian origin lie around Calixtlahuaca,[130] to the northwest of the levels. *Chinampa* cultivation here is a modern development.[131]

The floors of the basins (*vegas,* at 1500 to 2000 meters) within and immediately to the east of the Sierra Madre Occidental also appear to have been under grass at the beginning of the sixteenth century,[132] while many of the tributary valleys have been terraced for cultivation.[133] In parts of the Sierra Madre Oriental, areas of heavy sod above about 1700 meters could not easily be cultivated even with the early wooden plow, and tilled land was largely confined to basin slopes before the introduction of the heavy steel plow.[134]

The earliest accounts of the basin of Puebla-Tlaxcala refer to shallow lakes bordered by wet grassland. Over almost the entire area of the levels drainage is necessary for successful cultivation.[135] In the northern part particularly this has been achieved by ditching, and the result is a pattern of long, narrow fields. G. C. Wilken maintains that these are essentially the same as the *chinampas* of the valley of Mexico, and, furthermore, that they are probably of pre-Columbian origin. The state of Tlaxcala was one of the most heavily populated parts of Mexico when the Spaniards arrived[136] and shortage of hill land may well have led to attempts to drain

121. Ower, 1927, 384; J. E. Thompson, 1931, 228-29, and 1966, 358; Lundell, 1940, 9-11.

122. Romney *et al.,* 1959, 110-15; Willey, *et al.,* 1965, 24, 31. See also Reina, 1967, 3.

123. The pre-conquest site of Chamula lay on the Cerro Ecatepec, above modern San Felipe (Calnek, 1961, 8).

124. L. E. Guzmán, 1962, 398-406.

125. R. M. Adams, 1961, 341-43; Borhegyi, 1965a, 31, 41-43, and 1965b, 68.

126. R. M. Adams, 1961, 341. Borhegyi (1965b, 69) also refers to intensive cultivation of the basin levels of highland Guatemala during the late classic period.

127. Stevens, 1964, 274.

128. The basin of Cherán may be an exception (Beals, 1946, 22). The northern part of the *Bajío* lay beyond the limits of aboriginal agriculture (Chevalier, 1963, 3, 13).

129. Carrasco, 1952, 16.

130. García Payón, 1941, 210-11.

131. West and Armillas, 1950, 172.

132. West, 1964, 48; Howard and Griffiths, 1966, 14.

133. L. Herold (1965), who also comments upon earlier observations.

134. Dicken, 1936, 173, 175.

135. Wilken, 1969, 215-41; Pfeifer, 1966, 86-107.

136. Cook and Simpson, 1948, 18-38; Gibson, 1952, 138-42.

and cultivate the levels (which account for less than a quarter of the basin). But at present there is no proof of this,[137] and it has to be borne in mind that the bottom lands were almost certainly more waterlogged in the sixteenth century than they are today.[138] Accelerated erosion of the surrounding volcanic slopes, in spite of terracing,[139] has improved the condition of the levels, but a decisive shift in agricultural site values may not have occurred before the conquest.

THORN SCRUB AND DESERT

Northeast Mexico: At the beginning of the sixteenth century, agriculture was absent or only poorly developed over the arid eastern half of the plateau of northern Mexico. The floors *(bariales)* of the desert basins are often saline.[140] Further south, in the extreme east of the Mesa Central, the Llanos de San Juan comprise a group of level basins that are still partly occupied by salt marsh.

Valleys of Tehuacán and Oaxaca: The floors and lower slopes of several of the large intermontane valleys of southern Mexico are semi-arid.[141] High evapotranspiration reduces the value of a generally low annual rainfall. The natural vegetation is open thorn scrub and cactus rather than grass. The availability of stream or underground water has at all times strongly influenced the distribution of agriculture. In the broad valley of Tehuacán, sedentary cultivation was early associated with the tributary *barrancas*[142] where patches of fresh alluvium are periodically flooded. In many of the *barrancas* simple cross-channel terracing served to concentrate both soil and water behind series of rock dams. Subsequently, agriculture appears to have spread along the banks of streams and, in association with the building of canals (c. 200 B.C. - A.D. 800), into adjacent sections

of the valley floor.[143] The smaller and higher terraces are now mostly abandoned and partly destroyed where the intermittent streams have reestablished themselves. Furthermore, the springs above the town of Tehuacán, which have long been used for purposes of irrigation, are highly mineralized, and some of the older canals and adjacent fields also lie abandoned as the result of the accumulation of salts followed by wind erosion.[144] Agriculture is now spreading over the middle and upper slopes (above 1800 meters) of the flanking *sierras* at the expense of pine-oak woodland.

Over the floor of the valley of Oaxaca the average annual rainfall (500 to 700 mm) is similar to that of Tehuacán. The former valley has, however, a higher water table which in places cuts the surface to form small areas of marsh.[145] The earliest settlement sites (8000 to 1500 B.C.) in the valley were caves in the high piedmont, occupied by folk who depended on plant collecting and finally on vegeculture or incipient cultivation.[146] On the higher alluvial terraces the water table lies only 2 to 10 meters below the surface and here wells were sunk for the purpose of hand irrigation *(riego a brazo)* during the first farming phase (1500 to 600 B.C.). The villages occupied spurs and sandy rises away from possible flooding. As population increased, well irrigation and flood-water farming[147] and also forms of dry farming, spread more widely over the floor of the valley. At about the same time, higher ground, especially along the more important tributary valleys, was occupied and irrigated by means of canals. Terracing too may have commenced during this period or a little later. J. A. Neely has described agricultural terraces at Hierve el Agua (near San Lorenzo Albarrados), in the extreme south of the valley, that were in use from *circa* 500 B.C. to A.D. 1350.[148] Other abandoned terraces, including some near Mitla, belong to the Monte Albán V period (c. A.D. 1350).[149] Presently cultivated land immediately behind the town of Mitla is arranged in broad, sloping terraces.

---

137. The earliest indication of swamp cultivation is in a description (1614) by Alonso de la Mota y Escobar (Wilken, 1969, 238): "There are many farms owned by the Spaniards. They sow maize around what they call the swamp of Tlaxcala and now have started to sow irrigated wheat...." See West and Armillas (1950, 172) for "listas de tierra levantadas, llamadas *melgas*" in various parts of central and southern Mexico. Wilken (1969, 235) also mentions other areas of "drained fields." J. R. Parsons (1971, 220, 223, 226) argues strongly that parts of the Texcocan lakeshore plain were drained during the Aztec period.
138. Wilken, 1969, 222, 239.
139. Observed along the eastern (Tlaxcala to Zacatelco) and western (San Cristóbal Tepongtla to Texmelucán) margins of the basin.
140. West, 1964a, 50; Stevens, 1964. 271.
141. For the history of land use in the valley of the Río Balsas, see Armillas, 1949, 85-113; Brand, 1943b, 225-31.
142. C. E. Smith, 1965, 76.

143. Isabel Kelly (1945), investigating the dry Autlán-Tuxcacuesco area of Jalisco, used an unusually early *visita* (1525) and the distribution of archaeological sites to reconstruct the late pre-Columbian settlement pattern. She found that two locations were preferred, "the valley fringes, frequently including the lower slopes of cerros and sierras" and "the open valley, adjacent to running water."
144. C. E. Smith, 1965, 68, 72-73; Byers, 1964, 151.
145. Lorenzo (1958-9, 56) found no soils of lacustrine origin, but "en dos zonas, Papalutla y Zimatlán-Zaachila, existen ciénegas que han obligado, en varias épocas del pasado, a efectuar labores de drenaje."
146. Flannery *et al.,* 1967, 450.
147. *Ibid.*; Spores, 1965, 971.
148. Neely, 1967, 15-17.
149. Anne V. T. Kirkby (personal communication), and 1973, 35.

Northern Chile and Northwest Argentina: The southern limit of aboriginal terracing lies in northern Chile and northwest Argentina, from the western flanks of the Andes (at 2500 to 4000 meters above sea level) to the basin and range country to the east of the Puna.[150] The average annual precipitation is of the order of 250 to 450 mm. The basin levels are particularly dry and mostly saline. The surrounding slopes, which support thorn scrub passing into tola heath *(Lepidophyllum quadrangulare)* at about 4000 meters, offer the only opportunity for subsistence agriculture. As in the case of the semi-arid valley of Tehuacán, it has been suggested that the earliest improved sites were along tributary *barrancas* where rock dams were built to trap flood water and alluvium and to form plots of deepened and relatively moist soils.[151] Later, apparently, outwash fans and hill slopes were terraced and irrigated by spring water led along canals.

Substantially more than 50 percent of all anciently terraced land in Chile and Argentina is now abandoned. A predominantly physical explanation for this retreat of cultivation appears more reasonable than for most other areas of terracing in the New World. A very small reduction in the average rainfall, or greater fluctuations between years, would very likely be critical for agriculture in peripheral locations, and there is also a strong possibility of a gradual lowering in the level of ground water leading to the disappearance of springs.

LOCAL CONSIDERATIONS

FORM AND CONSTRUCTION

Classification: The agricultural terraces of the aboriginal New World belong to three main types. One comprises fields supported by walls built across an embayment or a narrow valley that was originally occupied by an intermittent stream. The cropping surfaces are characteristically level, and water drains into the fill from the surrounding slopes. The catchment is usually many times larger than the area cultivated, which is an important advantage. Such cross-channel terracing represents a significant advance on methods of farming that make use of annual, but largely uncontrolled, accumulations of alluvium. The combination of effectiveness and essential simplicity of construction has prompted the suggestion that this is the earliest form of true terracing.[152]

The lateral or contour terrace has many variations. At one extreme, the natural slope is but little modified;[153]

at the other, substantial walls support perfectly level benches that may be irrigated. Wherever surfaces are level, the height of the wall (up to 9 meters) is related to the steepness of the natural slope and to the width of the bench; similarly the thickness of the wall, to the volume of the fill. The engineering skills required for level bench terracing may be considerable.

The third, and rarest, type is the valley-floor terrace.[154] The walls or excavated faces lie roughly at right angles to the direction of drainage, but the stream remains in being. Breaks of slope of natural terraces are sometimes incorporated in the system. The broad planting surfaces are level, and it appears that the purpose of such terracing was always to facilitate irrigation by water drawn off at some higher point.

Walls: Terraces carved entirely out of deeply weathered material or volcanic ash are usually unfaced or merely buttressed with stone (which in such areas is naturally scarce). The riser may slope back as much as 45 degrees, depending on the cohesiveness of the mantle, and consequently some considerable area of land is lost to cultivation. Benches cut in colluvial deposits or outwash fans are generally faced with stone.

Most agricultural terraces are bounded, forward and back, by stone walls behind which soil has been placed or has accumulated. The walls may be simply parallel lines of loose stone, taken from the field in the course of cultivation and tending to halt the downward movement of soil. This rarely produces a level surface.

The quality of the stonework generally improves with the height of the wall and the volume of the fill; it also must necessarily reflect the experience of the constructors. The steeper the natural slope, the deeper the foundations tend to be. The more massive walls usually consist of two faces separated by rubble.[155] The outer face — often inclined toward the rearward slope for greater strength[156] — has to be adequate to support the fill under conditions of high soil moisture. This is a particularly important consideration where terraces are irrigated. Dry stonework naturally allows the slow seepage of water from one level to the next, but drains also may be incorporated. The state terraces of the Incas, based on earlier Andean experience, furthering a policy

150. Field, 1966a.

151. Le Paige, 1958, 20; Wright, 1963, 65-74. Boman (2, 1908, 605) recognized the advantages of slopes for early agriculture.

152. Le Paige, 1958, 20; Spencer and Hale, 1961, 27, 29; Wright, 1962, 97, 99, and 1963, 66, 68, 70, 72.

153. The flattened surfaces *(bancales)* produced by the accumulation of soil behind lines of maguey, characteristic of the eastern part of the Mesa Central, Mexico, is described as "semi-terracing" by West (1970).

154. Cf. Zohary (1954, 22) and Mayerson (1960, 31), writing of the Negev.

155. Gamarra Dulanto and Maldonado, 1945, 50; Field, 1966a, 396.

156. Garcilaso de la Vega (1604), 1871, 4.

of land improvement, and built with *mit'a* labor, display all these features to perfection. Their special features include the use of trimmed stone;[157] service stairways, flanked by side walls, between flights of terraces; and steps set into the walls.[158] Building proceeded upslope, the width and height of the benches being carefully adjusted to the natural gradient.[159] The regularity and cyclopean scale of the structures are without parallel in the New World. In fact, much Inca terracing appears to overstep the bounds of mere utility and to take on symbolic significance.[160]

Fill: Cross-channel terraces were filled in succession by material washed down from adjacent slopes,[161] and the process may have been deliberately accelerated by the clearing of vegetation and loose stones.[162] It has been argued that in the valley of Nochixtlán (Mixteca Alta) post-classic cultivators (c. A.D. 1000+) removed surface *caliche* to facilitate the erosion of underlying red marl.[163] In places, buried walls point to the destruction or to the reorganization of earlier fields.[164]

Some valley-floor and contour terraces are carved largely out of unconsolidated deposits and the term "fill" is inappropriate, even where stone walls separate the cropping surfaces. However, most contour terraces have been filled by the downward movement of soil under cultivation (which may lead to bedrock being exposed toward the back of the terrace) and/or by the introduction of soil from elsewhere. Where terraces were gradually filled, the retaining walls too may have been heightened in stages.[165] Over steep and rocky slopes, hand-filling was often essential. It also allowed the nature of the fill, and thus in part the water balance, to

be controlled. The later Inca terraces were first packed with a mixture of rubble and clay *(tierra arcillosa)*.[166] This was covered by 30 to 40 cm of top soil *(tierra vegetal)* that sometimes had to be brought from a distance.[167] Cieza de León (c. 1550), writing of the Second Inca, Sinchi Roca, states that at first "the whole valley of Cuzco was barren . . . so they brought many thousands of loads of earth from the great forests of the Andes, and spread it all over the land."[168] The excavation of a terrace at Cubietas Viejas (British Honduras) has indicated that soil from an adjacent swamp was introduced.[169] A. C. S. Wright found that some terraces in northern Chile have a compact soil horizon at about 40 cm below the surface.[170] The purpose of this was probably to guard against solifluction, to reduce seepage, and to direct excess irrigation water toward one corner of the plot.[171] But in certain cases it may also have so restricted drainage as to contribute to the accumulation of injurious salts.

SOCIAL BASIS AND PURPOSE

The agricultural terraces of the aboriginal New World represent an enormous investment of time, energy, skill and imagination. Individually, however, they are mostly small and irregular in plan and distribution. They were undoubtedly constructed piecemeal by single families or small groups of families, and, unlike irrigation, their maintenance involved cooperation at a level no higher than that of the village community. The one important exception is the terracing organized by the Incas as part of a systematic and nationwide policy of land improvement and colonization.[172]

157. Pedro Pizarro (1571-2), 2, 1921, 305; Cobo (1653), 4, 1895, 188; Squier, 1877, 360.

158. Pedro Pizarro (1571-2), 2, 1921, 305, 332.

159. Garcilaso de la Vega (1604), 1871, 4; Cobo (1653), 4, 1895, 188.

160. This also may be true of Inca roads and storehouses (D. E. Thompson, 1968b, 72). There is an interesting comment in Toledo (1570-72) (1882, 196): "Y cuando no habia cosas útiles, les hacian trabajar en cosas inútiles, como era en echar rios por unas partes y por otras, y hacer paredes muy largas de una parte y de otra por los caminos, y escaleras de piedras de que no habia necesidad."

161. L. Herold, 1965, 22, 108, 124, 129, 130, 147; Field, 1966a, 39, 219, 228, 285, 428.

162. Suggested in studies of ancient agricultural terraces in the Negev and the Judean hills (Amiran and Kedar, 1956, 215; Shanan *et al.,* 1957 and 1958; Ron, 1966, 46).

163. Spores, 1969, 563-64.

164. L. E. Guzmán, 1962. 401; L. Herold, 1965, 122; Field, 1966a, 228. Earlier walls were observed by the present author in exposed sections of fill near Zapotitlán, Mexico *(infra* p. 69).

165. L. Herold, 1965, 114, 122.

166. S. S. Hill, I, 1860, 183; O. F. Cook, 1916b, 509; Bingham, 1922, 56-57; Horkheimer, 1958, 84; Valcárcel, 1959, 136; Bonavia, 1967-8, 272, and 1968a, 81. Cf. Stanislawski, 1962, 46-47.

167. Matienzo (1567), 1910, 12; Sarmiento de Gamboa (1572), 1907, 98; Squier, 1877, 360; Markham, 1880, 479-80; O. F. Cook, 1925, 105; M. Sáenz, 1933, 54; Bingham, 1948, 13; Bernedo Málaga, 1949, 104; Gade, 1975, 61; Pulgar Vidal, n.d., 77. Gamarra Dulanto and Maldonado (1945) maintain that the terraces near Chosica, Peru, were gradually filled with fine material from the slopes above; the coarser debris was apparently trapped behind specially constructed walls.

168. Cieza de León, 1883, 99.

169. Hopkins, 1968, 41.

170. Wright, 1963, 71.

171. Field (1966a, 102) observed that the planting surfaces of the terraces at Belén, Chile, slope away from an inner corner beside the water-drop channel.

172. Sarmiento de Gamboa (1572), 1907, 98; Garcilaso de la Vega (1604), 1871, 3-5, 324.

Level surfaces: It is above all evident that terracing produces plots of more or less level land, and such surfaces are essential where irrigation, except by hand, is also practiced. An association between terracing and irrigation in the dry highlands of Middle and South America might therefore be predicted. At the same time, it is very doubtful whether the mere convenience of level surfaces was anywhere an important consideration, for hand cultivation, unlike plow agriculture, is not notably hampered by broken terrain.

Erosion control: The inspection of numerous sites has produced little evidence that terraces were constructed primarily to check soil erosion. Piecemeal terracing is not a satisfactory answer to gully erosion over valley slopes, and, as Wright has pointed out, surface wash, involving the removal of small amounts of top soil, may at first increase fertility and thus conceal the harmful long-term consequences until it is too late to act effectively.[173]

Soil and soil moisture: Cross-channel terracing evidently took advantage of normal, and probably deliberately accelerated, soil erosion. The effect, and presumably the purpose, was to create plots of deepened soil. The accumulation of soil also seems to have been the object of much contour walling, and the effect was to forestall widespread erosion. Benches excavated in deep, unconsolidated deposits are comparatively rare. The majority of terraces apparently were designed to overcome the chief disadvantages of slopes for farming in areas with a pronounced dry season — thin soils and inadequate soil moisture.[174]

CROPS

It appears that terrace-building in the Andean valleys under the Incas had as its prime object the expansion of maize cultivation, wherever possible in association with irrigation.[175] On the eastern flanks of the Andes, a special kind of terracing for coca is probably of Inca

or earlier origin.[176] Above the normal altitudinal limit of maize (3200 to 3500 meters), in high valleys and over breaks of slope on the *altiplano,* unirrigated terraces presumably were used for the staple food crops — tubers (potatoes, oca, ulluca) and local grains (quinoa, cañahua) — as is the case today.[177] A viceregal ordinance of 1575 refers to the "gran cantidad de chacras de mayz y papas, que estan hechas de andenes."[178] Similarly, Pedro Simón (1626) mentions root crops and maize *(raices y maíz)* in connection with the terraces of the Timote in the Venezuelan Andes.[179]

In Middle America, maize was an even more important food crop than in the Andes, and, although there appears to be little direct information, one can probably assume a close association with terracing wherever this was practiced. Terraces near Chilchota (Michoacán), abandoned by 1579, had been used for maize.[180] Today, irrigated terraces in the Zapotec highlands of Oaxaca, around Lakes Pátzcuaro (Mexico) and Atitlán (Guatemala), and above Texcoco in the valley of Mexico, are planted to fruit trees and vegetables as well as maize.

The ultimate benefits of agricultural terracing were larger, more concentrated and less fluctuating yields. Where output was related to the urban market, through trading connections or systems of tribute, the increase in productivity served to compensate for generally poor transportation facilities. Moreover, by extending the range of ecological conditions, terracing probably helped to promote the varietal diversity that is such a marked feature of the cultivated plants of the New World.[181]

IRRIGATION

Canal irrigation first appears in the archaeological record of the Americas at about the same time as agricultural terracing — i.e., in the middle of the first millennium B.C. On the coast of Peru this is late in the middle formative (pre-classic) period (c. 400 B.C.).[182] Subse-

173. Wright, 1962, 99.

174. Raikes (1967, 5) includes terracing among examples of proto-engineering "for mitigating climatic stress." Kassas (1966, 155) emphasizes the importance of depth of soil in conserving moisture. See also Wright, 1962, 99; L. Herold, 1965, 132; Kirkby, 1973, 77.

175. Pedro Pizarro (1571-2), 1921, 305; Garcilaso de la Vega (1604), 1871, 3-5; Murra, 1958, 31, 1960, 395. For *chicha,* "un elemento sagrado," as well as "bread" grain. Boman (2, 1908, 604) and Bowman (1924, 321) thought that maize was probably the chief crop grown on the terraces of northern Chile and northwest Argentina. Field (1966a, 502) found little or no evidence of terracing "for special crops" in the same area.

176. Payne, I, 1892, 341; Métraux, 1946, 137.

177. Hodgson, 1951, 185, 187.

178. Ballesteros (ed), I, 1752, 148. See also Ortiz de Zúñiga (1562), 1, 1967, 216 *(maíz y trigo y papas),* and 2, 1972, 58, 83; Ramírez (1597), 1936, 41.

179. Simón, 2, 1892, 197. Maize was stored in subterranean silos — *mintoyes* — (Febres Cordero, 1920, 16; Acosta Saignes, 1952, 12-13, and 1958, 6).

180. Paso y Troncoso and Vargas Rea (eds), 2(7), 1944, 24.

181. On the promotion and recognition of genetic mutations under Andean conditions, see Wright, 1962, 100, and 1963, 73. Cf. Gade, 1975, 61. Maize, in particular, is very responsive to improvements in habitat (Mangelsdorf, MacNeish and Willey, 1964, 439).

182. Willey, 1955, 578; Towle, 1961, 112, 121; Collier, 1961, 105-106, and 1962, 169-70; Sherbondy de Tord, 1969, 117. See also B. J. Price, 1971, especially 14, 27.

quently, the various classic (Mochica, Nazca) and post-classic (Chimú, Ica, Inca) cultures developed elaborate systems for the distribution of ground and surface water.[183] Within the Andes the Inca rulers were responsible for the construction of important irrigation canals,[184] and again these superseded or supplemented earlier systems.[185] In Middle America, the first structural evidence for irrigation comes from the valley of Tehuacán (pre-classic, c. 900 - 200 B.C.),[186] and from a terraced site in the south of the valley of Oaxaca (c. 500 B.C.).[187] A pre-classic date has also been assigned to a "water distribution system" at Amalucan, Puebla.[188] So far as is known, there is nothing of comparable age in areas further north. Irrigation was practiced around classic Teotihuacán,[189] and in the Southwest of the United States from about the middle of the first millennium A.D. (Hohokam Culture).[190]

At the time of the Spanish Conquest, irrigation by canal or controlled flooding was widely but unevenly developed in the Andes,[191] from Venezuela to northern Chile and Argentina, and also in North and Middle America, from the Southwest of the United States, through the Sierra Madre Occidental, to central Mexico[192] and Chiapas. In the highlands of the New World, the distribution of irrigation and that of terracing were broadly similar, both being related to the distribution of seasonal or permanent aridity. In sixteenth-century sources, such as the *Crónicas* and the *Relaciones geográficas,* reports of irrigation greatly outnumber those of terracing, and it seems likely that some of the former concern places where the two techniques were combined.[193] Locally, they are known to have been combined, principally at sites within the central Andes (Inca), northwest Argentina and northern Chile (Diaguita, Atacameño, Humahuaca, Inca), the Sierra Nevada de Santa Marta (Tairona), the Venezuelan Andes (Timoto-Cuica), the basins of Mexico, Oaxaca, Tehuacán and Teotihuacán, and the Southwest of the United States (Hohokam, Pima, Papago).

ABANDONED TERRACES

A large proportion of the area at various times terraced for cultivation in the Americas is now abandoned.[194] This is clear from more or less broken walls and gullied fill and from heavily vegetated surfaces. Terraces are very liable to erode once parts of the supporting walls have collapsed, and in the case of cross-channel benches the former (intermittent) stream may re-establish itself. Many unbroken and only lightly covered terraces also are abandoned, but this can only be established by inquiry, for planting surfaces are sometimes left fallow for ten years or more.

Problems of a physical nature, chiefly connected with water supply, must have been encountered before, as well as after, the Spanish Conquest. Abandoned terraces are particularly common at the northern and southern ends of the overall distribution and also within less extensive arid regions such as the Mixteca Alta. The explanation may lie in critical fluctuations in rainfall and/or in a gradual lowering of the water table, and consequently a reduction in the supply of irrigation water. Moreover, irrigated lands, under conditions of high evaporation and where the water supply is barely adequate, are likely to suffer from the accumulation of harmful minerals,[195] and this in fact appears to be the reason for the abandonment of some terraced fields.[196]

The calamitous decline in the size of the aboriginal population after the Spanish Conquest was followed by changes in settlement pattern. Villages were abandoned

183. Cieza de Léon (c. 1550), 1864, 129, 236, 263; José, de Acosta (1590), 1880, 159, 267-68; Lizárraga (c. 1600), 1968, 43; Garcilaso de la Vega (1604), 1871, 147-48; Avila (1608), 1873, 144; Rivero y Ustariz and Tschudi, 1853, 250; Rossel Castro, 1942, 196-202; Regal, 1943, 210-13, 1945, 82, and 1970; Rowe, 1948, 31; Reparaz, 1958, 45, 57; Kinzl, 1963, 331-39; Sherbondy de Tord, 1969, 113-43.

184. Díez de Betánzos (1551), 1880, 103; Las Casas (1527-59) I, 1958, 199-200, and 2, 1958, 406; Borregán (1562-65), 1948, 81; Sarmiento de Gamboa (1572), 1907, 71, 132, 158; Cristóbal de Molina (1574-5), 1873, 19; Garcilaso de la Vega (1604), 1871, 3, 77 (for arable and pasture); Vázquez de Espinosa (c. 1628), 1942, nos. 1547, 1553, 1574; González Suárez, I, 1878, 196; Regal, 1945, 75-110; Murra, 1946, 810, and 1960, 395; Bernedo Málaga, 1949, 103-9; Zegarra, 1953, 173-74; Caballero Farfán, 1959, 127-30; Kobori, 1960, 419; Katz, 1960, 59-76; Baudin, 1962, 146-47.

185. Latcham, 1936, 615-16 (Atacameño, c. A.D. 900-1100).

186. MacNeish, 1961, 15, and 1967, 24; Coe and Flannery, 1964, 652 (classic, c. 200 B.C. - A.D. 800); C. E. Smith, 1965, 75; Woodbury, 1966, 346-47.

187. Neely, 1967, 15-17. See also Flannery *et al.,* 1967; Kirkby, 1973.

188. Fowler, 1969, 208-15.

189. Millon, 1954, 177-80, and 1957, 160-66; Sanders, 1965, 159, 174; B. J. Price, 1971, 19-20.

190. Castetter and Bell, 1951, 156; Ezell, 1960, 5, 36; Woodbury, 1961b, 552, and 1962, 303; Haury, 1962, 120-21; Willey, 1966a, 221-22.

191. Troll, 1958, 25-27.

192. Orozco y Berra (1880), 1950, 372; Armillas, 1949, 85-113; Palerm, 1954, 2-15, 64-74; Sanders and Price, 1968, 176-80.

193. Spencer (1964, 105) makes a similar suggestion in discussing agricultural terracing in China.

194. Wright (1963, 73) estimates that four-fifths of the ancient terraces of northern Chile are presently abandoned. For the whole of the Americas, the proportion can hardly be less than one-third.

195. Kellogg, 1953, 34.

196. Steward and Faron, 1959, 121; C. T. Smith, 1960, 406; C. E. Smith, 1965, 68; Neely, 1967, 15-17.

and communities regrouped under a policy of *congregación*. The outer limits of improved land contracted, and where terracing was characteristic the higher contour benches — relatively narrow, most difficult to irrigate, and in places poorly constructed — were first abandoned. Fields that require maintenance are particularly vulnerable under conditions of population decline. So too are irrigation works, and the neglect of canals, rather than any reduction in the supply of water at source, may, in particular cases, be the chief reason for the later "shortage" of water.

Physical considerations: Palaeoclimatic studies exist for only small areas of the highlands of Middle and South America, chiefly the valley of Mexico[197] and the *sabana* of Bogotá.[198] They give little support to the idea of a secular decline in rainfall over the last 2000 to 2500 years. On the other hand, short- and medium-term fluctuations in rainfall are known to have occurred,[199] and in many cases these could account for terrace abandonment where a climatic explanation, in whole or in part, seems to be appropriate.

A reduction in rainfall has been suggested to explain the abandonment of terraced fields in Peru,[200] southern Bolivia,[201] northern Chile and northwest Argentina,[202] in places where irrigation would have been impossible, or at least where there is no evidence of irrigation, and precipitation today is insufficient for cultivation. In the arid and semi-arid extremities of the distribution of terracing, a very small reduction in average rainfall for a decade or two, or alternatively greater fluctuations between years, could have had a quite disproportionate effect on the extent of cultivation.[203]

In the valley of Mexico, and probably throughout Middle America, the late pre-classic (formative) period (after c. 500 B.C.) appears to coincide roughly with relatively dry conditions, followed by periodic fluctuations in rainfall. This dry phase possibly formed the background to important developments in the control and the conservation of water — irrigation, *chinampa* farming and terracing.[204] Drier conditions tend to stimulate improvements in technique; subsequent fluctuations are likely to lead to the extension of cultivation and then to its retreat. This sequence of events may have been repeated several times in particular areas without necessarily involving the reoccupation of abandoned terraces.

As deserving of consideration as fluctuations in rainfall, at least in northern Chile and northwest Argentina, is the strong possibility of a steady fall in the level of ground water since the last pluvial phase of the Pleistocene.[205] Deforestation, followed by accelerated soil erosion and an increased rate of run-off, would have reinforced this trend. Local reports of springs drying up are fairly common throughout the highlands;[206] but, as has already been said, the evidence for this is often confused by the neglect of old irrigation works.[207]

Cultural considerations: The early Spaniards were frequently impressed by the density of Indian settlement,[208] and their estimates of population are generally being

197. Lorenzo, 1956; Willey, 1964. See also Armillas, 1966, 178.

198. Van der Hammen and González, 1960.

199. Hewett *et al.,* 1913, 43-70; Leighly, 1953, 11-15; Montes, 1958-9, 35-52; Yazawa, 1960, 413; Cowgill and Hutchinson, 1963a, 39, and 1963b, 281; Cardich, 1964, 30-40; Dollfus, 1965, 227-38; Pejme, 1966 (English summary); Hastenrath, 1967, 238, and 1968, 131-56.

200. Gamarra Dulanto and Maldonado (1945) concluded that the upper *andenes* in the ruined systems above Chosica must have depended on rainfall alone, and that terraces were filled by small and frequent additions of material washed in behind prepared walls; apparently soil was not taken from the valley bottom, as was the case in parts of the Sierra. See also Lanning, 1965, 68; C. T. Smith, 1960, 406.

201. Schmieder, 1926, 108; Rydén, 1952, 49.

202. Moreno, 1901, 585-86; Boman, 2, 1908, 603-604; Bowman, 1909, 267, 1924, 321; Márquez Miranda, 1939, 242; Gaignard, 1965, 310.

203. Armillas (1964, 317, and 1969, 701-702) argues that the northern frontier of agriculture retreated southward following "environmental deterioration" (i.e., the expansion of the North American arid zone) between the twelfth and the fifteenth centuries. Cf. J. N. Hill, 1966, 23-24.

204. Tolstoy, 1958, 70; Gibson, 1964, 5. See also Lorenzo, 1956, table; Mayer-Oakes, 1960, 173; Jiménez Moreno, 1966, 30.

205. Latcham, 1938, 107; Márquez Miranda, 1939, 108; Fernández de Lara, 1953, 156; Vita-Finzi, 1959, 402; Wright, 1963, 68.

206. Wright (1963, 68) writes, *apropos* of northern Chile: "In some localities [the ancient terraces] have been completely abandoned, probably because the springs or streams formerly nourishing them have dried up with the general drying out of the landscape. In other localities, formerly farmed, the volume of water is now adequate only to supply the lowest tiers of terraces."

207. Markham in Cieza de León, 1864, 237; Latcham, 1936c, 616; Reed, 1944, 209; Armillas, 1949, 85-113.

208. For example, Anon. (c. 1530), 1917, 18, 55; Motolinía (1541), 1951, 87; Cieza de León (c. 1550), 1864, 129, 360; Castellanos (1559), 1886, 141-62; Las Casas (1527-59), I, 1958, 31, 168, 178-79, 182, 186; Cervantes de Salazar (1554), 1953, 78.

confirmed by modern research.[209] During the fifteenth century in parts of central Mexico, numbers probably more than matched the long-term carrying capacity of the land at the prevailing level of technology.[210] However, during the sixteenth and early seventeenth centuries, population numbers fell very sharply over the greater part of the New World. The single most important cause was the introduction of certain diseases, particularly influenza,[211] smallpox and measles,[212] against which the native peoples had little or no natural resistance. The infectious diseases spread quickly, sometimes in advance of the Spaniards.[213] Periodically, outbreaks assumed epidemic proportions, and the mortality rate was almost invariably higher among Indians than Europeans.[214] As S. F. Cook has pointed out, the Indians were psychologically as well as physically ill-prepared for such disasters, for health conditions before 1492 appear to have been generally good, particularly in the highlands.[215] Syphilis, however, was found in both Mexico and Peru,[216] and along some of the coastal valleys of Peru a serious and sometimes fatal skin infection, known as *verruga peruviana,* was endemic.[217] J. Pulgar Vidal suggests that the presence of *verruga* may have been one reason for the abandonment of the terraced fields that border the flood plains of the lower Rimac and Cañete,[218] but whether this took place before or after the conquest is not clear.

According to S. F. Cook and W. Borah, the population of central Mexico (from the northern border of sedentary settlement to the isthmus of Tehuantepec) probably declined from about 25 million to 1 million, or by well over 90 percent, between 1519 and 1605.[219] A figure of 96 percent has been suggested for the Mixteca Alta.[220] C. Gibson calculated that there were about 500,000 people in the province of Tlaxcala in 1519 and a mere 75,000 in 1600.[221] Numbers in the valley of Mexico probably fell from 1-1.5 million in 1519 to a low of 70,000 in the middle of the seventeenth century.[222] The population of the central Andes declined by two-thirds or more between c. 1520 and c. 1570 and probably continued to fall until the end of the eighteenth century.[223] In the province of Chucuito, the proportion was already over half by 1567.[224] Reginaldo de Lizárraga (1540-1615) observed that in the valley of Chincha, Peru, there were 30,000 *indios tributarios* at the time of the Spanish Conquest, but "ahora no hay 600" [c. 1600].[225]

Population decline of this order meant that much cultivated land and many settlements were abandoned. Furthermore, the rural population became, in effect, more dispersed as other settlements were reduced in

209. Borah and Cook, 1963, 88; Borah, 1964, 379-87; Dobyns, 1966, 395-416; H. O. Wagner, 1968, 63-102, and 1969, 179-96. For more limited areas, see Smith and Kidder, 1943, 114; Goggin, 1943, 45; Brand, 1943, 227; J. J. Parsons, 1949, 29; Paddock, 1953, 26; A. L. Smith, 1955, 1; S. F. Cook, 1958, 19; Lowe, 1959, 1-2, 43; Borah, 1960, 159; Angulo Valdés, 1963, 62; Johannessen, 1963, 33; Bernal, 1965, 796; Cook and Borah, 1966, 229-39, and 1968. Sanders and Price (1968, 84) maintain that the estimates of sixteenth-century population by Cook and Borah are "much too high."

210. S. F. Cook, 1946a, 83; Borah and Cook, 1967, 719.

211. McBryde, 1940, 296-302.

212. Motolinía (1541), 1951, 87; López de Gómara (1552), 1, 1954, 83, and 2, 1954, 185-86; López de Velasco (1571-74), 1894, 99; Durán (1581), 1964, 323; Lazaro de Arregui (1621), 1946, 26-29; Oviedo y Baños (1723), 1940, 581. Smallpox appeared in Hispañiola in 1518 and in Mexico in 1520; Cortés (2, 1908, 6) mentions the disease in his Third Letter (1522).

213. McBryde, 1940, 296; Ezell, 1961, 15; Dobyns, 1963, 494, and 1966, 410; Craine and Reindorp (eds), 1970, 54.

214. Stearn and Stearn, 1945, 14-15; Dobyns, 1963, 507; Wachtel, 1971, 145-49. Gerhard (1972, 23) tabulates the epidemics that affected New Spain; similarly Gibson (1964, 448-51) for the valley of Mexico. The *Relación de Chinantla* (1579) refers to a heavy loss of population due to disease (Bevan, 1938, 139).

215. S. F. Cook, 1946, 335; Graña, 1940, 20. Malaria and tuberculosis were probably unknown (Dunn, 1965, 386-93; Sternberg, 1968, 417; Janssens, 1970, 102; cf. Graña, 1940, 17, Henschen, 1966, 98, 142); also bubonic plague (Morse, 1967, 250-58; Gade, 1967, 221). Concerning typhus and yellow fever, see Guerra, 1966, 330-31.

216. Ponce (1588), 1932, 353; Bloch, 1906, 57-79; Goff, 1967, 287-93; Crosby, 1969, 218-27; Janssens, 1970, 103-10.

217. Estete (1534-5), 1918, 17; Ortiz de Zúñiga (1562), 2, 1972, 177; Pedro Pizarro (1571-2), I, 1921, 151; Diego de Trujillo (1571), 1948, 48; Ruiz (1779), 1940, 37, 40; Raimondi, 1874, 161; Tschudi, 1847, 263-65; Hirsch, 2, 1885, 114-20; Patrón, 1889.

218. Pulgar Vidal, n.d., 78.

219. Cook and Borah, 1960, 49; Borah, 1962a, 172-78; Borah and Cook, 1963, 88, and 1967, 719; Gerhard, 1972, 22-24, and under individual *alcadías mayores.* Sanders and Price (1968, 77) put the population of Mesoamerica in 1519 at only about 15 million.

220. Cook and Borah, 1968, 32, 38. For the valley of Nochixtlán, see Spores, 1969, 566.

221. Gibson, 1952, 138, 142.

222. Sanders, 1956, 126, and 1965, 40 (tributary valley of Teotihuacán); Gibson, 1964, 6.

223. Bennett and Bird, 1949, 239; Steward and Faron, 1959, 149-50; Armillas, 1962, 130; C. T. Smith, 1971, 276; Wachtel, 1971, 135-40.

224. C. T. Smith *et al.,* 1968, 364; C. T. Smith, 1970, 453-64. See also Helmer, 1955-6, 12, 25, 34; Lipschutz, 1966, 229-47.

225. Lizárraga, 1968, 44.

size. This prompted attempts to concentrate population, sometimes at entirely new sites, for the purpose of easier administration, both civil and ecclesiastical. A policy of *congregación* or *reducción* was applied in Peru c. 1570[226] and in Mexico between 1598 (or a few years earlier) and 1606.[227] Its success varied, but there can be no doubt that the result was a further retreat of settlement and of cultivation, particularly from land that was marginal or difficult to maintain.[228] The latter included some terraced and irrigated fields.[229] Many

of the *pueblos viejos* mentioned in colonial documents date from the period of *congregaciones.*[230] Other sites that are similarly described today may have been abandoned earlier.[231] The association between hill-top *pueblos viejos* and abandoned terraces[232] deserves closer study. The Spaniards commonly resettled communities *(pueblos nuevos)* at piedmont sites, which were also favored for *hacienda* buildings, and from these centers many valley floors and basin levels were brought into cultivation with the aid of the plow.

226. Valdez de la Torre, 1921, 57, 75 ff; Cline, 1949, 349-69. Rowe (1957, 156) estimated that at least 1.5 million people were involved. Earlier, the Incas, "as soon as [they] had made themselves lords of a province, caused the natives, who had previously been widely scattered, to live in communities" (Polo de Ondegardo [*corregidor* of Cuzco, 1560], 1873, 155).

227. Cline, 1949, 349-69. Gibson (1964, 282) refers to 30 *congregaciones* in the valley of Mexico. See also Gamio, I, 1922, 378, 389; Simpson, 1934; Chevalier, 1963, 191; Carrasco, 1967, 75; Spores, 1967, 40-41. The mendicant orders organized re-settlement from the middle of the sixteenth century (Gibson, 1955, 585; for Chiapas, see Calnek, 1961).

228. In the words of one report (Simpson, 1934, 53), "the sites of the abandoned villages are good for sheep ranges and for nothing else; they can be granted."

229. Paddock, 1966a, 235, and in Dobyns, 1966, 437-38. See also Gibson, 1974, 6; Pulgar Vidal, n.d., 71-78.

230. Gamio, I, 1922, 378, 389; S. F. Cook, 1958, 12; Gibson, 1964, 282; Gorenstein, 1971, 336-37.

231. Schmieder, 1926, 115; E. Guzmán, 1934, 31; La Barre, 1948, 30; Bernal, 1953, 4.

232. Schmieder, 1926, 115; Márquez Miranda, 1939, 242; Gaignard, 1965, 310; Bonavia, 1967-8, 277.

PART III: REGIONS OF AGRICULTURAL TERRACING

1. NORTH AMERICA

A: Central Mexico

THE BASIN OF MEXICO

The valley of Mexico *(cuenca de México)* is the largest and historically the most important of the interior drainage basins of the Mesa Central (map 3.1). It is sharply defined to the southwest, south and east by high and predominantly volcanic ranges — the Sierra de Las Cruces, the Serranía de Ajusco, and the mountain chain that extends from Popocatepetl to beyond Tláloc. To the north, several broad tributary valleys or depressions lead toward comparatively low interfluves.

The basin began to assume its present form in the late Tertiary (Miocene/Pliocene) Era.[1] During the Pleistocene there was further volcanic activity and, in pluvial phases particularly, intensive subaerial erosion, leading to the rapid accumulation of large colluvial and stream deposits on the flanks and floor of the basin. The lake or group of lakes that formed at the base of the Serranía de Ajusco fluctuated in extent with the prevailing climatic conditions. At the time of the Spanish Conquest, the permanently inundated area was still very extensive, consisting of five periodically connected lakes — Chalco and Xochimilco in the south and, beyond the peninsula formed by the *cerros* Estrella and Santa Catarina, the more saline Texcoco, Xaltocan and Zumpango.[2] To reduce the danger of flooding around Tenochtitlán,[3] and at the same time to increase the height and control the flow of sweet water, a series of dikes and causeways had been built under the Aztecs. The most important of these was the dike of Nezahualcóyotl (c. 1450) which divided Texcoco into eastern and western basins.[4] A steady diminution in the area of the lakes as a whole may have commenced around the tenth century A.D.[5] In any event, the process gathered momentum after the Spanish Conquest,[6] until today only a small remnant of Texcoco remains. The basin floor is an almost level plain at a mean altitude of 2300 meters. The underlying fill consists of "alluvial gravels, sands and lacustrine clays, interspersed with beds of pumice and deposits of calcium carbonate, locally called *caliche.*"[7]

The climate of the central and southern parts of the basin is classified as "warm temperate/winter dry" (Köppen: Cwbg). The city of Mexico receives from 550 to 600 mm of rainfall per annum,[8] mostly between May and September. Winter drought rules out double cropping without irrigation. Irrigation is also desirable for single cropping, particularly in the north where the climatic type is closer to BS ("semi-arid") than to Cw and there are greater annual and seasonal fluctuations in rainfall. Although there is no evidence of any secular decline in precipitation over the last few hundred years, it may be assumed that deforestation of the slopes of the basin in late pre-Columbian and colonial times led to more marked seasonal variations in stream flow, and further that the disappearance of the lakes reduced the general level of humidity over the lower piedmont and increased the incidence of frost.

Agriculture, deforestation and, after the conquest, the grazing of livestock have entirely transformed the vegetation of the lower slopes of the basin. It is generally agreed however that, like parts of the middle slopes today (above the limits of regular cultivation), the primeval cover was forest of oak, cedar, cypress and pine.[9]

---

1. Linné, 1948; Sokoloff and Lorenzo, 1953, 50-55; Maldonado-Koerdell, 1954-5, 15-21; Mooser, White and Lorenzo, 1956; Cornwall, 1962, 55-58.

2. See the map accompanying Díaz del Castillo, 5, 1910. Maps collected by Apenes (1947) show the extent of water in the recent past; no. 36 (Manero, 1875) purports to illustrate the reduction in area since 1521.

3. Cervantes de Salazar (1554), 1953, 69; Boban, 2, 1891, 417.

4. The eastern side of Texcoco was more saline than the western. The beds of Xaltocan and Zumpango in the arid north have never been of any agricultural value; and following the recent draining of Lake Chalco, salt water has risen by capillary action, rendering much of the land here unproductive.

5. Muller, 1952, 13.

6. Motolinía (1541), 1950, 214. In 1607, work started to drain water from the basin toward the north (into the Río Tula); this immense scheme was not completed until the nineteenth century.

7. Cornwall, 1962, 56.

8. Page, 1930, 25; Ward, Brooks and Connor, 1938, J52-53 (series of data from 1841).

9. Maldonado-Koerdell, 1954-5, 19. See also Anon. (c. 1530), 1917, 58; Motolinía (1541), 1950, 206; Ojea (c. 1610), 1897, 2.

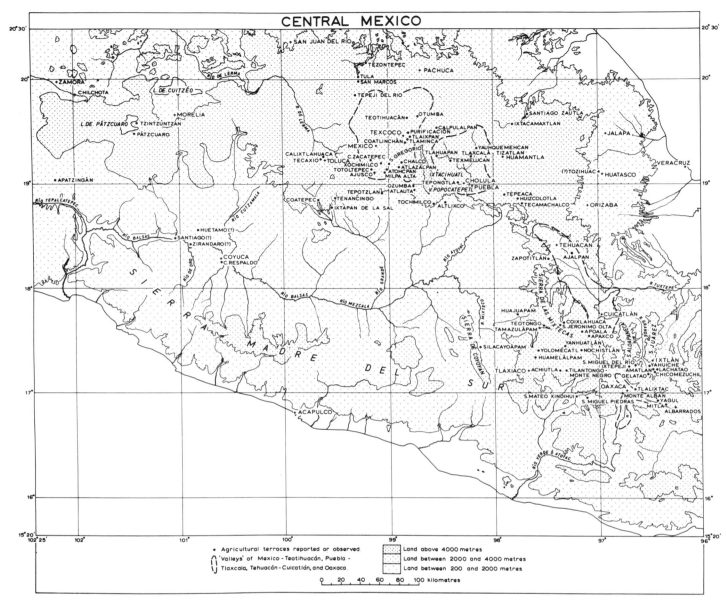

MAP 3.1

The basin was the heart of the federal empire of the Culhua-Mexica, and in 1519 it was probably more densely peopled than any other area of comparable size in the New World. W. T. Sanders estimated the population at between 1 and 1.5 million, or double the present total (excluding the metropolis).[10] About 1541, Toribio Motolinía (c. 1490-1569) observed that "all the slopes and environs of the ranges are thickly populated. Within [the basin] . . . there are forty large- and medium-sized towns."[11] The inhabitants relied heavily upon foodstuffs grown near at hand, around the margins of the basin, over the piedmont slopes and along the lake shores.[12] Here agri-

culture was strongly market-oriented. It was also notably intensive, involving the cultivation of *chinampas* (Ná-huatl: *chinámitl)* around or within the lakes and of terraced plots, many of them irrigated, on the adjacent slopes. That the Indians distinguished very carefully between different soil types[13] is some indication of the level of agricultural expertise.

12. Maize also reached Tenochtitlán as tribute from lands beyond the basin; on the eve of the Spanish Conquest, such supplies may have amounted to 300,000 bushels per annum (Anderson and Barlow, 1943, 416-17).

13. Such as — fertile alluvium, sandy alluvium, stony soil, soil enriched by decayed trees, soil enriched by decayed grass, soil enriched by dung, soil impregnated with salts (Gibson, 1964, 300). Seler (1904, 205-206) refers to hieroglyphs for types of soil.

10. Sanders, 1956, 126.

11. Motolinía, 1950, 205, 210.

Cortés (1520), Motolinía (1541) and Las Casas (c. 1550) refer to *huertas* in the vicinity of the city of Mexico.[14] Bernardino de Sahagún (c. 1570), Alonso de Molina (1571) and Diego Durán (1570-81) were among the first to use the word *chinampas*.[15] Recent discussions on their origin and construction have been summarized by C. Gibson.[16] *Chinampas* were artificial fields and house sites formed of aquatic vegetation, domestic refuse and fertile lake mud separated by "canals." Their height above the level of the lake had to be such as to ensure year-round irrigation and the removal of injurious salts, without, at the same time, inviting inundation. Fresh soil was added before each planting until the surface was too high and had to be lowered. The *chinampas* of the sixteenth century and later did not actually float, but some seed beds *(almácigos)* were in the nature of movable rafts.[17] While it is not certain that either antedates the eleventh or twelfth century, a much earlier origin has been suggested.[18] We do know that they came to occupy most of the shorelands of the sweet-water lakes (Xochimilco-Chalco-western Texcoco) and parts

of the more saline (particularly eastern Texcoco). By the beginning of the sixteenth century, however, *chinampa* cultivation was almost entirely confined to the former, in a wide belt extending from Tenayoca, 8 kilometers northwest of Tenochtitlán, to Coyoacán (an area now largely built over), and thence south and east around the shores of Xochimilco-Chalco. As the lakes contracted, so necessarily did *chinampa* farming,[19] until today it is concentrated in the area between Xochimilco *(xuchil,* flower; *milli,* plantation) and Mixquic (formerly on the shores of lake Chalco) in the extreme south of the basin.

In comparison with the *chinampas,* the terraced fields of the hill lands surrounding the basin of Mexico have attracted little attention. E. C. Brasseur de Bourbourg may have had terraces in mind when he wrote, *apropos* of the inhabitants of the basin, "ils entouraient leurs champs de murailles de pierres ou de haies d'aloès épineux."[20] Z. Nuttall included *andenes* among the "gardens of ancient Mexico,"[21] and P. B. Sears, W. T. Sanders, and J. R. Parsons have each referred to agricultural terracing here.[22] The most detailed studies are by E. R. Wolf and A. Palerm.[23]

The areas of terracing broadly correspond to the eastern and southern piedmonts. No evidence has so far been found, either in the field or in published accounts, of agricultural terraces on the western or northern sides of the basin (excepting the tributary valley of Teotihuacán). The eastern (Texcocan) piedmont, below the Cerro Tláloc, is crossed by a number of streams, and here alone are levelled fields commonly associated with canal irrigation. This is also the area with the most widespread evidence of abandonment of the higher flights of terraces.[24] The explanation may lie partly in the greater concentration of early *haciendas* here than in the hills behind lakes Xochimilco and Chalco. Abandonment has been followed by soil erosion, which is generally thought

14. Cortés, 1960, 41; Motolinía (1541), 1941, 202; Las Casas (1527-59), I, 1958, 172.

15. Sahagún, 4, 1956, 144-46; Alonso de Molina, 1944; Durán, 2, 1967, 448 ff. A document of 1562 mentions *chinampas* at Xochimilco (Scholes and Adams [eds], 1958, 106). See also José de Acosta (1590), 1880, 469; Alvarado Tezozómoc (1598), 1949, 37-38; Vargas Machuca, 1599, 148, 156 *(camellón y camellón);* San Antón Muñón [Chimalpahín] (c. 1607), 1965, 91; Torquemada (1615), 2, 1723, 483; Vetancurt (1698), 1, 1960, 112, and 3, 1961, 153. Cf. Berlin (ed), 1948, 52 (? 1528, referring to the late fourteenth century). An obscure sentence in a very early *relación* of Andrés de Tapia (1519-20) (1963, 24) has been taken to refer to *chinampas,* and the "Maguey Map" (pre-Columbian to 1562) shows *chinampas* in what is now part of the built-up area of Mexico City. The "andenes llanos de rosas y flores" at Ixtapalapa (Díaz del Castillo [c. 1568], I, 1955, 261) are interpreted, doubtless correctly, as *chinampas* by Palerm, 1973, 28.

16. Gibson, 1964, 320-21, 557. In addition to the authorities cited, see Santamaría, 1912; Hrdlicka, 1912, 11-13; Butman, 1912, 132-33; Nuttall, 1920, 193-213; Callegari, 1925, 1057-62; Schilling, 1939; Meyer l'Epée, 1943, 376-77; Grove 1965, 23-29; Moriarty, 1968, 461-84; Armillas, 1971, 653-65; Calnek, 1972, 104-15; Palerm, 1973; Rojas, Strauss and Lameiras, 1974, 29 ff.; 142-43, 159-62. For *chinampas* in the tributary valley of Teotihuacán, see Sanders, 1965, 44-45.

17. Rafael Landívar (1781) (1948, 169-171) described the construction of "floating fields" on "wicker mats"; he may have been referring to seed beds. See also Durán (1581), 1964, 36-37; Anon. (*Códice Ramírez,* 1586-89), 1903, 37; Ojea (c. 1610), 1897, 3 ("unos huertos mobiles de 20 y 30 pies de largo y del ancho . . . en los quales siembran los almácigos de sus legumbres . . ."); Alva Ixtlilxochitl (c. 1640), I, 1891, 100 ("unas tierras de riego y huertas"), 221 ("el agua jardines").

18. Gibson (1964, 5) writes that drought "may have stimulated the adoption both of the aquatic gardens called *chinampas* and of systems of irrigation, possibly during the period of Teotihuacán I" (? final centuries B.C.). Cf. B. J. Price, 1971, 22; Blanton, 1972, 1325 (Ixtapalapa: Aztec evidence).

19. The distribution of mounds known as *tlatles* may be evidence of its former extent; pottery from *tlatles* has been assigned to the early centuries A.D. (late Teotihuacán I) (Apenes, 1943, 29-32). See also Parker, 1967, 515-22; Armillas, 1971, 657-58.

20. Brasseur de Bourbourg, 3, 1857-9, 634.

21. Nuttall, 1920, 193-94.

22. Sears, 1953a, 115, and 1953b, 160; Sanders, 1956, 116, and 1971, 10, 41; J. R. Parsons, 1971 (*infra,* f.n. 30).

23. Wolf and Palerm, 1955, 265-81; Palerm and Wolf, 1954-5, 337-49, and 1961, 239-96.

24. On the abandonment of high ground, see Gibson, 1964, 268.

to have increased after the conquest.[25] At the same time, many cultivated slopes today are unprotected by walling, and this was probably always so.[26]

The eastern piedmont: Texcoco, capital of the ancient Acolhuacán kingdom, lies near the eastern margin of the lacustrine levels. The urban zone may have had a population of 100,000 — similar to that of Tenochtitlán-Tlaltelolco — at the time of the Spanish Conquest.[27] Behind the town the land rises gently for 3 or 4 kilometers, then much more steeply at the base of the foothills of the Cerro Tláloc. The lower piedmont stretches northward, round the projecting Cerro Tlalte Huacán and into the valley of Teotihuacán; to the south it terminates against the Cerros Chimalhuacán and Texolotl. The upper zone consists of volcanic hills and high, nearly level surfaces that are cut by *barrancas* and flanked by aprons of outwash material. The area under discussion extends from Coatlinchán, 8 kilometers southeast of Texcoco, to Purificación, about the same distance to the northeast, and includes the line of hills behind San Miguel Tlaíxpan and San Nicolás Tlaminca (Tetzcutzingo, Cocotl, Tepeticpac, Moyotepec and San Joaquín). In this central section, terracing is more highly developed than elsewhere in the basin of Mexico.

East of Texcoco there are (i) broad, irrigated terraces on the lower piedmont; and (ii) irrigated and (iii) dry contour benches in the foothills. The last include many plots that have long been abandoned.

The unconsolidated deposits of the lower piedmont comprise silts and gravels separated by bands of coarser material. Fields are stepped between walls of earth and stone, 1 to 2 meters high, including a low bund. Irrigation water is led along open ditches. The levelled surfaces probably came into being gradually as soil under cultivation moved down slope and boundary walls were heightened. The chief crops today are maize and alfalfa.

In the hills beyond the lower piedmont, the broken or dismantled walls of terraces (fig. 3.1), flights of rutted or scrub-covered surfaces and blocked irrigation ditches point to fluctuations in the limits of agriculture. Entire groups of terraces have been abandoned, most commonly on high ground and over steep slopes with bedrock at or near the surface. Presently cultivated terraces are concentrated around the various hill villages, in embayments and on outwash fans where soils are relatively deep (fig. 3.2). Near Tlaíxpan and Tlaminca there are flights of well constructed and carefully maintained benches (fig. 3.3), characteristically high (2 to 3.5 meters), narrow (3 to 10 meters) and perfectly level. Many also serve as house sites. Irrigation water is led along stone-lined channels, the flow from one level to the next being controlled by sluices. Distribution is supervised by local "water commissioners" *(regidores de agua).*[28] Irrigated terraces are privately owned and traditionally linked with particular houses, but buying and selling do occur. Fruit, vegetables and flowers are grown for the metropolitan market, in addition to maize and wheat[29] which are also raised on some dry terraces.

Terracing for agriculture in the basin of Mexico may have commenced in the late pre-classic period, that is a century or so before the beginning of the Christian era. Along with irrigation and *chinampa* farming, it probably helped to make possible the striking expansion of population and urbanism in classic and post-classic times. The terraces and associated irrigation works of the Texcocan piedmont certainly antedate the Spanish Conquest.[30] Canals, carried over *barrancas* on great causeways, were built in the fifteenth century to bring water from the slopes of Tláloc to the terraced gardens on Tetzcutzingo,[31] a distance of about 12 kilometers. Irrigation was "fairly widespread" in the basin at the time of the conquest,[32] but declined in importance after 1519[33] with the reduction in the size of the Indian population, the

25. Wolf and Palerm, 1955, 277-78; Gibson, 1964, 304. Torquemada (1615) (I, 1723, 310) associated the cultivation of slopes with erosion and the exposure of subsoil *tepetate.* Tylor (1861, 160) mentions soil erosion following the cutting of timber.

26. In the eighteenth century, Clavijero (2, 1945, 268) drew attention to "tierras pendientes" that were not cultivated every year.

27. Nicholson, 1967, 63. J. R. Parsons (1970, 437, and fig. 10) writes: "By the time of the Spanish Conquest, population in the Texcoco region had reached an all-time high of something over 100,000."

28. Wolf and Palerm, 1955, 267.

29. Wheat was irrigated on Spanish, and to a lesser extent on Indian, properties in the late sixteenth century (Gibson, 1964, 552 n. 45; Nuttall, 1926, 78 [1580: Acolman]).

30. Wolf and Palerm, 1955, 267; Palerm and Wolf, 1954-5, 347. J. R. Parsons (1971) refers to ancient terracing in many parts of the Texcocan region; some structural remains possibly belong to the "terminal formative" (c. 250 B.C. - A.D. 100) or even the "late formative" (c. 550 - 250 B.C.) (J. R. Parsons, 1971, 31, 185). Blanton (1972, 1320) puts the "first occupation" of the southern piedmont around Ixtapalapa in the late and terminal formative.

31. Pomar (1582), 1891, 53-54; Alva Ixlilxochitl (c. 1640), 2, 1891-2, 210 ("sus gradas, parte de ellas hecha de argamasa, parte labrada en la misma peña"); Bullock, 1825, 389-91; Reyes, 1888, 129-50; Mendizabal, 1925, 86-95; McAfee and Barlow, 1945-8, 113-14; Coy, 1966, 543-49; J. R. Parsons, 1971, 123-4, 146-51.

32. Gibson, 1964, 310. Palerm (1954, 3-4, 9-10, 66, 70) lists references to irrigation in sixteenth-century sources. See also Palerm, 1973, and Rojas, Strauss and Lameiras, 1974.

33. Tylor, 1861, 160; H. S. Reed, 1944, 209.

Fig. 3.1 Broken and abandoned terraces, 4 kilometers east of Texcoco, basin of Mexico

Fig. 3.2 Terraced fields near Texcoco, basin of Mexico

Fig. 3.3 Terrace wall (c. 1.5 meters), San Miguel Tlaíxpan, basin of Mexico

seizure of land by the Spaniards and the introduction of animal husbandry. The grazing of cattle, sheep and goats on abandoned Indian holdings no doubt contributed to the destruction of terrace walls.

The southern piedmont: The levels of the former lake Xochimilco-Chalco terminate abruptly against the foothills of the Serranía de Ajusco. Behind the break of slope the topography is related to geologically recent vulcanism, represented by ash and cinder cones and innumerable overlapping lava flows. During the Pleistocene, streams scoured and etched these surfaces. The small basins, floored with colluvial and lacustrine deposits, are mostly well drained and may have been cultivated at an early date. Soils developed *in situ* are fine and liable to "blow" in the dry season. They are fertile, rich in base minerals, but of uneven depth and usually lie over unweathered basement rock with little intervening subsoil.

Stone is the chief building material throughout the southern piedmont. Roughly shaped blocks are used in house construction, to surface tracks that would otherwise invite erosion, and for boundaries of all kinds, including terrace walls. There is now little constructional timber in the vicinity of most villages.

The valley slopes and undulating basaltic plateaux of the entire piedmont (from San Pablo Atlazalpan, southwest of Chalco, westward to Ajusco and probably beyond)[34] are covered with thousands of small, terraced fields, carefully adjusted to the topography and descending, behind Xochimilco and San Gregorio Atlapulco, to the very edge of the *chinampa* zone.[35] In contrast to the eastern piedmont, there is little evidence of abandonment.

The terraces are of three types. Firstly, the broken flanks of old lava flows and the slopes of the valleys of incised streams are sites for benches with high supporting walls. The planting surfaces are usually level, but limited in extent (in places only a few square meters) and irregular in outline. Secondly, over the gentler slopes, including the plateaux tops, wider terraces with lower walls and inclined surfaces are characteristic. And, thirdly, cross-channel terracing is everywhere common. The contour terraces, although primarily prepared for purposes of cultivation, are also occasionally used as house sites, and some of the lakeside villages have spread into the terraced zone.

On the sharply rising ground immediately behind the lacustrine levels fields mostly take the form of narrow, bench-like terraces. They are fertilized with animal drop-

34. Palerm (1961, 299) reports "terrazas agrícolas" of late Aztec date from the Cerro Zacatepec in the center of the Pedregal, northwest of Ajusco.

35. The province of Chalco was an important supplier of tribute maize to Tenochtitlán (Molíns Fábrega, 1954, 305).

Fig. 3.4 Cross-channel terraces, San Gregorio, basin of Mexico

ings and domestic refuse and are also occasionally fallowed. The tops of the supporting walls generally rise a little above the planting surfaces and consequently storm water is first impounded and then gradually absorbed. There is in fact little surface drainage. The craggy terrain clearly presented problems for the terrace builders who were obliged to take advantage of sharp breaks of slope and of small hollows where soil had accumulated naturally. In places, bedrock outcrops at the back of terraces, but inquiry produced no evidence of soil ever being introduced to supplement the fill.

Embayments and cuts in the highland edge have almost all been terraced by means of massive, cross-channel walls, up to 6 meters high and securely locked into the adjacent slopes (fig. 3.4).

Terracing is also a feature of the lands of the upland villages 5 to 10 kilometers south of the levels. Milpa Alta lies to one side of a basin, the floor of which is now divided into large rectangular fields. The surrounding terraces are characteristically broad and sloping, with walls that have been gradually heightened to between 1 and 2 meters. The rounded hills are deeply weathered, and bedrock is little in evidence except along sunken tracks between fields.

Ajusco stands on the edge of another small basin. Terracing is less well developed here than around Milpa Alta but similar in kind. The more broken territory of the neighboring village of San Andrés Totoltepec presented a greater challenge and here there are many small,

Fig. 3.5 Terraced fields, San Andrés Totoltepec, basin of Mexico

level benches. Plots of no more than 100 square meters are buttressed by exceptionally high walls (4 to 5 meters) (fig. 3.5), and isolated terraces are flanked by side walls built into the slope (fig. 3.6).

The construction of a new terrace wall was observed at Totoltepec (fig. 3.7). The foundations were 2.5 meters wide and lay a meter below the surface. The forward face of selected stone was being backed by rubble, and the top of a completed section of the wall stood 1.5 meters above the ground on the up-slope side.

THE VALLEY OF TEOTIHUACÁN

The climate of the valley of Teotihuacán is semi-arid (average annual precipitation, 575 mm), and irrigation accompanied by terracing has probably been an important feature of settlement here since classic times.[36] Water was drawn from springs and from the Río Teotihuacán. Although the extent and intensity of cultivation fluctuated with population density, the terraced fields of the Aztec period, based on earlier systems, appear to have covered the greater part of the valley.[37]

The slopes of the middle valley provide ample evidence of the retreat of cultivation. The severely degraded higher ground west of the archaeological zone is crossed by numerous broken walls, the remains of broad contour terraces (fig. 3.8). Here and there, gully and wind erosion have exposed the underlying *caliche*. Below and between the areas of contour terracing lie flights of abandoned and partly destroyed cross-channel plots, flanked by silted canals and small reservoirs. In this, the lower part of the piedmont, there are also terraces of fairly recent construction which are in regular use but unirrigated. The broad planting surfaces usually occupy embayments between deeply eroded ridges.

The hills overlooking the upper valley of Teotihuacán near Aguatepec (5 kilometers southeast of Otumba) are covered with low, sloping terraces *(bancales)*.[38] Many are planted to maguey,[39] but scarred surfaces and parallel lines of stone again indicate a retreat from the higher, marginal land at different times in the past.

36. Millon, 1954, 177-80, and 1957, 160-66; Armillas, Palerm and Wolf, 1956, 396-99; Millon, Hall and Díaz, 1961, 494-521; Palerm, 1961, 297-302; Sanders, 1965, 174.

37. Sanders, 1965, 39.

38. Aerial photographs. *Cia. Mexicana Aerofoto SA* — Series Otumba y Tláloc, OT 18-20, 26-28, 39-41 (April, 1948).

39. Similarly, near Calpulalpan, 20 kilometers to the southwest. Cf. West, 1970, 361-69.

Fig. 3.6 Tapered side wall of a terraced field, San Andrés Totoltepec, basin of Mexico

Fig. 3.7 Construction of a new terrace wall, San Andrés Totoltepec, basin of Mexico

Fig. 3.8 Old terraced surfaces, western slopes of the valley of Teotihuacán, central Mexico

West   East

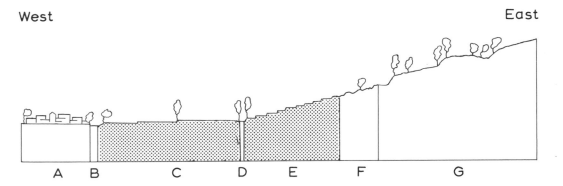

Diagram 3.1
LAND-USE ZONES: VALLEY OF THE RÍO TULA, MEXICO

A   Tula

B   Río Tula

C   Irrigated valley-floor and contour terraces

D   Main irrigation canal

E   Contour terraces

F   Abandoned terraces

G   *Monte*

THE VALLEY OF THE RÍO TULA

The climate of the valley in the neighborhood of Tula itself is semi-arid (BS kwg). The average annual rainfall is probably substantially less than 500 mm.[40] Irrigation is practiced wherever possible, and it was reported near here in the sixteenth century.[41] The river is incised to a depth of several meters below the valley floor which is composed of material washed down from the adjacent limestone uplands. S. F. Cook has postulated two periods of accelerated erosion.[42]

The floor of the valley is stepped back in a series of broad, irrigated fields (diag. 3.1). Terracing continues over the eastern slopes of the valley in the form of successively narrower benches faced with limestone and volcanic blocks to a height of 2 to 3 meters (figs. 3.9,

3.10). Above the main irrigation canal, dry terraces (for wheat and maguey) are interspersed with house gardens that are irrigated by hand. Broken walls and abandoned fields cover some of the higher slopes. The plateaux tops (on one of which stand the remains of the ancient Tula) are almost bare of soil and support only light xerophytic scrub. Here the grazing of goats alone is possible.[43]

THE BASIN OF TOLUCA

The village of Calixtlahuaca and the pre-classic site of Tecaxic[44] lie together at the base of the hills that form the western boundary of the high basin of Toluca. The floor of the basin is almost flat and a high water table gives rise, in places, to marsh and, during the wet season, extensive sheets of water. The large fields are surrounded by drainage ditches. Ancient settlements occupy piedmont sites.

---

40. No local data have been found, but Ward, Brooks and Connor (1938, J52) give the annual average rainfall of Querétaro (1878-1927) as 503 mm, and of Pachuco (1893-1927) as 366 mm.

41. Palerm, 1954, 6.

42. S. F. Cook, 1949a, 51-53 (c. A.D. 1000-1200, and c. A.D. 1400-1600).

43. Aerial photographs *(Cia. Mexicana Aerofoto SA* — Series 1532 [Valle de Mexquital], especially nos. 119-123, 136-139) show that valley-side terracing extends southward to at least Tepeji del Río and northward to the neighborhood of Tezontepec.

44. García Payón, 1941, 210-12.

Fig. 3.9   Terraced fields, 2 kilometers south of Tula, central Mexico

Fig. 3.10   Bench terraces (1.5 meters high), 2 kilometers south of Tula, central Mexico

Above Calixtlahuaca — in the vicinity of the Aztec temples of Quetzalcóatl and Tláloc — there is an area of terraced fields and house gardens. The walls of earth and stone are poorly maintained and many surfaces have been wholly or partly destroyed by gully erosion. Bedrock is exposed along the back-slopes of some of the higher fields, and it is possible that in the past soil was brought from the basin floor.

THE SOUTHERN PIEDMONT OF THE MESA CENTRAL

The highlands south of the basins of Mexico and Toluca descend from the neo-volcanic axis toward sedimentary and older igneous rocks in the upper drainage of the Río Balsas. The subtropical piedmont zone is crossed by numerous permanent streams, and the more developed systems of terracing are associated with irrigation.

Tenancingo: Tenancingo dates from a *congregación* of 1593,[45] but the terraces of the Cerro Tres Cruces, immediately above the town, are thought to be pre-Columbian in origin.[46] They have been shaped in the course of cultivation. The faces incorporate, at most, a few lines of stone, either for support or to give extra height. The majority of the planting surfaces slope at angles of more than 10 degrees (fig. 3.11). Ditches to carry off storm water feed into channels lying between flights of terraces.

Between the Cerro Tres Cruces and the poorly drained bottom lands east of Tenancingo there are irrigable terraces[47] separated by walls of earth and stone. Broad level surfaces are still being prepared in this area. Figure 3.12 shows a new riser (one of a series of half a dozen) excavated at the base and completed to a height of 2 meters with a wall of sod.

Coatepec: Coatepec lies on a shelf of old outwash material between two incised streams, the Río Malinaltenango and one of its tributaries. Above the township, most of the cultivated area is arranged in large, valley-floor terraces, flanked by sunken approach roads. The surfaces have been leveled between risers that are 1 to 2.5 meters high and crowned with maguey. Irrigation water is led from one or other of the streams at points further up the valley. The chief crops are maize, wheat, beans and alfalfa. Again, the lower ground is poorly drained and only partly cultivated.

Tepoztlán: Agricultural terracing is well developed around Tepoztlán, an important place in both pre-Columbian and colonial times. Within the built-up area there is a close pattern of terraced house-and-garden plots. Some of the walls are 3 meters or more high and include very large boulders. The outwash slopes below the village have been shaped into broad, irrigable fields, separated by walls 1 to 2 meters high. The latter resemble the terraces of Coatepec and account for the greater part of the cultivated area.

Ozumba-Chimalhuacán-San Miguel Atlauta: In this area, to the west of Popocatepetl, innumerable irregular terraces have been formed in the course of cultivation; the risers are mostly of earth and heavily vegetated. Series of terraces are, however, commonly separated by massive stone walls flanking sunken roads.

Tochimilco-Atlixco: Tochimilco lies on the lower, southern slopes of Popocatepetl. Motolinía (1541) observed that "the soil [of Tochimilco] is very good and the region is densely populated."[48] Most of the cultivated area is elaborately terraced and systematically irrigated. The terraces within and immediately around the village are broad level benches, supported by walls 2 to 4 meters high (fig. 3.13). Equally substantial side walls line the roads serving the village. Many plots are either wholly or partly planted to fruit trees, notably aguacate *(Persea americana)*.

As the natural slope decreases to the south and east of the village, the fields become larger and the walls lower. Similar terraces were observed in the upper part of the basin of Atlixco[49] to the east of Tochimilco. Possibly there is no significant break in the distribution.

B: East Central Mexico

THE BASIN OF PUEBLA-TLAXCALA

The basin of Puebla-Tlaxcala comprises a group of depressions, three-quarters surrounded by volcanic highlands: the *bloque de Tlaxcala* to the north, La Malinche to the east, and the Popocatepetl-Ixtaccíhuatl-Tláloc range to the west. Some of the depressions contain residual lakes and all are potentially swampy. Fields in the Tlaxcalan levels are accompanied by deep drainage ditches.

---

45. Simpson, 1934, 40.

46. Wolf, 1959, 75. See also Patiño, 1940, 877; H. H. Bennett, 1944, 67.

47. Fabila (1947, 263) estimated the irrigated area around Tenancingo at more than 2000 hectares.

48. Motolinía, 1951, 326; similarly Durán (c. 1576-79), 1971, 255, writing of the area around Popocatepetl.

49. "In the old days before the Spaniards came a very great part of this valley was uncultivated. . . . Now the land is all being occupied by the Spaniards with their flocks and by the natives with farms" (Motolinía [1541], 1951, 269). Cf. Durán (1581), 1964, 231.

Fig. 3.11 Cerro Tres Cruces, Tenancingo, central Mexico

Fig. 3.12 New terrace wall (2 meters high: excavated base, capped with sod), Tenancingo, central Mexico

Fig. 3.13 Terrace wall (c. 4 meters), Tochimilco, central Mexico

In the adjacent hill country, woodland once covered large areas that are now either under crops or used as rough grazing following accelerated soil erosion.[50]

On the western side of the basin, terraced fields commence at the first important break of slope. Around the village of San Cristóbal Tepongtla (5 kilometers west of Cholula), terracing is associated with areas of deeper soil in small embayments (fig. 3.14) and along the lower slopes of tributary valleys. The intervening headlands are mostly under grass, but broken walls and eroded banks suggest cultivation in the past. The terraces that remain are supported by earth and stone walls 1.5 to 2 meters high. Few of the planting surfaces are level and dry farming is the rule.[51] On the other hand, to the northwest of Texmelucan (notably in the vicinity of Tlahuapan), there are irrigated terraces between earth borders, as well as narrow, stone-faced benches on which fruit trees are grown.

North of Tlaxcala, as far as Tlaxco, agricultural terracing is poorly developed. Effective cross-channel benches do exist, for example around San Pablo Yauhquemehcán, but the amount of land involved is negligible. Low banks of earth and maguey are more common. Gully and sheet erosion have done great damage in this area and the illegal cutting of pinewood threatens further destruction.

Tlaxcala lies in the northeastern corner of the main basin; here and to the south the dissected lower slopes of La Malinche form the eastern peidmont. Soils are deep in low-lying pockets but quick to erode on unprotected slopes. On the *cerros* around Tlaxcala substantial walls have been built or excavated along the contour (figs. 3.15, 3.16).[52] The terraces so formed are in some cases irrigated. Similar fields may be observed at intervals along the length of the eastern piedmont. There is, however, considerable variation in the quality of terracing. For example, terraces of the kind just described surround a lake- and marsh-filled depression 5 kilometers

---

50. Pfeifer, 1966, 91.

51. The climate is "warm temperate" (Cwbg/i); the average annual rainfall is between 800 and 900 mm (Ward, Brooks and Connor, 1938, J53).

52. Caso (1927, 139) reported "restos de antiguos terraplenes" around the site of Tizatlán, 5 kilometers to the northeast of Tlaxcala. See also Vega, 1927.

Fig. 3.14 Old terraced fields (partly in use), San Cristóbal Tepongtla, near Cholula, east central Mexico

to the south of Tlaxcala; but on the higher, more exposed slopes, around the hill village of San Sebastián Atlahpa, the supporting banks are low, inexpertly constructed and frequently broken. Erosion channels are steadily spreading into cultivated land, and in an attempt to prevent this a number of "dams" have been built. Bedrock or calcareous *caliche* is also exposed along the back-slopes of old terraces, many of which are now completely abandoned.

In the shallow valleys of the plateau between the basins of Puebla, Huamantla and Tehuacán, slopes have been leveled, primarily to facilitate irrigation. There are good examples in the neighborhood of Tepeaca, Huizcolotla and Tecamachalco. The principal walls are often separated by several lower boundaries, suggesting that the present levels are the result of the subdivision of larger fields.

THE EASTERN PIEDMONT OF THE MESA CENTRAL

Carl Sartorius (c. 1850), who lived near Huatusco de Chicuellar, referred to abandoned terraces in the grass- and scrub-covered foothills of the Mesa Central. Thus, "when the tall grass is burnt down, we can see that the whole country was formed into terraces with the assistance of masonry, everywhere provision had been made against the ravages of the tropical rains; they were carried out on every slope, descending even to the steepest spots, where they are often only a few feet in width. In the flat valleys are countless remains of dams and reservoirs, mostly of large stones and clay, many of solid masonry, naturally all rent by the floods at the lowest part, and filled with earth."[53] No terraces, in use or abandoned, were observed in journeys through the piedmont, but in an area to the south of Tozihuac (above the Río Chichiquila and 20 kilometers northwest of Huatusco) aerial photographs[54] show parallel earthworks on slopes that have been cleared of scrub. P. Armillas has reported abandoned terraces near Ixtacamaxtlán[55] in the upper valley of the Río Apulco; and downstream, toward Santiago Zautla, terraced fields are still in use (fig. 3.17).[56]

53. Sartorius, 1961, 10.
54. *Cia. Aerofoto Mexicana SA* — Series 1329 (Camino Huatusco-Jalapa) nos. 71-73 (November, 1956).
55. Armillas, 1961, 267.
56. Aerial photographs. *Cia. Mexicana Aerofoto SA* — Series 1611 (Santiago Zautla) nos. 1-5, 11-15 (August, 1961).

Fig. 3.15 Terraced fields, Cerro de Ocotlan, Tlaxcala, east central Mexico

Fig. 3.16 Terrace wall (c. 2.5 meters) of trimmed blocks, Cerro de Ocotlan, Tlaxcala, east central Mexico

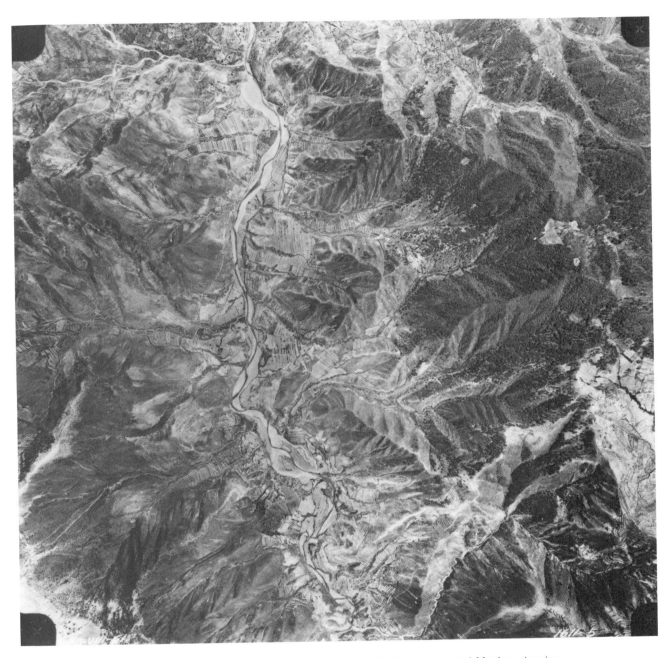

Fig. 3.17 Valley of the Río Apulco, above Santiago Zautla, east central Mexico, showing
terraced fields *(Cia. Mexicana Aerofoto S. A.)*

C: West Central Mexico

THE WESTERN HIGHLANDS AND THE BASIN OF THE BALSAS-TEPALCATEPEC

The plateau of central Mexico extends westward between the Lerma-Santiago depression (the *Bajío*) to the north and the basin of the Balsas-Tepalcatepec to the south. The greater part lies between 1000 and 2500 meters above sea level. The climate is "warm temperate" (Cw: average annual rainfall 700 to 900 mm) and the natural vegetation is (or was) pine-oak woodland. Huetamo, at 427 meters in the valley of the Balsas, is more tropical (AW'g) with about the same total rainfall[57] but considerably higher evapotranspiration. The lower parts of the middle Balsas-Tepalcatepec basin (at 100 and 250 meters) are distinctly arid (BS), and irrigation and the use of saturated bottom lands *(cultivo en humedales)* have been of some importance from at least the early colonial period.[58]

R. H. Lister has referred to "terraces" on the Cerro El Respaldo, 1 kilometer to the south of Coyuca de Catalán on the banks of the Río Balsas.[59] The *cerro* is a small ridge of sandstone rising 20 to 30 meters above the level of the floodplain. Over the northern face of the ridge there are several leveled surfaces, each of about 300 square meters and supported by walls 1.5 to 3 meters high. Less than half the total area is cultivated today; the rest is under xerophytic scrub. The Cerro El Respaldo appears to be an old settlement and agricultural site (although the fields could not have been irrigated, except by hand) antedating the reclamation of the floodplain.

Both Lister and D. Osborne mention prehistoric "terracing" downstream of Coyuca. Near Zirándaro, at the confluence of the Balsas and the Río del Oro, there are four levels "with about a 2-meter drop between the floors."[60] Opposite Santiago "the Balsas river front is terraced or has otherwise been built up for about 500 meters up and downstream."[61] Here too *yácatas* are "commonplace." These are raised platforms of earth and refuse which may be explained as habitation sites in formerly marshy areas.[62]

Further west, in the tributary *cuenca* of the Tepalcatepec, J. M. Goggin[63] and Isabel Kelly[64] reported terracing around Apatzingán, but came to no conclusion regarding its purpose. Goggin favored neither farming nor defense, but considered that "terraced hillsides, because of their broad distribution in the valley and the local variation in type, are outstanding in interest." The sites extend from the Cerro de la Nueva Italia (south of Parácuaro) in the east, to Los Cimientos (near Tepalcatepec) in the west, and also include the Cerro Cuitzinguio and the Cerro de la Huerra, a few kilometers to the southwest and northeast of Apatzingán respectively. The *cerros* are isolated, rocky eminences, mainly volcanic, in the broad plain of the Tepalcatepec. The only terraced site examined by the present author lies 1.5 kilometers east of Apatzingán on the slopes of the Cerro de San Miguel, part of an old lava flow *(malpaís)*. Behind the first rise there is a U-shaped depression, and beyond this steeper and higher slopes. The latter are dotted with short, unaligned walls, up to 3 meters high and supporting small platforms of earth.

These rocky "islands" within the basin of the Balsas-Tepalcatepec had certain obvious advantages as settlement sites in prehistoric times. They were defensible and could be improved by simple terracing. The piedmont slopes may also have been cultivated. The chief attraction of the extensive levels lay in the possibility of irrigation or in the presence of periodically saturated soils. Where neither existed — back from the main rivers and on the low interfluves between tributaries — hill sites seem to have been preferred.

THE BASIN OF LAKE PATZCUARO

Lake Pátzcuaro lies near the center of the plateau of Michoacán. At the time of the Spanish Conquest the lake region was also the nucleus of the area in which Tarascan was spoken.[65] The chief town of the Tarascans, Tzintzúntzan, stood back from the lake, to the northeast of a volcanic peninsula.

The slopes opposite the archaeological site of Tzintzúntzan were evidently cultivated more intensively in the past than today. Thorn scrub covers abandoned terraces, particularly on the higher ground, and some cultivated fields are almost surrounded by deep and encroaching *barrancas*. The patchwork of fields, in use and abandoned, is related to the uneven terrain, the distribution of deeper soils,[66] and to the piecemeal process of terrace construction in which excavation has been more important than the building of stone walls.

57. Average 880 mm (1909-27) (Ward, Brooks and Connor, 1938, J56).

58. Armillas, 1949, 85-113; Aguirre Beltrán, 1952, 42; Palerm, 1954; Palerm and Wolf, 1957, 12, 19.

59. Lister, 1947-8, 69. *Coyucán* was an important place in the southern marches of the Tarascan state (Osborne, 1943, 61).

60. Osborne, 1943, 67.

61. Near the ruins of Mexiquito (Osborne *op. cit.;* Lister, 1947-8, 69). On Mexiquito, see Armillas, 1944, 261-62. Osborne also refers to terracing near Huetamo.

62. Brand (1939, 144) notes that *yácata* is a local term for "ruin" in the *tierra caliente* of Michoacán.

63. Goggin, 1943, 46.

64. I. Kelly, 1947, 172, 191.

65. Brand, 1943a; West, 1948.

66. Ten varieties of soil are recognized and named within the territory of Tzintzúntzan (Foster, 1948, 58).

The northern and western slopes of the above-mentioned peninsula, overlooking the lake, are worked from the hamlets of Ichupio, Tarerio and Ucasanéstacua. The stepped gardens *(hortalizas)* of the narrow shorelands are intensively cultivated; "a primitive type of irrigation makes possible continuous planting throughout the year."[67] Above the fertile *orillas* the land rises steeply for 150 to 250 meters and then more gently. On the steeper slopes there are flights of bench terraces supported by substantial stone walls. These terraces were probably partly filled with soil brought from the surrounding area. There are also many primitive sloping terraces where large boulders left *in situ* form part of the foundations.

THE VALLEY OF THE RÍO CHILCHOTA

There is a small but interesting area of agricultural terracing in the valley of the Río Chilchota (or Duero) on the northern margin of the Tarascan plateau. The part known as *La Cañada* extends for about 10 kilometers above the town of Chilchota. R. C. West observed: "The western end of the valley (near Chilchota) is marked by an ancient lava flow, which once partially blocked normal drainage. Subsequent deposition of alluvium — possibly lacustrine — behind the lava dam has resulted in the present wide, flattish floor of the valley's western half."[68] Above the main fill, low outwash fans lie around the mouths of lateral *arroyos*. The south-facing slopes of the valley are deeply eroded; considerable areas are bare of vegetation, with bedrock exposed, but where some soil remains there are scattered *milpas*. The contrast with the well-conserved and irrigated valley floor is most striking.

After the lava dam had been breached, the Río Chilchota began to excavate the alluvio-gravel fill, shaping it into a series of terraces; and in swinging back and forth between the sides of the old valley, the river has trimmed the edges of many of the outwash fans. Today it is entrenched 3 to 10 meters into the immediately adjacent levels.

The *relación geográfica* (1579) for the township of Chilchota refers to narrow stone-faced terraces *(gradas)* that apparently had been abandoned for some considerable time.[69] These have not been identified, but agricultural terraces of a different kind cover the floor and lower slopes of the valley (diag. 3.2). The remnants of

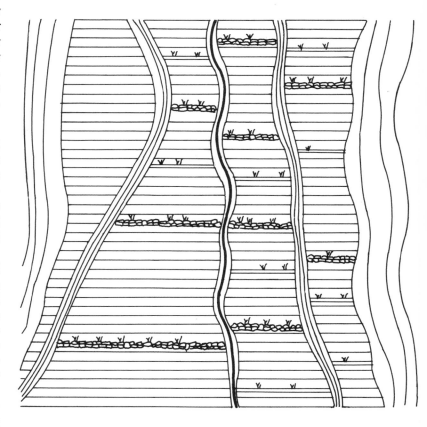

Diagram 3.2

PART OF LA CAÑADA, RÍO CHILCHOTA, MICHOACÁN, MEXICO

Río Chilchota

Sides of river terraces

} Walls of agricultural terraces

Cultivated

---

67. Foster, 1948, 67. Around Huecoria, the water table is only a few feet below the surface, and stream water is also diverted to fields (Belshaw, 1967, 9). Hand irrigation was practiced in pre-Columbian times; water was taken from wells and from ditches that led back from the lake (Palerm and Wolf, 1957, 12). The "chronicles of Michoacán," compiled 1539-41, several times refer to seed beds (Craine and Reindorp [eds], 1970, especially 132 — "We used to make seedbeds over on the shore").

68. West, 1947, 4.

69. Paso y Troncoso and Vargas Rea (eds), 2(7), 1944, 24.

river terraces form the basis of broad, contour-stepped fields (fig. 3.18). The valley-floor terraces appear to have been approximately leveled between substantial walls and then subdivided to produce virtually level planting surfaces. Water from the Río Chilchota, which maintains a strong flow into the middle of the dry season, is drawn off at successively lower levels, and there can be little doubt that terracing was undertaken to facilitate irrigation[70] of the fertile and well-drained valley floor.

Fig. 3.18 Valley of the Río Chilchota, above Chilchota, Michoacán, Mexico; contour terraces and (right center) cross-channel terraces

D: Northwest Mexico and the Southwest of the United States

The Sierra Madre Occidental forms the backbone of western Mexico (map 3.2). Above 2200 meters, where the annual rainfall normally exceeds 500 mm,[71] the natural vegetation is pine-oak woodland.[72] Areas of agricultural terracing lie partly in this cool, temperate zone and partly around the margins of the *cordillera,* or within interior basins, where the lower and less reliable rainfall supports a steppe vegetation of scrub oak, grama grasses, mesquite, acacia shrub and cacti. In the latter areas, the smaller streams are intermittent and soils deep enough for cultivation are concentrated in narrow flood plains and on outwash fans along the lower slopes of hills. Here simple methods of water control developed in association with terracing.

SOUTHWEST CHIHUAHUA AND NORTHERN SINALOA

The agricultural terraces of southwest Chihuahua and northern Sinaloa, on the western flanks of the Sierra Madre, were first recognized by Carl Lumholtz. He described check dams of stone up to 3 meters high in *arroyos* leading into the valley of the Río Fuerte and near Cusárare on a tributary of the Urique.[73] C. W. Pennington, in his study of the Tarahumar Indians of this area, draws attention to primitive contour terraces where soil is allowed slowly to accumulate behind stone walls. Along the Urique "a major portion of food" is still produced on such fields.[74]

To the south and east of the territory of the Tarahumar, stone-faced terraces line parts of the Río Florida and the Río Tunal.[75] Comparatively advanced farming folk (La Quemada and Chalchihuites) spread along the eastern piedmont of the Sierra Madre Occidental before A.D. 1000, but it is not certain that these particular terraces were constructed for the purpose of cultivation.

NORTHWEST SONORA AND NORTHERN CHIHUAHUA

Another group of terraced sites, now mainly abandoned, lies around the northern margins of the Sierra Madre. A. F. Bandelier, who first reported cross-channel terraces in the Pima-Papago-Opata territory of northwest Sonora,[76] was told that their purpose was to store moisture for cultivation by increasing the depth of soil.[77] O. H. Howarth, writing a few years later (apparently without knowledge of Bandelier's work) described "terraced gardens in the beds of steep gullies of the Sonoran mountains . . . in fact soil dams, into which the torrents had washed the best alluvial matter from the surface. . . . A succession of level plots of the highest fertility was thus secured by utilizing the operations of nature" (1895).[78] This is possibly the earliest description of the part played by natural processes in terrace building.

The most detailed studies of agricultural terracing in northwest Mexico, and probably of anywhere in the New World, concern the upper catchment of the Río

70. See Palerm, 1954, 11 (160) [*Suma de visitas*].

71. Page, 1930; Bennett and Zingg, 1935, 4-5; Wallén, 1955.

72. Leopold, 1950, 510-11, and 1952, 61-63.

73. Lumholtz, 1902, 73, 137. Blackiston (1905, 360; 1906, 10) observed both contour and cross-channel terraces (with 5-meter walls) in (?) Cave valley off the Río Piedras Verdes.

74. Pennington, 1963, 48-49. Pennington (1969, 59-60) also mentions cross-channel terraces in the neighboring Tepehuan territory.

75. Kelley, 1956, 129, 132. See also Hewett, 1936, 55, 58.

76. For the distribution and economy of these people, see Sauer, 1933 and 1935; also the map of the Pimería Alta, 1687-1711, in Bolton, 1919.

77. "Pima Indians of Sonora assert that they were garden beds [cultivated] without irrigation and with the help of summer showers alone" (Bandelier, 1892, 61).

78. Howarth, 1895, 435.

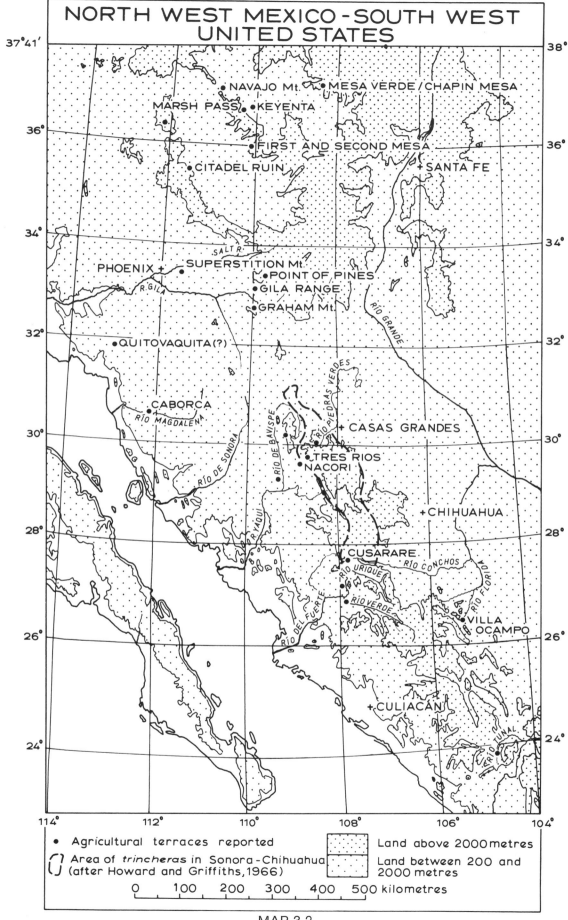

NORTH WEST MEXICO-SOUTH WEST UNITED STATES

- • Navajo Mt.
- • MESA VERDE/CHAPIN MESA
- MARSH PASS • • KEYENTA
- • FIRST AND SECOND MESA
- • CITADEL RUIN
- + SANTA FE
- SALT R.
- PHOENIX + • SUPERSTITION Mt.
- • POINT OF PINES
- R. GILA
- • GILA RANGE
- • GRAHAM Mt.
- RÍO GRANDE
- • QUITOVAQUITA (?)
- RÍO PIEDRAS VERDES
- • CABORCA
- RÍO MAGDALENA
- RÍO DE BAVISPE
- RÍO PIEDRAS VERDES
- RÍO DE SONORA
- + CASAS GRANDES
- • TRES RIOS
- • NACORI
- + CHIHUAHUA
- R. YAQUI
- • CUSARARE
- RÍO CONCHOS
- RÍO URIQUE
- RÍO DEL FUERTE
- • RÍO VERDE
- RÍO FLORIDA
- • VILLA OCAMPO
- RÍO PETATLAN
- + CULIACÁN
- RÍO TUNAL

| • | Agricultural terraces reported | | Land above 2000 metres |
| (] | Area of *trincheras* in Sonora-Chihuahua (after Howard and Griffiths, 1966) | | Land between 200 and 2000 metres |

0   100   200   300   400   500 kilometres

MAP 3.2

Fig. 3.19 Agricultural *trincheras,* near Río Piedras Verdes, northwest Mexico (L. Herold, 1965)

Fig. 3.20 Hopi terrace gardens, near Wipo Springs, First Mesa, Arizona (G. R. Stewart, 1940)

Gavilan, southwest of Casas Grandes, Chihuahua.[79] Here precipitation increases with altitude from 375 mm to 625 mm per annum, but the only areas cultivated today are occasional strips of alluvium along streams. The great majority of the terraces are of the cross-channel *(trinchera)* type (fig. 3.19). The walls, up to 2 meters high, are sometimes sited at nick points so that "a maximum of fill could be controlled by a minimum of trinchera wall construction."[80] The normal processes of deposition and mass wasting appear to explain the formation of cropping surfaces. No evidence of artificial filling was found.

Southwest of the Río Gavilan, similar cross-channel terraces have been recognized around Nacori[81] and in the Sierra de Teras[82] (within the great bend of the Río Bavispe). Like those of the Gavilan, they mostly lie within the zone of oak, pine and juniper forest and have long been abandoned.

How far agricultural terracing extends west of the Río Bavispe is not entirely clear. There are reports for the Papaguería as far as Caborca on the Río Magdalena.[83] But the question is complicated by the presence north and west of the Río Sonora of terraces, also known as *trincheras,* of a different kind. These are narrow, contour benches, with little or no fill, and apparently designed as house sites and fortifications.[84] The builders are thought to have farmed the surrounding flood-plains and outwash fans where terracing is unnecessary. The *cerros de trincheras* were essentially settlement sites.

THE SOUTHWEST OF THE UNITED STATES

There are two main areas of aboriginal terracing in the deserts and steppes of the Southwest: the valley systems of the middle and upper Gila and Salt rivers, and the Colorado Plateau, north and east of Flagstaff.

The valleys of the middle and upper Gila and Salt rivers: In Hohokam times (100 B.C. - A.D. 1400), there developed in the Gila-Salt basin the most advanced system of canal irrigation in North America.[85] This survived in part under the Pima[86] who also terraced for agriculture and practiced flood-water farming. The cross-channel terraces[87] are very similar to those already described for the northern Sierra Madre. While the Pima and the Papago leveled fields artificially in preparation for the use of flood-water,[88] the terraced plots appear to have been formed by the gradual accumulation of water-borne alluvium.

Colorado Plateau: Several hundred contour and cross-channel terraces have been identified at Mesa Verde (Colorado)[89] where farming probably ceased *circa* 1300.[90] From Citadel Ruin in the San Francisco Mountains of northern Arizona, G. R. Stewart and M. Donnelly reported abandoned terraces that were partly filled with domestic refuse.[91] Probably the best examples of terraces still in use are to be found around Hopi settlements on First Mesa (fig. 3.20).[92] Traditional agricultural practices have survived more completely among the Hopi and Zuni than elsewhere in the Southwest.

79. L. Herold, 1965 and 1966. See also Bandelier, 1892, 62; Sayles 1936, 38; McCabe, 1955, 75-90; Howard and Griffiths, 1966.

80. L. Herold, 1965, 147.

81. Lumholtz, 1902, 21-22.

82. Bandelier, 1892, 62; Lumholtz, 1902, 45; Sauer and Brand, 1931 (photographs).

83. L. Herold, 1965, 1.

84. Schumacher, 1882, 227-29; McGee, 1895, 372 (Papaguería of Sonora-Arizona); Sauer and Brand, 1931; Ives, 1936, 257 (Quitovaquita, Sonora); Hoover, 1941, 228, 231; A. F. Johnson, 1963-4, 178, and 1966, 32-33; Harlem, 1964, 339-50.

85. Haury, 1936, 48-50, and 1962, 122; Halseth, 1936, 42; Woodbury, 1961b, and 1962, 302; E. K. Reed, 1964, 182. Schroeder (1966) discusses the diffusion of cultural features, including irrigation, from Mexico toward the Southwest after c. A.D. 600.

86. Bartlett, 1854, 232-33, 242-43; Bandelier, 1892, 104, 254; Castetter and Bell, 1942, 59, 151; Ezell, 1961, 36; Woodbury, 1962, 302.

87. Stewart, 1940, 217; Woodbury, 1961a, 11-12, and 1962, 302-304.

88. Castetter and Bell, 1942, 161, 169. On flood-water farming, see Bryan, 1929, 444-56, and 1941, 219-42; Spicer, 1961, 12, 50.

89. Stewart, 1940, 214; Stewart and Donnelly, 1943, 34; J. Herold, 1961, 103-108, 111; Woodbury, 1962, 304; Rohn, 1963, 441-56; Erdman, Douglas and Marr, 1969, 57-58.

90. J. Herold, 1961, 111. On the abandonment of settlements in arid North America c. A.D. 1300-1400, see Hewett, Henderson and Robbins, 1913; Bryan, 1941, 72, 74; O'Bryan, 1952, 153-57; Stevens, 1964, 292; Armillas, 1969, 697-704. Woodbury (1962, 304) places the beginning of terracing in the Southwest in the eleventh century or earlier. According to L. Herold (1965, 1), the [abandoned] terraces of northern Mexico were constructed between c. 1100 and 1450.

91. Stewart and Donnelly, 1943, 42-43. For brief references to abandoned terraces elsewhere in northern Arizona and in southern Utah, see Kidder and Guernsey, 1919, 64 (Marsh Pass, Arizona); Stewart and Donnelly, 1943, 37 (Navajo Mountain); Brew, 1946, 10 (Alkali Ridge, Utah); Woodbury, 1962, 304 (Kayenta, Arizona).

92. Forde, 1931a, 364-5; Colton, 1932, 16; Stewart, 1940, 201-20, 329-40; Hack, 1942, 34-37.

2. MIDDLE AND CENTRAL AMERICA

A: Southern Mexico and Southwest Guatemala

THE MIXTECA ALTA AND THE BASIN OF TEHUACÁN

The highlands west of the basins of Oaxaca and Tehuacán-Cuicatlán (map 3.1) form part of the continental divide. The ethno-linguistic province known as the Mixteca Alta extended from the Sierra de Coicoyán (or Coyoyán) eastward to a little beyond the main watershed, the Sierra de las Mixtecas.[1]

The average annual rainfall of this area at present is of the order of 500 mm to 750 mm, which is about the minimum necessary for the cultivation of maize on soils of reasonable depth without irrigation. Considerable fluctuations in the total amount are, however, experienced locally,[2] and the effectiveness of the rainfall is further reduced by the wide extent of bare, eroded surfaces. The "natural" vegetation is pine-oak forest, but this has largely disappeared, and what remains, mainly above 2500 meters, is exploited for firewood and building material. The consequences of sheet and gully erosion are more apparent here than in any other part of Mexico. In late pre-Columbian times, the Mixteca Alta supported a dense population "which may have exceeded the long-term carrying capacity of the land."[3] Numbers fell precipitously between *circa* 1530 and 1620,[4] and conditions that must have led to further erosion included the abandonment of peripheral holdings, inadequate maintenance of terrace walls and irrigation works, and the introduction of livestock. About the middle of the seventeenth century, Thomas Gage noted "the great abundance of cattle" in the Mixteca.[5]

Large areas of the Mixteca Alta have at some time or other been terraced for agriculture. The following account is based on field observations around Coixlahuaca, Nochixtlán, Huajuápam, Tamazulápam-Teotongo, Yolomécatl and Huamelúlpam, and on published statements concerning Achiutla and Tilantongo-Monte Negro. There are also areas of old terracing near Silacayoápam on the western margins of the Mixteca Alta.[6] Aerial photographs further extend the known distribution between Coixlahuaca and Nochixtlán and in the highlands to the west of the basin of Oaxaca.

Northern and western Mixteca Alta: Tamazulápam, Teotongo and Tejúpam occupy piedmont sites overlooking the head waters of the Río Loro. The soils here are of limestone origin and of good texture but thin except in natural embayments. The whole area displays "numerous indications of ancient habitation. . . . There is little question that a large population lived here for a very long period before the Conquest."[7] S. F. Cook estimated the population of Tamazulápam in 1520 at approximately 72,000, and of the whole valley at 120,000; it is scarcely one-tenth of this today.

Southwest of Tamazulápam, broken walls and heavily degraded surfaces indicate the valleyward retreat of cultivation (fig. 3.21). Isolated cross-channel benches also

---

1. There are useful sketch maps of the Mixteca in Diguet, 1906; Dahlgren de Jordan, 1954; Paddock, 1966a, 86; Spores, 1967, 7, 21, 99. Cook and Borah (1968) includes an important discussion of the extent of the Mixteca Alta.

2. 85 mm to 575 mm at Coixlahuaca between 1906 and 1913 (S. F. Cook, 1958, 9).

3. Borah, 1960, 159; Cook and Borah, 1968. Paddock (1964, 464-65, 1966b, 369) adduces (on the evidence of Cortés, Cobo, Vázquez de Espinosa, Gage and Burgoa) generally better conditions in the sixteenth and seventeenth centuries than today; see also, López de Velasco (1571-4), 1894, 229, and García Pimentel, 1904, 62. The *Relaciones geográficas* similarly suggest a deterioration since the latter half of the sixteenth century (Cabrero Fernández, 1962, 688-94, and 1964, 135). S. F. Cook (1949 and 1958b) and Bernal (1965, 796) argue that soil erosion was already extensive by 1500.

4. Cook and Borah, 1968. There were large-scale epidemics in 1520, 1531, 1545 and 1576 (Dahlgren de Jordan, 1954, 29).

5. Gage (1648), 1928, 119. Indians could keep large animals only for field labor and transport. Permission was needed even to graze sheep and goats on unoccupied land *(baldios);* nevertheless the Indians owned large numbers by the end of the sixteenth century (Miranda, 1958, 788, 794; Spores, 1967, 83).

6. A. Caso, personal communication, 1966.

7. S. F. Cook, 1949b, 4. For two former settlement sites (Yatachió and Pueblo Viejo), see Bernal, 1953.

Fig. 3.21 Abandoned terraces, Tamazulápam, Mixteca Alta, Mexico

have been abandoned. The most productive terraces —
here, and very possibly in the entire Mixteca Alta —
lie to the northeast of Tamazulápam in the basin of the
Loro. Slopes of southwesterly aspect and of less than
10 degrees gradient have been carefully organized into
a series of contour and valley-floor fields between walls
1 to 2.5 meters high (fig. 3.22). Water from springs that
feed the Loro is distributed by stone-lined channels.

Huamelúlpam and Yolomecátl stand at just over 2000
meters near the center of the Mixteca Alta. The grits
and shales around Huamelúlpam disintegrate to form
comparatively deep soils. Presently cultivated areas include some steep and unprotected slopes, contour terraces along the lower slopes of the hills, and cross-channel
terraces in *barrancas* and broader embayments. The
contour terraces represent only a part of the area at
different times prepared for cultivation in a similar way.
Broken walls now run through woodland, and old agricultural surfaces are occasionally "exhumed" for temporary *milpa*. Cross-channel terracing is more highly
developed and almost wholly in use. Along *barrancas*,
retaining walls are curved toward the higher ground for

greater strength, and in embayments (fig. 3.23) leveling,
partly to facilitate irrigation, has involved considerable
movement of soil.

Yolomécatl is situated in an area with strong karstic
features. The slopes of the enclosing hills include large
outcrops of bare limestone, and other parts are only
lightly covered with fine gray soils. Cultivation is now
mainly concentrated on the floors of small basins or
poljes where fields are regularly irrigated. The lower
slopes are terraced, but without much attention to leveling. To an even greater extent than at Huamelúlpam,
broken terrace walls on the middle and upper slopes
bear witness to changes in the limits of agriculture. Dam-
ming some of the *barrancas* has again proved more re-
warding than contour terracing. The cross-channel terraces are usually small and some amount to only a few
square meters. The fill clearly has been derived from
the interfluves which are often deeply eroded.[8]

8. Terracing similar to that of Yolomécatl may be observed
   around San Miguel Tixa and San Felipe Ixtapa.

Fig. 3.22   Irrigated terraces, Tamazulápam, Mixteca Alta, Mexico; the crop is alfalfa

Fig. 3.23   Terraced fields, San Martin Huamelúlpam, Mixteca Alta, Mexico

Southern and eastern Mixteca Alta: This area includes the numerous tributary valleys of the south-flowing Río Ixtayutla (or Verde). Aerial photographs of the upper Cuanana (near San Mateo Xindihui) and of the Peñoles (near San Miguel Piedras), some 50 kilometers west of Oaxaca, show a large number of terraced fields.[9] Cross-channel structures are strongly represented; the great majority are well defined and clear of vegetation. As in other parts of the Mixteca Alta, the higher contour terraces show most evidence of abandonment or long neglect.

Alfonso Caso has reported old "terraces" at Monte Negro-Tilantongo.[10] They appear to have been used as house sites and for agriculture as early as *circa* 600 B.C. Francisco de Burgoa (1674), in describing the area between Tilantongo and Achiutla, remarked upon terraced fields "like staircases" that were still in use.[11]

Agricultural terracing covers large areas in the southern half of the Sierra de las Mixtecas, from north and west of Nochixtlán to Coixlahuaca. Nochixtlán is situated at the head of a valley opening soutward.[12] The surrounding slopes are extensively eroded and much formerly cultivated land has been lost. Agriculture is now chiefly associated with valley bottoms and basin floors where deep soils have accumulated. Cross-channel terraces occupy embayments, and low terraces along the piedmont also are cultivated. On the higher slopes there are remains of old contour benches.[13]

Aerial photographs[14] show well developed terracing to the northeast of Nochixtlán, as well as east of Yanhuitlán,[15] west of Apoala and Santa María Apasco, and south and west of Coixlahuaca. This again is predominantly limestone country and the soils of the interfluves are thin and stony. The more humid hilltops are wooded, but at lower levels the vegetation is open, xerophytic

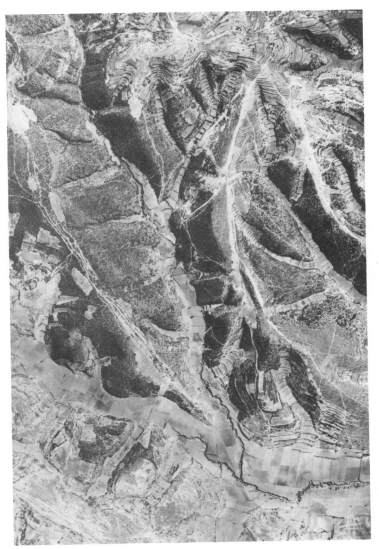

Fig. 3.24 Cross-channel and contour terraces, 8 kilometers east of Yanhuitlán, Mixteca Alta, Mexico
(Cia. Mexicana Aerofoto, S.A.)

scrub. What roughly level land there is, is distributed in small *poljes* and at intervals along valleys. The accumulation of cultivable soil has been assisted by cross-channel terracing, and long series of small, stepped fields lead into the highlands (fig. 3.24). The great majority are still cultivated, unlike the contour terraces which have been widely abandoned.

The lands of Coixlahuaca probably showed evidence of over-cultivation in the late fifteenth century when the town itself was a very important place.[16] Their condition today is in many respects typical of the limestone

9. *Cia. Mexicana Aerofoto SA* — Series 1581 (Río Verde), nos. 157-59, 187-92, 195-97 (December 1960).

10. Caso, 1938, 55, *plano* 8; and personal communication, 1966.

11. Burgoa, I, 1934, 275. Diguet (1906, 27) estimated the population of Achiutla c. 1500 at 14,000, compared with barely 2000 in Achiutla and Tilantongo c. 1900. Spores (1967, 44) reports cultivated terraces at Mogote del Cacique, 5 kilometers east of Tilantongo.

12. Observations west to San Juan Sayultepec and northeast to San Pedro Quilitongo.

13. E. Guzmán (1934, 31) and Spores (1967, 38) mention terraces around the *pueblo viejo* (abandoned c. 1561) of Nochixtlán.

14. *Cia. Mexicana Aerofoto SA* — Series 1529 (Nochixtlán y Cuicatlán), January 1960.

15. E. Guzmán (1934, 18, 23, 31) and Spores (1967, 34, 81) refer to "terraces" around and to the east of Yanhuitlán (Yacuita, Chachoapan). Yanhuitlán was the largest town in the Mixteca Alta in 1565-70 (Spores, 1967, 240).

16. Durán (1581), 1964, 117. The present village covers part of the ancient settlement, and the great church of the Dominicans stands on the base of a pre-Columbian pyramid (Bernal, 1948-9, 6). Coixlahuaca fell to the Mexicans between 1440 and 1468.

Fig. 3.25 Abandoned terraces, Coixlahuaca, Mixteca Alta, Mexico; bare limestone outcrops in middle distance

areas of the Mixteca Alta. Soil erosion is widespread and water scarce (the Río Blanco almost disappears in the dry season). Cutting for firewood and the grazing of goats appear to be chiefly responsible for the reduction in the area of woody vegetation in recent times.

The Río Blanco is incised within the main valley, setting a low base level for the many tributary *barrancas,* and the small area of level land is subject to both lateral and headward erosion. The deep soils of the valley bottom hold enough moisture to permit the cultivation of maize, but some fields are irrigated. Cross-channel terraces are rare in comparison with areas to the south of Coixlahuaca. Nevertheless, several *barrancas* have been dammed to form tiers of small fields separated by massive walls up to 4 meters high. The adjacent slopes are often completely bare of soil.

Contour terraces are prominent in the vicinity of Coixlahuaca. Those that have been developed on outwash fans below the town are managed much like the adjacent bottom lands. On the other hand, the higher terraces are at best cultivated once in every six or seven years, and many are virtually abandoned (fig. 3.25). In places, the rock pavement is exposed within terraces, and surfaces are deeply gullied where walls have collapsed (fig. 3.26). The finer soil particles are constantly being removed by wind erosion.

Barranca Grande (basin of Tehuacán): The highlands of which the Sierra de las Mixtecas forms a major part continue northward to beyond the Río Hondo where they flank the northern end of the basin of Tehuacán. From this basin has come the earliest evidence of plant domestication[17] and of irrigation[18] in Middle America. Forms of water control, involving terracing, were also developed in the narrow valleys of the highland margins.[19]

The branching watercourses of the Barranca Grande are completely dry in winter but liable to flood in the wet season, and flash floods have been responsible for the final destruction of abandoned fields. A tributary *barranca* immediately to the northeast of Zapotitlán contains several groups of cross-channel terraces, all more or less eroded (fig. 3.27). Soil has been swept down

17. MacNeish, 1962; Byers, 1964a and b.

18. Possibly 900-200 B.C. [Santa María phase], certainly 200 B.C.-A.D. 800 [Palo Blanco phase] (Mangelsdorf *et al.,* 1964, 444; C. E. Smith, 1965, 68-75; MacNeish, 1967, 24). Information has come from 150 sites (Paddock, 1966a, 195). Palerm (1954), in his study of irrigation in sixteenth-century Mexico, lists several places within and to the east of the basin of Tehuacán: Tehuacán itself, Coxcatlán, Teotitlán del Camino, Quiotepec, Cuicatlán, Pápalo and Atatlahuacá.

19. C. E. Smith, 1965, 62, 65, 70, 76.

Fig. 3.26   Broken terrace wall (3.5 meters), Coixlahuaca, Mixteca Alta, Mexico

Fig. 3.27   Abandoned cross-channel terraces, Zapotitlán, near Tehuacán, Mexico

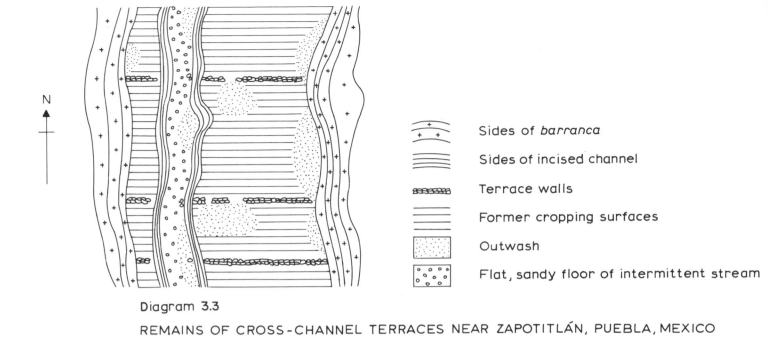

Sides of *barranca*

Sides of incised channel

Terrace walls

Former cropping surfaces

Outwash

Flat, sandy floor of intermittent stream

Diagram 3.3

REMAINS OF CROSS-CHANNEL TERRACES NEAR ZAPOTITLÁN, PUEBLA, MEXICO

Fig. 3.28 Abandoned cross-channel terraces, cut by an *arroyo,* Zapotitlán, near Tehuacán, Mexico

from one level to the next following the partial collapse of walls. Moreover, the high terraces are flanked by a stream bed (fig 3.28; diag. 3.3) of later origin and 2 to 4 meters below the top of the artificial fill. Walls can sometimes be matched across the cutting, in the sides of which sections of buried walls are also exposed, indicating successive planting surfaces. Where the *barranca* broadens out, there are traces of old contour terraces — parallel lines of stone, at most a few courses high, and 10 to 20 meters apart. Any soil that accumulated behind these walls has been subsequently removed, and the intervening surfaces are indistinguishable from the unterraced slopes.

OAXACA

The valley of Oaxaca-Tlacolula comprises several broad depressions, drained by the headwaters of the Río Atoyac. It has been suggested that uplift of the southern coastal ranges isolated the Oaxaca valley system and led to the formation of a group of lakes.[20] Legend[21] and the various marshy tracts that exist today or have been reported in the past[22] appear to lend support to this theory. However, recent work has shown the valley deposits to be alluvial rather than lacustrine and of Pleistocene and later origin.[23] The fill almost completely covers an uneven foundation of old metamorphic rocks and Tertiary volcanics which rise steeply along the northeastern side of the basin and form part of the watershed of the north-flowing Río Grande.

The valley of Oaxaca has a transitional (Aw/Cw) climate, becoming more arid (probably BS) toward the east (in the rain shadow of the Sierra de Juárez) around and beyond Tlacolula. Oaxaca, at 1550 meters above sea level, has an annual rainfall of between 500 mm and 700 mm, of which 85 percent or more falls between April and November. The Sierra to the north and east receives substantially more rain (800 mm to 900 mm at Ixtlán de Juárez) and the seasonality of the regime is somewhat less marked. The climate here belongs to the Cw type and the natural vegetation on slopes between 1800 and 3000 meters is typically pine-oak woodland.[24]

The valley of Oaxaca-Tlacolula: The remarkably high water table over parts of the valley floor permitted the development, at least as early as 700 B.C., of hand irrigation based on shallow wells.[25] Villages were sited on rocky outliers or piedmont spurs, principally, it seems, to avoid the risk of flooding. Settlement near perennial streams within the piedmont probably came somewhat later (c. 600-200 B.C.) when canal irrigation also commenced.

At the time of the Spanish Conquest, the valley and surrounding mountains of Oaxaca were occupied by Mixtec and Zapotec peoples. The area has a long and involved history of occupation, as evidenced by numerous archaeological sites,[26] including three of the first importance — Mitla, Yagul and Monte Albán. None of these sites lies on the floor of the valley. Monte Albán occupies a leveled hilltop 6 kilometers west of the city of Oaxaca, and Yagul and Mitla belong to the eastern piedmont of the valley of Tlacolula. According to O. Schmieder, the Spaniards found large parts of the valley unoccupied (but not without claimants) and here they established *haciendas*. Indian settlements were generally nucleated and regrouping *(congregación)* was unnecessary; the present distribution, at least around the margins of the basin, is pre-Columbian in origin.[27]

The hills on the northeastern side of the valley, from Tlalixtac de Cabrera to beyond Mitla, show traces of more extensive cultivation in the past than today.[28] The greater part of Mitla's cultivated land lies on the valley floor, but the rising ground immediately behind the town is covered with broad, stone-faced terraces that are mostly still in use (fig. 3.29). The bedrock is limestone and the soil on unterraced slopes is thin. Terracing is best developed in shallow embayments. Some of the higher and more steeply sloping plots have not been cultivated for many years and may be regarded as abandoned.

Fields that have been roughly terraced extend northwestward along the piedmont to beyond Yagul. There are also many cross-channel terraces in small *barrancas;* some of the supporting walls have collapsed and a high proportion of the fields are now abandoned.

20. Schmieder, 1930, 5. Swinson (1955, 10) describes the levels around Yagul as an "old lake bottom."

21. "Not only do ancient writers speak of projects by Zapotec sovereigns to drain the valley, but the belief persists in the folklore of today" (Bernal, 1965, 794). See also Caso, 1962, 4.

22. The *relación de Tlacolula* (1579) states (Swinson, 1955, 17), "this town lies on flat ground. It is unhealthful because of the dampness of the nearby marsh."

23. Lorenzo, 1960, 49-63.

24. Bravo, 1960, 42-43.

25. Lorenzo, 1960, 58; Flannery *et al.,* 1967, 445-54; Kirkby, 1973, 127.

26. Bernal (1965, 795) remarks that agricultural terraces are "commonly" associated with archaeological sites in the Zapotec region.

27. Teotitlán del Valle (or *Xaguixe,* "at the foot of the mountain") was the first town founded by the Zapotecs in the valley of Oaxaca (Caso, 1962, 4).

28. For a general account of Zapotec agriculture, see Mendieta y Núñez, 1949, 451-89.

Fig. 3.29 Terraced fields, Mitla, valley of Oaxaca, Mexico

At Hierve el Agua near San Lorenzo Albarrados (about 30 kilometers east of Mitla) a flight of agricultural terraces has been dated to "before 300 B.C. and expanding through all subsequent periods of Oaxaca prehistory." The "dry-laid stone terraces had been irrigated by means of small canals which carried the water down to the fields and along the tops of the terrace walls."[29] Travertine dissolved in the spring water eventually made the terraces unfit for agriculture but preserved the canals.

Abandoned agricultural terraces at Monte Albán have been mentioned by several scholars.[30] On the east, northeast and southeast facing slopes of the hill there are parallel lines of broken walls, in places up to 1.5 meters high. The planting surfaces, 15 to 40 meters wide, could never have been level. In the same area there are also several small valleys that have been cross-terraced, almost certainly for purposes of cultivation.

The highlands of Oaxaca: The Sierras Aloapaneca, Juárez and Ixtlán together form the watershed of the upper Río Grande. The area so defined is one of powerful relief and difficult communications. There is very little level ground for agriculture. The narrow bottom lands of the tributary valleys of the Río Grande are attractive for the strips of fertile alluvium and the ease of irrigation. Villages are sited on mountain-side benches 200 to 400 meters above the adjacent streams. Changes in the settlement pattern are apparent from the many abandoned *pueblos.*[31]

Terracing is an important feature of the agricultural scene in this part of the Zapotec highlands. To the west, among the Mixe Indians, terraces are prepared for house sites[32] but not, apparently, for fields. The terraces of the Zapotec country range from the primitive to the very advanced. The latter are cultivated continuously or with only short periods of fallow, the former at intervals of five to seven years. Crops are also taken for

29. Flannery, *et al.,* 1967, 451-53; Neely, 1967, 15-17 ("alguna de las primeras evidencias de la agricultura de riego hasta ahora descubiertas en Mesoamérica").

30. See Armillas, 1948, 106; Bernal, 1965, 805. The earliest reference discovered is by Bandelier, 1884, 319 ("the brink of the eastern declivity, which there is steep and interrupted by cultivation terraces").

31. Pérez García, I, 1956, 58-59, 63; Schmieder, 1930, 48. Pérez García includes a *plano topográfico* (1870) of the lands of San Juan Chicomezúchil; and Schmieder's map of the Serrano-Tzapotec settlements is valuable for the minor topographic names.

32. Beals, 1945, 9, 15 (Ayutla).

Fig. 3.30 Irrigated terraces, San Juan Chicomezúchil, Zapotec highlands, Oaxaca, Mexico

two or three years together from unterraced slopes. This combination of different systems of cultivation, from permanent and sometimes irrigated fields to temporary *milpa,* is characteristic of much of central and southern Mexico. The vegetation of the area under consideration has been strongly influenced by man. But on account of the scattered distribution of *milpas,* and because of the comparatively high rainfall which favors the rapid regeneration of woody species, soil erosion is not a serious problem, at least in comparison with northwest Oaxaca and the Mixteca Alta.

Attempts to create level, cultivable ground are most evident in the immediate vicinity of Lachatao, Yahuiche, and particularly San Juan Chicomezúchil. Stretches of alluvium along the Río San Juan (or Teté), upstream from its confluence with the Río Grande, are divided into small, valley-floor terraces. Chicomezúchil itself occupies a ridge between the Río San Juan and the Río Yahuiche. The south-facing slopes of the ridge are expertly terraced (fig. 3.30); walls up to 3.5 meters high support level surfaces that are regularly irrigated.[33] Some of the plots within the village are essentially orchards with vegetables and field crops planted between the trees (zapote [*Calocarpum mammosum*], níspero [*Achras sapodilla*] and aguacate [*Persea americana*]). Two crops of maize, beans or alfalfa can be grown in any one year. House gardens, and irrigated land generally, receive most of whatever fertilizer is available.

In the vicinity of Lachatao[34] one again finds level benches with high and well-constructed walls, but according to local informants there is now "insufficient water for irrigation." At Yahuiche the nearer fields are both terraced and irrigated, and around all three villages, dry, sloping terraces (cropped after several years of fallow) comprise an important part of the cultivated area.

Above Lachatao and Chicomezúchil, and between the former and Amatlán, there are the remains of agricultural terraces, some of which probably belonged to settlements that have been abandoned. O. Schmieder observed that west of Lachatao "the entire top [of a hill known as *Ye-tha*] is carefully terraced with stone walls, several meters high."[35] There is no trace of former dwellings but the tradition of a *pueblo viejo* survives.

33. Irrigation was practiced at Chicomezúchil in the sixteenth century (Palerm, 1954, 13); Pérez García (1, 1956, 151) refers to "una zanja antigua de agua."

34. According to Pérez García (2, 1956, 227), "uno de los lugares más pedregosos de los pueblos del Distrito."

35. Schmieder, 1930, 48.

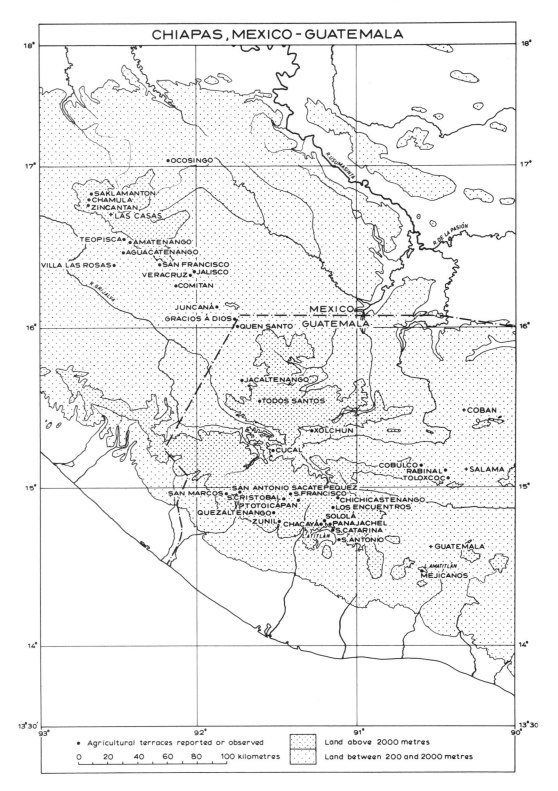

CHIAPAS, MEXICO - GUATEMALA

18°

17°
•OCOSINGO

•SAKLAMANTON
•CHAMULA
•ZINCANTAN
+LAS CASAS

TEOPISCA• •AMATENANGO
•AGUACATENANGO
VILLA LAS ROSAS• •SAN FRANCISCO
VERACRUZ• •JALISCO
•COMITAN

JUNCANÁ• MEXICO
GRACIOS Á DIOS• GUATEMALA
16° •QUEN SANTO

•JACALTENANGO

•TODOS SANTOS
+COBAN

•XOLCHÚN

•CUCAL
COBULCO• •RABINAL• +SALAMA
•TOLOXCOC

15° SAN ANTONIO SACATEPEQUEZ
SAN MARCOS• •S.FRANCISCO•
•S.CRISTOBAL• •CHICHICASTENANGO
•P.TOTOICAPAN •LOS ENCUENTROS
QUEZALTENANGO• SOLOLÁ•
ZUNIL• •PANAJACHEL
CHACAYÁ• •S.CATARINA
L.ATITLÁN •S.ANTONIO
+GUATEMALA

L.AMATITLÁN
MEJICANOS

14°

R.USUMASINTA
R.DE LA PASIÓN
R.GRIJALVA

13°30'
93°   92°   91°   90°   13°30'

• Agricultural terraces reported or observed   Land above 2000 metres

0   20   40   60   80   100 kilometres   Land between 200 and 2000 metres

MAP 3.3

No agricultural terracing was observed in the highlands between the Pacific coast and the valley of Oaxaca. However, the *relación geográfica* for Ozolotepec (1580) alludes to terraces *(llanadas, llanos hechos a mano)* built for the purpose of cultivation and involving irrigation.[36] These still await investigation.

CHIAPAS-CUCHUMATANES

Old agricultural terracing has been reported from widely separated sites in Chiapas and northern Guatemala. The known distribution, incorporating additional field observations, is shown in map 3.3.

Chamula-Saklamantón, Chiapas: North of Chamula,[37] on the high plateau of central Chiapas, lie a succession of limestone basins. The slopes are wooded; the floors, on the other hand, are mostly grass-covered and appear never to have been cultivated. The basin that forms the nucleus of the *paraje* of Saklamantón is a good example. Here cultivation is entirely confined to embayments and small tributary valleys across which substantial walls have been built (figs. 3.31, 3.32). The terraces so formed are worked from hamlets that occupy adjacent cols and hilltops. There are also some new or reconstructed terraces on outwash fans between Chamula and Saklamantón. Proficiency in the use of stone is strikingly displayed, not only in boundary walls, but in the lined and funnel-shaped wells of this area.

Amatenango-Aguacatenango, Chiapas: Terraces cover the slopes of a dry valley behind the *finca* San Nicolás in the basin of Amatenango. The walls, although everywhere much broken and almost hidden by dense deciduous scrub, stand in places to a height of 2.5 meters. They appear to have supported level or gently-sloping surfaces 50 to 75 meters long. There is evidence of a former settlement along the top of the ridge and the terraces probably served as house sites as well as fields.

The basin of Aguacatenango[38] lies 10 kilometers south of Amatenango. The break of slope between the level floor and the surrounding hills is masked by aprons of unconsolidated material and by wider fans at the mouths of *arroyos*. The center of the basin is occupied by a lake which fluctuates considerably in area and divides in two during the dry season. It is drained subterraneanly. The basin of Aguacatenango, like that of Amatenango-Teopisca, is fundamentally a large *polje*. The bottom lands are now partly cultivated and partly under pasture.

36. Paso y Troncoso (ed), 4, 1905-6, 141.
37. Chamula is the center *(cabecera)* of a *municipio;* dependent territories are known as *parajes*.
38. P. L. Wagner, 1962, 253-74 (fig. 6).

Fig. 3.31 Cross-channel terraces (lower wall c. 2 meters), Saklamantón, near Chamula, Chiapas, Mexico

Fig. 3.32 Cross-channel terraces, Saklamantón, near Chamula, Mexico

On the western side of the basin, each of a dozen or more short, tributary valleys contains flights of cross-channel terraces.[39] The level surfaces are occasionally cropped, but the more heavily vegetated slopes (easily cleared by burning and of high initial fertility) are preferred for temporary *milpa*. Parts of the retaining walls have collapsed (fig. 3.33) and in places cuttings reveal buried walls, from which it could be argued that plots were occasionally overwhelmed by material swept from the valley sides and/or that the terraced area was several times reorganized. In any event, it appears from details of construction that the retaining walls were gradually heightened.

Beyond the mouths of the *arroyos,* a succession of stone walls, no more than half a meter high but up to 100 meters long, run roughly parallel to the margins of the basin. Although without much effect on the naturally gentle slope, they have served to impound outwash material.

Terraces arranged concentrically around hills on the southwestern side of the basin have been interpreted by L. E. Guzmán as house and garden plots. The level top of one of these hills *(Hlehlum)* is partly covered with low walls that suggest house foundations. As has been said, such high sites are still typical of the hamlets and isolated farmsteads to the north of Chamula where bottom lands remain largely uncultivated. The settlement features and agriculture of Saklamantón and Aguacatenango may represent conditions characteristic of, respectively, pre- and post-Columbian times. The regular plan of Aguacatenango, like that of most other important villages, but not Chamula, displays strong Hispanic influence. R. M. Adams suggests that a trend toward the siting of settlements on lower ground commenced in the central highlands of Chiapas in late pre-Columbian times and that this movement was reinforced by a policy of *congregación* under the Spaniards.[40] Such resiting would not, however, automatically lead to the abandonment of terraced fields. This came rather with the greater, perhaps first, utilization of the wet bottom lands, facilitated by the introduction of the plow and domestic animals. The terraces apparently belong to the middle

---

39. L. E. Guzmán, 1958, 266, 1962, 398-406.

40. R. M. Adams, 1961, 350.

Fig. 3.33   Broken terrace wall and eroded fill, Aguacatenango, Chiapas, Mexico

and late classic periods (c. A.D. 700 to 1000). That they were built by a population that occupied hilltop sites is also probable.[41]

Comitán-San Francisco, Chiapas: The limestone hills immediately to the north of Comitán have been extensively terraced for agriculture.[42] Contour benches are ranged behind walls 1 to 2 meters high. Some flights are now entirely covered with scrub oak; more often, however, only the higher and smaller plots have been abandoned.

The *colonia* of San Francisco[43] lies within a *polje,* 20 kilometers northwest of Comitán. The surrounding hills are heavily wooded and the timber (oak, cypress and pine) is exploited commercially. To the west of the village, a hill stands a little forward of the main *cuesta.* It is terraced on three sides from top to bottom. On the top, commanding a view of the basin, there are the remains of a small pyramid and traces of other buildings. So far as is known, this site has not hitherto been described. The terraces, wide at the base of the hill, become narrower and higher (up to 5 meters) as the angle of the slope increases (figs. 3.34, 3.35). To enable the upper part of the hill to be occupied at all, some form of leveling was probably essential. The purpose of the lower and broader terraces, however, can scarcely have been simply to provide house sites, and in fact there is no evidence of this. They are best explained as former agricultural terraces. The walls all appear to rest on rock which is now exposed at the back of many terraces on the middle slopes of the hill. Cultivable soil may originally have been brought from the floor of the basin.

In the broken country between San Francisco and Comitán, around Ajayash and Chacaljocón, and also near Zapaluta to the south of Comitán, inconspicuous boundary walls check soil movement at the lower ends of fields. The cultivation of unterraced slopes is, however, the rule.

---

41. Lowe (1959, 15, 70) and Lowe and Mason (1966, 239) report terracing, possibly agricultural, on the flanks of the Grijalva depression to the southwest of the plateau of central Chiapas. Narrow, stone-faced terraces around the archaeological site of Tonolá, overlooking the coastal plain of Chiapas, also may have been for cultivation (Palacios, 1928, 18; Hewett, 1936, 139), but Ferdon (1953, 2) thinks not, although the adjacent levels are "subject to a certain amount of rainy season flooding."

42. "Comitán appears in the conquest lists of Ahuitzotl, and is described as one of the largest and wealthiest towns of Chiapas by its first *encomendero*" (Calnek, 1961, 4). One kilometer northwest of Comitán, on a hill known as *Hun-Chabin,* there are the remains of pyramids as well as terraces (Palacios, 1928, 54, 63).

43. The name that appears on the Map of Hispanic America (1:1 million). Locally the place is known as Abelardo San Rodríguez, constituted a *colonia* in 1931; it occupies the site of the former *finca* San Francisco.

Fig. 3.34 Terrace wall (c. 3 meters), San Francisco, Chiapas, Mexico

Fig. 3.35 Prepared stone in the corner of a terrace wall, San Francisco, Chiapas, Mexico

Ocosingo-Gracias á Dios, Chiapas-Guatemala: O. F. Cook reported in 1909 that "terraces . . . cover many square miles of unoccupied land in the semi-arid plateau region of Chiapas, between the Guatemalan boundary and Comitán, as well as between Comitán and Ocosingo. This terraced region is now covered partly by fire-swept grass lands and partly by scattered growths of pines and oaks, where the fires are less severe. . . . The walls [of the terraces] are only a few feet high, though the area enclosed may be several acres in extent. . . . The probability is that the complete leveling of the land was found useful to prevent the running off of any of the rather slight rainfall. . . . While the terraces are not high, the walls are often half a mile or more in length. The leveling of the land must have required vastly more labor than the building of the walls, but the work may have been done gradually if the regular practice of hoeing the earth toward the wall were followed."[44]

The archaeological site of Quen Santo appears to include the remains of agricultural terraces.[45] C. Basauri observed numerous "diques artificiales" between Juncaná and the Guatemalan border,[46] and a sketch map published by F. Blom shows cross-channel terraces "between San Cristóbal and Teopisca to Gracias á Dios."[47] The distribution of old terraced fields almost certainly extends beyond Gracias á Dios to the foothills and valleys of the Alto Cuchumatanes.

Todos Santos Cuchumatán, Guatemala: The village of Todos Santos lies at a height of 2,480 meters in the valley of the Río Limón on the western flanks of the Sierra de los Cuchumatanes.[48] The site is essentially an outwash fan cut by several *arroyos.* But the deep colluvial and alluvial material has been reshaped to produce level house-and-garden plots supported by walls up to 3.5 meters high and incorporating large boulders in the foundations. Around the village there are also many sloping terraces that have developed in the course of cultivation. R. Stadelman reported that some of the walls had been heightened in recent years.[49]

O. F. Cook has referred to high, narrow terraces near Jacaltenango,[50] 20 kilometers to the northwest of Todos Santos. The western slopes of the Alto Cuchumatanes are little known and invite further study.

B: West Central Guatemala

THE WESTERN HIGHLANDS

The basin of Quezaltenango-Totonicapán: Pedro de Alvarado observed in 1524 that the basin of Quezaltenango, or *Xelahum,* was as thickly populated and as widely cultivated as that of Tlaxcala in Mexico.[51] Nevertheless, it appears that parts of the floor (like that of Tlaxcala) were marshy.[52] The towns of colonial origin occupy piedmont sites, and today both the floor and the slopes of the surrounding hills are intensively cultivated. The soils, almost wholly derived from light-colored volcanic ash *(talpetate),* are deep and remarkably cohesive. Building stone is not readily available except along streams and around the summits of certain hills. The only stone-faced terraces observed lie on high slopes to the south of the city of Quezaltenango. Elsewhere, and particularly around Totonicapán, terraces have developed in the course of cultivation. The sloping surfaces are separated by unfaced, but thickly overgrown, walls.

The ridging of soil along the contour is widely practiced in the western highlands of Guatemala (figs. 3.36, 3.37). The ridges are 1 to 2 meters apart and about .5 of a meter high. The pattern changes in detail from year to year in the course of rehoeing. Ridging probably developed after the introduction of the large, square-bladed hoe *(azada)*[53] from the ancient practice of piling up soil around individual maize plants. On the watershed between the Río Samalá and the Río Motagua at 2500 to 3000 meters above sea level (near the altitudinal limit of maize) ground that has been ridged is now under grass and pine forest.

Zunil: The valley of the Río Samalá leads southwestward from the basin of Quezaltenango. Around the village of Zunil (diag. 3.4) enormous quantities of stone have been removed from the bed of the river for the construction of boundary walls. Terraces extend from the house-and-garden sites downslope to the river, from which water is led to the lower fields. Several outwash fans also have been terraced (fig. 3.38).

44. O. F. Cook, 1909, 18; 1921, 317; McBryde, 1945, 17 ("stone-faced terraces" near Ocosingo). Officials of Santa Margarita referred in conversation (1966) to abandoned terraces in the vicinity of Colonia Veracruz and Colonia Jalisco, about 15 kilometers to the northeast of the *municipio.*

45. Seler, 1901, 84, 97.

46. "En toda la parte comprendida entre Juncaná y la frontera con Guatemala, se ven multitud de diques artificiales, hechos para defender la tierra de los deslaves producidos por las lluvias. Lugares dedicados por los antiguos mayas a la agricultura" (Basauri, 1931, 12).

47. Blom, 2, 1927, 429.

48. Ricketson (1940, 351) mentions two archaeological sites near Todos Santos. For an account of the township, see Oakes, 1951.

49. Stadelman, 1940, 101.

50. O. F. Cook, 1909, 18.

51. Alvarado, 1924, 59.

52. Piñeda (1594), 1908, 436.

53. In 1950, plows were available on only 7.3 percent of farms in Guatemala; the department of Totonicapán had the lowest proportion, 0.1 percent (Whetton, 1961, 139).

Fig. 3.36 Ridged fields, Chichicastenango, Guatemala

Fig. 3.37 Terraces and (foreground) ridging, Chichicastenango, Guatemala;
the terraced plots are ridged at right angles to the retaining walls

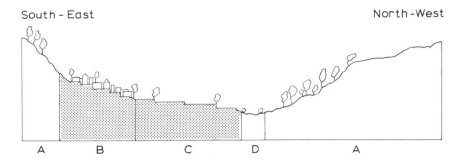

South-East   North-West

A   B   C   D   A

Diagram **3.4**
LAND-USE ZONES: VALLEY OF RÍO SAMALÁ AT ZUNIL, GUATEMALA

A   *Monte* and maize *milpas*
B   Zunil: house-and-garden terraces
C   Contour and valley-floor terraces
D   Bed of Río Samalá

Fig. 3.38 Terraced outwash fan, Zunil, near Quezaltenango, Guatemala

The basin of San Marcos: Although the floor of the basin of San Marcos (diag. 3.5) is now the center of agricultural operations, the surrounding hills have been extensively terraced and most of the lower surfaces are still cultivated. The broad terraces behind the town are set in weathered volcanic ash. Soil has been gradually hoed forward between field boundaries. The ash stands up well at depths below .5 of a meter and the terrace faces are also protected by grass and low scrub. Proceeding up slope, bedrock first appears in *barrancas* and along sunken lanes and stone is used for the walls of small valley-floor terraces and to increase the height of contour benches to about 1.5 meters. Within the succeeding zone of pasture and pine forest there are parallel lines of stone, a course or two high, that are probably the remains of old agricultural terraces.

The basin of Lake Atitlán: Some of the finest agricultural terracing in Middle America is to be found around the shores of Lake Atitlán. The lands of Santa Catarina Palopó and San Antonio Palopó and the valley of the Río Novillero between Los Encuentros and Panajachel are of special interest. S. K. Lothrop has reported terraced house sites along the south shore[54] as well as archaeological terraces, of unknown or unspecified function, near Santiago Atitlán.[55]

Fertile colluvial and lacustrine deposits in embayments along the eastern shore of the lake have been formed into low, stone-faced terraces *(tablones)* (fig. 3.39) to facilitate irrigation. They closely resemble the

54. Lothrop, 1928, 384.
55. *Ibid.,* 378, 1933, 17-18, 78. For the terraces of the basin of Lake Atitlán, see also McBryde, 1945, 30-32; Wilken, 1971, 434-36.

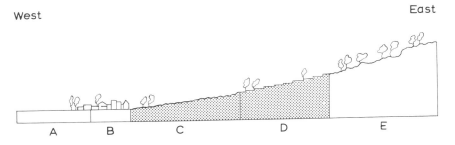

Diagram **3.5**

LAND-USE ZONES: BASIN OF SAN MARCOS, GUATEMALA

A   Basin floor, large rectangular fields
B   San Marcos
C   Excavated terraces, sunken lanes
D   Walled terraces
E   Abandoned terraces, pasture, woodland

Fig. 3.39 Terraced fields, San Antonio Palopó, basin of Lake Atitlán, Guatemala

South-West   North-East

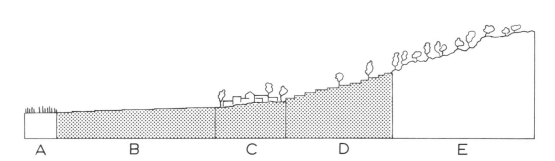

Diagram **3.6**

LAND-USE ZONES : BASIN OF LAKE ATITLÁN AT SAN ANTONIO
PALOPÓ, GUATEMALA

A   Reed beds

B   Colluvial/alluvial/lacustrine deposits, low contour terraces

C   San Antonio Palopó: house-and-garden terraces

D   Field terraces

E   *Monte* and broken terraces

Fig. 3.40 Flights of stone-faced terraces, San Antonio Palopó, Guatemala

hortalizas beside Lake Patzcuaro (*supra,* p. 57). Above the shorelands there is another terraced zone (diag. 3.6) to which the villages also belong. Sets of contour benches have been constructed where the limestone and volcanic soils are comparatively deep. The highest surfaces have not been cultivated for many years and they effectively belong to the *monte.* The majority of the terraces are, however, in regular use. Some are faced with stone (figs. 3.40, 3.41); others are essentially cuttings in deep soils derived from volcanic ash (fig. 3.42).

Long flights of contour terraces, partly stone-faced, cover south- and east-facing slopes above the Río Novillero. The best examples lie below Sololá (fig. 3.43) and are worked from San José Chacayá and the hamlet of Chuchexio.

The basin of Lake Amatitlán: The archaeological site of Mejicanos on the southwestern shore of Lake Amatitlán "consists of four mounds . . . hemmed in on three sides by steep mountains which still show traces of pre-Columbian agricultural terracing."[56] This probably dates

56. Borhegyi, 1959, 105. Shook (1952, 5) noted "extensos trabajos de terracería en el talud del terrano" 1 kilometer east of Amatitlán.

Fig. 3.42 Excavated terraces (c. 1.5 meters high), Santa Catarina Palopó, basin of Lake Atitlán, Guatemala

Fig. 3.41 Terraces (2 meters high, 5 meters wide), San Antonio Palopó, Guatemala

Fig. 3.43 Terraced fields near Sololá, Guatemala

from the late pre-classic (a time of rising population in the Guatemalan highlands)[57] or the early classic, the major period of occupation at Mejicanos. Terracing has also been associated with the occupation of hill sites during the late classic (c. A.D. 700 to 1000).[58] S. W. Miles in his study of the Pokom-Maya, who occupied the area around and to the north and east of Lake Amatitlán in the sixteenth century, drew attention to widespread evidence of "terracing."[59]

THE CENTRAL PLATEAU

Contour ridging was observed around Chichicastenango and Santa Cruz del Quiché, and it has been reported by O. F. Cook from Cobulco.[60] Cook also noted "small, isolated, walled-in fields . . . on the spurs of hills about Salama," and "stone enclosures and . . . terraces [on] the upper slopes of ruin-crowned mountains, like that above Rabinal."[61] A. L. Smith mentions "terracing" at the archaeological site of Toloxcoc,[62] southwest of Rabinal, but whether this was for agriculture is not clear. Other sites where the evidence is doubtful include Xolchún[63] and Cucal[64] in the department of Huehuetenango.

C: Central America

THE VACA PLATEAU, BRITISH HONDURAS

According to C. L. Lundell, "no other area of similar size in the Yucatan Peninsula shows as much evidence of Maya occupation as the limestone plateau [of British Honduras]."[65] This evidence partly consists of abandoned agricultural terraces that probably belong to the late classic or the post-classic period.[66]

The plateau is covered with broadleaf forest,[67] and the "comparatively small flora" suggested to Lundell that this area was abandoned several centuries later than the northern Petén.[68] Soils on the middle and upper slopes of the hills are thin, immature and easily eroded.[69]

The area of reported terracing (map 3.4) extends eastward from the valley of the Río Chiquibul to that of the Río Macal,[70] and from Benque Viejo (450 meters) in the north to Retiro (1350 meters) in the south.[71] In 1928 T. W. F. Gann wrote concerning the area around Benque Viejo: "We passed great numbers of ancient terraces along the hillsides, where the earth had been retained in place by semi-circular walls built of great blocks of limestone, and the *arrieros* told us that these terraces, which had evidently been used by the ancient Maya for agricultural purposes, extended for many miles in all directions, connoting, at one time, a large population and intensive agriculture throughout a country now completely uninhabited and covered by a dense growth of forest."[72] Flights of over 50 terraces have been observed. The walls of "rough blocks of limestone"[73] range in height from .5 of a meter to over 3 meters[74] and some are now buried under 2 to 3 feet of soil.[75]

THE MAYAN LOWLANDS, MEXICO

"Tens of thousands of relic terraces . . . encompassing an area exceeding 10,000 square kilometers" have recently been reported from the Río Bec area of southern Campeche and Quintana Roo.[76] They cover the slopes of low limestone hills, between Nicolás Bravo and Xpujil-Becan.[77] The terraces are chiefly of the "linear sloping, dry field" type, supported by limestone walls; the rest are cross-channel plots in hillside ravines. The former, according to B. L. Turner, "were probably constructed as impediments to the erosion of the very shallow (5 to 45 cm) topsoils. . . ." The region experiences torrential rain during the wet season, and many of the terraces

57. Borhegyi, 1965b, 62, 65.

58. Borhegyi, 1965a, 30.

59. Miles, 1957, 752.

60. O. F. Cook, 1909, 10.

61. *Ibid.,* 21.

62. A. L. Smith, 1955, 54.

63. *Ibid.,* 15, fig. 10d (stone-faced terraces); Burkitt, 1930, 41-72.

64. A. L. Smith, 1955, 9.

65. Lundell, 1940, 9.

66. J. E. Thompson, 1965, 358.

67. Ower, 1928, 496. *Map of Natural Vegetation, British Honduras* (Directorate of Overseas Surveys, London, 1958).

68. Lundell, 1940, 10-11; 1942, 169-70.

69. Lundell, 1940, 9. The *Provisional Soil Map of British Honduras* (Directorate of Overseas Surveys, London, 1958) shows "skeletal soils" over calcareous bedrock.

70. Possibly to the Río Sibun (Ower, 1927, 384, who appears to have been the first to comment on these terraces).

71. Lundell (1940, 9) estimated the area as approximately 400 square kilometers.

72. Gann, 1928a, 145, 156. Hopkins (1968, 41) states that a test dig was undertaken at Cubietas Viejas in 1961, and the results suggested that humus-rich swamp soils had been spread over the terraces. Gann (1928b, 210-12) also observed stone-faced "terraces" on the upper slopes of the south bank of the Río Pusilhà near Chumuchà.

73. J. E. Thompson, 1931, 228-29.

74. Lundell, 1940, 9.

75. Romney, 1959, 113.

76. Turner, 1974, 118-24, and 1976, 73-82. See also Matheny, 1976, 639.

77. Turner's papers appeared after the present work had been largely prepared for publication; consequently his sites are not listed in the appendix; nor were they used in the preparation of fig. 2.1 (table) and map 2.2.

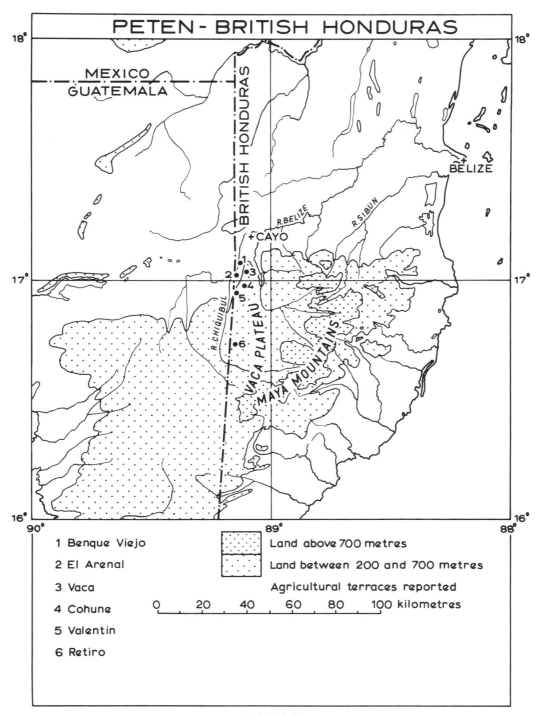

PETEN - BRITISH HONDURAS

MEXICO
GUATEMALA

BRITISH HONDURAS

BELIZE

R.BELIZE

R.SIBUN

+CAYO

1
2 •3
•4
5
R.CHIQUIBUL
•6

VACA PLATEAU

MAYA MOUNTAINS

1 Benque Viejo
2 El Arenal
3 Vaca
4 Cohune
5 Valentin
6 Retiro

Land above 700 metres

Land between 200 and 700 metres

Agricultural terraces reported

0   20   40   60   80   100 kilometres

MAP 3.4

incorporate devices (guide walls, seepage outlets, and laterally sloping embankments) to facilitate drainage and to control the distribution of run-off water. As the author of the report points out, terracing on such a scale has an important bearing on the question of the agricultural and demographic foundations of the ancient Maya civilization. Agricultural terracing (and raised field cultivation) in the Río Bec area is thought to have commenced c. A.D. 500-600 (Sabucan phase), to have been most important in the late classic (Bejuco [c. A.D. 600-730] and Chintok [c. A.D. 730-830] phases), and to have declined in significance during the terminal classic (Xcocom phase, c. A.D. 830-1050).

THE VALLEY OF THE RÍO GRANDE DE CHOLUTECA, HONDURAS

The only known report of terracing to the southeast of the area of Maya settlement concerns the valley of the Río Grande de Choluteca in southern Honduras. Here D. Stone briefly noted "stone and earth filled agricultural terraces" that are clearly old but possibly post-conquest.[78]

78. Stone, 1957, 92 (Mogotillo or Palo Verde, near El Matasano). Meggers and Evans (1963, table 2) refer to agricultural terracing in Panama ("very late pre-Conquest"), but no authority for this is given.

3. SOUTH AMERICA

A: Venezuela

LA CORDILLERA DE LOS ANDES

At the beginning of the sixteenth century, a large part of the Venezuelan Andes[1] (map 3.5) was occupied by culturally advanced folk who spoke variants of Timoto-Cuica. Juan Rodríguez Suárez, in a letter written in 1558 and preserved by Father Pedro Simón (1626), went so far as to compare their buildings with those of Rome![2] Simón himself refers to agricultural terraces *(poyos á trechos)* for maize and root crops.[3]

In 1894 Febres Cordero observed flights of grass-covered terraces, each 3 to 4 *varas* wide and faced with stone, near Aricagua, 40 kilometers to the south of Mérida.[4] The distribution of old agricultural terracing extends, so far as is known, from Aricagua and Acequias in the southwest[5] to Jajó and Tuñame in the northeast, that is broadly through the central part of the *cordillera*.[6] In origin, terracing, like irrigation and the construction of storage reservoirs *(quimpúes, estanques)*, appears to belong to the late pre-Columbian period.[7]

The valleys of the Chama and the Motatán almost bisect the Andes lengthwise. The watershed between the two, the *páramo* Mucuchíes, though high (c. 4000 meters), is not a serious obstacle to movement and it was not a cultural divide in pre-Columbian times. The upper sections of both rivers are flanked by extensive river terraces and outwash fans. Where these are cultivated, the lower field boundaries have checked the movement of soil.[8] Sloping terraces are characteristic (figs. 3.44, 3.45), but around Chachopo, in a narrow section of the Motatán, high level benches have been constructed, and further downstream (notably near Timotes) there are flights of old valley-floor terraces.[9]

B: Colombia

THE ALTIPLANO OF BOYACÁ-CUNDINAMARCA

The *altiplano* of Boyacá-Cundinamarca lies in the heart of the Cordillera Oriental[10] (map 3.6). It consists of a dozen or more aggraded levels at heights of from 2500 to 2700 meters, enclosed or largely enclosed by hill tracts and bold *sierras* rising to over 3500 meters. These intermontane basins belong to the lower part of the *tierra fria*. The mean annual temperature of the *sabana* of Bogotá is 13 to 14 degrees centigrade, and being only 4 to 6 degrees latitude north of the equator there is little variation throughout the year. Rainfall generally exceeds 700 mm per annum with maxima in April-May and October-November.[11]

---

1. A. L. Cárdenas, 1960-1, 139-49.

2. Simón, 2, 1882-92, 197 ("eran innumerable gente y población de las Sierras, y que había tantos edificios como en Roma").

3. *Ibid* (observed c. 1612-13): *poyos* or *apoyos*, "supports"; *á trechos*, "at intervals."

4. Febres Cordero, 1920, 15 ("En un viaje que hicimos a Aricagua en 1894, admiramos estos restos monumentales de la civilización indígena, recorriendo a caballo varias gradas de un empinado cerro cortado en planos sucesivos hasta la cúspide, de tres o cuatro varas de ancho cada uno, que formaban en conjunto una vasta escalinata cubierta de pasto natural, que apenas dejaba entrever los cimientos de piedra, llamados *catafós* por los aborígenes").

5. Jahn, 1927, 318; Osgood and Howard, 1943, 91; Lares (1883) 1952, 17 ("Los Tiguiñoes recogían en las faldas de los montes con cerdados de piedra en forma de anfiteatro la tierra vegetal para sembrar en ella. Todavía se encuentran en las cercanías de Acequias gran número de estos cercados. ...").

6. Brito Figuero (1963, 48) in a sketch map entitled *La economía indígena Venezolana en el siglo XV*, shows "agricultura con riego sistemático, cultivo en terrazas" from the Colombian border to an area northeast of Trujillo. Cf. Troll, 1930, 451; Brito Figueroa, 1962, 8, 46; Kleiss, 1967, 271-72 *(catafós. quimpúes)*: E. Wagner, 1967b, 227-37 *(catafós, quimpúes)*, and 1969, 284.

7. Aguado (1581), 2, 1917, 226; Salas, 1916, 25-26, and 1956, 106; Acosta Saignes, 1952, 54, 1958, 6, and 1961, 20, 31; Sanoja, 1963, 74; Chaves, 1963, 131.

8. For the stonework of the area, see Gasparini, 1962, 28-29; for details of crops, Lares (1883) 1952, 17; Briceño Iragorry, 1946-47, 16; Salas, 1956, 103-16; Rouse and Cruxent, 1958, 264; Acosta Saignes, 1958, 7; Grant *et al.*, 1963, 6; E. Wagner, 1967a, 83.

9. Terracing of recent origin may be observed in the vicinity of Mucuchíes, Mucurubá and Jajó.

10. For an account of the geology and physical geography, see Hettner, 1892.

11. Henry, 1922, 189-90; Eidt, 1952, 489-503.

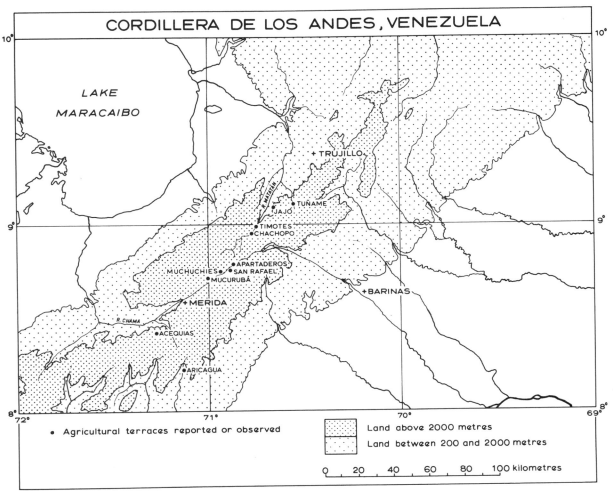

MAP 3.5

At the time of the Spanish Conquest the *altiplano* was controlled by the Chibcha, and early reports indicate a comparatively dense population.[12] Accounts of the area from the middle of the sixteenth century to the beginning of the nineteenth also refer to several lakes and to stretches of marsh.[13] T. Van Der Hammen and E. González have shown that the sediments of the *sabana* of Bogotá are 200 to 400 meters thick.[14] Although mostly of lacustrine origin, they include layers of peat and alluvium (indicating that the lake was at times replaced by marsh) and are overlain, at a point near the northwestern outskirts of the city of Bogotá, by 3.45 meters of humic clays deposited during intermittent inundations. Pollen trapped in the upper 2.45 meters, representing the Holocene (? 8100 B.C.), suggests alternating wet (*Alnus* dominant) and dry (*Myrica* dominant) periods. The gradual increase in the proportion of Gramineae over tree species above the 70 cm level (? 600 B.C. to early post-conquest) is particularly important for Van Der Hammen and González interpret this in terms of the introduction and spread of agriculture. They rule out a physical explanation on the grounds that the climate of this period (Holocene VIII) was neither dry nor particularly cold, conditions that apparently produced high percentages of Gramineae during parts of the Late Glacial.

12. Aguado (1581) 1906, 118-19. Population data are summarized by Eidt (1959, 378-80) who computes 643,000 for the Chibcha area (25,500 square kilometers) or about 25 per square kilometer. See also Jaramillo Uribe, 1964, 240-51; and for the Chibcha economy, Trimborn, 1930, 10-11.

13. Castellanos (1559) I, 1886, 111, 280; Rodríguez y Freile (1636) 1961, 35, 37; Fernández Piedrahita (1668-88), I, 1942, 47; Cochrane, 2, 1825, 5; Hamilton, I, 1827, 129. Cf. Triana, 1922, 27-34 ("Paisaje prehistórico de la altiplanicie").

14. Van Der Hammen and González, 1960, 261-315. Findings based on the examination of part (32.2 meters) of a 266-meter core, with three carbon-14 dates from the top 2.5 meters; altitude at the surface, 2560 meters.

Fig. 3.44   Terraced outwash fan, near Mucuchíes, Mérida, Venezuela (G. Gasparini, 1962)

Fig. 3.45 Terraced fields on an alluvio-gravel bench, Apartaderos, Mérida, Venezuela

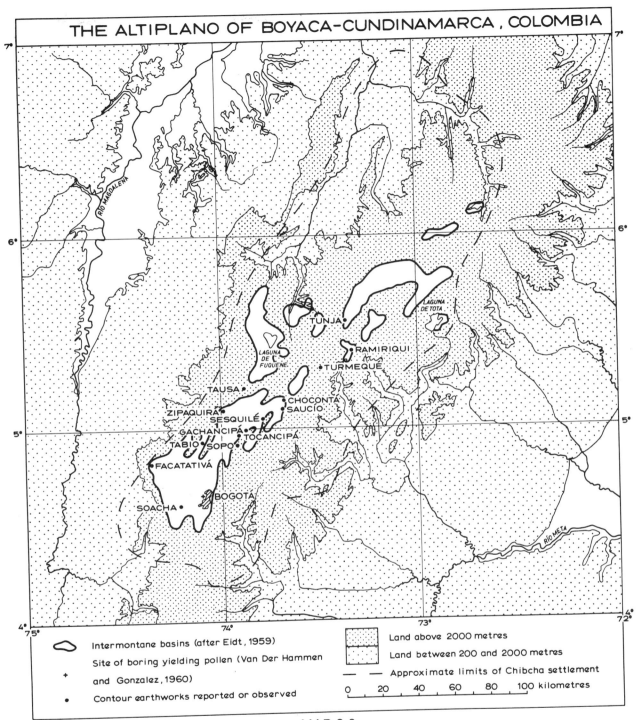

THE ALTIPLANO OF BOYACA-CUNDINAMARCA, COLOMBIA

RIO MAGDALENA

LAGUNA DE TOTA

TUNJA

LAGUNA DE FUQUENE

RAMIRIQUI

TURMEQUE

TAUSA

CHOCONTA

ZIPAQUIRA

SAUCIO

SESQUILÉ

GACHANCIPÁ

TOCANCIPÁ

TABIO SOPO

FACATATIVÁ

BOGOTA

SOACHA

RIO META

⬭ Intermontane basins (after Eidt, 1959)

＋ Site of boring yielding pollen (Van Der Hammen and Gonzalez, 1960)

• Contour earthworks reported or observed

[⠿] Land above 2000 metres

[ ] Land between 200 and 2000 metres

— — Approximate limits of Chibcha settlement

0   20   40   60   80   100 kilometres

MAP 3.6

The *sabana* of Bogotá, according to the same authors, was densely forested until cleared for agriculture.[15] The latter inference is at least questionable so far as the levels are concerned. The hydrological problems were already formidable, and clearing would have led to more frequent flooding. Old planting ridges do extend into the levels,[16] but the virtual absence of woodland at the time of the conquest may also have been the result of prolonged cutting for firewood and for house building.[17] Van Der Hammen and González further claim that "the beginnings of intensive agriculture in the *sabana* of Bogotá can now be dated, with the aid of a Carbon 14 date, as A.D. 1650 ±160), that is somewhat after the arrival of the Spaniards." This presumably refers to the introduction of animal husbandry about the middle of the sixteenth century rather than to intensive cultivation.

"Agricultural terraces" were reported from piedmont sites by E. W. Haury and C. J. C. Cubillos in 1953,[18] and they have since been the subject of closer study by S. M. Broadbent.[19]

On the lower slopes of the basins in the southwestern half of the Chibcha domain there are various earthworks — ditches, ridges, mounds and terraces — many of which clearly belong to an earlier period of occupation.[20] The terraces are entirely unfaced,[21] and consequently there is some difficulty in distinguishing these features from the effects of soil slumping and soil creep. The chief pointers to man's influence are the regular form and distribution of certain terraces, house foundations and spoil heaps containing prehistoric pottery, notably at Pueblo Viejo (Facatativá), and associated ditches that must have been dug.

Silted-up ditches and low banks may be widely observed on slopes of from 10 to 20 degrees around Tabío, Gachancipá, Tocancipá, Chocontá and Facatativá. The contour banks are about 1 meter high and 2 meters wide and either incorporate a ditch (fig. 3.46) or lie immediately above one. As Broadbent points out, such ditches are still constructed to improve drainage for arable and pasture. Low ridges (without ditches) on steeply sloping ground between Santa Rosita and Chocontá appear to mark the lower boundaries of former fields.

The terraces closely resemble the lynchets of southern England. There are examples above Gachancipá, and others have been reported from Pueblo Viejo. Two and a half kilometers south of Tocancipá, a group of terraces (each about 3 meters high, 10 to 20 meters wide and 80 to 150 meters long) stand out very prominently (fig. 3.47); both the flattened surfaces and the risers are cultivated and the area has yielded prehistoric pottery. Similar features, now under grass, line the Cerros de Loma Grande, 4 kilometers west-southwest of Saucío[22] and overlooking the wet bottom lands of the Río Sisga (fig. 3.48). Such terraces could be the combined result of ditching, soil creep, and the gradual hoeing forward of soil. Furthermore, where terraces were also settlement sites,[23] the accumulation of domestic refuse probably contributed to their formation.

15. *Ibid.,* 311. The maps of "natural vegetation" prepared by Espinal and Montenegro (1963) show *bosque seco montaño bajo* (temperature range 12 to 18 degrees centigrade, annual precipitation 500 to 1000 mm) over most of the *sabana.* See also Jenny, 1948, 7-8.

16. Eidt, 1959, 374-92. Broadbent (1968, 135-47) examined evidence of old fields, chiefly on marginally higher ground in the vicinity of Suba. West (1959, 279-82), while mainly discussing *eras* (ridges arranged against the slope) in other parts of the Colombian Andes, drew attention to Aguado's reference (1581) (1906, 297) to *camellones* for cultivation in Chibcha territory. Joaquín Acosta (1848, 204) also remarks, "Aun se ven terrenos incultos hoy en la llanura de Bogotá, ó que solo sirven para crias de ganados, surcados por anchos camellones que son vestigios de antiguos cultivos de estos pueblos eminentemente agrícolas. . . ." The opportunities for fishing were probably an important inducement to settlement within the levels (Broadbent, 1966, 7, and 1968, 142).

17. The typical Chibcha settlement was a small cluster of huts surrounded by a wooden palisade (Joaquín Acosta, 1848, 207; Bueno, 1963, 27, 34; G. Reichel-Dolmatoff, 1965, 158). Building in stone was rare, and virtually absent altogether around Bogotá; a minor exception "en forma de cámaras subterráneas" from the *municipio* of Guatavita has been noted by Broadbent (1963, 81-88). See also Markham, 1912, 19; Nachtigall, 1958, 33.

18. Haury and Cubillos, 1953, 83-86; Haury, 1953, 77 (at Facatativá, Soacha, Guatavita, Tocancipá, Zipaquirá, Tausa, Chocontá and Tunja). Earlier, Kirchhoff (1943, 101, 106) listed "terrazas para cultivo" among the elements of Chibcha culture.

19. Broadbent, 1963, 501-504, and 1965. The terraces at Zipaquirá and Tausa were not re-examined by Broadbent, and she concluded that those at Guatavita were natural features. For earlier investigations at Gachancipá and Tocancipá, see Bolinder, 1937, 130-32. Gachancipá, Tocancipá, Pueblo Viejo (Facatativá), Tabío, Saucío (Chocontá) and Tunja were visited in 1966.

20. The dry season becomes more marked toward the northeast where, according to Restrepo (1895, 122), canal irrigation ("acequias de los ríos para regar") was practiced in pre-Columbian times.

21. The bedrock at Tocancipá, Gachancipá and Facatativá weathers to a fine material and loose building stone is not widely available; stone could, however, have been quarried at points where the *cuesta* projects forward into the basin of Bogotá.

22. Fals-Borda (1962, 87-88) describes "terraces" about 7 feet wide and 20 to 60 feet long in flights of two or three "on Arrayenes (9 kilometers northwest of Saucío) and one other hill in Saucío."

23. Haury and Cubillos, 1953, 53. Fals-Borda (1962, 87) notes references to hill settlement in Chibcha legend. Cf. Fernández Piedrahita (1668-88) I, 1942, 33. Most modern settlements lie around the margins of the levels.

Fig. 3.46 Bank and ditch, Gachancipá, Sabana de Bogotá, Colombia

Fig. 3.47 Terraces, 2.5 kilometers south of Tocancipá, Sabana de Bogotá, Colombia

Fig. 3.48 Earthworks, including terraces, near Saucío, Sabana de Bogotá, Colombia

NORTHERN COLOMBIA

In 1925 J. A. Mason referred to stone-faced terraces in the Santa Marta massif[24] (map 3.7). In the same year, A. F. R. Wollaston described "wide artificial terraces for old cultivation and the remains of large irrigation channels or aquaducts ingeniously cut along the hill-sides" south of San Miguel[25] (fig. 3.49). Mason associated these features with the Tairona culture and this has been confirmed by the work of G. Reichel-Dolmatoff. The Tairona, who occupied the northern slopes of the Sierra Nevada in late pre-Columbian times, were chiefly remarkable in that, alone of the prehistoric peoples of Colombia, they made much use of stone for house foundations, roads, canals, reservoirs and drains as well as agricultural terraces.[26] The terraces are each about 1 hectare in area, 4 to 6 meters wide, and supported by generally low walls.[27] They are found in the arid foot-hills, along with irrigation ditches,[28] and on the higher and wetter slopes of the massif.[29] The discovery of hand mills in terrace fill suggests that maize was cultivated. The Cágaba, who occupy the area today, practice irrigation and, like the Ica, "terrace with undressed stone to provide level ground for coca cultivation."[30] On the other hand, the old terraces are avoided, apparently for supernatural reasons.[31] On the southeastern side of the Sierra Nevada *terrazas de cultivo* with walls 2 meters high are associated with the archaeological site of La Mesa.[32]

24. Mason, 1925, 161.

25. Wollaston, 1925, 103.

26. In addition to Mason and Reichel-Dolmatoff (*infra,* fn. 27-29, 32-33), see Seifriz, 1934, 483; W.C. Bennett, 1944b, 92, 1946a, 52; Calle Orozco, *n.d.,* 102.

27. Mason (1922-23), 1931-9, 123; G. Reichel-Dolmatoff, 1954b, 166-67, 173 (Pueblito: retaining walls from 50 cm to 3 meters high). There is a sketch in Bueno (1963, 44) and photographs in G. Reichel-Dolmatoff (1953) and Nachtigall (1961, Abb. 23, 25).

28. G. Reichel-Dolmatoff, 1950, 97 ("canales y zanjas bien trazados").

29. G. Reichel-Dolmatoff, 1961, 84; G. and A. Reichel-Dolmatoff, 1961, 6, 202, 205.

30. Park, 1946, 879. Cf. Reclus, 1881, 298; Taylor, 1931, 539-58.

31. G. Reichel-Dolmatoff, 1950, 97-98 ("Las terrazas están tabuizadas. En las tradiciones tribales juegan un papel importante como sitios sagrados y actualmente se encuentra en el centro de muchas terrazas un lugar donde se depositan ofrendas. Pero sembrar en las terrazas está absolutamente prohibido y si, como pasa en ocasiones, algún sembrado se extendiera contra la voluntad de su dueño sobre una de estas construcciones, el sacerdote de la población interviene inmediatamente"). See also G. and A. Reichel-Dolmatoff, 1951, 196.

32. G. and A. Reichel-Dolmatoff, 1959, 162. There is some evidence that these terraces were irrigated.

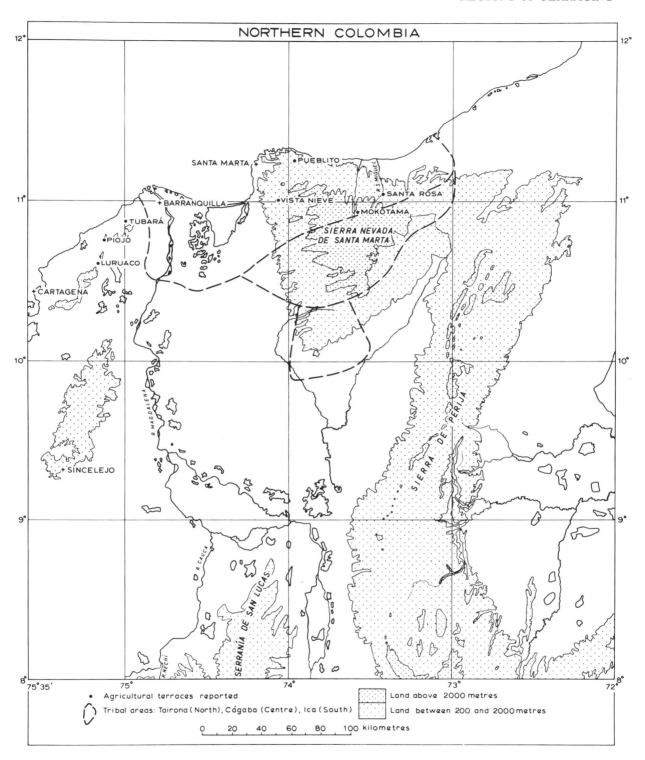

MAP 3.7

Fig. 3.49 Agricultural terraces, above the Río San Miguel, Sierra Nevada de Santa Marta, Colombia (H. Nachtigall, 1961.)

G. Reichel-Dolmatoff[33] has reported stone-faced terraces in the foothills of the Serranía de San Lucas; near the headwaters of the Río Nechí;[34] and in the hills around Tubará,[35] Piojó, Luruaco and "other places between Barranquilla and Cartagena." But unlike the Tairona terraces, "these rudimentary architectural features are hardly more than an occasional adaptation to the broken terrain, and they are not accompanied by a higher cultural development in other respects."

C: Ecuador

WESTERN ECUADOR

The Cerro de Hojas and the Cerro Jaboncillo lie in the semi-arid hill country of western Ecuador (map 3.8). M. H. Saville observed in 1907: "On many slopes [of the Cerro de Hojas] terraces are one below the other, resembling an enormous flight of huge steps."[36] It appears that these were agricultural terraces and that they were constructed by the stone-working Manteño people (c. A.D. 1000-1500).[37]

The amphitheater of hills (part of the Cerro Jaboncillo) to the north of El Cerro comprises an upper and very steep section, moistened by cloud condensation and mostly wooded; an intermediate zone of generally moderate slopes, xerophytic scrub and coarse grass; and a gently sloping lower section to which the village itself belongs. Within the intermediate zone there are flights of roughly level surfaces 10 to 15 meters wide. These are clearly artificial and some of the risers are marked by lines of stone. In addition, the broken walls and eroded fill of old cross-channel terraces occupy the middle courses of several *barrancas*. None of the terraces is cultivated today.

LA CORDILLERA DE LOS ANDES

Abandoned agricultural terraces have been observed in the valley of the Río Matoqui below Sigsipamba and to

---

33. G. Reichel-Dolmatoff, 1965, 124.

34. Also Wassén, 1936, 31.

35. Also Angulo Valdés, 1951; Nachtigall, 1961, 98, Abb. 24; Meggers and Evans, 1963, table 2 (c. A.D. 1000).

36. Saville, I, 1907, 22. Uhle (1931) makes no reference to terraces.

---

37. Estrada, 1962, 22, 86-87, 104, with a sketch map showing areas of terracing in the Cerro Jaboncillo and the Cerro de Hojas; Estrada and Evans, 1963, 85; Meggers, 1966, 124. The area was only briefly visited by the present author in 1966.

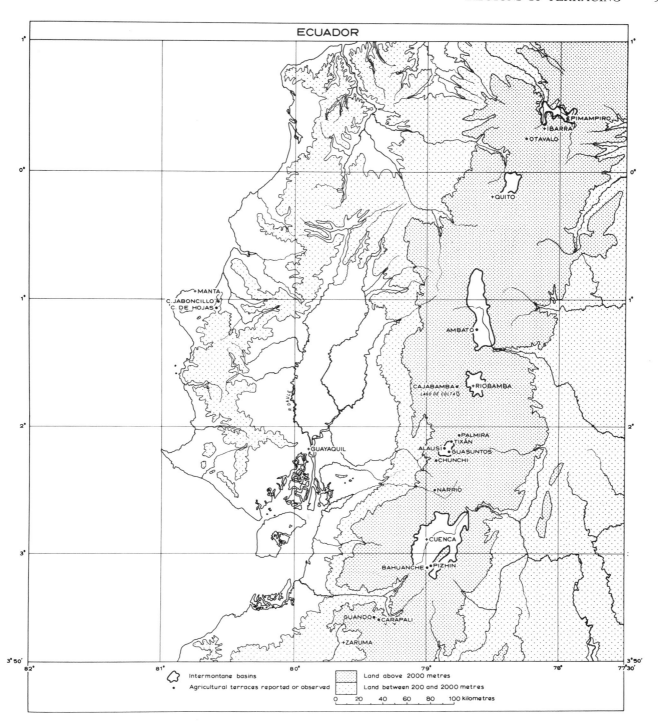

ECUADOR

PIMAMPIRO
IBARRA
OTAVALO

QUITO

MANTA
C. JABONCILLO
C. DE HOJAS

AMBATO

R. DAULE

CAJABAMBA   RIOBAMBA
LAGO DE COLTA

PALMIRA
TIXÁN
ALAUSÍ   GUASUNTOS
CHUNCHI

GUAYAQUIL

NARRÍO

CUENCA

BAHUANCHE   PIZHIN

GUANDO   CARAPALI

ZARUMA

Intermontane basins

Agricultural terraces reported or observed

Land above 2000 metres

Land between 200 and 2000 metres

0   20   40   60   80   100 kilometres

MAP 3.8

the southeast of Pimampíro.[38] Around Otavalo steep slopes are cultivated without recourse to terracing. There are, however, small areas of sloping terraces overlooking the northern end of Lake San Pablo. Cuttings in the deep volcanic soil acquire an adobe-like surface and stand up well.

On the western slopes of the basin of Latacunga fields are buttressed with stone walls placed *en échelon;* they are also often ridged in a manner that has been described for the western highlands of Guatemala (*supra* p. 76).

The area of greatest interest lies between Cajabamba and Chunchi.[39] Above the wet margins of Lake Colta fields have been leveled behind rough walls. There are also valley-floor terraces, faced with stone and irrigated, in the neighborhood of Tixán and an extensive zone of sloping terraces along the Río Alausí and its tributary the Zula, especially around Guasuntos. Near Palmira hillside "steps," first described in 1918, seemed to D. Collier and J. V. Murra "nothing but agricultural terraces."[40]

Further to the south, W. C. Bennett has reported "terracing" at three archaeological sites near Cumbe.[41] Similarly, Collier and Murra observed "terraces" in the head valleys of the Río Jubones. At Guando "the northern and southern approaches to a flat ridge are terraced, and some of the terraces are faced with stone . . . 1.5 to 3 meters high."[42]

---

38. D. A. Preston, photograph and personal communication; although regarded locally as Inca, they may, according to Preston, belong to an earlier period. The Incas are credited with agricultural improvements in Ecuador, especially the introduction or extension of canal irrigation (Vázquez de Espinosa [c. 1628] 1942, no. 1574; W. C. Bennett, 1946a, 13; Murra, 1946, 810). González Suárez (I, 1878a, 196; 1878b, 68) noted the remains of aqueducts in Azuay province. See also Larrea, 1965.

39. Part of the region to which Crespo Toral (1926, 31) refers: "En las pendientes, para utilizar la tierra de los deslaves, para detenerla igualmente que los abonos, dispóngase el sembrado en terrazas paralelas, en platabandas orilladas por cabuyos, cercas de piedra, árboles o juncos, a manera de los aborígenes sobre todo del norte, como se puede observar hoy mismo principalmente en la región de los antiguos puruháes." *(Puruhá* covered what is now the province of Chimborazo and part of the province of Bolivar-Murra, 1946, 788). Jijon y Caamaño (2, 1927, 152), discussing *Los Puruháes, contemporaneos de los Incas:* "Acequias para regadío menciona el Anónima autor de la *Descripción de Riobamba,* en San Andrés, Guano, Penipe, Quimiac y Achambo."

40. Collier and Murra, 1943, 18.

41. W. C. Bennett, 1946d, 64-65 (Pizhín, Bahuanche, and Condurcaca or Yuracaca). Leveling for house sites is suggested; at Condurcaca there are "alignments of stones, but no actual construction work."

42. Collier and Murra, 1943, 31-32, 71.

D: Peru-Bolivia

THE NORTHERN HIGHLANDS OF PERU

In 1829 H. L. Maw drew attention to "marks of old cultivation . . . furrows or ridges" between Caxamarca (Cajamarca) and Chachapoyas[43] (map 3.9). Southeast of Cajamarca, near Cajabamba, "the remains of ancient human activity [are] abundant, particularly in the shape of walls forming *andenes.*"[44] Agricultural terracing around archaeological sites on the eastern flanks of the Andes has been reported by L. Langlois (valley of the Río Utcubamba),[45] B. Flornoy and H. and P. Reichlen (valley of the Río Marañon),[46] D. Bonavia (valley of the Río Abiseo),[47] and P. Rojas Ponce (Pajatén).[48] The *Visita de la provincia de León de Huánuco* (Ortiz de Zúñiga, 1562) refers to cultivated *andenes* in several villages to the east of the upper Marañon. At Pajatén, according to Rojas Ponce, "the lower slopes of the hill, from the point where it is bounded by the Jelache River to the Santa Cruz, are entirely covered with large agricultural terraces, and we imagine that all the rest of this region is similar; that is to say, it was a great 'granary' which could have fed thousands of people." Similar terracing is known from the central and southern sections of the Peruvian *montaña* (*infra,* pp. 94, 122).

C. Wiener (1880) was impressed by the "traces de *andenes*" around Lake Tuctucocha near Cabana (90 kilometers south of Cajabamba).[49] At Pueblo Viejo and Parián in the Callejón de Huailas (between the *cordilleras* Negra and Blanca) there are abandoned terraces associated with irrigation works.[50] In the Cordillera Blanca, H. Kinzl observed "the remains of old human settlements high above the present-day line of habitation. They are most frequent on the high plateaus at the northwest foot of the mountain range, but are also to be found far into the high valleys at present uninhabited. Most numerous are perhaps the old terraces bearing fields above the present-day borderline of cultivation. . . . Not every field run wild may be designated as 'given up.' There are, however, many places where this is certainly the

---

43. Maw, 1829, 43, 50.

44. McCown, 1945, 277.

45. Langlois, 1933, 126-28 (*andenes* with walls 1.5 to 3 meters high).

46. Flornoy, 1955-6, 62, 63, 65; H. and P. Reichlen, 1950, 226 ("terraces de culture").

47. Bonavia, 1968b, 14, 62, 68.

48. Rojas Ponce, 1966, 121, and 1967, 14.

49. Wiener, 1880, 171 (with field sketch).

50. Doughty, 1968, 10, 153. See also W. C. Bennett, 1944a, 12, 14 ("artificial stone terraces" at three sites near Huaras); Ishida, 1960, pl. 26 (western flanks of the Cordillera Negra); Dobyns, 1963, 494.

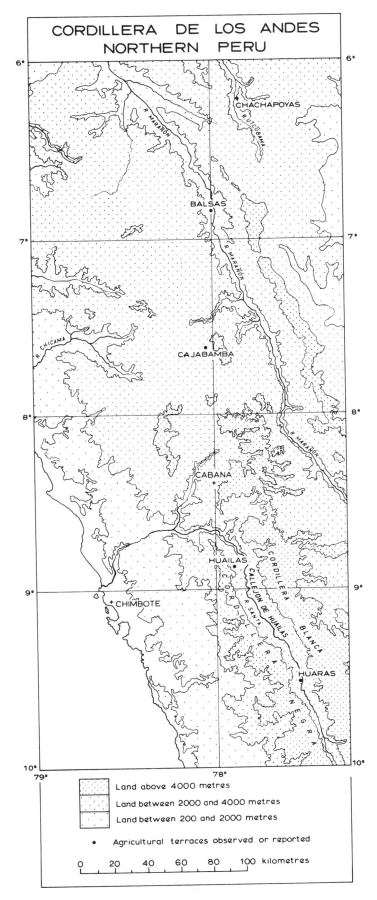

CORDILLERA DE LOS ANDES
NORTHERN PERU

Land above 4000 metres

Land between 2000 and 4000 metres

Land between 200 and 2000 metres

• Agricultural terraces observed or reported

0   20   40   60   80   100 kilometres

MAP 3.9

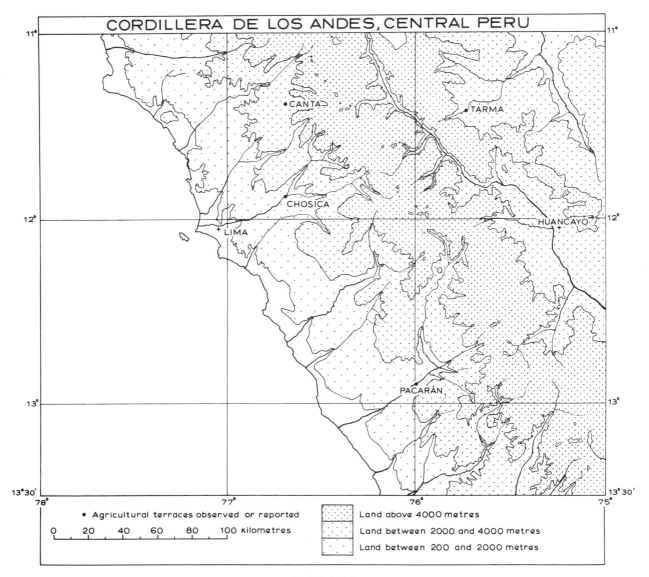

- Agricultural terraces observed or reported

0   20   40   60   80   100 kilometres

Land above 4000 metres

Land between 2000 and 4000 metres

Land between 200 and 2000 metres

MAP 3.10

case. Often the Glacial moraine walls at the opening of the high valleys, or the terminal moraines of the Glacial Period farther to the interior, are covered with terraces bearing former fields on which are sometimes also found the remains of old huts."[51]

The lower sections of the northern coastal valleys, with their impressive evidence of long occupation and advanced floodplain irrigation, have naturally attracted much attention.[52] The mountainous interior is comparatively unexplored, but it seems clear that terracing for agriculture was widely practiced in pre-Columbian times.

THE CENTRAL HIGHLANDS OF PERU

Scholars have referred in passing to *andenes* along the valley of the Río Chancay[53] and in the province of Canta generally;[54] along the *quebrada* of Chilca[55]; near Pacarán on the Río de Cañete;[56] and in the valley of the Río Mantaro[57] (map 3.10).

The valley of the Río Rimac: The remarkable agricultural terraces between Chosica and the confluence of the Río Rimac and the Río Eulalia (fig. 3.50) were observed by T. J. Hutchinson about 1870. He briefly described two locations — Moyabamba (Moyapampa) and an area around the ruins of Parárá in the *quebrada* of Yanacotá.[58] In 1945 L. Gamarra Dulanto and A. Maldonado discussed in some detail the form and significance of these terraces.

51. Kinzl and Schneider, 1950, 31.

52. From the valley of the Río Casma, Tello (1956, 24) reported: "En las faldas de los cerros contiguos aparecen restos de terrazas que a lo lejos simulan andenerías agrícolas."

53. Horkheimer, 1962 (no pagination).

54. Paz Soldán, I, 1862, 324.

55. Engel, 1966, figs. 14, 66, 85.

56. Pulgar Vidal, *n.d.,* 78.

57. Ishida, 1960, pl. 27.

58. Hutchinson, 2, 1873, 47, 53; he compares the terraces of Moyapampa with those of "Cuzco."

Fig. 3.50 Valleys of the Río Rimac and Río Eulalia, above Chosica, Peru, showing abandoned agricultural terraces on south-facing slopes
(*Servicio Aerofotográfico Nacional,* Perú)

There are terraces at Santa Inés on the left bank of the Rimac; in a *quebrada* (? Yanacotá) behind Chosica; and most notably at Moyapampa where, according to Gamarra Dulanto and Maldonado, the *andenes* cover about 60 hectares. All but a very small fraction are abandoned. Agriculture today is virtually confined to the level bottom lands and depends on irrigation. Rainfall is negligible (average 5 mm per annum), but the terraced areas lie within the *zona de lomas* where in winter (June to October) the heavy coastal mist or *garúa* imparts some moisture to the ground.[59]

The terraces here are essentially contour benches but, having been developed over broad embayments in the valley walls (fig. 3.51), they also have some of the

Fig. 3.51 Abandoned terraces, near Chosica, Peru

characteristics of cross-channel terraces. It has been argued that stone dams and sluices on the higher slopes served to trap coarse material and to direct silt-laden water behind retaining walls. Excavation of portions of this fill by Gamarra Dulanto and Maldonado revealed little or no stratification, suggesting small and frequent additions of sediment. Examination of some of the many sections exposed by gully erosion supports this conclusion. Gamarra Dulanto and Maldonado also showed by chemical and mechanical analyses that soluble nitrates and the finest material of the fill are concentrated behind terrace walls and 80 cm or more below the surface. The dry masonry and drains incorporated in the walls

allowed excess water to pass from one terrace to the next. If the suggested method of construction by controlled sedimentation is correct, it implies that the rainfall at the time was significantly higher and more regular than at present. There is also some evidence that irrigation water was conducted from springs and from points higher up the Río Rimac.

The retaining walls are between 1 and 3 meters high, the inner and outer faces being separated by rubble. Staircases between flights and steps set in the walls facilitated movement within the terraced area. In places, the former cropping surfaces are below the tops of the retaining walls. This could be the result of wind erosion, or perhaps the terraces were never entirely filled, either by accident or design, in the latter case to leave a forward bund. The ordered arrangement of terraces in flights suggests considerable experience in building. Irregularities of slope were overcome by angled straight sections and the use of end walls.

The broken walls of more primitive terraces may be observed along both sides of the valley of the Rimac upstream from the confluence with the Río Eulalia as far as Casapalca (about 3200 meters above sea level).

The basin of Tarma: The basin of Tarma (at about 3000 meters) comprises the valleys of the headwaters of the Río Palca which drains northeastward into the Río Paucartambo. The main axis of the basin runs from northwest to southeast along a belt of Palaeozoic sandstones. The high western margins extend into the mass of Jurassic and Triassic limestones that here forms the backbone of the *cordillera.*

Around the Inca site of Tarmatambo,[60] J. J. Von Tschudi noted water conduits and "walled fields" overgrown with puna grass.[61] In fact, the slopes of the valleys above Tarma are terraced to the altitudinal limits of cultivation. To the south of the town, small areas of low-lying scrub and rough pasture were probably more extensive before drainage was controlled for purposes of irrigation. Minor breaks of slope have been emphasized by boundary walls to form large, valley-floor terraces. The walls of the adjacent valley-side benches (fig. 3.52) are partly cut out of the hillside and partly constructed of stone and blocks of adobe. Although grass and low scrub give support and protection to excavated faces, many are undercut and deeply scalloped by rain water. The lower surfaces are irrigated by means of canals brought along the hillsides.[62]

59. The *garúa* is mentioned by López de Gómara (1552) I, 1954, 327 *(rocío);* Matienzo (1567) 1910, 91; Ramírez (1597) 1936, 13; Martín de Murúa (1590) 2, 1962, 148, 150; Lizárraga (c. 1600) 1968, 11; Cobo (1653) I, 1956, 87-90. Cutting for domestic fuel has destroyed most of the xerophytic forest of the *lomas,* 500 to 700 meters above sea level (Beek and Bramao, 1968, 107).

60. Wiener, 1880, 234; Regal, 1945, 102.

61. Tschudi, 1847, 495.

62. The average annual rainfall at Tarma is about 650 mm, which makes irrigation for maize desirable but not essential. See Drewes and Drewes, 1957, 10.

Fig. 3.52 Terraced fields and house sites, near Tarma, Peru

Irrigated, valley-floor terraces extend for about 10 kilometers to the west of Tarma, and the flanking slopes are covered with innumerable stone-faced benches to near the crest of the limestone plateau at about 3700 meters. The valley of the Río Palca below Tarma (toward the *montaña*) was not investigated. There are, however, reports of old agricultural terracing to the east of Huancayo and Ayacucho[63] and along the valley of the Río Chanchamayo.[64]

THE SOUTHERN HIGHLANDS OF PERU

The highlands of southern Peru (map 3.11) are formed partly of immense lava flows, deeply dissected and crowned by volcanic cones. Underlying sedimentary

63. Bonavia, 1964, 20, 39, 1967-8, 271-78, and 1968a, 80; Bonavia and Rabines, 1967, 62, 67. W. C. Bennett (1953, 24), describing the site of Wari (25 kilometers NNE of Ayacucho), states that "terraces are abundant everywhere, from 2 to 5 meters high, and aligned with the contours of the slopes. The facings are well made of selected, rough stone."

64. Lathrap, 1970, 176; also 1962-3, 196-202.

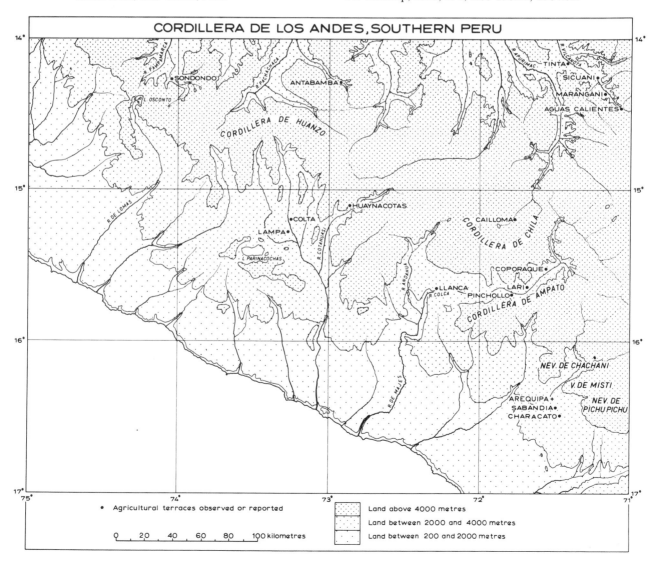

MAP 3.11

Fig. 3.53 Terraced fields around an abandoned village, valley of the Río Colca, Peru (P. A. Means, 1932)

rocks of Jurassic and Cretaceous age are exposed along the middle courses of the rivers that flow into the Pacific. The axis of the highlands follows the Cordillera de Huanzo and the Cordillera de Chilca which rise to over 6000 meters. Drainage to the north and east of this axis is toward the Río Apurimac, while to the south and west half a dozen smaller river systems lead toward the Pacific. Within the upper reaches of valleys on both sides of the watershed, almost inaccessible gorge sections alternate with valley basins. In these basins, agricultural terraces cover very large areas and a wide variety of slopes.

The climate of the region is arid or semi-arid; rainfall generally decreases from northeast (about 500 mm per annum) to southwest. Desert scrub ("maleza desértica montano bajo") in the western foothills is replaced at higher altitudes by steppe ("estepo montano") and *páramo* vegetation.[65]

Terraced fields, some in use and others abandoned, are a characteristic feature of the upper valleys (3500 to 4500 meters) of the Río Antabamba (near Antabamba

itself),[66] the Río Apurimac (near Cailloma),[67] and the Río Pampamarca (the *quebrada* Sondondo, westward to Lake Osconta).[68] On the Pacific side of the watershed, terracing has been practiced on a vast scale (i) within the basin of Lake Parinacochas[69] and on the slopes of the Nudo Sarasara;[70] (ii) in the valleys of the Lampa,[71] Coathuasi[72] and Arma;[73] and (iii) to the southeast in the valleys of the Andahua[74] and Colca (fig. 3.53).[75] Baltasar

65. Tosi, 1960 *(mapa ecológico del Perú).*

66. Aerial photograph, *Museo e Instituto Arqueológico,* Cuzco.

67. Shippee, 1932b, fig. 8.

68. Vitangurt, 1940, 33-34.

69. Bingham, 1922, 84.

70. Vitangurt, 1940, 34 ("tierras de cultivo incásico," abandoned for up to four centuries).

71. Bingham, 1922, 84 (Colta).

72. Bowman, 1916, figs. 27, 131; Bingham, 1922, 54.

73. Bowman, 1916, 56, and fig. 30 (Salamanca): "The floor and slopes . . . are more completely terraced than any other valley I know of."

74. Shippee, 1932b, 581, fig. 3, pl. IV.

75. Johnson and Platt, 1930, figs. 26, 27; Means, 1932, figs. 2, 3; Shippee, 1932b, figs. 13, 14 — around Llanca, Lari, Pincholla, Yanque and Coporaque.

Fig. 3.54 Terraced fields, in use and abandoned, near Arequipa, Peru (*Servicio Aerofotográfico Nacional, Perú*)

Ramírez (1597) reported terracing combined with irrigation in the highlands to the east of Coathuasi,[76] and a *relación* of 1586 for the province of Collaguas (upper Colca) refers to unirrigated *andenes*.[77] The remains of agricultural terraces have been identified at Churajón (approximately 30 kilometers southeast of Arequipa) and around the related archaeological sites of Sarito de Pucará and Huatalacac.[78] At Churajón "the *andenes* are constructed of big stones, each terrace measuring on an average 1 meter high and 3.5 meters wide."

Arequipa: Some of the most advanced agricultural terracing still in use in the New World is to be found in the vicinity of Arequipa. Here the headwaters of the Río de Vitor, descending from the slopes of the Nevado de Chacháni, the Volcán de Misti and the Nevado de Pichu Pichu, lead into a bowl-like depression open to the southwest. The main valleys to the south and west of Arequipa, and that of the Río Chili on which the city stands, are filled with old fluvial material in which streams are incised. The intervening ridges are steep-sided and, above the limits of cultivation, almost bare of vegetation (fig. 3.54). The average annual rainfall is about 110 mm. Agriculture depends on water drawn from streams fed by melting snow and led in stone-lined channels *(acequias)* along the middle slopes of the ridges. Ramírez (1597) observed "acequias muy grandes" at Arequipa.[79]

---

76. Ramírez, 1936, 41.

77. Ulloa Mogollón, 1885, 46.

78. Ishida, 1960, 281, 467-69 (c. A.D. 1100); Bernedo Málaga, 1949, 108.

79. Trimborn, 1936, 44. Bernedo Málaga (1949) names terraced sites in the upper Vitor and the Tambo (to the southeast). Around Arequipa there are now about 20,000 acres (mostly terraced) under irrigation (C. T. Smith, 1960, 406).

The terraces in the vicinity of Arequipa — generally attributed to the Incas[80] — are of two main kinds. Firstly, parts of the old floodplains have been divided into large, valley-floor terraces, stepped between walls of earth and stone up to 4 meters high. They resemble the terraces behind Ollantaitambo in a tributary valley of the Urubamba; in both cases, the task of leveling must have been enormous. Secondly, there are many flights of superbly constructed valley-side benches (figs. 3.55, 3.56, 3.57); the supporting walls, with built-in steps, are of trimmed blocks arranged in courses (fig. 3.58). These terraces have been largely hand-filled, first with rubble (now occasionally exposed in eroded sections) and then with cultivable soil; their "superimposed" character is clearly apparent where they terminate against end walls (fig. 3.59).

The terraces in use extend about half way up the sides of the ridges (fig. 3.60). Beyond this, broken walls and eroded fill indicate changes in the limits of cultivation (fig. 3.61). Some of the abandoned flights approach

---

80. According to Markham (1862, 80), Arequipa was colonized by Inca Mayta; the present city was founded by Pizarro in 1540. Juan Polo de Ondegardo (1873, 163-64), *corregidor* of Cuzco in 1560, reported that "in the *Collao*, where no maize can be raised, the people had lands on the coast *(suyus),* and sent men down to till them, near Arequipa for instance."

Fig. 3.55 Irrigated terraces near Arequipa, Peru; the crop is alfalfa

Fig. 3.56 Irrigated terraces, near Arequipa, Peru

Fig. 3.57 Irrigated terraces, Sabandia, Arequipa, Peru

Fig. 3.58 Terrace wall (c. 3 meters), trimmed blocks in courses,
near Arequipa, Peru

Fig. 3.59 Superimposed bench terraces, Sabandia, Arequipa, Peru

Fig. 3.60 Terraces in use (lower and middle slopes) and abandoned
(upper slopes), Sabandia, Arequipa, Peru

Fig. 3.61 Broken and abandoned terraces (2.5 meters wide), Sabandia, Arequipa, Peru

the crests of the ridges, and on the parched and undulating tops (known as *pampas*) there are lines of stone (fig. 3.62) that are not easily explained except as old field boundaries. To judge from the condition of the terrace walls, the process of abandonment has been gradual. Probably the soils of some areas became too saline for cultivation under conditions of high evaporation and inadequate irrigation. It appears that there is less water available to farmers today than at certain periods in the past. This could be due to lower precipitation in the form of rain and snow, or to the drying up of springs following seismic disturbances, or to a deterioration in the standard of management after the Spanish Conquest, or, as is most probable, to some combination of these circumstances. Several broken dams and silted reservoirs were observed around Sabandia and Characato (fig. 3.63).

THE VALLEYS OF THE RÍO VILCANOTA-URUBAMBA

The Río Vilcanota (map 3.12) drops 1000 meters between Aguas Calientes, below the Nudo de Vilcanota (the watershed with the basin of Titicaca), and the village of Vilcabamba, a distance of 150 kilometers. The Urubamba (as the same river is known below Vilcabamba) falls 2000 meters in about the same distance, notably in a series of gorges that separate U-shaped sections with well-developed floodplains. The annual precipitation along the Vilcanota is of the order of 550 to 700 mm. The basin of Cuzco receives about 820 mm. Above Machu Picchu, the Urubamba lies in the rain shadow of the Cordillera Vilcabamba; rainfall along the floor and lower slopes of the valley is apparently considerably less than for the area as a whole (750 to 1100 mm, increasing northward) and systems of irrigation long antedate the Spanish Conquest.

The basins of Zurite, Cuzco and Oropesa: Cieza de León (c. 1550),[81] Bartolomé de Las Casas (1527-1559),[82] Pedro Pizarro (1571-2)[83] and the anonymous author of the *Descripción general del Reino del Perú* (c. 1620)[84] refer to *andenes* near Cuzco itself.[85] Cieza also described the basin of Zurite (or Anta, anciently *Xaquixaguana*). It had once been "very populous," and the marshy floor was crossed by a "broad and deep causeway" of Inca construction. The hillside "fields were divided from each other by broad walls."[86] This is a clear allusion to *andenes*,

81. Cieza de León, 1883, 160.

82. Las Casas, I, 1958, 194.

83. Pedro Pizarro, 2, 1921, 305.

84. Lewin (ed), 1958, 91.

85. Similarly Garcilaso de la Vega (1604) 1871, 470. Ishida (1960, 487-96) lists 45 sites with *"andenes* or terraces" within 5 kilometers of Cuzco. See also Rowe, 1944, 51 (Llaullipata). At Sapantiana there are "pequeños andenes desenterrados" (photograph, *Museo e Instituto Arqueológico,* Cuzco). Brundage (1967, 92, 94, 95) mentions Inca house-and-cultivation terraces at Cusipata and Patallacta, now within the built-up area of the city.

86. Cieza de León, 1864, 320-21.

Fig. 3.62 Former field boundaries (?) on the plateau above Sabandia, Arequipa, Peru

Fig. 3.63 Silted reservoir and broken dam
(5 meters high), Characato, Arequipa, Peru

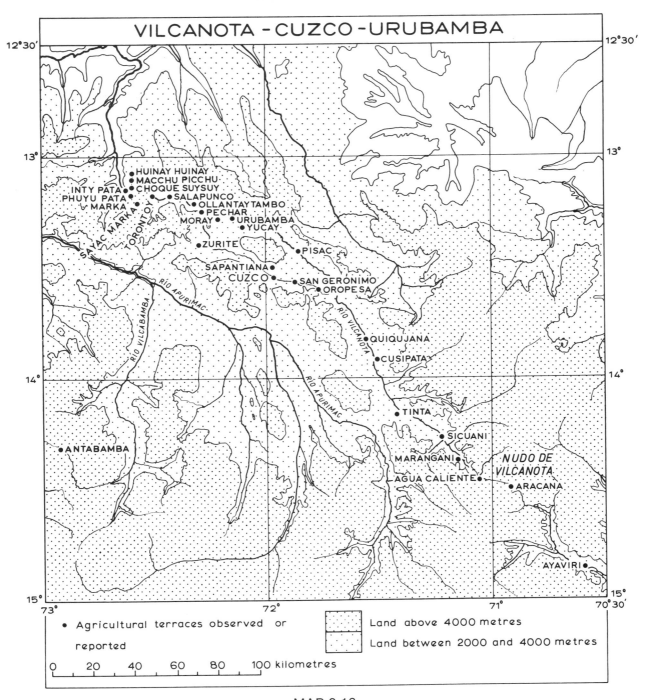

VILCANOTA - CUZCO - URUBAMBA

• Agricultural terraces observed or reported

Land above 4000 metres

Land between 2000 and 4000 metres

0   20   40   60   80   100 kilometres

MAP 3.12

the remains of which can be observed on the ground and on aerial photographs.[87] From the basin of Oropesa, H. Bingham reported agricultural terraces of cut stone, some of which were being cultivated by the people of Quispicanchi.[88]

The valley of the Río Vilcanota: Traces of former cultivation extend almost to the head of the Vilcanota and over higher ground along the length of the valley. The slopes around Aguas Calientes (4038 meters) are lined with broken walls. On the other hand, between Aguas Calientes and Maranganí,[89] and also around Tinta,[90] there are several areas of irrigated valley-floor terraces. Cultivated cross-channel terraces occupy *barrancas* near Sicuani (where parts of the floodplain are still unreclaimed marsh), and at Cusipata and Quiquiana steep-sided outwash fans have been terraced.[91]

The valley of the Río Urubamba: In the valley of the Urubamba certain landforms are regularly repeated: alluvio-gravel levels (fig. 3.64), steep valley walls above aprons of colluvial material, and outwash fans around the mouths of tributary valleys. The terraces that cover parts of all the sloping surfaces are among the most remarkable in the world.

Pisac: Pisac itself has a typical grid plan of the colonial period. The plaza and church lie close to the piedmont, and it appears that the town has been gradually extended across the floodplain which is now almost wholly reclaimed and divided into large, irrigated fields. The river follows a remarkably straight course, between strengthened banks, on the south side of the valley.

The terraces of advanced construction are confined to the south-facing side of the valley which receives less insolation than the opposite slopes and is more thickly vegetated. A composite outwash fan to the northwest of Pisac has been re-shaped by excavation and forward filling into a series of levels (figs. 3.65, 3.66) supported

Fig. 3.64 Valley of the Río Urubamba, near Pisac, Peru

by walls 1.5 to 4 meters high. These terraces are still regularly cultivated. Secondly, above Pisac, there are several flights of 20 to 30 valley-side benches on slopes of 35 to 50 degrees (fig. 3.67); some have been carried to the very edge of precipices (fig. 3.68). The supporting walls are commonly between 2.5 and 3.5 meters high (exceptionally as much as 5.5 meters). Like the valley-side terraces at Arequipa, those of Pisac are fully superimposed, that is their construction involved little or no excavation except for the foundations of the walls. The spaces behind the walls must have been artificially filled. The former cropping surfaces are roughly level with the tops of the walls and either bare of vegetation or lightly covered with *ichu* grass. Flights of terraces, manifestly planned as a whole, are separated longitudinally by end walls enclosing stone stairways and water channels.

On a commanding spur above the terraces lie the remains of the Inca fortress and palace of Inti-Huatana (fig. 3.69) and, to one side of this, an abandoned settlement (fig. 3.70). Today, only a few of the valley-side

---

87. *Museo e Instituto Arqueológico,* Cuzco. There was a *hacienda* called Andenes near Zurite (Paz Soldán, 1877). See also Markham, 1856, 93; Squier, 1877, 535; Ishida, 1960, 500.

88. Bingham, 1922, 135, 141 (ruined terraces above the Inca site of Rumiccolca); Rowe, 1944, 53 ("This part of the Cuzco valley, around the small lake of Lucre [Muyna] and down the road to Andahuaylillas on the other side of Rumiccolca, is full of terraces and buildings indicating intensive occupation").

89. See Ishida, 1960, 505.

90. See O. F. Cook, 1916b, 522.

91. Poindexter (1930, 87) mentions "well finished" terraces along the Vilcanota.

Fig. 3.65 and 3.66   Terraced outwash fan, Pisac, Peru;
walls of terraces 1.5 to 4 meters high

Fig. 3.67   Abandoned terraces (c. 2.5 meters high) Pisac, Peru

Fig. 3.68   Abandoned terraces, Pisac, Peru

Fig. 3.69 Fortress and palace of Inti-Huatana, above Pisac, Peru

Fig. 3.70 Abandoned settlement below Inti-Huatana, Pisac, Peru; cultivated terraces to the left

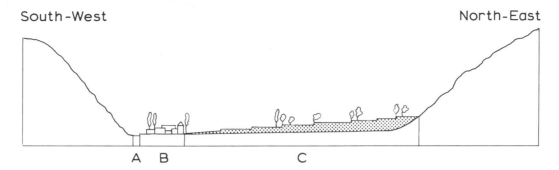

South-West   North-East

Diagram 3.7

VALLEY OF THE RÍO URUBAMBA AT YUCAY, PERU

A   Río Urubamba

B   Yucay

C   Terraced outwash fan

benches, below the *pueblo viejo* and overlooking a right-bank tributary of the Urubamba, are in use. The reasons for abandonment have not been precisely determined, but they may be expected to lie in the failure of the system of irrigation and/or in soil sterility produced by the accumulation of harmful salts.

Other terraces around Pisac are structurally unremarkable. On the highest slopes, potatoes and oca are grown, for several years in succession, in small, irregular fields. The boundary walls have checked the downward movement of soil, but the angle of slope of only a small proportion of the cultivated area is thereby affected. The drier, north-facing side of the valley also has been terraced, but the walls and surfaces are in a poor condition and only some of the lower plots are cultivated.

Yucay: At Yucay,[92] 40 kilometers downstream from Pisac, the Río Urubamba lies under the south wall of the U-shaped valley. The river appears to have been pushed across the floodplain by the advance of a large outwash fan, at the foot of which stands Yucay (diag. 3.7). The floodplain is under cultivation except for some unreclaimed marsh; the fields are large, and bounded by adobe walls 1 to 3 meters high. The dry and precipitous north-facing slopes of the valley are almost bare of vegetation and show no signs of ever having been cultivated.

The outwash fan has been completely terraced. The supporting walls are megalithic features, up to 9 meters high and in some cases incorporating a recessed stairway (fig. 3.71). Where the walls are stepped back, the

Fig. 3.71 Stairway in a terrace wall (c. 7 meters high), Yucay, Peru

92. For a general description, see Gade, 1968, 12-19.

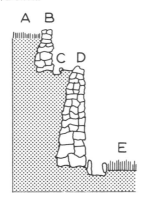

Diagram 3.8

DOUBLE TERRACE WALL, YUCAY, PERU

A   Upper cropping surface

B   Upper wall (3·5 metres)

C   Intermediate level, canal, pathway

D   Lower wall (8 metres)

E   Irrigation ditch & lower cropping surface

narrow, intermediate level usually carries an irrigation ditch and also serves as a pathway; in one example of this, the two sections together stand 11.5 meters high (diag. 3.8). The quality of the masonry is inferior to that of Pisac, but this is probably due less to any difference in building skill than to the use at Yucay of water-smoothed boulders and cobbles instead of quarried stone.

The terraced fields of Yucay (fig. 3.72) are intensively cultivated, with fruit trees planted between crops of maize, beans, vegetables and alfalfa. Water, drawn from the *arroyo* at the head of the fan, is applied both to the larger, central fields and to the benches that border the floodplain (fig. 3.73).

Ollantaitambo: Between Ollantaitambo and the township of Urubamba the lower reaches of tributary valleys are choked with alluvium and rock waste — an indication of more pluvial conditions in the geologically recent past. Ollantaitambo itself occupies part of a large outwash fan. This has been terraced, and so too have (i) the lower slopes of the main valley (the terraces on the north-facing side are, however, either abandoned or in a poor state of repair) (fig. 3.74) and (ii) the floor of the tributary valley behind the town. The valley-floor terraces (fig. 3.75) account for a large proportion of the

Fig. 3.72 Terraced outwash fan, Yucay, Peru

Fig. 3.73 Terraced flank of an outwash fan, Yucay, Peru

Fig. 3.74 Ollantaitambo, Peru: abandoned or poorly maintained terraces on north-facing slopes of the valley of the Urubamba; remains of an Inca bridge in the foreground

Fig. 3.75 Valley-floor terraces behind Ollantaitambo, Peru; walls 2 to 3 meters high

area presently cultivated. When the work of leveling commenced, the surface of the fill must have been littered with fragments of stone. The construction of the retaining walls (up to 3.5 meters high and 200 meters long) would have helped to overcome this problem, but, as in the case of Yucay, the chief reason for terracing was undoubtedly to facilitate irrigation.

The well-known terraces around the Inca fortress of Ollantaitambo cover a rock slope of about 40 degrees. It was probably these to which Pedro Pizarro (1571-2) referred when he wrote of "many very high *andenes,* very steep and strong."[93] They are similar to the terraces below Inti-Huatana at Pisac. The almost vertical walls would have assisted defense, and platforms faced with large blocks of prepared stone continue the sequence into the fortress itself.

The Urubamba below Ollantaitambo: Below Ollantaitambo, agricultural terracing has been reported from Salapunco[94] and Torontoy,[95] and from several Inca sites close to the final high mountain section of the Urubamba. Here the river cuts across the Cordillera Vilcabamba in a series of deeply incised meanders to reach the eastern piedmont of the Andes, the *montaña.* Along the lower half of the gorge, the rain-shadow effect of the range is considerably reduced and north-facing slopes, with ample insolation, have advantages for agriculture.

P. Fejos has studied some of the abandoned terraces of this area. His descriptions of Phuyu Pata Marka and Choquesuysuy are among the most detailed available:

The system of terraces at Phuyu Pata Marka is very extensive and comprises a great majority of all the structures at the site. Each terrace is built of coarse rocks at the bottom and smaller ones towards the top which are overlaid by a varying thickness of clay and humus, usually about two-thirds of a meter in depth. This material is held in place by an outer wall, 60 to 74 centimeters thick, constructed of stone, and usually sloping back towards the terrace at an angle of 15 to 20 degrees from the vertical. In most of the terrace walls, the stonework is comparatively rough. Although in all cases the stones have been carefully selected to fit into one another, they are small and

have been very little trimmed except in the corners. Because of irregularities in the rocks, most of which are of white granite, the surfaces of the walls are rough and gaps of from 2.5 to 5 centimeters are frequently to be found. Along the tops of the walls, however, rather flat slabs of uniform size have been used to give the walls a finished appearance. . . . There seems little doubt that Phuyu Pata Marka was a small town and that the terraces were used for agricultural purposes.[96]

And at Choquesuysuy:

Terraces were found on the alluvial soil on either side of the *quebrada,* extending from the water's edge to a height of about 67 meters above the river. On the higher terraces, the alluvial soil becomes much thinner and bed rock is visible in many places. There are twenty-three rows of terraces east of the *quebrada,* ranging in width from 5 to 18 meters. These are well preserved except in the center of the area, where water from the upper slopes has washed down and broken the terraces to a width of some 8 meters, and in the vicinity of the stream, where erosion has also taken place. West of the *quebrada,* the number of terraces is twenty-four, but they are much narrower than those on the east. Again, some erosion has taken place near the stream and in addition all terraces along the bank of the Urubamba 70 meters from the stream and beyond are now covered with wash from the slope above, so that it is impossible to determine how far the western terraces extend.

The terraces on both sides of the *quebrada* are built of good masonry formed from hammer-broken boulders. The terrace walls at this site, unlike all the rest, are vertical rather than slightly sloping. The walls of the west terrace are plain, but those east of the *quebrada* bear two added features: steps composed of projecting stones as at Inty Pata and vertical grooves in the terrace walls. These grooves, which have a square cross section, are about 20 centimeters deep. Since they often occur one above the other, they might be presumed to be water drains were it not for the fact that they connect with no channels on the terraces and their tops are not modified to receive a stream of water.[97]

93. Pedro Pizarro, 2, 1921, 332. Photographs in the *Museo e Instituto Arqueológico,* Cuzco, show the walls in poor repair; during the work of reconstruction Inca pottery was found (Llanos, 1936, 123; Pardo, 1946, 47-73).

94. Llanos, 1936, 153; Ishida, 1960, 498; photographs in the *Museo e Instituto Arqueológico,* Cuzco.

95. O.F. Cook, 1916a, 290; Ishida, 1960, 498. See also Bowman, 1916, 77, and cf. Gade, 1975, 21 n. 7.

96. Fejos, 1944, 28.

97. *Ibid.,* 48. Fejos also describes (*ibid.,* 32) masonry-lined gutters and spouts at Sayac Marka. He provides a plan of the terraces at Inty Pata, "sunny slope" (figs. 3.76, 3.77), and notes the occurrence of isolated groups of terraces unassociated with house sites "along the sides of the valley between Machu Picchu mountain and the ridge to the south."

Fig. 3.76 Agricultural terraces, Inty Pata, valley of the Urubamba, Peru (P. Fejos, 1944)

Fig. 3.77 Agricultural terraces, Inty Pata, valley of the Urubamba, Peru (P. Fejos, 1944)

Fig. 3.78 Agricultural terraces, Machu Picchu, valley of the Urubamba, Peru

The terraces at Machu Picchu (fig. 3.78) occupy northeast- and northwest-facing slopes of 30 to 45 degrees. The spaces behind the walls have been artificially filled, doubtless in the manner described for Phuyu Pata Marka. Long flights of benches are separated by end walls, stairways and, in some cases, spillways. There are also irrigation channels along some of the retaining walls (fig. 3.79). The terraces apparently are inclined a little from the horizontal in alternate directions between one surface and the next. In this way water could be brought down a whole flight of benches.[98]

Moray: The terraces of Moray,[99] at a height of about 3500 meters on the plateau between the valleys of the Urubamba and the Cuzco, are entirely unique.[100] They are arranged (i) in three circles (fig. 3.80: *A, B* and *C*); (ii) around an "amphitheater" (*D*) to the south of circle *A,* and (iii) across slope *E.* The base of flight *E* is ap-

proximately level with the top of the "amphitheater," which in turn lies above circle *A.* The circles are 40 to 45 meters in diameter (measured between the walls of the lowest terrace) and in each case there are six concentric cropping surfaces. The "amphitheater" consists of five benches, and the area that it encloses, like that within each circle, is almost level. Many of the walls, particularly of circle *C,* are in poor repair and overgrown, but it is clear from what remains that the planting surfaces (4 to 10 meters wide) were all originally level. The benches on slope *E* are the most massive (2 to 3.5 meters high and 7 to 25 meters wide) and are structurally intact.

98. M. Sáenz (1933, 54) refers to the irrigation of *andenes* by canal and by hand ("La irrigación de los andenes se hacía por canales cuando era posible, pero en muchas ocasiones el agua de llevaba a mano, en cántaros"). See also Bingham, 1916, 445; Latcham, 1923, 9; Suárez Polar, 1934, 15; Baudin, 1962, 147; Pulgar Vidal *n.d.,* 100-102.

99. See Rowe, 1944, 53-54; Ishida, 1960, 50.

100. The nearest settlement of any size is the village of Maras, 6 kilometers to the southeast. Agricultural terraces have been reported (Núñez del Prado, 1949, 200) from Chinchero, east of Maras and 25 kilometers northwest of Cuzco ("Existe otro tipo de tierras que son consideradas por los indios como de alta calidad, las mismas que se encuentran constituídas por las plataformas de andenería incaica. Dichas tierras, casi exclusivamente están asignadas a la Iglesia").

Fig. 3.79 Irrigation channel below a terrace wall, Machu Picchu, valley of the Urubamba, Peru

Fig. 3.80 Moray, Peru (Shippee, 1932a)

Fig. 3.81 Cultivated floor of a doline, Moray, Peru

Fig. 3.82 Water drop (?) in a terrace wall, Moray, Peru

All but a small fraction of the terraces are now abandoned. The exceptions are part of the two highest benches of circle *B* (adjacent to the cultivated area between *A* and *B*) and possibly some of the terraces at *E*; in addition, half of the level area within the "amphitheater" was under barley in 1966. The floors of the circles show no signs of cultivation in the recent past but, being comparatively moist, they have a good cover of grass even in the dry season and are preferred by grazing animals.

On the limestone plateau around Moray, surface water is largely confined to several deep *quebradas.* In places, these open out to form dolines in which residual soils have collected (fig. 3.81) and where there are pools for most of the year. Whether the terraced area at Moray was originally part of a single *quebrada* (possibly stepped in the direction of flow, that is toward the Urubamba) or consisted of two or three dolines could probably only be determined by borings. If the former was the case, a large amount of material must have been transported to separate the three circles. The necks of land between *A* and *B* and *B* and *C,* as well as the narrower ridge to the west of circle *C* (the lowest of the three), may be largely artificial. The terraces were probably built around

an area, or rather several areas, of cultivable soil that could be used as fill for the upper benches particularly. In any event, there must have been a considerable amount of excavation, if only to achieve the remarkable symmetry of form.

The recessed slopes are relatively sheltered, and cultivation is favored on this account, but for maize some form of irrigation would probably have been essential. If the floors of the circles were normally covered with water,[101] perhaps hand irrigation was practiced. Since, however, the work of terracing clearly had involved a great deal of labor, as well as much forethought, one would expect to find that water was brought by canal to a point where it could be distributed over the planting surfaces. So far as is known, no such canal has been reported, and on the site itself the only evidence for gravity-flow irrigation appears to be a water drop in the wall of one of the terraces of circle *B* (fig. 3.82) and certain long depressions that may have been lateral distributaries behind the tops of the walls at *E*.

---

101. Rowe (1944, 54) observed water in circle *B*.

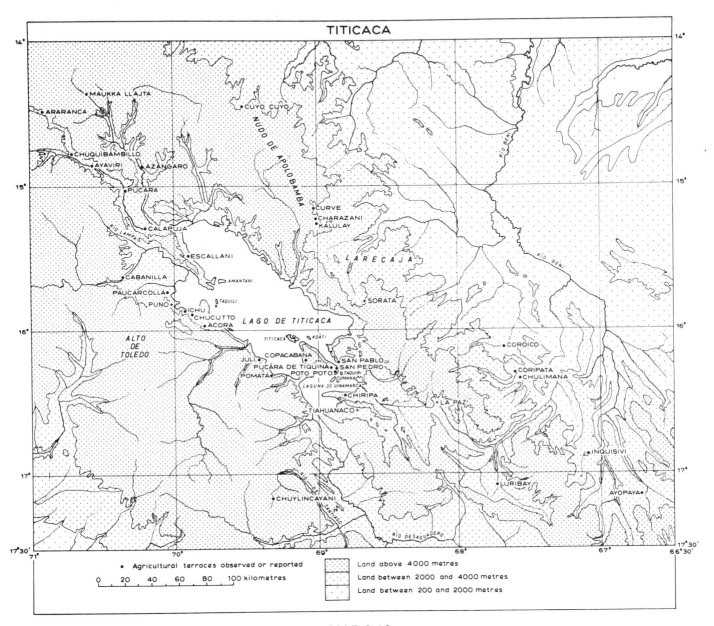

MAP 3.13

THE BASIN OF LAKE TITICACA AND THE HIGHLANDS OF APOLOBAMBA-PUPUYA

The basin of Lake Titicaca and the surrounding highlands (map 3.13) is the *Collao (Colla-suyo)* of the early chronicles and the homeland of the Aymara-speaking peoples. Tiahuanaco, near the southern shores of the lake, was a place of more than regional importance; during the eleventh and twelfth centuries A.D. its influence extended as far afield as coastal Peru and northwest Argentina.[102] But of the economy of the society that produced Tiahuanaco almost nothing is known for certain. The *Collao* later formed part of the Inca empire, and at the time of the Spanish Conquest the territory surrounding Lake Titicaca was heavily populated.[103]

Terraced fields are an important feature of the southern and western shores of Lake Titicaca and of several of the islands. They have also been observed along valleys

102. Debenedetti, 1912.

103. Sancho (1535) 1917, 162; C. T. Smith, 1970, 453-64.

to the southwest[104] and the distribution may extend without interruption into northern-most Chile. To the north and northeast of the lake, there are reports of terracing from the vicinity of the Nudo de Apolobamba and the Nevado de Pupuya (on either side of the Peru-Bolivia border).

The basin of Lake Titicaca: Lake Titicaca[105] lies at about 3800 meters above sea level. The large body of water has an ameliorating effect on the climate, particularly that of the islands.[106] The shorelands have been improved by ridging,[107] but the areas of ridged fields under grass indicate wider cultivation by this method in the past than today. The ridges, like the terraces, of the Titicaca region date from different periods; likewise their abandonment was probably piecemeal and not wholly related to the introduction in the sixteenth century of cattle and sheep which increased the value of pasture.[108]

The terraces of the basin of Titicaca are typically small, contour benches supported by substantial stone walls from 1 to 3.5 meters high. The cropping surfaces are mostly level but irrigation was nowhere observed.[109] Individual terraces vary in length from 5 to 50 meters. There is little indication of planned development of entire slopes but rather of gradual extension by families and small communities. Moreover only a small proportion of the terraced fields (probably less than 25 percent of those not completely abandoned) is worked in any one year. Around Chucuito such land is usually cultivated only once or twice in six or seven years.[110] At the end of this time fields are lightly covered with puna grass *(Stipa ichu)* and grazing animals are partly responsible for the destruction of terrace walls.

The *cuestas* overlooking the southern part of the lake are extensively terraced but many of the higher flights appear to be abandoned. Along both sides of the straits of Tiquina, above the *pueblos* of San Pedro and San Pablo, and around the peninsula of Copacabana, terraces commonly extend from hill crest to shoreline.[111] Pathways take advantage of the frequent changes of alignment and connect adjacent surfaces. The chief crops are quinoa,[112] barley and the local tubers, oca, ullucu and potatoes.

South of the straits of Tiquina, agricultural terracing has been reported from the islands of Taquiri[113] and Cumana[114] in the Laguna de Uinamarca. There are also terraces, presumed to have been agricultural, near the archaeological site of Chiripa (? c. 500 B.C.) on the shores of the *laguna,*[115] and below the Pucará de Khonkho[116] some 50 kilometers to the south.

Terraces cover large areas of the island of Titicaca (Isla del Sol)[117] where maize can be more successfully grown than along the outer shores of the lake. Some of the terraces resemble those of the Urubamba valley. Below the "Fountain of the Inca" (in a sheltered embayment near the peninsula of Yumani), a flight of steps separates two sets of terraces. The upper benches are about as high as they are wide (approximately 3.5 meters). The walls have been carefully constructed and some are stepped back for greater strength. A paved water channel lies at the base of each wall, but, like the feeder drains, many are now blocked and the system of drainage has almost entirely broken down. Most of the lower terraces are water-logged and others are heavily overgrown. Nevertheless very few walls have collapsed and some of the middle and upper terraces are cultivated. On the broad, lake-facing slopes to the south of the *pila* (around the site of Pilco-Kayma) there are tiers of sloping terraces of more ordinary construction which likewise are still in use.

Agricultural terraces line the southwestern shores of Lake Titicaca from the base of the Copacabana peninsula to Paucarcolla, 10 kilometers to the north of Puno. They are especially prominent around Pomata, Juli,

104. Squier, 1877, 260, 269. Bowman (1924, 322) noted *andenes* in the Cayrani valley (? Chuyuncayani or upper Santiago).

105. Monheim, 1956.

106. There is some evidence that the water level has fallen in recent times (Raimondi [1864], 1908, 453; Agassiz, 1875, 268; Squier, 1877, 330; Neveu Lemaire, 1909, xlix-liii; Gilson, 1938, 534; Helmer, 1951, 121).

107. Gilson, 1938, 535; Parsons and Denevan, 1967, 100; Smith, Denevan and Hamilton, 1968, 353-67.

108. The juxtaposition of terraces and planting ridges has also been reported from the Jos Plateau of Nigeria (Netting, 1968, 59). Terraces and *chinampas* lie adjacent to each other on the southern edge of the basin of Mexico (*supra* p. 44).

109. Soria Lens (1954, 87) writes of old irrigation canals (not specifically connected with terracing) near the Río Desaguadero. La Barre (1948, 85) maintains that irrigation was never important among the Aymara.

110. Forbes (1870, 263) reported the cropping of terraces every fifth year. See also Kuczynski Godard, 1945, 32.

111. Casanova (1942, 340) refers to "la extraordinaria cantidad de andenes de cultivo," mostly abandoned, around Mocashi on the south side of the peninsula. Rydén (1947, 370) observed agricultural terraces at Poto-Poto, 3 kilometers south of San Pedro, and at the Pucará de Tiquina 4 kilometers to the north.

112. Cañahua *(Chenopodium pallidicaule)* appears to have declined in importance since the sixteenth century (Helmer, 1951, 131).

113. Rydén, 1947, 343-45.

114. W. C. Bennett, 1936, 460.

115. Towle, 1961, 134; Steward and Faron, 1959, 84.

116. Rydén, 1947, 327 (terraces for agriculture and buildings).

117. Bandelier, 1910, 5 ff. Ramos Gavilán (1621) (1886, 21) mentions the planting of coca here; this may imply terracing. For Coati (Isla de la Luna), see Squier, 1877, 360.

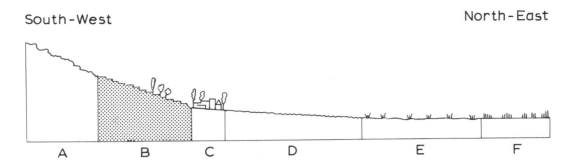

South-West   North-East

A B C D E F

Diagram 3.9

LAND-USE ZONES: BASIN OF LAKE TITICACA, NEAR CHUCUITO, PERU

A   Broken terraces, rock outcrops, *ichu* grass

B   Cultivated terraces

C   Settlement

D   Plough cultivation

E   Uncultivated wet land

F   Totora reed beds

Acora and Chucuito (diag. 3.9, fig. 3.83), places of considerable importance in pre-Columbian times.[118] Elsewhere, communities consisting of only three or four farms appear to have been responsible for much terrace construction.[119]

Between Puno and Paucarcolla, there are countless abandoned terraces;[120] cultivation is confined to some of the lower surfaces and to adjacent portions of the valley bottoms. Puna grass covers many square kilometers of old cropland. On the more exposed slopes wind erosion has removed all traces of former cultivation, and, where walls have collapsed, gully erosion has further destroyed the cropping surfaces (fig. 3.84). Old agricultural terraces have also been briefly reported from two islands off the Bay of Puno, Amantani[121] and Taquili.[122]

Fig. 3.83 Terraced plots overlooking Lake Titicaca, near Chucuito, Peru

118. Tschopik, 1946, 4, 7. Chucuito was the chief town of the Lupaqa kingdom (Murra, 1968, 115-51; Helmer, 1951, 121-122, 127). A. Kidder (1943, 13) and Kuczynski Godard (1945, 31-32) refer to terraces at Ichu, between Puno and Chucuito.

119. According to Tschopik (1946, 4), the majority of the Aymara lived in "clustered extended family compounds" at the time of the Spanish Conquest.

120. Bandelier (1905, 57) and also, apparently, S. S. Hill (1, 1860, 326) mention terraces here.

121. A. Kidder, 1943, 16.

122. Cano, 1952, 40; Matos Mar, 1957, 235, 239.

Fig. 3.84 Abandoned and eroded terraces between Puno and Paucarcolla, Peru

North of Paucarcolla a level *pampa,* formerly part of the lake, extends as far as the Río Cabanilla and the Río de Coata and westward along the valley of the Lampa. Large areas were at one time cultivated, judging from the amount of ridging. The piedmont hamlets are surrounded by small, sloping fields and in some cases a few terraces. The high ground north of the Coata-Lampa and above Cabanilla shows traces of old terracing which may extend eastward to the lake at Escalani.[123] Between Puno and Azangaro, C. R. Markham found "remains of *andenería,* or terraces for cultivation, rising in every direction tier above tier up the sides of the hills. But it is now almost exclusively a grazing country."[124] Along the valley of the Río de Pucará there are ridged fields, particularly near Lare, as well as terraces; the latter extend as far as Araranca (4127 meters) below the Nudo de Vilcanota. Abandoned terraces are particularly widespread on the slopes above Pucará itself and at Ayaviri.[125] They have similarly been reported around the archaeological site of Maukka-Llajta (10 kilometers northwest of Nuñoa).[126]

The highlands of Apolobamba-Pupuya: Valley-side terraces appear to be an important feature of the highlands to the northeast of Lake Titicaca, particularly beyond the watershed with the Amazon drainage system. There are large areas around Charazani, Kalulay and Curve,[127] and at Cuyo Cuyo (fig. 3.85) near the head of the Río Sandia.[128] Terraced fields in the vicinity of Sandia itself and at Patambuco have been described by W. H. Isbell. He writes of "super agricultural terracing . . . ruined villages and agricultural earthworks. . . . After the forest is cleared, long-forgotten stone-faced terraces come to light and serve the modern farmer much as they must have served their builders centuries ago. In fact, from the highest mountain sides to the tropical river edges, the ancient terraces are still farmed by a sizeable population of Quechua-speaking Indians. . . . Agricultural terracing is associated with all but the smallest [archaeological] sites and covers an enormous proportion of the land in the upper reaches of the mountain streams. . . . It is apparent that a great part of the valley of the Inambari River, from about 1200 meters to perhaps 800 meters above sea level, was in the past intensively cultivated on artificially leveled and stone-faced terraces. . . . The extensive terracing of the tropical *montaña* suggests that intensive agriculture was made necessary by the pressure on the land of a large population."[129]

Terracing for food crops probably spread from the Sierra to the flanks of the basin of the Amazon in pre-Inca times.[130] The distinctive terraces used in the cultivation of coca *(Erythroxylon coca)* may represent a secondary development within the *montaña.*

THE EASTERN YUNGAS

The Cordillera Real rises above the *altiplano* to the southeast of Lake Titicaca. The lower eastern flanks of the range are known as Las Yungas — a warm, moist and heavily forested region, comprising the *Medio Yunga* between about 2800 and 2200 meters above sea level, and the *Yunga Verdadero* below 2200 meters.[131]

In this part of Bolivia, agricultural terracing is widely associated with the cultivation of coca *(koka, cuca).* The

123. A. Kidder, 1943, 16.

124. Markham, 1862, 190.

125. A pre-Columbian town (Tschopik, 1946, 4); Pucará, too, was an important place (A. Kidder, 1943, 13). For an account of the economy today, see Sabogal Wiesse, 1961, 39-63.

126. Franco Inojosa and González, 1936, 158-59.

127. Vellard, 1963, 69, and pls. 3, 4 and 5.

128. Hodgson, 1951, 185; Isbell, 1968, 109. Markham (1862, 218) observed *andenería* "the upper tiers from 6 to 8 feet wide, but gradually becoming broader."

129. Isbell, 1968, 108-14.

130. Lathrap, 1962-3, 201; Evans and Meggers, 1968, 108; Bonavia and Rabines, 1967, 62. Earlier, however, the direction of cultural movement, including the spread of agriculture, may have been from the lowlands to the highlands (Lathrap, 1965, 798, and 1972, 13-23).

131. M. Cárdenas, 1941, 453.

Fig. 3.85 Terraces for tuber crops, Cuyo-Cuyo, Peru (Hodgson, 1950-1)

leaves of coca (containing cocaine, with anoretic and stimulative properties) are chewed, usually mixed with unslaked lime or ash derived from quinoa stalks *(llipta, llacta)*. Cultivation of the shrub long antedates the Spanish Conquest. Coca leaves were used medicinally and in religious ceremonies under the Incas[132] and production was controlled by the state.[133] The Spaniards encouraged, or at least permitted, wider use of the leaf, especially among Indians drafted into the silver mines,[134] and thence the practice spread until today it is found throughout the *altiplano*.

Erythroxylon coca[135] has a life cycle of about thirty-five years; the leaves of the mature shrub (pruned to heights of 50 to 75 cm) are normally picked three times a year. The chief areas of cultivation lie below 2500 meters. Coca terraces[136] — roughly 1 meter high and the same wide — occupy slopes of up to 60 degrees.[137] Some are faced with stone.[138] At the back of each step

132. Díez de Betánzos (1551) 1880, 67, 94, 104, 127; Cristóbal de Molina (c. 1552) 1968, 82; Murúa (1590) 1946, 288, 298; Santa Cruz Pachacuti-yamqui Salcamayhua (c. 1613) 1874, 79, 81; Gagliano, 1968, 230; Martin, 1970, 422-37.

133. Helmer (1549) 1955-6, 11, 14, 35; Jiménez de la Espada (ed) (1557) I, 1965, 177, 179; Polo de Ondegardo (c. 1560) 1873, 158; Santillán (1563-4) 1879, 115-18; Matienzo (1567) 1910, 89-90; José de Acosta (1590) I, 1880, 245; Garcilaso de la Vega (1604) 1871, 215, 372; L. N. Sáenz, 1938, 18; La Barre, 1948, 26; Gutierrez-Noriega, 1949, 143-45; Golte, 1970, 471-78. The Yungas formed part of the eastern frontier of the Inca realm from the middle of the fifteenth century (Nordenskiöld, 1917, 104; Bonavia and Rabines, 1967, 61-69).

134. Cieza de León (c. 1550) 1864, 353, 391; Capoche (1585) 1959, 175-76; Lizárraga (c. 1600) 1968, 63; Lewin (ed) (c. 1620) 1958, 21; Gagliano, 1963, 43-63.

135. Gosse, 1861; Gutierrez-Noriega and Von Hagen, 1951, 145-52.

136. Francisco Hernández (1571-6) (2, 1959, 238) describes coca *en hileras* (rows or ? tiers). According to Forbes (1870, 265), coca was "more seldom" grown on level ground (in furrows, *uachos,* separated by walls, *umachas)* than on terraced slopes. Markham (1862, 234, and 1880, 148) states that the former was a recent development.

137. Mortimer, 1901, 266; Brabant, 1908, 134; Troll, 1930, 396; M. Sáenz, 1933, 160.

138. Weddell, 1853, 519; Gibbon, 1854, 181-82; Forbes, 1870, 265; Markham, 1862, 229, 234; 1880, 148; La Barre, 1948, 68. See also Bowman, 1916, 77, and cf. Gade, 1975, 21 n. 7.

Fig. 3.86 Unfaced coca terraces, near Chulumani, Bolivia

there is a trench (fig. 3.86) into which seedlings are trans-planted.[139] The general purpose is to increase absorption of rain water while at the same time maintaining good drainage.[140] For this frequent hand cultivation is also desirable.[141] Ramírez (1597) wrote of "eras muy labradas" and of "limpiando y excabando la tierra" for coca,[142] which may be the earliest allusion to terracing.

The production of coca is now concentrated around Coroico, Coripata and Chulumani. L. Soria Lens also refers to coca terraces further north in the Yungas of Larecaja and to the south in the Yungas of Inquisivi, Aropaya (Independencia) and Loayza (Luribay).[143]

The coca terraces around Chulumani are known as *gradas* — or *takhanas* by the local Aymara-speaking population. Shaped with an adze-like implement (fig. 3.87), they are arranged in long sets, each about 10 meters wide (fig. 3.88). Sets of different age lie in close proximity, from freshly prepared series (fig. 3.89) to slopes on which the steps are now barely recognizable. Coffee shrubs are sometimes planted at irregular intervals along the *gradas* and mature fruit trees also may be specially reserved.

139. Matienzo (1567) (1910, 89-90), Hernández (1571-6) (2, 1959, 238), Ramírez (1597) (1936, 38), and Garcilaso de la Vega (1604) (1871, 373) mention the use of seed beds *(colchas)* or nurseries *(almácigas)*.

140. Parodi (1935, 125) writes, "son gradas semejantes a enormes escaleras. ...En tal forma el suelo es muy aereado, y por consiguiente ideal para aquellos cultivos; además el agua se infiltra, no lava la tierra y queda más tiempo a disposición de las plantas." See also Hooker, 1835, 166; Troll, 1930, 329; M. Sáenz, 1933, 166.

141. Hoes and "a small wooden shovel" are used (La Barre, 1948, 68; Walle, 1920, 176-78). Matienzo and Hernández remark upon the need for frequent working of the soil.

142. Ramírez, 1936, 38.

143. Soria Lens, 1954, 89. Vázquez de Espinosa (c. 1628) (1942, nos. 1630, 1885) mentions the cultivation of coca in Larecaja. In the province of Sandia, Markham (1862, 229) observed "stone terraces of coca." Luribay lies to the south of the Cordillera Real but is connected with the Yungas proper by the valley of the Río La Paz. For early evidence of the wider cultivation of coca in the *montaña* (but without reference to terracing) see Pedro Pizarro (1571-2) 2, 1921, 363; Vázquez de Espinosa (c. 1628) 1942, nos. 1044 (Colombia), 1547, 1550 (Peru), and 1682, 1688 (Bolivia); Cosme Bueno (c. 1770), 1951, 44, 45, 47, 48, 62, 64, 70, 110, 111, 117; Ernst, 1890, 230-43; Sauer, 1950, 540. Walger (1917) and Cooper (1949) include maps of the distribution of coca cultivation.

Fig. 3.87 Implements used in making coca terraces; locally manufactured

Fig. 3.88 Sets of coca terraces, Chulumani, Bolivia

Fig. 3.89 Recently prepared coca terraces (middle distance), Chulumani, Bolivia

E: Chile and Argentina

The semi-arid zone around the *altiplano* of northern Chile and northwest Argentina (map 3.14) has declined in importance since late pre-Columbian times.[144] There is every indication of a large reduction in the area of cropped land, partly, perhaps, on account of fluctuations in rainfall (presently about 250 mm to 500 mm per annum) or a gradual lowering of the water table.[145] The soils of the region are generally thin, and sites favorable for agriculture and terracing, such as outwash fans, the floors of tributary *arroyos* and piedmont tracts close to springs, are limited in extent and widely scattered.

CHILE

"Practically all cultivation [along the Andean piedmont of northern Chile] is accomplished through the use of terracing and irrigation."[146]

There are four main groups of terraced sites: *A,* east of Arica, along the middle and upper reaches of a number of small rivers, from the Río Lluta in the north to the Quebrada de Vitor in the south; *B,* inland from the Salar de Pintados and the Salar de Sur Viejo (both *A* and *B* flank the Cordillera Occidental); *C,* in the Calama basin and particularly around the headwaters of the Río Salado; and *D,* between the Salar de Atacama and the Cordillera de los Andes.

According to C. Field, about 60 percent of the terraces within zone *A* are abandoned, and the proportion for the entire piedmont is probably no less than this. Cross-channel terraces are best developed at Socaire *(D),* where some of the lower plots are still in use.[147] There are also well-constructed valley-floor terraces at Poroma and Tarapaca *(B).* Contour terraces (mostly stone-faced and artificially filled) are, however, more characteristic of the piedmont and of the southern Andes generally. The remarkably uniform *andenes* at Belén *(A)* and at Toconce, Topain,[148] Aiquina (fig. 3.90) and Cupo (fig. 3.91) in the Calama basin suggest Inca in-

fluence. Toconce "has the greatest display of intensive terracing with stylistic unity in Chile . . . a monument to extension of terracing by dogged persistence or, more likely, by determined planning and rule";[149] yet only about 15 percent of the total area of terraced land, namely that part most convenient for irrigation and closest to the village, is presently cultivated. This is a difficult site and some of the higher terraces were probably never adequately filled.

South of the Salar de Atacama, terracing is confined to a few valleys in the coastal range (as far as the Río Choapa) and much of it may date from colonial and modern times. Along the Río Elqui and the Río Huasco there is a notable development of narrow, excavated benches, in places supported by a few courses of stone. Most of these terraces are irrigated and many are planted to vines.

ARGENTINA

The terraced fields of Argentina have a discontinuous distribution within the Puna de Atacama and the basin-and-range country to the east of the Puna.[150] In the extreme north, there are two areas of terracing. The more westerly includes the Pucará de Rinconada (3950 meters), Casabindo,[151] Sayate and Cochinoca. The terraces are typically stone-faced benches. According to I. Bowman, those around the Pucará de Rinconada could not be satisfactorily irrigated today,[152] and the question of how, if at all, water was supplied to the terraces of Sayate and Casabindo was left in doubt by E. Boman in his account of the area in 1908.[153] Field concluded that irrigation was practiced to some extent at Casabindo and Cochinoca.

---

144. Much of the following discussion is based on Field (1966a). There are also descriptions of terraced sites (mostly in Argentina) in Boman (1908), Debenedetti *et al.* (1918, 1933-5), Bowman (1924), Ardissone (1928, 1943, 1944, 1945), Casanova (1934, 1936), Latcham (1938), Márquez Miranda (1939), Krapovickas (1955), Rohmeder (1955), Lafón (1956-7), Le Paige (1958), González and Reguiro (1960), Cigliano and Márquez Miranda (1961), Wright (1963), Gaignard (1965), and Suetta (1967).

145. *Supra* p. 36.

146. Field, 1966a, 61. For a general account of pre-Hispanic agriculture in Chile, see Latcham, 1936a.

147. Partly mapped by Field (1966a, 212, 217), showing broken walls, surviving fill and a few intact fields.

148. According to Le Paige (1958, 31), the terraces here "están dominadas por la acequia principal y separadas por pequeñas acequias de 15 a 20 cm de ancho, descendiendo cada 6 pasos. Estas últimas están constituídas por dos series de piedras planas de pie; es decir, que hay por lo menos 20 km de acequias pequeñas."

149. Field, 1966a, 180. See also Walcott, 1925, 345-66.

150. The archaeology of northwest Argentina is summarized in W. C. Bennett *et al.,* 1948. For pre-Hispanic agriculture, see Parodi, 1935, 115-67.

151. Rosen, 1904, 573, and 1924, 15.

152. Bowman, 1924, 320.

153. Boman (1908, 601-606) discusses the views of Tschudi (hand irrigation) and Rosen (canals), but inclines to the likelihood of climatic change. Bowman (1924, 321) writes: "The traces of water conduits encountered on the terraces of Sayate are interpreted as indicating the practical beginnings of a system of conserving the natural rainfall from terrace to terrace without permitting it to run off violently as it would do if left to take its natural course to the floor of the ravine."

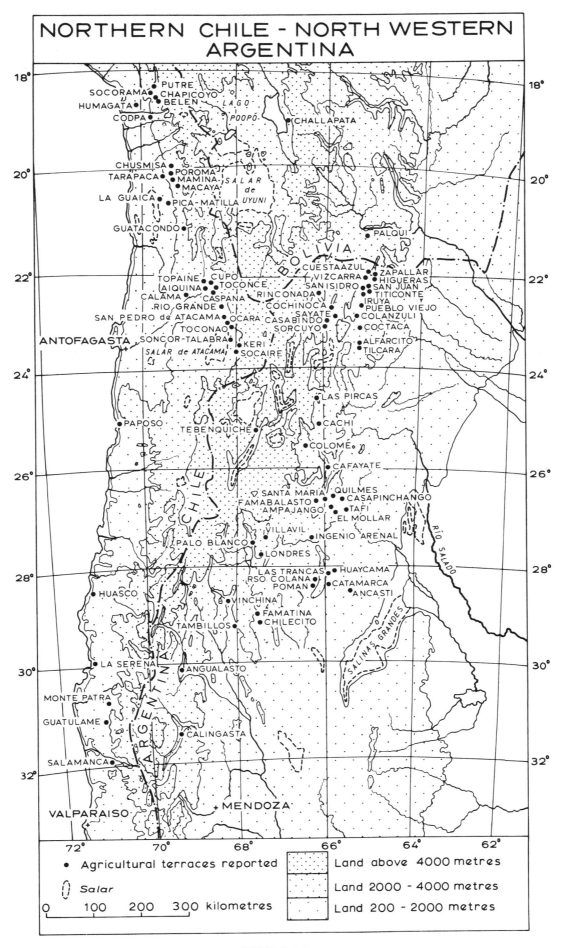

NORTHERN CHILE - NORTH WESTERN ARGENTINA

18°

SOCORAMA PUTRE
CHAPICOYO
HUMAGATA BELEN   LAGO
CODPA   POOPÓ   CHALLAPATA

20°

CHUSMISA
TARAPACA POROMA   SALAR
          MAMINA   de
          MACAYA
LA GUAICA PICA-MATILLA UYUNI

GUATACONDO   PALQUI

                        BOLIVIA

                        CUESTAAZUL ZAPALLAR
TOPAINE CUPO   VIZCARRA   HIGUERAS
AIQUINA   TOCONCE   SANISIDRO   SAN JUAN
CALAMA   CASPANA   RINCONADA   TITICONTE
RIO GRANDE   COCHINOCA   IRUYA
SAN PEDRO de ATACAMA OCARA SAYATE PUEBLO VIEJO
          TOCONAO CASABINDO   COLANZULI
SONCOR-TALABRA   SORCUYO   COCTACA
ANTOFAGASTA   KERI   ALFARCITO
          SALAR de ATACAMA SOCAIRE TILCARA

24°

                        LAS PIRCAS

PAPOSO   CACHI
        TEBENQUICHE

                        COLOMÉ

                        CAFAYATE

26°

                ▽ SANTA MARIA QUILMES CASAPINCHANGO
        FAMABALASTO   CASAPINCHANGO
          AMPAJANGO   TAFI
                   EL MOLLAR
                VILLAVIL
        PALO BLANCO   INGENIO ARENAL
                LONDRES

                LAS TRANCAS HUAYCAMA
                RSO. COLANA
                POMAN CATAMARCA
HUASCO   ANCASTI
        VINCHINA
           FAMATINA
        TAMBILLOS CHILECITO

        SALINAS GRANDES

LA SERENA
        ANGUALASTO

MONTE PATRA

GUATULAME
           CALINGASTA

SALAMANCA

VALPARAISO   + MENDOZA

72°   70°   68°   66°   64°   62°

• Agricultural terraces reported   Land above 4000 metres

◯ Salar   Land 2000 - 4000 metres

0   100   200   300 kilometres   Land 200 - 2000 metres

MAP 3.14

Fig. 3.90 Cultivated (alfalfa, maize) and irrigated terraces, Aiquina, Chile (C. Field, 1966a)

Fig. 3.91 Cultivated and irrigated terraces, Cupo (c. 3,300 meters), Chile (C. Field, 1966a)

Fig. 3.92 Abandoned terraces, Coctaca, Argentina (C. Field, 1966a)

The Quebrada Humahuaca includes two of the best known sites — Coctaca and Alfarcito. The benches of Coctaca[154] (fig. 3.92) are remarkable for their extent and regularity, suggesting careful planning and considerable experience in building. Like those of Alfarcito, they were irrigated by means of canals and sluices, but are now largely uncultivated. L. R. Parodi described the system of irrigation at Alfarcito as "las obras hidráulicas más ingeniosas de nuestra agricultura autóctona."[155] North of Humahuaca, agricultural terraces have been reported from Iruya[156] and from the Cordillera de Santa Victoria. The distribution undoubtedly extends into the eastern Puna of Bolivia. O. Schmieder noted abandoned terraces around the (? Inca) site of Palqui, northwest of Tarija and near the Río San Juan del Oro.[157] He could find no evidence of irrigation although cultivation would be impracticable without it today. Further north again, I. Bowman observed well-maintained and irrigated terraces on piedmont slopes near Challapata.[158]

South of the Quebrada Humahuaca there are five main areas of terracing: the Valle de Calchaquí[159] (Colomé and Las Pircas); the intermontane basin of Santa María or Campo Arenal (Ampajango, Quilmes, Pajanguillo,

154. Ardissone, 1928, 166; Gatto, 1934, 51; Casanova, 1934, 29-30 *(andenes* "construídos para mantener la tierra vegetal y approvechar más el agua"); Suetta, 1967, 1-9.

155. Parodi, 1935, 150. Debenedetti (1918, 293) suggests that "El Alfarcito fué exclusivamente destinado a la agricultura por una población que fijó su residencia fuera de la comarca, posiblemente en la vecina quebrada de Humahuaca." See also Imbelloni, 1926, fig. 105; Lafón, 1956-7, 43-59.

156. Márquez Miranda, 1939, 97, 106, 108. Debenedetti and Casanova (1933-5, 16-18) describing Titiconte, north of Iruya, observed "seis enormes terrazas escalonadas suavemente en la meseta de Titiconte, cuya superficie medida es de 11 hectáreas aproximadamente"; also "28 terrazas o gradas con sus correspondientes muros de contención, construídos sólidamente con lajas ajustadas en seco, pero perfectamente seleccionadas y distribuídas. Estos muros de contención no son continuos ni su altura es la misma. Muchos se han desmoranado, en parte, por la acción de las aguas pluviales filtradas; las piedras arrastradas han formado pequeños conos de deyección que permiten, con toda claridad y fijeza, precisar su procedencia."

157. Schmieder, 1926, 108. See also Rosen, 1924, 98 (Tarija).

158. Bowman, 1909, 182-83.

159. Ten Kate, 1894, 17.

Famabalasto and Ingenio de Arenal)[160] and the mountains to the east of the basin (Caspinchango and Tafí[161]); the southern and western piedmonts of the Sierra Curampaja (Londres and Palo Blanco); the foothills of the Sierra Ambato and the Sierra Ancasti (Pomán, Rosario Colano, Huaycamo, Ancasti and Las Trancas);[162] and the piedmont of the Sierra Famatina (Vinchina, Tam-

billos, Chilecito, Famatina and Campanas). Additionally, at Tebenquiche, within the Puna and near the northern end of the Salina de Antofalla, P. Krapovickas has reported *andenes* accompanied by irrigation ditches.[163]

As in Chile, excavated terraces are only common in the south where some are modern. Cross-channel terraces, although observed by Field at several widely scattered sites, notably Ancasti,[164] are nowhere typical. Stone-faced contour benches cover by far the largest area and probably well over 50 percent are abandoned and in various stages of decay. In the Rincón de Quilmes less than one-tenth of the terraced area is now cultivated.[165] It is possible that the great majority of the terraces in Argentina were irrigated, but clear evidence of this is absent from many sites.

160. Cigliano and Márquez Miranda, 1961, 153; Gaignard, 1965, 306-10.

161. González and Reguiro, 1960, 490-93. El Mollar (the most important site in the Tafí valley) includes "thousands of stone lines that mark the sites of ancient agricultural terraces. These are predominantly straight but there are also some curved ones. The stone lines are laid transversely to the slope of the hill." Similarly Santamarina, 1945, 14-15 ("grandes terrazas de cultivos construídas en las partes en donde el terreno ofrece major declive. . . . Estos andenes, especies de escalones con bordes de piedras, se encuentran a distancias que varían entre 5.8 y 10 metros aproximadamente, siguiendo las líneas sinuosas del terreno").

162. Ardissone, 1944, 93-107.

163. Krapovickas, 1955, 12 ("los *andenes* eran alimentados por acequías que, siguiendo el curso del arroyo, se continúan hasta arriba").

164. See also Ardissone, 1943, 6-7, and 1945, 383-416.

165. Field, 1966a, 358.

PART IV: DISCUSSION

Agricultural terracing belongs predominantly to the arid and semi-arid highlands of the New World. Toward the very dry northern and southern extremities of the overall distribution it may coincide with the local beginnings of cultivation based on irrigation. However, the earliest terraced sites almost certainly lie in less arid regions, from which dates around the middle of the first millennium B.C. are presently available. There were probably several, and possibly many, centers of origin of the most elementary terracing, for the pre-conditions were not notably specialized.

Soil and water: The intermontane levels were generally unfavorable for aboriginal cultivation. The reclamation of waterlogged bottom lands seems to have been a late and essentially localized development. Old and compact and/or saline soils, supporting grass or scrub, also were unpromising. On the other hand, patches of fresh alluvium along small valleys and *barrancas* probably invited cultivation, and their attractiveness could be enhanced by terracing that made use of natural processes. Cross-channel terracing served to concentrate the soil and water resources of limited catchments. Contour terracing stabilized valley- and basin-side cultivation over larger and more consolidated areas. In both cases, the most important effect was to increase the depth of soil and thereby its capacity to absorb and conserve moisture. Terracing everywhere preserved the normal advantages of cultivating slopes — good drainage and relatively frost-free surfaces — and, at the same time, countered the major disadvantages — thin soils, inadequate soil moisture, and gradients more or less unsatisfactory for purposes of irrigation.

The supply or control of water was also a central consideration in the preparation of agricultural surfaces in some of the flatlands of the New World: excavated fields *(hoyas)* to tap underground water in the lower valleys of coastal Peru, and ridged fields *(camellones)* in extensive lowlands and some intermontane basins to control the flow and distribution of surplus water. *Hoyas* and *camellones* are in several respects complementary to terraces, but all three denote attempts to create, by the movement of earth, physical conditions favorable for plant growth. They belong to the same category of cultural features as the hilling of soil around maize and the

preparation of mounds for tuber crops. Agricultural earthworks on whatever scale represent, like irrigation systems, the "investment of energy to produce more energy" in contrast to "monumental pyramids and massive walls [which take] energy out of circulation."*

Technology: Cross-channel terracing was associated with active soil erosion, possibly accelerated by the deliberate clearing of vegetation and stones. The stones could be used in the construction of retaining walls — a relatively easy task on gently sloping *barranca* floors between natural rock emplacements. In places, the presence of heightened walls and, especially, of buried walls, point to changes in the extent and arrangement of planting surfaces. Perhaps the artificial ponding of water, and thereby the accumulation of fertile alluvium, suggested the building of permanent soil dams along the courses of intermittent streams. Contour terracing, too, may have been prompted by the accumulation of soil behind rock outcrops, fallen trees, the walls of dwellings and, in the Andes, animal pounds. The next step could have been the deliberate alignment of loose stones where it was necessary or customary to remove these in the course of cultivation.

The artificial filling of contour terraces to produce a level surface represented an important advance. The preparation of a satisfactory soil profile was an operation calling for considerable knowledge and experience. So, too, was the construction of retaining walls across uneven terrain and under conditions of marked seasonal variation in the moisture content of the fill. The absence of stone seems rarely to have restricted terrace building, but the kinds of stone available (such as river cobbles, igneous fragments and slabs of sedimentary rock) help to account for differences in the height, width and structural characteristics of the walls. Terraces of selected stone are very common. Trimming to form regular courses is best exemplified at Inca sites, but is found elsewhere, for example near Texcoco and Tlaxcala (Mexico). Perhaps refinements in agricultural terracing owe something to the use of the platform or "terrace" in architecture. Certainly the standard of construction

_____

*B. J. Price, 1971, 35.

132

appears to be related to stone-working skills in general, with major centers in Mexico/Middle America and the central Andes. The Incas carried the art of stone working and terrace building to the point where it ceased to have mere utilitarian value. It combined aesthetic appeal with a demonstration of imperial power and might also be partly interpreted as an obsession arising from the intrinsic difficulty of shaping stone without tough metal implements.

Many contour terraces have been partly excavated, but excavation alone is comparatively rare. Slopes of deeply weathered volcanic ash, highly permeable and cohesive upon exposure to the atmosphere, have been shaped into terraces, for example within the intermontane basins of western Guatemala. Where no stone is employed, the sloping faces of the terraces represent land lost to cultivation. Valley-floor terraces and contour terraces built on aprons of unconsolidated material and over outwash fans also involve excavation, but in such cases stone is usually available and has been widely employed in wall construction. The movement of exceptionally large amounts of earth must have been necessary in the case of some valley-floor terraces, such as those behind Ollantaitambo (Peru).

Valley-floor and contour terraces shaped in deep alluvium or colluvial deposits are (or were) commonly associated with canal irrigation. To increase the depth of soil could hardly, in such cases, have been a reason for terracing. Canal irrigation was also practiced on many filled terraces, and it probably served to raise the standard of construction generally. A level or graded surface was desirable for the even distribution of water, and questions of drainage, soil profile and wall construction assumed greater importance where irrigation was practiced. Although by no means all terraces were irrigated, there was a broad correspondence between the distribution of terracing in the highlands of the New World and the distribution of irrigation, either by controlled flooding or by canals. The extent of hand irrigation is scarcely determinable, but it could have been of considerable importance where more elaborate methods were impossible or inappropriate.

Irrigation and terracing rested upon similar skills and experience. Terracing not merely stabilized existing cultivation, it also served to extend agriculture into climatically marginal areas, and this was particularly the case where terracing and irrigation were combined. Consequently any significant reduction in water supply, for whatever reason, was likely to be followed by a comparable reduction in the cultivated area.

Economy: At the time of the Spanish Conquest, the overwhelming majority of the population of the New World depended upon agriculture, although very large areas were still lightly occupied by hunting and collecting folk. The unstable northern frontier of agriculture extended deep into Mexico (map 2.1). Within the agricultural zone as a whole there were large and important differences in food staples, methods of cultivation and plant reproduction, but only in the central Andes was animal husbandry of any consequence. In areas of high civilization and dense population, agriculture was a well-understood art. There was much curiosity about the natural world and a remarkable corpus of knowledge concerning the behavior and properties of plants and the ecological conditions appropriate to each. Moreover, agriculture had considerable social status as an occupation. The "good" farmer was widely admired. It is against this generally favorable background that the presence of specialized forms of farming, and advances in agriculture generally, have to be considered.

Terracing fitted well into the prevailing pattern of pre-Columbian agriculture. Fields were characteristically small. Cultivation depended upon hand implements, which effectively limited the scale of individual operations and, to some extent, the general distribution of cultivation, but not the quality or intensity of land use. This ranged from temporary, bush-fallow agriculture to continuously worked and artificially fertilized house gardens. The leveled house-and-garden plot was probably a starting point for some valley-side terracing. Around the homestead, experimentation would be encouraged by daily observation, and any improvements could be most easily maintained. Early advances in the direction of terracing may perhaps be traced to the dumping of refuse, to the tending of special plants, and to irrigation by hand. The construction of a wall around a hillside croft must often have produced the appearance of a terrace.

There were many "systems" of pre-Columbian agriculture, and several might be found within the limits of a single highland township. Terraced fields were usually combined with other, mostly less intensive, forms of cultivation. Terracing, especially with irrigation, must have led to improved yields and, possibly more important, to less fluctuation between years. It also had the effect of concentrating production, which was an important advantage where transportation facilities (between field and homestead, and between town and country) were everywhere poor. Terracing alone was not a basis for continuous cultivation but, like fixed-plot agriculture generally, it undoubtedly served to regularize the cycle of land use and to shorten the period of fallow. It introduced greater variety and thereby greater security into the overall pattern of farming. Probably there was always a tendency — widely observable today — for the nearer (and better maintained) terraces to be used more intensively than those further afield. The former are often close in form and function to house gardens, to which they may also be adjacent.

There is almost no direct information on what crops were grown on terraced fields in pre-Columbian times. But from later reports, and from the very wide extent of terracing, it can safely be assumed that the staple food crops had high priority. The special kind of terracing associated with the cultivation of coca is an interesting exception. It was probably derived from more generalized Andean forms.

Terracing is found in two major agricultural provinces of the New World, one dominated by the cultivation of seed crops, chiefly maize, and the other by temperate tuber crops, including the potato. Maize, beans and squash, a Middle American trio, often grown together in the same plot, are very responsive to improved physical conditions (deeper soil, more moisture, greater freedom from frost) and higher standards of cultivation. Tubers generally require deep and free-draining soil, and ridging or mounding, as well as terracing, provided this. It is probable that some terraces, like house gardens, were reserved for special varieties of food crops, and for such as condiments, plants with ceremonial significance, and preferred fruit trees. In any event, the extension of ecological conditions through terracing, combined with improved standards of management, must have encouraged the selection of new varieties. The attention given to individual plants under hand cultivation was probably the basis for the large number of varieties present in the aboriginal New World.

Society: Terraced fields, however extensive, cover only a fraction of the highlands of Middle and South America. The distribution is related to that of population at different times in the past and more specifically to the distribution of settlement. Beyond this, it becomes a question of perception by the individual, community or, exceptionally, the state of the benefits to be derived from terracing, and of the will and technical resources to overcome the problems of construction. Culturally and geographically, the process was very selective.

It is obviously difficult to generalize concerning highland settlement in pre-Columbian times. There is considerable archaeological evidence of changes in regional patterns. Nevertheless, two categories of site appear to have been especially common: piedmont sites, above valley bottoms or intermontane levels; and hill-top or ridge-top sites (now frequently abandoned). The latter invited the cultivation of surrounding slopes which might later be improved by contour terracing and/or by the building of cross-channel terraces in adjacent *barrancas*. Piedmont sites offered a choice between sharply contrasting terrain. It is suggested that the piedmont zone itself and then the adjacent slopes were generally preferred to the flatlands. About 1500, many basin levels appear to have been entirely uncultivated. The most notable exceptions probably lay in those parts of the Andean *altiplano* where the *taclla* was employed.

Terracing characteristically involved a large investment of time and labor. It therefore probably contributed to social stability, complementing the security gained by the improvement and diversification of agriculture. Selective improvements in land use must also have reinforced any tendency to social stratification based on property. Terraced fields were a territorially defined and assignable asset which also required regular care and attention. In such ways an attachment to place and a sense of continuity through time might be induced and fostered.

How terrace building was organized can usually only be inferred from the nature of the enterprise and the surviving pattern of fields (in use and abandoned). It was a task that lent itself to piecemeal and discontinuous effort by nuclear or extended families. In some areas, the local landowning group (*calpulli* in Mexico, *ayllu* in Peru) was probably important. Irrigation often involved cooperation at the village or inter-village level, but the only clear example (albeit a very important one) of large-scale planning and the use of directed labor in terracing is provided by the work of the Incas.

Terracing *per se* does not imply high population densities. To estimate former densities from abandoned terraces one must know over what period they were constructed and whether or not they were left fallow for several years in succession (as is commonly the case today). At the same time, terraced agriculture, combined with irrigation, apparently did support high rural densities in the major centers of New World civilization. Here too, from the classic period onward, there was a growing urban, or at least non-agricultural, population that was maintained by tribute or through a system of markets. This suggests that rising population numbers encouraged improvements in land use, and that such improvements, in turn, permitted the growth of population and greater occupational specialization. The initiation and maintenance of substantial field-works also meant a more fully employed peasantry. Consequently, the precipitous, and ultimately very large, reduction in the size of the Indian population in the two centuries or so after the Spanish Conquest was followed by a comparable, or even proportionately greater, contraction in the area of cultivated land. Population decline after c. 1520 was undoubtedly the chief cause of the abandonment or gross neglect of terraced fields, and the process was carried further by the implementation of policies of *congregación* and by the gradual expansion of agriculture on level terrain. The reasons for abandonment before the conquest were probably chiefly

134

physical, specifically critical fluctuations in rainfall or available ground water (the incidence of this being directly related to the general level of aridity) and deterioration in soil fertility or soil texture on account of continuous cropping, wind erosion, poorly structured fill, and the accumulation of harmful minerals under conditions of inadequate irrigation and/or drainage. Abandoned terraces are highly vulnerable to gully erosion, and many are now barely recognizable landmarks in the settlement history of the New World.

Postscript: The study of agricultural terracing in the New World has scarcely begun. The Andes north of the Inca realm and the *montaña* generally deserve more attention. In the Maya province, several areas invite research: the northeastern half of the highlands of Chiapas, the adjacent flanks of the Alto Cuchumatanes, Baja Verapaz, and the Vaca plateau of British Honduras. From central Mexico, we have Carl Sartorius's enigmatic reference to extensive areas of abandoned terraces along the eastern piedmont. Conversely, the association between terracing and irrigation is still well exemplified, but little explored, at sites along the southern slopes of the neo-volcanic range. Integrated systems of great age also survive near Texcoco, within the basin of Atitlán (Guatemala), and around Arequipa (Peru).

APPENDIX

SITES WITH AGRICULTURAL TERRACING

ORDER OF ENTRIES

SYMBOLS AND ABBREVIATIONS

Place names in italics indicate that information is based wholly or in part on field observations.

c.	hill, ridge *(cerro)*
v.	valley (also *barranca, quebrada, cuenca, arroyo*)
*	not located on map
**	located outside areas covered by regional maps
(?)	*agricultural* terraces ?
/	area between . . . and . . .

FORM

ct	contour terraces
cc	cross-channel terraces
vf	valley-floor terraces
sf	stone-faced

USE

wu	wholly or largely in use
sa	substantial abandonment
wa	wholly or almost wholly abandoned
i	wholly or partly irrigated today
fi	formerly irrigated (field and/or documentary evidence)

AREA	FORM				USE					AUTHORITY
MEXICO										
CENTRAL MEXICO										
Ajusco	ct	cc		sf	wu					
Atlixco	ct				wu			i		
Calpulalpan	ct				wu					
Cerro Zacatepec (Pedregal)										Palerm, 1961
Chalco/Atlapulco/San Gregorio/Xochimilco	ct	cc		sf	wu					
Chalco/Ozumba	ct				wu					
Coatepec			vf		wu			i		
Coatlinchán	ct			sf				i		
Ixtapan de la Sal	ct				wu					
Laurel*	ct									McBride, 1923
Maquixco Alto	ct	cc		sf	wu			i		Sanders, 1965
Milpa Alta	ct	cc		sf	wu					
San Pablo Oxtotepec San Pedro Atohopan San Lorenzo										aerial photograph
Otumba/Aguatepec	ct			sf		sa				
Ozumba/Chimalhuacán/ San Miguel Atlauta	ct				wu					
San Andrés Totoltepec	ct	cc		sf	wu					
San Miguel Tlaíxpan/ Purificación	ct			sf		sa		i	fi	Alva Ixtlilxochitl (c. 1640), 1891-2; Palerm and Wolf, 1954-5, 1961; Palerm, 1955
San Nicólas Tlaminca	ct			sf		sa		i		Wolf and Palerm, 1955; Palerm and Wolf, 1961; Coy, 1966
Tecaxio/Calixtlahuaca	ct			sf	wu					García Payón, 1941
Tenancingo	ct				wu					Patiño, 1940; H. H. Bennett, 1944; Wolf, 1959
Teotihuacán v.	ct	cc		sf		sa		i	fi	Sanders, 1965, 1968, 1971
Tepeji del Río/ Tezontepec	ct			sf	wu					aerial photograph
Tepotzlán	ct		vf		wu					
Tetzcutzingo c.	ct			sf			wa		fi	Wolf and Palerm, 1955; Palerm and Wolf, 1961; Coy, 1966

AREA	FORM					USE					AUTHORITY
	ct	cc	vf	sf		wu	sa	wa	i	fi	
Tochimilco	ct			sf		wu			i		
Tula/San Marcos	ct			sf		wu			i		S. F. Cook, 1949 b.
Xochimilco	ct	cc		sf		wu					Sanders, 1971
EAST CENTRAL MEXICO											
Iztacamaxtitlán/ Santiago Zautla	ct					wu					Armillas, 1961; aerial photograph
San Cristóbal Tepongtla	ct	cc		sf		wu					
San Pablo Yauhquemehcán	ct	cc		sf		wu					
Tepeaca/Huizcolotla/ Tecamachalco	ct			sf		wu			i		
Texmelucán	ct	cc				wu			i		
Tlahuapan	ct			sf		wu			i		
Tlaxcala/Tizatlán/ San Sebastián Atlahpa	ct			sf		wu					Caso, 1927; H. H. Bennett, 1942
Tozihuac (?)	ct							wa			aerial photograph
WEST CENTRAL MEXICO											
Apatzingán				sf				wa			Goggin, 1943; I. Kelly, 1947
Chachahuatlán (?)	ct			sf				wa			I. Kelly, 1949
Chilchota	ct		vf	sf		wu			i	fi	Paso y Troncoso and Vargas Rea (eds.) (1579), 1944; West, 1947; Armillas, 1961
Huetamo (?)											Osborne, 1943
Respaldo c.	ct			sf			sa				Lister, 1947-8
Santiago (?)											Osborne, 1943
Tzintzúntzan/ Pátzcuaro	ct	cc		sf		wu			i		West, 1947
Zirándaro (?)				sf							Osborne, 1943
NORTH WEST MEXICO											
Bavispe v.		cc		sf				wa			Lumholtz, 1902; Sauer and Brand, 1931; Howard and Griffiths, 1966
Caborca											L. Herold, 1965
Casas Grandes											McCabe, 1955; Johnson, 1963

AREA	FORM			USE				AUTHORITY
Florida v. (?)			sf					Kelley, 1956
Fuerte v.		cc	sf	wu				Lumholtz, 1902
Gavilan v.	ct	cc	sf			wa		McCabe, 1955; L. Herold, 1966
Nacori		cc	sf					Lumholtz, 1902
Piedras Verdes (Cave) v.	ct	cc	sf			wa		Lumholtz, 1902; Blackiston, 1905-6; L. Herold, 1965; Howard and Griffiths, 1966
Quitovaquita (?)			sf			wa		Ives, 1936
Tres Ríos		cc	sf			wa		Howard and Griffiths, 1966
Tunal v. (?)			sf					Kelley, 1956
Verde v. (canyon)		cc	sf	wu				Pennington, 1969
THE MIXTECA								
Achiutla/Tilantongo			sf	wu				Burgoa (1674), 1934
Ajalpan						wa		Byers, 1964
Coixlahuaca	ct	cc	sf		sa			
Huajuápan/Nochixtlán	ct	cc	sf					
Mogote del Cacique								Spores, 1967
Nochixtlán v.	ct	cc			sa			Peña, 1950; Spores, 1967, 1969
Santiago Apoala	ct	cc	sf		sa			aerial photograph
Santiago Yolomécatl	ct	cc	sf	wu			i	
Silacayoápam								A. Caso *pers. comm.*, 1966
San Jerónimo Otla	ct	cc	sf		sa			aerial photograph
Santa María Apaxco	ct	cc	sf		sa			aerial photograph
San Martin Huamelálpam	ct	cc	sf	wu			i	
San Mateo Xindihui/ San Miguel Piedras	ct	cc	sf		sa			aerial photograph
Tamazulapám	ct	cc	sf	wu			i	
Tehuacán Basin								MacNeish, 1962; Smith, 1965; Jiménez Moreno, 1966
Teotongo	ct		sf		sa			
Tilantongo/Monte Negro								Caso, 1938, *pers. comm.,* 1966; Armillas, 1948; Jiménez Moreno, 1966; Spores, 1967
Yanhuitlán	ct	cc	sf		sa			aerial photograph
Zapotitlán	ct	cc	sf			wa		

AREA	ct	cc	sf	wu	sa	wa	i	fi	AUTHORITY
OAXACA									
Amatlán	ct		sf		sa				
Guelatao	ct		sf		sa				
Hierve el Agua	ct		sf			wa		fi	Neely, 1967; Flannery *et al.*, 1967
Ixtepeji	ct		sf		sa				
Lachatao	ct	cc	sf		sa				Schmieder, 1930
Mitla	ct		sf		sa				
Monte Albán (Atzompa)	ct		sf			wa			Bandelier, 1884; Armillas, 1948; Bernal, 1966
Ozolotepec								fi	Paso y Troncoso (ed.) (1580), 1905; Spores, 1966
San Juan Chicomezúchil	ct	cc	sf		sa		i		
San Miguel del Río	ct		sf		sa				
Yagul/Tlalixtac de Cabrera	ct		sf	wu					
Yahuiche	ct		sf	wu			i		
CHIAPAS									
Aguacatenango	ct	cc	sf		sa				R. M. Adams, 1961; L. E. Guzmán, 1962
Amatenango	ct		sf			wa			
Chamula/Saklamantón	ct	cc	sf		sa				
Chamula/Zinacantán		cc	sf			wa			
Chincultik			sf			wa			Palacios, 1928
Colonia Jalisco	ct		sf			wa			local information
Colonia Veracruz	ct		sf			wa			local information
Comitán	ct		sf		sa				O. F. Cook, 1909, 1919; Blom, 1927; Palacios, 1928; Lundell, 1940
Gracias á Dios		cc							Blom, 1927
Grijalva v. (?)									Lowe and Mason, 1966
Juncaná (?)						wa			Basauri, 1931
La Venta v.		cc							Lowe and Mason, 1966
Ocosingo			sf						O. F. Cook, 1909, 1919; Lundell, 1940; McBryde, 1945
San Francisco	ct		sf			wa			
Teopisca	ct	cc	sf			wa			Blom, 1927

AREA	FORM					USE					AUTHORITY
Tonolá (?)	ct										Palacios, 1928; Hewett, 1936; Ferdon, 1953
Villa Las Rosas	ct										R. M. Adams, 1961; Hill, 1964
THE UNITED STATES											
Alkali Ridge		cc		sf							Brew, 1946
Chapin Mesa	ct	cc		sf				wa			Rohn, 1963
Citadel Ruin	ct			sf				wa			Stewart and Donnelly, 1943
First Mesa	ct	cc		sf			wu				Stewart, 1940; Hack, 1942
Gila v.	ct			sf						fi	Stewart, 1940; Woodbury, 1962
Graham Mountains											Woodbury, 1962
Kayenta											Woodbury, 1962
Marsh Pass											Kidder and Guernsey, 1919
Mesa Verde	ct	cc		sf							Stewart, 1940; Stewart and Donnelly, 1943; J. Herold, 1961; Erdman *et al.*, 1969
Navajo Mountains	ct										Stewart and Donnelly, 1943
Point of Pines		cc		sf							Woodbury, 1961 a, 1962
Second Mesa		cc									Colton, 1932; Woodbury, 1962
Superstition Mountains											Woodbury, 1962
GUATEMALA											
ALTO CUCHUMATANES AND VERA PAZ											
Cobulco											O. F. Cook, 1909
Jacaltenango							wu				O. F. Cook, 1909; Lundell, 1940
Quen Santo				sf							Seler, 1901
Rabinal				sf							O. F. Cook, 1909
Todos Santos	ct	cc	vf	sf			wu				Stadelman, 1940

AREA	FORM				USE			AUTHORITY
WEST CENTRAL GUATEMALA								
Chacayá	ct			sf	wu		i	
Chichicastenango	ct				wu			
Cucal (?)								A. L. Smith, 1955
Mejicanos						wa		Borhegyi, 1959
Quezaltenango	ct			sf	wu			
San Antonio Sacatepequez	ct		vf	sf	wu			
Santa Catarina Palopó/ San Antonio Palopó	ct			sf	wu		i	Lothrop, 1933
Santa Cruz del Quiche								O. F. Cook, 1909
San Marcos	ct		vf	sf	wu			
Sololá/Panajachel	ct			sf	wu		i	Lothrop, 1933; McBryde, 1945
Toloxcoc (?)								A. L. Smith, 1955
Totonicapán/San Cristóbal/ San Francisco el Alto	ct				wu			O. F. Cook, 1909; McBryde, 1945
Xolchún (?)				sf				Burkitt, 1930; A. L. Smith, 1955
Zunil	ct	cc		sf	wu		i	
BRITISH HONDURAS								
Arenal				sf		wa		
Benque Viejo				sf		wa		
Chalillo*				sf		wa		Ower, 1927; Gann, 1928; Lundell, 1940; J. E. Thompson, 1931, 1965; Romney *et al.*, 1959; Rice, 1974
Cohune				sf		wa		
Retiro				sf		wa		
Vaca				sf		wa		
Valentin				sf		wa		
Cubietas Viejas				sf				Hopkins, 1968

AREA		FORM				USE		AUTHORITY
HONDURAS								
Choluteca v.				sf				Stone, 1957
VENEZUELA								
Acequias				sf				Lares, 1883 and 1952; Jahn, 1927; Alvarado, 1945
Apartaderos/San Rafael	ct	cc	vf	sf	wu			Vogt, 1946
Aricagua				sf				Febres Cordero, 1894 and 1926; Acosta Saignes, 1952
Chachopo	ct		vf	sf	wu			
Jajó	ct			sf	wu			Vogt, 1946
Mucuchíes/Mucurubá	ct		vt	sf	wu			Gasparini, 1962
Timotes			vt	sf	wu			
Tuñame								local information
COLUMBIA								
BOYACÁ-CUNDINAMARCA								
Chocontá	ct						wa	Haury, 1953; Haury and Cubillos, 1953; Broadbent, 1964, 1965
Chulo v.								Haury and Cubillos, 1953
Facatativá (Pueblo Viejo)	ct						wa	Haury, 1953; Haury and Cubillos, 1953; Broadbent, 1964
Gachancipá	ct					sa		Haury and Cubillos, 1953; Donkin, 1968
Saucío	ct						wa	Fals-Borda, 1962; Donkin, 1968
Tabío	ct						wa	Broadbent, 1964
Tocancipá	ct				wu			Haury, 1953; Haury and Cubillos, 1953; Broadbent, 1964, 1965; Donkin, 1968
Tunja								Haury, 1953; Haury and Cubillos, 1953

AREA	FORM				USE				AUTHORITY
NORTHERN COLOMBIA									
La Mesa	ct			sf			wa		G. and A. Reichel-Dolmatoff, 1959
Luruaco				sf					G. Reichel-Dolmatoff, 1965
Nechí v.				sf					G. Reichel-Dolmatoff, 1965
Piojó				sf					G. Reichel-Dolmatoff, 1965
Pueblito				sf			wa		G. Reichel-Dolmatoff, 1954, b.
San Lucas Mountains				sf					G. Reichel-Dolmatoff, 1965
Santa Rosa/Mokotáma	ct			sf			wa	fi	Wallaston, 1925; Reichel-Dolmatoff, 1950, 1953; G. and A. Reichel-Dolmatoff, 1951
Tubará	ct			sf					Angulo Valdés, 1951, 1963; Nachtigall, 1961; G. Reichel-Dolmatoff, 1965
Vista Nieve (?)				sf					Mason, 1931-9
ECUADOR									
Ambato	ct			sf	wu				
Bahuanche (?)									W. C. Bennett, 1946
Cajabamba/Tixán/Alausí/ Guasuntos/Chunchi	ct			sf	wu			i	
Carapali (?)									Collier and Murra, 1943
Cerro de Hojas	ct	cc		sf			wa		Saville, 1907; Estrada, 1962
Cerro Jaboncillo	ct	cc		sf			wa		Estrada, 1962
Guando (?)				sf					Collier and Murra, 1943
Otavalo	ct				wu				United States Department of Agriculture, 1943
Palmira									Collier and Murra, 1943
Pimampíro	ct			sf			wa		D. A. Preston *pers. comm.* and photograph
Pizhín (?)									W. C. Bennett, 1946
Puruhá (Narrío)				sf					Crespo Toral, 1926; Collier and Murra, 1943

AREA	FORM				USE			AUTHORITY
PERU								
BASIN OF TITICACA, PUCARÁ VALLEY, AND HIGHLANDS OF APOLOBAMBA-PUPUYA								
Acora	ct		sf		sa			
Amantani Island								A. Kidder, 1943
Araranca	ct		sf			wa		
Ayaviri	ct		sf			wa		
Cabanilla	ct		sf			wa		
Calapuja	ct		sf			wa		
Capachica peninsula	ct							C. T. Smith *et al.*, 1968
Chucuito	ct		sf		sa			Tschopik, 1951
Chuquibambillo		cc	sf			wa		
Cumana Island								W. C. Bennett, 1936
Cuyo Cuyo	ct		sf		sa			Markham, 1862; Mortimer, 1901; Hodgson, 1951; Isbell, 1968
Escallani (Sillustani)								Pardo, 1942; A. Kidder, 1943
Hacienda Machacmarca	ct							C. T. Smith *et al.*, 1968
Ichu	ct		sf		sa			A. Kidder, 1943; Kuczynski Godard, 1945
Lampa v.	ct		sf			wa		
Maukka-Llajta								Franco Inojosa and González, 1936
Patabuco	ct		sf		sa			Isbell, 1968
Pomata/Juli	ct		sf		sa			
Pucará (?)	ct		sf			wa		Montesinos (c. 1640), 1920
Puno/Azangaro	ct		sf		sa			Markham, 1862
Puno/Paucarcolla	ct		sf		sa			S. S. Hill, 1860
Sandia	ct		sf		sa			Isbell, 1968
Taquili Island								Cano, 1952; Matos Mar, 1957
VALLEYS OF THE RÍO VILCANOTA-URUBAMBA								
Andenes								Ishida, 1960
Aguas Calientes/Marangani	ct	wa			sa			Ishida, 1960

AREA	FORM					USE					AUTHORITY
Calca											Ishida, 1960
Chinchero	ct					wu					Núñez del Prado, 1949
Choquesuysuy	ct			sf				wa			Fejos, 1944; Ishida, 1960
Cusipata	ct			sf		wu					
Cuzco	ct			sf							Cieza de León (c. 1550), 1883; Las Casas (1527-59), 1958; P. Pizarro (1571-2), 1921
Huinay Huinay	ct			sf				wa			Ishida, 1960
Inty Pata	ct			sf				wa			Fejos, 1944; Ishida, 1960
Larapa											Ishida, 1960
Llaullipata								wa			Rowe, 1944; Ishida, 1960
Machu Picchu	ct			sf				wa		fi	O. F. Cook, 1916 a.; Ishida, 1960
Moray	ct			sf			sa			fi	Rowe, 1944; Ishida, 1960
Ollantaitambo/Urubamba	ct		wa	sf			sa		i	fi	P. Pizarro (1571-2), 1921; Wiener, 1880; Bowman, 1916; Bingham, 1925; O. F. Cook, 1925; Poindexter, 1930; Pardo, 1946; Trimborn, 1959; Ishida, 1960
Oropesa Basin (Pikillacta, Rumiccolca)				sf				wa			Bingham, 1922; Rowe, 1944; Caballero Farfán, 1959; Ishida, 1960
Panticalla v.								wa			O. F. Cook, 1916 a.
Pechar	ct			sf		wu					Ishida, 1960
Phuyu Pata Marka	ct			sf				wa			Fejos, 1944; Ishida, 1960
Pisac	ct			sf			sa		i	fi	O. F. Cook, 1925; Rowe, 1946; Tosi, 1960; Ishida, 1960
Quiquijana	ct			sf		wu					
Salapunco	ct			sf				wa			Llanos, 1936; Ishida, 1960; photograph
Sapantiana	ct			sf							Ishida, 1960; photograph
Sayac Marka	ct			sf							Fejos, 1944; Ishida, 1960
San Gerónimo	ct							wa			Platt, 1942; Ishida, 1960
Sicuani		cc		sf			sa				
Tambomachay											Ishida, 1960
Tinta	ct						sa		i		O. F. Cook, 1916 b.

AREA	FORM			USE					AUTHORITY
Torontoy									O. F. Cook, 1916 a.; Ishida, 1960
Yucay	ct		sf	wu				i	Squier, 1877; Bingham, 1922; Rowe, 1946; Ishida, 1960
Zurite Basin (Xaquixaguana)	ct		sf		sa				Cieza de León (c. 1550), 1864; Markham, 1856; Ishida, 1960; photograph
NORTHERN HIGHLANDS									
Abiseo v. (?)	ct		sf			wa			Bonavia, 1968 b.
Balsas			sf			wa			Reichlen, 1950
Blanca, Cordillera	ct		sf			wa			Kinzl, 1950
Cajabamba	ct	.	sf			wa			McCown, 1945
Cajamarca/Chachapoyas (?)									Maw, 1829
Casma v.	ct								Tello, 1956
Huánuco Basin**									Lathrap, 1970
Atcor	ct			wu					
Auchi	ct			wu					
Chacabamba	ct			wu					
Chinchacocha	ct			wu					
Guacor	ct			wu					Ortiz de Zúñiga (1562), I, 1967, II, 1972
Guaya	ct			wu					
Queros	ct			wu					
Tancor	ct			wu					
Yacán	ct			wu					
Huaraz (Ayapampa, Kekamarca, Wilkawain)			sf						W. C. Bennett, 1944a
Huailas (Pueblo Viejo, Parián)	ct					wa	fi		Doughty, 1968
Jesús/Rondos (Kénac, Chicrin, Konje)	ct		sf		sa				Flornoy, 1955-6
Negra, Cordillera									Dobyns, 1963
Pajatén	ct		sf			wa			Rojas Ponce, 1966, 1967
Tuctucocha Basin	ct		sf						Wiener, 1880
Utcubamba v. (?)									Langlois, 1933; W. C. Bennett, 1944a

AREA	FORM				USE					AUTHORITY
CENTRAL HIGHLANDS										
Caballoyuq**	ct			sf			wa			Bonavia, 1964
Canta										Paz Soldán, 1862
Chancay v.										Horkheimer, 1962
Chanchamayo v.										Lathrap, 1970
Chosica (Palomar)	ct	cc		sf			wa		fi	Gamarra Dulanto and Maldonado, 1945; Regal, 1945; Horkheimer, 1958
Condoruchku**	ct			sf			wa			Bonavia, 1967-8, 1968 b.
Matukalli**	ct			sf			wa			Bonavia, 1964
Moyopampa	ct			sf			wa		fi	Hutchinson, 1873; Latcham, 1936; Gamarra Dulanto and Maldonado, 1945
Pacarán				sf			wa		fi	Pulgar Vidal, n.d.
Poma-Ticlio							wa		fi	Pulgar Vidal, n.d.
Raqaraqay**	ct			sf			wa			Bonavia, 1964
Santa Inés	ct			sf			wa		fi	Gamarra Dulanto and Maldonado, 1945; Horkheimer, 1958
Tarma/Tarmatambo	ct	cc	vf	sf	wu			i		Tosi, 1960; Dyer, 1962
Uchuihuamanga**	ct			sf			wa			Bonavia, 1967-8, 1968 b.
Wari (?)	ct			sf			wa			W. C. Bennett, 1953
Yanacotá v. (Parárá)	ct			cf			wa		fi	Hutchinson, 1873; Gamarra Dulanto and Maldonado, 1945
SOUTHERN HIGHLANDS										
Andahua v.	ct			sf		sa				Shippee, 1932b; Armillas, 1961
Antabamba	ct			sf						aerial photograph
Cailloma	ct			sf						Shippee, 1932b
Churajón	ct			sf					fi	Regal, 1945; Bernedo Málaga, 1949; Ishida, 1960; Rowe, 1963
Colca v.	ct			sf		sa				Johnson and Platt, 1930; Shippee, 1932b; W. C. Bennett, 1946a
Coporaque	ct			sf		sa				Shippee, 1932b
Cotahuasi v. (Huaynacotas)	ct			sf		sa		i		Bowman, 1916; Bingham, 1922
Huatalacac	ct			sf			wa			Ishida, 1960
Lampa v. (Colta)										Bingham, 1922

AREA	FORM			USE					AUTHORITY
	ct	vf	sf	wu	sa	wa	i	fi	
Lari	ct		sf						Shippee, 1932 b
Llanca	ct		sf						Shippee, 1932 b
Mollebaya	ct		sf					fi	Bernedo Málaga, 1949
Parinacochas Basin									Bingham, 1922
Piaca	ct		sf					fi	Bernedo Málaga, 1949
Pincholla	ct		sf						Johnson and Platt, 1930; Shippee, 1932b; Kubler, 1946
Pocsi	ct		sf					fi	Bernedo Málaga, 1949
Puquina	ct		sf					fi	Bernedo Málaga, 1949
Quinistacas	ct		sf					fi	Bernedo Málaga, 1949
Sabandia/Characato (Arequipa)	ct	vf	sf		sa		i		Paz Soldán, 1862; C. T. Smith, 1960
Salamanca	ct		sf	wu					Bowman, 1916
Sarito de Pucará*	ct		sf			wa			Ishida, 1960
Yanque*	ct		sf						Means, 1932
Yarabamba	ct		sf					fi	Bernedo Málaga, 1949

BOLIVIA

ALTIPLANO AND
HIGHLANDS OF
APOLOBAMBA-PUPUYA

AREA	FORM			USE					AUTHORITY
	ct	vf	sf	wu	sa	wa	i	fi	
Apolobamba Highlands									Vellard, 1963
Arque	ct		sf	wu			i		
Challapata	ct			wu					Bowman, 1909
Charazani v.	ct		sf						Vellard, 1963
Chiripa			sf						Steward and Faron, 1959; Towle, 1961
Copacabana	ct		sf	wu					Vellard, 1963
Cumana Island									W. C. Bennett, 1936
Curve v.	ct		sf						Vellard, 1963
Kululay	ct		sf						Vellard, 1963
Koati Island (Isla de la Luna)					sa				Bingham, 1922; Cano, 1952
Mocachi	ct		sf		sa				Casanova, 1942
Muyuquira	ct		sf	wu			i		
Poto Poto	ct		sf						Rydén, 1947
Pucará de Khonkho	ct		sf			wa			Rydén, 1947
Pucará de Tiquina	ct		sf						Rydén, 1947
San Pablo	ct		sf	wu					Vellard, 1963
San Pedro	ct		sf	wu					Vellard, 1963
Sacaba	ct		sf	wu			i		
Santiago v.	ct				sa				Squier, 1877; Bowman, 1924

AREA	FORM				USE				AUTHORITY
Taquiri Island	ct		sf						Rydén, 1947
Titicaca Island (Isla del Sol)	ct		sf		sa			fi	Squier, 1877; Bandelier, 1905 a., 1910; Gregory, 1913; Cano, 1952; Vellard, 1963
EASTERN YUNGAS									
Apita*									Soria Lens, 1954
Ayopaya (Independencia)									Soria Lens, 1954
Chulimani	ct				wu				La Barre, 1948
Coripata	ct		sf		wu				La Barre, 1948
Coroico	ct				wu				La Barre, 1948
Curihuati*									Soria Lens, 1954
Espiritu Santo	ct		sf						Gibbon, 1854
Inquisivi									Soria Lens, 1954
Larecaja									Soria Lens, 1954
Loayza (Luribay)									Soria Lens, 1954
Lomagrande*									Soria Lens, 1954
Los Angeles*									Soria Lens, 1954
Palqui						wa			Schmieder, 1926
Santa Barbara*									Soria Lens, 1954
Wara*									Soria Lens, 1954
Wila Wila*									Soria Lens, 1954
CHILE									
Aiquina	ct		sf		wu		i	fi	Walcott, 1925; Wright, 1963; Field, 1966 a.
Belén	ct		sf			sa	i		Wright, 1963; Field, 1966 a.
Calama							i		Field, 1966 a.
Calar	ct								Le Paige, 1958
Caspana	ct								Le Paige, 1958
Chapicoyo	ct		sf						Field, 1966 a.
Chusmisa			sf						Field, 1966 a.
Codpa	ct		sf				i		Wright, 1963; Field, 1966 a.
Cupo	ct		sf				i		Field, 1966 a.

AREA	FORM				USE			AUTHORITY
Guatacondo	ct	cc	sf				i		Field, 1966 a.
Guatulame	ct		sf				i		Field, 1966 a.
Hatchar	ct								Le Paige, 1958
Huasco	ct		sf				i		Field, 1966 a.
Humagata	ct		sf				i		Field, 1966 a.
Keri	ct							fi	Le Paige, 1958
La Guaica									Field, 1966 a.
La Serena	ct						i		Field, 1966 a.
Macaya	ct		sf				i		Field, 1966 a.
Mamina	ct	cc	sf				i		Field, 1966 a.
Monte Patria			sf				i		Field, 1966 a.
Ocara	ct								Le Paige, 1958
Paposo	ct		sf				i		Field, 1966 a.
Pica-Matilla	ct		sf				i		Field, 1966 a.
Poroma	ct	cc	sf				i		Field, 1966 a.
Putre	ct		sf				i		Field, 1966 a.
Río Grande	ct					wa			Le Paige, 1958
Salamanca	ct		sf				i		Field, 1966 a.
Socoroma	ct		sf				i		Field, 1966 a.
Socaire	ct	cc	sf				i		Field, 1966 a.
Soncor y Talabre	ct								Le Paige, 1958
San Pedro de Atacama	ct		sf				i		Field, 1966 a.
Talikuma	ct								Le Paige, 1958
Tarapaca	ct		sf				i		Field, 1966 a.
Toconao	ct		sf		sa		i		Field, 1966 a.
Toconce v.	ct	cc	sf		sa		i		Walcott, 1925; Field, 1966 a.
Topain	ct					wa		fi	Le Paige, 1958
ARGENTINA									
Alfarcito	ct	cc	sf		sa		i	fi	Debenedetti, 1918; Parodi, 1935; Casanova, 1936, 1946; Bennett *et al.*, 1948; Bennett and Bird, 1949; Lafón, 1956-7; Field, 1966 a.
Ampajango	ct		sf				i		Field, 1966 a.

AREA	FORM				USE				AUTHORITY
	ct	cc	sf		sa	wa	i	fi	
Ancasti (Cuerva v.)		cc	sf			wa			Ardissone, 1943, 1945; Bennett and Bird, 1949; Field, 1966 a.
Angualasto							i		Field, 1966 a.
Cafayete									Ardissone, 1945
Calingasta									Field, 1966 a.
Casabindo	ct		sf				i		Boman, 1908; Rosen, 1904, 1924; Casanova, 1946; Field, 1966 a.
Caspinchango	ct		sf				i		Field, 1966 a.
Chilecito	ct						i		Field, 1966 a.
Cochinoca	ct		sf				i		Field, 1966 a.
Coctaca	ct	cc	sf		sa		i	fi	Ardissone, 1928; Casanova, 1934, 1936, 1946; Gatto, 1934; Parodi, 1935; Bennett *et al.,* 1948; Bennett and Bird, 1949; Field, 1966 a.; Suetta, 1967
Colanzulí									Márquez Miranda, 1939
Colomé	ct		sf						Field, 1966 a.
Cuesta Azul									Márquez Miranda, 1939
Famabalasto		cc	sf						Field, 1966 a.
Famatina	ct	cc	sf				i		Field, 1966 a.
Higueras									Márquez Miranda, 1939, 1954
Huaycama	ct		sf						Field, 1966 a.
Ingenio Arenal	ct		sf						Cigliano and Márquez Miranda, 1961; Field, 1966 a.
Iruya	ct		sf				i		Márquez Miranda, 1939; Field, 1966 a.
Las Pircas			sf						Field, 1966 a.
Las Trancas	ct		sf			wa		fi	Ardissone, 1944; Field, 1966 a.
Londres	ct						i		Field, 1966 a.
Pajanguillo	ct		sf						Field, 1966 a.
Palo Blanco	ct	cc	sf				i		Field, 1966 a.
Pelado*	ct		sf						Field, 1966 a.
Poman	ct	cc	sf				i		Field, 1966 a.
Pucará de Rinconada									Bowman, 1924
Pueblo Viejo									Márquez Miranda, 1939

AREA	FORM					USE				AUTHORITY
Quilmes	ct			sf		sa		i		Field, 1966 a.
Rosario Colana	ct			sf				i		Field, 1966 a.
Sayate v.				sf						Boman, 1908; Bowman, 1924; Casanova, 1946
San Isidro										Márquez Miranda, 1939
San Juan										Márquez Miranda, 1939
Santa María v.			vf	sf						Gaignard, 1965
Sorcuyo	ct			sf			wa			Casanova, 1936
Tafí del Valle	ct	cc		sf			wa			Santamarina, 1945; Rohmeder, 1955; González and Regueiro, 1960; Field, 1966 a.
Tala v.										Larrouy, 1914
Tambillos	ct									Field, 1966 a.
Tebenchique									fi	Krapovickas, 1955
Tilcara (El Pucará)	ct			sf			wa			Bennett *et al.,* 1948; Casanova, 1970
Titiconte				sf					fi	Debenedetti and Casanova, 1933-5; Márquez Miranda, 1939; Bennett *et al.,* 1948
Villavil	ct							i		Field, 1966 a.
Vinchina	ct							i		Field, 1966 a.
Vizcarra										Márquez Miranda, 1939
Zapallar										Márquez Miranda, 1939

LITERATURE CITED

ACOSTA, JOAQUÍN
1848   *Compendio histórico del descubrimiento y coloniza-ción de la Nueva Granada en el siglo décimo sexto,* Paris

ACOSTA, JOSÉ DE
1880   *The Natural and Moral History of the Indies* [1590], trans. and ed. C. R. Markham, Hakluyt Society, 60, 61, London

ACOSTA SAIGNES, M.
1952   "El área cultural prehispánica de los Andes Vene-zolanos" *Archivos Venezolanos de Folklore,* I, 45-80 (published separately, Caracas, 1952, 30 pp.)
1958   "Los timoto-cuicas, un pueblo previsivo" *El Farol,* 20, 2-7
1961   *Estudios de Etnología Antigua de Venezuela,* Cara-cas

ADAMS, R. M.
1961   "Changing settlement patterns of territorial organi-zation in the Central Highlands of Chiapas, Mexico" *American Antiquity,* 26, 341-60

ADAMS, R. N.
1966   *A Community in the Andes: Problems and Progress in Muquiyanyo,* American Ethnological Society, New York

AGASSIZ, A.
1875   "Hydrographic sketch of Lake Titicaca" *Proceed-ings of the American Academy of Arts and Sciences,* 3, 283-92

AGUADO, PEDRO DE
1906   *Recopilación historial resolutoria de Sancta Marta y Nuevo Reino de Granada de las Indias del Mar Océano* [1581], Biblioteca Historia Nacional, 5, Bogotá
1916-17   *Historia de Santa Marta y Nuevo Reino de Granada* [1581], 2 volumes, Real Academia de la Historia, Madrid

AGUIRRE BELTRÁN, G.
1952   *Problemas de la población indígena de la Cuenca del Tepalcatepec,* Instituto Nacional Indigenista, (México): Memorias, 3

ALLEN, P. (ed)
1842   *History of the expedition under the command of Cap-tains Lewis and Clarke* (1804-1806), 2 volumes, New York

ALVA IXTLILXOCHITL, FERNANDO DE
1891-2   *Obras Históricas* [c. 1640], ed. A. Chavero, 2 vol-umes, México

ALVARADO, L.
1945   *Datos Etnográficos de Venezuela,* Caracas

ALVARADO, PEDRO DE
1924   *An account of the conquest of Guatemala in 1524,* trans. and ed. S. J. Machie, Cortés Society, 3, New York

ALVARADO TEZOZOMOC, FERNANDO DE
1949   *Crónica Mexicayotl* [c. 1598] (traducción directa del Náhuatl por Adrian León) México, 1949

ALVAREZ DEL VILLAR, J.
1952   "Esquema geobotánico de Chiapas" *Boletín de la Sociedad Mexicana de Geografía y Estadística,* 73, 97-124

AMARAM, D. W.
1937   "Eastern Chiapas" *Geographical Review,* 27, 19-36

AMBROSETTI, J. B.
1904   *El Bronce en la Región Calchaquí,* Anales del Museo Nacional de Buenos Aires, 11, 163-314

AMIRAN, D. H. K.
1966   "Man in Arid Lands, II: Patterns of Occupance" in E. S. Hills (ed) *Arid Lands: A Geographical Apprais-al,* U.N.E.S.C.O., Paris, 239-54

AMIRAN, D. H. K., and Y. KEDAR
1959   "Techniques of ancient agriculture in the Negev of Israel" *XVIIIe. Congrès International de Géographie* (Rio de Janeiro, 1956), *Actes de Congrès,* I, 206-17

ANCONA, L. H.
1933a   "El ahuautle de Texcoco" *Anales del Instituto de Biología* (México), 4 (1), 51-69
1933b   "Los jumiles de cuautla *Euschistus zopilotensis"* *Anales del Instituto de Biología* (México), 4 (2), 103-8

ANDA, L. DE
1951   "El cultivo de maíz en Chiapas" *Ateneo,* I, 64-71

ANDAGOYA, PASCUAL DE
1865   *Narrative of the proceedings of Pedrarias Davila in the provinces of Tierra Firme or Castilla del Oro, and the discovery of the South Sea and the coasts of Peru and Nicaragua* [c. 1540], trans. and ed. C. R. Mark-ham, Hakluyt Society, 34, London

ANDERSON, E., and R. H. BARLOW
1943   "The maize tribute of Moctezuma's Empire" *Annals of the Missouri Botanical Garden,* 30, 413-20

ANDREWS, E. W.
1943   *The Archaeology of Southwestern Campeche,* Car-negie Institution of Washington, Contributions to American Anthropology and History, 8, publication 546, 1-100

ANGHIERA, PIETRO MARTIRE D'
1912   *De Orbe Novo Decades* [c. 1516], trans. and ed. F. A. MacNutt, 2 volumes, London

ANGULO VALDÉS, C.
1951   *Arqueología de Tubará,* Divulgaciones del Instituto de Investigación Etnológica 2, Barranquilla
1963   "Cultural Development in Colombia" in B. J. Meggers and C. Evans (eds) *Aboriginal Cultural Development in Latin America: An Interpretative Review,* Smithsonian Miscellaneous Collections, 146, Washington, 55-66

ANONYMOUS
1889   "Coca" *Royal Botanical Gardens, Kew: Bulletin of Miscellaneous Information,* 25, 1-13
1903   *Manuscrit Ramírez: Histoire de l'origine des Indiens que habitent la Nouvelle Espagne selon leurs traditions,* ed. and trans. D. Charnay, Recueil de Voyages et de Documents pour servir à l'Histoire de la Géographie depuis le XIIIe. jusqu'à la fin du XVIe. siècle, 19, Paris
1917   *Narrative of some things of New Spain and of the Great City of Temestitan, Mexico, written by the anonymous conqueror, a companion of Hernan Cortés* [c. 1530], trans. and ed. M. H. Saville, Cortés Society, 1, New York
1943   "Soil conservation in South America" *Agriculture in the Americas,* 3, United States Department of Agriculture, Washington

ANTEZANA, O.
1952   "Las heladas y la agricultura" *Nimbus,* 3, 17-30

APENES, O.
1943   "The *tlateles* of Lake Texcoco" *American Antiquity,* 9, 29-32
1947   *Mapas antiguos del Valle de México,* México

ARDISSONE, R.
1928   "Coctaca" *Gaea: Anales de la Sociedad Argentina de Estudios Geográficos,* 3, 160-66
1943   "Construcciones agrícolas indígenas en Ancasti" *Gaea: Boletín de la Sociedad Argentina de Estudios Geográficos,* 5, 6-7
1944   "Andenes en la Cuenca del Torrente de Las Trancas" *Relaciones de la Sociedad Argentina de Antropología,* 4, 93-109
1945   "Las Pircas de Ancasti: Contribución al conocimiento de los restos de andenes en el Noroeste de la Argentina" *Gaea: Boletín de la Sociedad Argentina de Estudios Geográficos,* 7, 383-416

ARMILLAS, P.
1944   "Mexiquito, gran ciudad arqueológica en la cuenca del río de las Balsas" *El México Antiguo,* 6, 261-62
1946   "Los Olmeca-xicalanca y los sitios arqueológicos del soroeste de Tlaxcala" *Revista mexicana de estudios antropológicos,* 8, 137-45
1948   "A sequence of cultural development in Meso America" *Memoirs of the Society for American Archaeology,* 4, 105-11
1949   "Notas sobre sistemas de cultivo en Meso-américa: cultivos de riego y humedad en la cuenca del río de las Balsas" *Anales del Instituto Nacional de Antropología e Historia* (México), 3, 85-113
1951   "Mesoamerican fortifications" *Antiquity,* 25, 77-86
1961   "Land use in pre-Columbian America" in L. D. Stamp (ed) *A History of Land Use in Arid Regions,* U.N.E.S.C.O., Paris, 255-76
1962   *Program of the History of America, I: The Native Period in the History of the New World,* Instituto Panamericano de Geografía e Historia, Comisión de Historia, publicación 265
1964   "Northern Mesoamerica" in J. D. Jennings and E. Norbeck (eds) *Prehistoric Man in the New World,* Chicago, 291-330
1966   "Los orígenes del cultivo en el Nuevo Mundo: antecedentes y procesos de desarrollo" *XXXVI International Congress of Americanists* (Sevilla, 1964): *Proceedings,* I, 175-80
1969   "The arid frontier of Mexican civilization" *Transactions of the New York Academy of Sciences,* 31, 697-704
1971   "Gardens on swamps" *Science,* 174, no. 4010, 653-65

ARMILLAS, P., A. PALERM, and E. R. WOLF
1956   "A small irrigation system in the Valley of Teotihuacán" *American Antiquity,* 21, 396-99

ASCHMANN, H.
1955-6   "Hillside farms, valley ranches: land clearing costs and settlement patterns in South America" *Landscape,* 5, 17-24
1960   "The subsistence problem in Mesoamerican history" *Social Science Monographs* 10: *Middle American Anthropology,* 2, Pan American Union, Washington, 1-11

AVILA, FRANCISCO DE (compiler, 1598-1608)
1873   *A narrative of the errors, false gods, and other superstitions and diabolical rites in which the Indians of the province of Huarochiri lived in ancient times* [1608], in C. R. Markham (trans. and ed) *Narratives of the Rites and Laws of the Yncas,* Hakluyt Society, 48, 121-47, London
1966   *Dioses y Hombres de Huarochiri: narración quechua recogida por Francisco de Avila* [?1598] (traducción: José María Arguedas), Lima

BAESSLER, A.
1906   *Altperuanische Metallgeräte,* Berlin

BALDWIN, M. *et al.*
1954-5   "Soil Erosion Survey of Latin America" *Journal of Soil and Water Conservation,* 9-10, 158-68, 214-19, 223-29, 237, 275-80

BALLESTEROS, T. DE (ed)
1752   *Ordenanzas del Perú,* Lima

BANDELIER, A. F.
1884   *Report of an Archaeological tour of Mexico in 1881,* Papers of the Archaeological Institute of America, 2
1892   *Final Report of Investigations among the Indians of the Southwestern United States carried on mainly in the years from 1880 to 1885,* Papers of the Archaeological Institute of America, 3, 4,
1905a   "The basin of Lake Titicaca" *Bulletin of the American Geographical Society,* 37, 449-60
1905b   "The aboriginal ruins at Sillustani, Peru" *American Anthropologist,* 7, 49-68
1910   *The Islands of Titicaca and Koati,* Hispanic Society of America, New York

BARBER, R. K.
1932 *Indian Labor in the Spanish Colonies,* Historical Society for New Mexico, Publications in History, 6, Albuquerque

BARLOW, R. H.
1949a "El Codice Azcatitlan" *Journal de la Société des Americanistes de Paris,* 38, 101-35
1949b *The extent of the empire of the Culhua-Mexica,* Ibero Americana, 28, University of California, Berkeley

BARON CASTRO, R.
1959 "El desarrollo de la población hispano-americana, 1492-1950" *Cahiers d'histoire mondiale,* 5, 325-43

BARRIENTOS, C. E.
1923 "La agricultura en el Imperio de los Incas" *Revista de Arqueología* (Lima), I, 15-19

BARTLETT, J. R.
1854 *Personal narrative of explorations and incidents in Texas, New Mexico, California, Sonora, and Chihuahua,* 2 volumes, London and New York

BASAURI, C.
1931 *Tojolabales, Tzeltales y Mayas,* México

BATAILLON, C.
1966 "L'axe néovolcanique dans la géographie du Mexique central" *Revista Geográfica,* 64, 17-28

BAUDIN, L.
1927 "Les communautés agraires du Pérou précolombién" *Revue d'Histoire Economique et Sociale,* 15, 302-20
1929 "L'organisation économique de l'Empire des Incas" *Revue de L'Amérique Latine,* 17, 385-93
1962 *El Imperio Socialista de los Incas,* 5th. ed., Santiago de Chile

BAZAN PÉREZ, T.
1939 "La Mixteca y sus condiciones actuales" *Boletín de la Sociedad Mexicana de Geografía y Estadística,* 51, 297-315

BEALS, R. L.
1932 *The comparative ethnology of northern Mexico before 1750,* Ibero Americana, 2, University of California, Berkeley
1945 *Ethnology of the Western Mixe,* University of California Publications in American Archaeology and Ethnology, 42, Berkeley and Los Angeles
1946 *Cherán: A Sierra Tarascan Village,* Smithsonian Institution, Institute of Social Anthropology, 2, Washington

BEARD, J. S.
1944 "Climax vegetation in Tropical America" *Ecology,* 25, 127-58
1953 "The savanna vegetation of northern Tropical America" *Ecological Monographs,* 23, Durham, N.C. 149-215

BEEK, K. J., and D. L. BRAMAO
1968 "Nature and Geography of South American Soils" in E. J. Fittkau *et al.* (eds) *Biogeography and Ecology in South America,* I: Monographiae Biologicae, 18, The Hague, 82-112

BELSHAW, M.
1967 *A village economy: land and people of Huecorio,* New York

BENNETT, H. H.
1925 "Some geographical aspects of western Ecuador" *Annals of the Association of American Geographers,* 15, 126-47
1942 "Soil erosion and its control" *Proceedings of the Eighth American Science Congress,* 5, 331-47
1944 "Food comes from the soil" *Geographical Review,* 34, 57-76

BENNETT, W. C.
1936 *Excavations in Bolivia,* Anthropological Papers of the American Museum of Natural History, 35, New York, 329-509
1944a *The North Highlands of Peru: Excavations in the Callejón de Huaylas and at Chavín de Huántar,* Anthropological Papers of the American Museum of Natural History, 39, New York
1944b *Archaeological Regions of Colombia,* Yale University Publications in Anthropology, 30, New Haven
1946a "The Andean Highlands: An Introduction" in J. H. Steward (ed) *Handbook of South American Indians,* 2, Smithsonian Institution, Bureau of American Ethnology, Bulletin 143, Washington, 1-60
1946b "The archaeology of the Central Andes" *ibid.,* 61-147
1946c "The Atacameño" *ibid.,* 599-618
1946d *Excavations in the Cuenca Region, Ecuador,* Yale University Publications in Anthropology, 35, New Haven
1949 "Engineering" in J. H. Steward (ed) *Handbook of South American Indians,* 5, Smithsonian Institution, Bureau of American Ethnology, Bulletin 143, Washington, 53-65
1950-1 "Cultural unity and disunity in the Titicaca Basin" *American Antiquity,* 16, 89-98
1953 *Excavations at Wari, Ayacucho, Peru,* Yale University Publications in Anthropology, 49, New Haven

BENNETT, W. C. and J. B. BIRD
1949 *Andean culture history,* The American Museum of Natural History, handbook series, 15, New York

BENNETT, W. C., E. F. BLEILER, and F. H. SOMMER
1948 *Northwest Argentina Archaeology,* Yale University Publications in Anthropology, 38, New Haven

BENNETT, W. C., and R. M. ZINGG
1935 *The Tarahumara: An Indian Tribe of Northern Mexico,* Chicago

BERLIN, H. (ed)
1948 *Anales de Tlatelolco* (from *La historia de Tlatelolco desde los tiempos mas remotos* [1528]), México

BERNAL, I.
1948-9 "Exploraciones en Coixlahuaca, Oaxaca" *Revista Mexicana de Estudios Antropológicos,* 10, 5-76
1953 *Excavations in the Mixteca Alta,* Mesoamerican Notes, 3
1958 "Archaeology of the Mixteca" *Boletín Estudios Oaxaqueños,* 7, 1-12
1965 "Archaeological synthesis of Oaxaca" in G. R. Willey (ed) *Handbook of Middle American Indians,* 3, Austin, 788-813

BERNEDO MÁLAGA, L.
1949 *La cultura puquina o prehistoria de la provincia de Arequipa,* Lima

BERTONIO, L.
1612   *Vocabulario de la Lengua Aymara,* Juli, Perú

BEVAN, B.
1938   *The Chinantec: report on the central and southeastern Chinantec region,* I: *The Chinantec and their habitat,* Instituto Panamericano de Geografía e Historia, 24, México

BINGHAM, H.
1916   "Further explorations in the land of the Inca" *National Geographic Magazine,* 29, 431-73
1917   "The Inca Peoples and their Culture" *XIX International Congress of Americanists* (Washington, 1915): *Proceedings,* 253-60
1922   *Inca Land,* London
1948   *The Lost City of the Incas,* New York

BISHKO, C. J.
1952   "The Peninsular background of Latin American cattle ranching" *Hispanic American Historical Review,* 32, 491-515

BLACKISTON, A. H.
1905   "Cliff dwellings of northern Mexico" *Records of the Past,* 4, 355-61
1906   "Cliff ruins of Cave Valley, northern Mexico" *Records of the Past,* 5, 5-11

BLANTON, R. E.
1972   Prehispanic adaptation in the Ixtapalapa region, Mexico," *Science,* 175, no. 4028, 1317-26

BLOCH, I.
1906   "Der Ursprung der Syphilis (Morbus americanus)" *XIV International Congress of Americanists* (Stuttgart, 1904): *Proceedings,* I, 57-79

BLOM, F.
1927   *Tribes and Temples,* 2 volumes, New Orleans
1932   "Archaeological and other maps of Middle America" *Ibero-Amerikanisches Archiv,* 6, 288-92

BLÜTHGEN, J.
1964   *Allgemeine Klimageographie,* Lehrbuch der Allgemeinen Geographie, 2, Berlin

BOBAN, E.
1891   *Documents pour servir à l'histoire du Mexique,* 2 volumes, Paris

BOLINDER, G.
1937   "Archaeological researches in the tableland about Bogotá" *Ethnos* (Stockholm), 2, 130-32

BOLLAERT, W.
1863-4   "Observations on the past and present populations of the New World" *Memoirs of the Anthropological Society of London,* I, 73-119

BOLTON, H. E. (ed)
1919   *Kino's Historical Memoir of the Pimería Alta, 1683-1711,* Cleveland

BOMAN, É.
1908   *Antiquités de la région andine de la République Argentine et du Désert d'Atacama,* 2 volumes, Mission Scientifique G. de Créqui Montfort et E. Sénéchal de la Grange, Paris

BONAVIA, D.
1964   "Investigaciones en la Ceja de Selva de Ayacucho" *Arqueológicas,* 6, 1-55
1967-8   "Investigaciones arqueológicas en el Mantaro Medio" *Revista del Museo Nacional* (Lima), 35, 211-94
1968a   "Nucleos de población en la Ceja de Selva de Ayacucho" *XXXVII International Congress of Americanists* (Mar del Plata, 1966): *Proceedings,* I, 75-83
1968b   *Las Ruinas de Abiseo,* Universidad Peruana de Ciencias y Tecnología, Lima

BONAVIA, D., and R. RABINES
1967   "Las fronteras ecológicas de la civilización andina" *Amaru,* 61-69

BORAH, W.
1960   "Sources and possibilities for the reconstruction of the demographic process in the Mixteca Alta" *Revista Mexicana de Estudios Antropológicos,* 16, 159-71
1962a   "Population decline and the social and institutional changes of New Spain in the middle decades of the sixteenth century" *XXXIV International Congress of Americanists* (Vienna, 1960): *Proceedings,* 172-78
1962b   "América como modelo? El impacto demográfico de la expansión europea sobre el mundo no europea" *Cuadernos Americanos,* 6, 176-85 (reprinted in English in *XXXV International Congress of Americanists* (Mexico, 1962): *Proceedings,* 3, 1964, 379-87)

BORAH, W., and S. F. COOK
1960   *The population of Central Mexico in 1548: an analysis of the Suma de visitas de pueblos,* Ibero Americana, 43, University of California, Berkeley
1963   *The aboriginal population of Central Mexico on the eve of the Spanish Conquest,* Ibero Americana, 45, University of California, Berkeley
1967   "New demographic research on the sixteenth century in Mexico" in H. F. Cline (ed) *Latin American History: Essays on its Study and Teaching, 1898-1965,* 2, Austin and London, 717-23 (earlier published as "La despoblación del México Central en el siglo XVI" *Historia Mexicana,* 12, 1962, 1-12)

BORDA, M. L.
1942   *Historia del Tucumán: Siglo XVI,* Tucumán

BORHEGYI, S. F. DE
1956   "Settlement patterns in the Guatemalan Highlands: past and present" in G. R. Willey (ed) *Prehistoric settlement patterns in the New World,* Viking Fund Publications in Anthropology, 23, New York, 101-106
1959   "Underwater archaeology in the Maya highlands" *Scientific American,* 200, 100-113
1964   "Pre-Columbian cultural similarities and differences between the highland Guatemalan and tropical forest Mayas" *XXXV International Congress of Americanists* (Mexico, 1962): *Proceedings,* I, 215-24
1965a   "Archaeological synthesis of the Guatemalan highlands" in G. R. Willey (ed) *Handbook of Middle American Indians,* 2, Austin, 3-58
1965b   "Settlement patterns in the Guatemalan highlands" *ibid.,* 59-75

BORREGÁN, ALONSO
1948   Crónica de la conquista del Perú [1562-65], ed. R. Loredo, Escuela de Estudios Hispano-Americanos de Sevilla, 48, Sevilla

BOWMAN, I.
1909a   "Man and climatic changes in South America" Geographical Journal, 33, 267-78
1909b   "The highland dweller of Bolivia" Bulletin of the Geographical Society of Philadelphia, 7, 159-84
1916   The Andes of southern Peru, New York
1924   Desert Trails of Atacama, American Geographical Society, special publication 5, New York

BRABANT, W. VAN
1908   La Bolivie, Paris

BRAINERD, G. W.
1956   "Changing living patterns of the Yucatan Maya" American Antiquity, 22, 162-64

BRAND, D. D.
1942   "Recent archaeological and geographic investigations in the basin of the Río Balsas, Guerrero and Michoacán" XXVII International Congress of Americanists (Mexico, 1939): Proceedings, I, 140-47
1943a   "An historical sketch of anthropology and geography in the Tarascan region: I" New Mexico Anthropologist, 6-7, 37-108
1943b   "Primitive and modern economy in the middle Río Balsas, Guerrero and Michoacán" Proceedings of the Eighth American Science Congress, 9, 225-31
1952   "Bosquejo histórico de la geografía y la antropología en la región Tarasca" Anales: Museo Michoacano, 5, 43-163

BRASSEUR DE BOURBOURG, E. C.
1857-9 Histoire des nations civilisées du Mexique et de l'Amérique-Centrale, 4 volumes, Paris

BRAUNGART, R.
1881   Die Ackerbaugeräthe in ihrer praktischen Beziehungen wie nach ihrer urgeschichtlichen und ethnographischen Bedeutung, Heidelberg

BRAVO, H.
1960   "Algunos datos acerca de la vegetación del Estado de Oaxaca" Revista Mexicana de Estudios Antropológicos, 16, 31-47

BREW, J. O.
1946   Archaeology of Alkali Ridge, southeastern Utah, Papers of the Peabody Museum of American Archaeology and Ethnology, 21, Cambridge, Mass.

BRICEÑO IRAGORRY, M.
1946-7 "Procedencia y Cultura de los Timoto-Cuycas" Acta Venezolana, 2, 1-23.

BRIGHAM, W. T.
1887   Guatemala: the land of the Quetzal, New York

BRINTON, D. G., H. PHILLIPS, and J. C. MORRIS (eds)
1893   "The tribute roll of Montezuma" Transactions of the American Philosophical Society, 17(3), 53-61

BRITO-FIGUEROA, F.
1962   Población y economía en el pasado indígena venezolano, Caracas

1963   La estructiva económica de Venezuela Colonial, Caracas

BROADBENT, S. M.
1963   "Construcciones megalíticas en el territorio Chibcha" Revista Colombiana Antropología, 12, 81-88
1964   "Agricultural terraces in Chibcha territory, Colombia" American Antiquity, 29, 501-504
1965   Investigaciones arqueológicas en el territorio Chibcha, Bogotá
1966   "The site of Chibcha Bogotá" Ñawpa Pacha, 4, 1-13
1968   "A prehistoric field system in Chibcha territory" Ñawpa Pacha, 6, 135-47

BRONSON, B.
1966   "Roots and the subsistence of the Ancient Maya" Southwestern Journal of Anthropology, 22, 251-79

BROWN, C. B.
1926   "On stone implements from North West Peru" Man, 26, 97-101

BRUMAN, H. J.
1967   "Man and Nature in Mesoamerica: the ecologic base" in B. Bell (ed) Indian Mexico Past and Present, Latin American Center, University of California, Los Angeles, 13-23

BRUNDAGE, B. C.
1967   Lords of Cuzco: a history and description of the Inca people in their final days, Norman

BRUNET, J.
1967   "Geologic studies" in D. S. Byers (ed) The Prehistory of the Tehuacán Valley, I: Environment and Subsistence, Austin and London, 66-90

BRUSH, C. F.
1962   "Pre-Columbian alloy objects from Guerrero, Mexico" Science, 138, 1336-38

BRYAN, K.
1929   "Flood water farming" Geographical Review, 19, 444-56
1941   "Pre-Columbian agriculture in the South West as conditioned by periods of alluviation" Annals of the Association of American Geographers, 31, 219-42

BUCK, P. H.
1949   The coming of the Maori, Wellington

BUDOWSKI, G.
1966   "Some ecological characteristics of higher tropical mountains" Revista Interamericana de Ciencias (Turialba), 16, 159-68

BUENO, COSME
1951   Geografía del Perú virreinal [c. 1763-80], Lima

BUENO, T. A.
1963   Precolombia, Bogotá

BUKASOV, S. M.
1930   The cultivated plants of Mexico, Guatemala and Colombia, Leningrad

BULLARD, W. R.
1964   "Settlement pattern and social structure in the southern Maya lowlands during the Classic Period" XXXV International Congress of Americanists (Mexico, 1962): Proceedings, I, 279-87

BULLOCK, W.
1824   *Six months residence and travels in Mexico,* London

BUNZEL, R.
1952   *Chichicastenango: a Guatemalan village,* American Ethnological Society, New York

BURGOA, FRANCISCO DE
1934   *Geográfica Descripción* [1674], Publicaciones del Archivo General de la Nación, 25, 26, México

BURKITT, R.
1920   "The Hills and the Corn" *The University Museum Anthropological Publications* (University of Pennsylvania, Philadelphia), 8, 183-227

1930   "Explorations in the highlands of western Guatemala" *The Museum Journal* (University of Pennsylvania, Philadelphia), 21, 41-72

BUSCHAN, G.
1922   *Illustrierte Völkerkunde,* I, Stuttgart

BUTMAN, C. H.
1912   "Xochimilco and its lake of gardens: Aztec irrigation of the sixteenth century" *Scientific American Supplement,* 74, 132-33

BYERS, D. S.
1964   "An introduction to the Tehuacán archaeological-botanical project" *XXXV International Congress of Americanists* (Mexico, 1962): *Proceedings,* I, 147-52

1967   "Climate and Hydrography" in D. S. Byers (ed) *The Prehistory of the Tehuacán Valley, I: Environment and Subsistence,* Austin and London, 48-65

CABALLERO FARFÁN, P.
1959   "Supervivencias agrarias del Tahuantinsuyo. La agricultura, base del poderío incaico" *Revista del Instituto Americano de Arte* (Cuzco), 9, 1959, 121-52

CABELLO DE BALBOA, MIGUEL
1838   *Histoire du Pérou* [1586] in H. Ternaux-Compans *Voyages, Relations et Mémoires originaux pour servir à histoire de la découverte de l'Amérique,* 4, Paris

CABRERO FERNÁNDEZ, L.
1962   "La economía básica de los Indios de la región Mixteca a través de las Relaciones Geográficas de Indias" *XXXIV International Congress of Americanists* (Vienna, 1960): *Proceedings,* 688-94

1964   "Descripción física de la Mixteca en las relaciones geográficas del siglo XVI" in *Homenaje a Fernando Márquez Miranda,* Madrid, 129-37

CALEY, E. R., and D. T. EASBY
1964   "New evidence of tin smelting and use of metallic tin in pre-Conquest Mexico" *XXXV International Congress of Americanists* (Mexico, 1962): *Proceedings,* 507-17

CALLE OROZCO, J., and L. R. RODRÍGUEZ LAMUS
n.d.   *Prehistoria,* Medellin

CALLEGARI, G. V.
1925   "Xochimilco, la Venezia dell'Anáhuac" *La Vie d'Italia e dell'America Latina* (Milan), 2, 1925, 1057-62

CALNEK, E. E.
1961   *Distribution and location of the Tzeltal and Tzotzil pueblos of the highlands of Chiapas from the earliest times to the present* (mimeographed), University of Chicago

1972   "Settlement pattern and chinampa agriculture at Tenochtitlán" *American Antiquity,* 37, 104-15

CANO, W.
1952   *Estudio geográfico, histórico y sociológico del Lago Titicaca,* Buenos Aires

CAPOCHE, LUIS
1959   *Relación General de la Villa Imperial de Potosí* [1585], Biblioteca Autores Españoles, Madrid

CÁRDENAS, A. L.
1960-1   "La Cordillera de los Andes" *Revista Geográfica* (Universidad de los Andes, Mérida), 2, 139-49

CÁRDENAS, M.
1941   "Aspecto general de la vegetación de Bolivia" *Chronica Botanica,* 6, 452-53

CARDICH, A.
1964   *Lauricocha: fundamentos para una prehistoria de los Andes centrales,* Centro Argentino de Estudios Prehistóricos, Buenos Aires

CARNEIRO, R. L.
1961   "Slash and burn cultivation among the Kuikuru and its implications for cultural development in the Amazon basin" in J. Wilbert (ed) *The evolution of horticultural systems in native South America: causes and consequences,* Antropológica, supplement 2, Caracas, 47-67

CARRASCO, P.
1952   *Tarascan folk religion: an analysis of economic and religious interactions,* Middle American Research Institute, Tulane University, New Orleans

1960   "Middle American Ethnography" in *Social Science Monograph 10: Middle American Anthropology,* 2, Pan American Union, Washington, 37-50

1967   "The Mesoamerican Indian during the Colonial Period" in B. Bell (ed) *Indian Mexico Past and Present,* Latin American Center, University of California, Los Angeles, 72-86

CARVAJAL, GASPAR DE
1934   *The discovery of the Amazon, according to the account of Friar Gaspar de Carvajal and other documents* [1541-2], comp. J. Toribio Medina, ed. H. C. Heaton, American Geographical Society, special publication 17, New York

CASANOVA, E.
1934   "Observaciones preliminares sobre la arqueología de Coctaca" *XXV International Congress of Americanists* (La Plata, 1932): *Proceedings,* 25-38

1936a   "La Quebrada de Humahuaca" in F. Márquez Miranda (ed) *Historia de la Nación Argentina,* I, Buenos Aires, 207-49

1936b   "El Altiplano Andino" *ibid.,* 251-75

1936c   "Investigaciones arqueológicas en Sorcuyo, Puno de Jujuy" *Anales del Museo Argentino de Ciencias Naturales,* 39, 423-56

1942   "Dos yacimientos arqueológicos en la península de Copacabana" *Anales del Museo Argentino de Ciencias Naturales,* 40, 333-99

1946   "The cultures of the Puna and the Quebrada of Humahuaca" in J. H. Steward (ed) *Handbook of South American Indians,* 2, Smithsonian Institution, Bureau of American Ethnology, Bulletin 143, Washington, 619-31

1970   *El Pucará de Tilcara,* Universidad de Buenos Aires, Museo del Pucará de Tilcara, publicación no. 1, Buenos Aires

CASO, A.
1927   "Las ruinas de Tizatlán, Tlaxcala" *Revista Mexicana de Estudios Históricos,* I, 139-72

1938   *Exploraciones en Oaxaca: Quinta y sexta temporadas, 1936-1937,* Instituto Panamericano de Geografía e Historia, México

1962   "The Mixtec and Zapotec cultures" (translation by J. Paddock of *Culturas mixtecas y zapotecas,* México, 1942) *Boletín Estudios Oaxaqueños,* XXI, 1-20

1963   "Land tenure among the ancient Mexicans" *American Anthropologist,* 65, 863-78

1965   "Lapidary work, goldwork, copperwork: Oaxaca" in G. R. Willey (ed) *Handbook of Middle American Indians,* 3, Austin, 896-930

CASTELLANOS, JUAN DE
1886   *Historia del Nuevo Reino de Granada* [1559], ed. D. Antonio Paz y Mélia, 2 volumes, Madrid

CASTETTER, E. F., and W. H. BELL
1942   *Pima and Papago Indian Agriculture,* Albuquerque

CERDA SILVA, R. DE LA
1956   *Los Indígenas mexicanos de Tuxpan, Jalisco: Monografía histórica, económica y etnográfica,* Instituto de Investigaciones sociales, Universidad Nacional de México, México

CERVANTES DE SALAZAR, FRANCISCO
1914   *Crónica de la Nueva España* [1560-75], Hispanic Society of America, New York

1914-36   *Crónica de la Nueva España* [1560-75], 3 volumes, Madrid

1953   *Dialogues* [1554], Austin

CHAUNU, P.
1964   "La population de l'Amérique indienne" *Revue Historique,* 232, 111-18

CHAVES, L. F.
1963   *Geografía Agraria de Venezuela,* Caracas

CHERVIN, A.
1908   *Anthropologie Bolivienne,* 3 volumes, Paris

CHEVALIER, F.
1963   *Land and Society in Colonial Mexico,* Berkeley and Los Angeles

CIEZA DE LEÓN, PEDRO DE
1864   *The travels of Pedro Cieza de León AD 1532-50 contained in the First Part of his Chronicle of Peru,* trans. and ed. C. R. Markham, Hakluyt Society, 33, London

1883   *The Second Part of the Chronicle of Peru by Pedro Cieza de León* [c. 1550], trans. and ed. C. R. Markham, Hakluyt Society, 68, London

1959   *The Incas.* ed. V. W. Von Hagen, Norman

CIGLIANO, E. M., and MÁRQUEZ MIRANDA, F.
1961   "Problemas arqueológicos en la zona del Ingenio del Arenal" *Revista del Museo de la Plata: Sección Antropología,* 5, 123-69

CLARK, J. COOPER (ed)
1938   *Codex Mendoza and Matrícula de Tributos,* 3 volumes, London

CLARKE, W. C.
1966   "From extensive to intensive cultivation: a succession from New Guinea" *Ethnology,* 5, 347-59

CLAUSON, G.
1953   *Communal Land Tenure,* Food and Agriculture Organization, Agricultural Survey 17, Rome

CLAVIJERO, A. F. J.
1917   *Historia Antigua de México* [c. 1780], 2 volumes, México

1945   *Historia Antigua de México* [c. 1780], 4 volumes, México

CLINE, H. F.
1949   "Civil congregations of the Indians in New Spain, 1598-1606" *Hispanic American Historical Review,* 29, 349-69

1964   "The *Relaciones Geográficas* of the Spanish Indies" *Hispanic American Historical Review,* 44, 341-74

1968   "The Oztoticpac lands map of Texcoco, 1540: further notes" *XXXVII International Congress of Americanists* (Mar del Plata, 1966): *Proceedings,* 119-53

CLOUDSLEY-THOMPSON, J. L., and M. J. CHADWICK
1964   *Life in Deserts,* London

COBO, BERNABÉ
1890-95   *Historia del Nuevo Mundo* [1653], ed. Marcos Jiménez de la Espada, Sociedad de Bibliófilos Andaluces, 4 volumes, Seville

1956   *Obras,* Biblioteca de Autores Españoles, 2 volumes, Madrid

COCHRANE, C. S.
1825   *Journal of a residence and travels in Colombia during the years 1823 and 1824,* 2 volumes, London

COE, M. D.
1962   "Costa Rican Archaeology and Mesoamerica" *Southwestern Journal of Anthropology,* 18, 170-83

1963   "Cultural development in Southeastern Mesoamerica" in B. J. Meggers and C. Evans (eds) *Aboriginal Cultural Development in Latin America: An Interpretative Review,* Smithsonian Miscellaneous Collections, 146, Washington, 27-44

COE, M. D., and K. V. FLANNERY
1964   "Microenvironments and Mesoamerican prehistory" *Science,* 143, 650-54

COE, W. R.
1957   "Environmental limitation on Mayan culture: a re-examination" *American Anthropologist,* 59, 328-35

COLLIER, D.
1955   "Development of civilization on the coast of Peru" in *Irrigation Civilizations: a comparative study,* Social Science Monographs, I, Pan American Union, Washington, 19-27

1961   "Agriculture and civilization on the coast of Peru" in J. Wilbert (ed) *The evolution of horticultural systems in native South America: causes and consequences,* Antropológica, supplement 2, Caracas, 101-109

1962   "The Central Andes" in R. J. Braidwood and G. R. Willey (eds) *Courses toward Urban Life,* Edinburgh, 165-76

COLLIER, D., and J. V. MURRA
1943   *Survey and Excavations in Southern Ecuador,* Anthropological Series of the Field Museum of Natural History, 35, Chicago

COLLINGWOOD, R. G.
1957-8   "Digging sticks and their use in Java" *Antiquity,* 31, 39-40

COLTON, H. S.
1932   *A survey of prehistoric sites in the region of Flagstaff, Arizona,* Smithsonian Institution, Bureau of American Ethnology, Bulletin 104, Washington

COMAS, J.
1956   "Principales contribuciones indígenas precolombinas a la cultura universal" *Cahiers d'histoire mondiale,* 3, 196-230

COOK, JAMES
1784   *A voyage to the Pacific Ocean in the years 1776-80,* 3 volumes, Dublin

COOK, O. F.
1909   "Vegetation affected by agriculture in Central America" *United States Bureau of Plant Industry, Bulletin 145,* Washington

1916a   "Agriculture and native vegetation in Peru" *Journal of the Washington Academy of Sciences,* 6, 284-93

1916b   "Staircase farms of the Ancients" *National Geographic Magazine,* 29, 474-534

1920   "Footplough agriculture in Peru" *Annual Report of the Smithsonian Institution for 1918,* Washington, 487-91

1921   "Milpa Agriculture" *Annual Report of the Smithsonian Institution for 1919,* Washington, 307-26

1925   "Peru as a centre of domestication. Tracing the origin of civilization through domesticated plants" *Journal of Heredity,* 16, 33-46, 95-110

1937   "Campos de cultivo en *andenería* de los antiguos" *Revista Universitaria* (Cuzco), año 26, no. 72, 205-20, no. 73, 98-145

COOK, S. F.
1942   "The population of Mexico in 1793" *Human Biology,* 14, 499-515

1946a   "Human sacrifice and warfare as factors in the demography of pre-Colonial Mexico" *Human Biology,* 18, 81-102

1946b   "The incidence and significance of disease among the Aztecs and related tribes" *Hispanic American Historical Review,* 36, 320-35

1947-8   "The interrelation of population, food supply and building in pre-Conquest Central Mexico" *American Antiquity,* 13, 45-52

1949a   *The Historical Demography and Ecology of the Teotlalpan,* Ibero Americana, 33, University of California, Berkeley

1949b   *Soil Erosion and Population in Central Mexico,* Ibero Americana, 34, University of California, Berkeley

1958   *Santa María Ixcatlán: habitat, population, subsistence,* Ibero Americana, 41, University of California, Berkeley

1960   "Reconstruction of extinct populations" *Revista Mexicana de Estudios Antropológicos,* 16, 173-82

COOK, S. F., and W. BORAH
1947   "The rate of population change in Central Mexico, 1550-70" *Hispanic American Historical Review,* 37, 463-70

1960   *The Indian Population of Central Mexico, 1531-1610,* Ibero Americana, 44, University of California, Berkeley

1966   "On the credibility of contemporary testimony on the population of Mexico in the sixteenth century" in *Homenaje a Roberto J. Weitlaner,* Mexico, 229-39

1968   *The Population of the Mixteca Alta, 1520-1960,* Ibero Americana, 50, University of California, Berkeley

COOK, S. F., and B. SIMPSON
1948   *Population of Central Mexico in the Sixteenth Century,* Ibero Americana, 31, University of California, Berkeley

COOPER, J. M.
1946   "The Araucanians" in J. H. Steward (ed) *Handbook of South American Indians,* 2, Smithsonian Institution, Bureau of American Ethnology, Bulletin 143, Washington, 687-760

1949   "Stimulants and Narcotics" in J. H. Steward (ed) *Handbook of South American Indians,* 5, Smithsonian Institution, Bureau of American Ethnology, Bulletin 143, Washington, 525-58

CORTÉS, HERNANDO
1908   *Hernando Cortés: his five letters of relation to the Emperor Charles V,* trans. and ed. F. A. MacNutt, 2 volumes, Cleveland

1960   *Cartas de Relación,* México

COWGILL, U. M.
1961   "Soil fertility and the Ancient Maya" *Transactions of the Connecticut Academy of Arts and Sciences,* 42, 1-56

COWGILL, U. M., and G. E. HUTCHINSON
1963a   *El Bajo de Santa Fé,* Transactions of the American Philosophical Society, 53(7), Philadelphia

1963b   "Ecology and Geochemistry of the Maya Lowlands" *Southwestern Journal of Anthropology,* 19, 268-86

COY, P. E. B.
1966   "Tetzcotzinco: usurped and neglected" *Man,* I, 543-49

CRAINE, E. R., and R. C. REINDORP (trans. and eds.)
1970   *The Chronicles of Michoacán* [compiled 1539-41, ? by Martin de Jesús de la Coruña], Norman

CRESPO TORAL, R.
1926   *Geografía Agrícola de la Antigua Provincia del Azuay,* Cuenca

CRISTÓBAL DE MOLINA (EL ALMAGRISTA)
1968   *Relación de muchas cosas acaescidas en el Perú* [c. 1552], in Francisco Esteve Barba (ed) *Crónicas Peruanas de Interes Indígena,* Biblioteca de Autores Españoles, 209, Madrid, 1968, 61-95

CRISTÓBAL DE MOLINA (EL CUZQUEÑO)
1873   *An account of the fables and rites of the Yncas* [1574-5], trans. and ed. C. R. Markham, Hakluyt Society, 48, 3-64, London

1916   *Relación de las fábulas y ritos de los Incas* [1574-5], Lima

CROSBY, A. W.
1967   "Conquistador y Pestilencia: the first New World pandemic and the fall of the great Indian empires" *Hispanic American Historical Review*, 47, 321-37

1969   "The early history of syphilis: a reappraisal" *American Anthropologist*, 70, 218-27

CRUXENT, J. M.
1966   *Apuntes sobre las Calzadas de Barinas-Venezuela*, Caracas

CUATRECASAS, J.
1934   *Observaciones geobotánicas en Colombia*, Trabajos del Museo Nacional de Ciencias Naturales, Serie Botánica, 27, Madrid

1958   "Aspectos de la vegetación natural de Colombia" *Revista de la Academia Colombiana de Ciencias Exactas, Físicas y Naturales*, 10, 221-64

CULIN, S.
1907   *Games of the North American Indians*, Twenty-fourth annual report of the Bureau of American Ethnology, Washington

CUNNINGHAM, J. F.
1948   *Observations on the agriculture of Guatemala*, n.p.

CUNOW, H.
1937   *Geschichte und Kultur des Inkareiches*, Amsterdam

DAHLGREN DE JORDAN, B.
1954   *La Mixteca: su cultura e historia prehispánica*, México

DARK, P.
1958   *Mixtec Ethnohistory: a method of analysis of the codical art*, Oxford

DEBENEDETTI, S.
1912   *Influencias de la cultura de Tiahuanaco en la región del noroeste argentino*, Publicaciones de la Sección Antropológica de la Facultad de Filosofía y Letras, 11, Buenos Aires

1918   "Las ruinas prehispánicas de El Alfarcito" *Boletín de la Academia Nacional de Córdoba*, 23, 287-318

DEBENEDETTI, S., and E. CASANOVA
1933-5   *Titiconte*, Publicaciones del Museo Antropológico y Etnográfico de la Facultad de Filosofía y Letras: Serie A., 3, Buenos Aires, 7-35

DEEVEY, E. S.
1957   "Limnologic studies in Middle America with a chapter on Aztec limnology" *Transactions of the Connecticut Academy of Arts and Sciences*, 39, 213-328

DENEVAN, W. M.
1962   "Informe preliminar sobre la geografía de los Llanos de Mojos, nordeste de Bolivia" *Boletín de la Sociedad Geográfica e Histórica de Sucre*, 48, 91-113

1963   "Additional comments on the earthworks of Mojos in Northeastern Bolivia" *American Antiquity*, 28, 540-45

1964   "Pre-Spanish earthworks in the Llanos de Mojos of Northeastern Bolivia" *Revista Geográfica*, 60, 17-24

1966a   "A cultural ecological review of the former aboriginal settlements in the Amazon Basin" *Professional Geographer*, 18, 346-51

1966b   *The aboriginal cultural geography of the Llanos de Mojos of Bolivia*, Ibero Americana, 48, University of California, Berkeley

DENNIS, H. W.
1967   *The effect of trincheras upon agriculture in the Pompa Basin, Sierra Madre Occidental, Mexico*, unpublished MA thesis, University of Denver

DE YOUNG, M.
1958   *Man and Land in the Haitian Economy*, University of Florida, Gainesville

DÍAZ DEL CASTILLO, BERNAL
1908-16   *The True History of the Conquest of New Spain* [c. 1568], ed. Genaro García, trans. A. P. Maudslay, Hakluyt Society, 23-25, 30, 40, London

1955   *Historia Verdadera de la Conquista de la Nueva España* [c. 1568], ed. Joaquín Ramírez Cabañas, 2 volumes, México

DIBBLE, C. E. (ed)
1951   *Códice Xolotl*, Publicaciones del Instituto de Historia, 22, México

DICKEN, S. N.
1936   "The basin settlements of the Middle Sierra Madre Oriental, Mexico" *Annals of the Association of American Geographers*, 26, 157-78

DICKINSON, J. C.
1969   "The Eucalypt in the Sierra of Southern Peru" *Annals of the Association of American Geographers*, 59, 294-307

DÍEZ DE BETÁNZOS, JUAN
1880   *Suma y Narración de los Incas* [1551], Biblioteca Hispana-Ultramarina, V, Madrid

DÍEZ DE SAN MIGUEL, GARCÍA
1964   *Visita hecha a la provincia de Chucuito, por Garcí Díez de San Miguel en el año 1567* (ethnological commentary by J. V. Murra), Documentos regionales para la etnología y etnohistoria Andinas, tomo 1. Ediciones de la Casa de la Cultura del Perú, Lima

DIGUET, L.
1906   "Contribution à l'étude géographique du Méxique précolombien: Le Mixtécapan" *Journal de la Société des Americanistes de Paris*, 3, 15-43

DISSELHOFF, H. D.
1967   *Daily Life in Ancient Peru*, New York

1968   *Oasenstädte und Zaubersteine im Land der Inka: archäologische Forschungsreisen in Peru*, Berlin

DOBYNS, H. F.
1963   "An outline of Andean epidemic history to 1720" *Bulletin of the History of Medicine*, 37, 493-515

1966   "Estimating aboriginal American population" *Current Anthropology*, 7, 395-416

DOLLFUS, O.
1965   "Effets des fluctuations et des accidents climatiques sur l'écologie humaine du Pérou" *Journal de la Société des Americanistes de Paris*, 54, 227-38

1967   "Le rôle de la nature dans le developpement péruvien" *Annales de Géographie*, 76, 714-33

DONKIN, R. A.
1968   "Ambiente y Poblamiento Precolombinos en el Altiplano de Boyaca Cundinamarca, Colombia" *Boletín de la Sociedad Geográfica de Colombia*, 26, 199-207

DONKIN, R. A. (continued)
1970   "Pre-Columbian field implements and their distribution in the highlands of Middle and South America" *Anthropos*, 65, 505-29

DORANTES DE CARRANZA, BALTASAR
1902   *Sumaria relación de las cosas de la Nueva España* [1604], México

DOUGHTY, P. L., and M. F.
1968   *Huaylas: an Andean district in search of progress*, Cornell Studies in Anthropology, Ithaca

DOZIER, C. L.
1958   *Indigenous Tropical Agriculture in Central America: Land Use, Systems, and Problems*, National Academy of Sciences, publication 594, Washington

DOZIER, E. P.
1961   "The Río Grande Pueblos" in E. H. Spicer (ed) *Perspectives in American Indian Culture Change*, Chicago

DREWES, W. U., and A. T. DREWES
1957   *Climate and related phenomena of the eastern Andean slopes of Central Peru*, Syracuse University Research Institute

DUMOND, D. E.
1961   "Swidden agriculture and the rise of the Maya civilization" *Southwestern Journal of Anthropology*, 17, 301-16

DUNN, F. L.
1965   "On the antiquity of malaria in the western hemisphere" *Human Biology*, 37, 386-93

DURÁN, DIEGO
1867-80   *Historia de las Indias de Nueva España* [1581], 2 volumes and atlas, México

1964   *The Aztecs: the history of the Indies of New Spain by Fray Diego Durán* [1581], trans. and ed. D. Heyden and F. Horcasitas, New York

1967   *Historia de las Indias de Nueva España e Islas de la Tierra Firme* [1581], ed. A. M. Garibay, 2 volumes, México

1971   *Book of the Gods and Rites* [c. 1576-79] *and The Ancient Calendar* [1579], trans. and ed. F. Horcasitas and D. Heyden, Norman

EALAND, C. A.
1915   *Insects and Man*, London

EASBY, D. T.
1962   "Two 'South American' metal techniques found recently in Western Mexico" *American Antiquity*, 28, 19-24

EIDT, R. C.
1952   "La climatología de Cundinamarca" *Revista de la Academia Colombiana de Ciencias Exactas, Físicas, y Naturales*, 8, 489-503

1959   "Aboriginal Chibcha settlement in Colombia" *Annals of the Association of American Geographers*, 49, 374-92

1968   "The Climatology of South America" in E. J. Fittkau *et al*, (eds) *Biogeography and Ecology in South America*, I, Monographiae Biologicae, 18, The Hague, 54-81

ENGEL, F.
1957   "Early sites in the Pisco valley of Peru: Tambo Colorado" *American Antiquity*, 23, 34-45

1965   *Historia Elemental del Perú Antiguo*, Lima

1966   *Geografía Humana Prehistórica y Agricultura Precolombiana de la Quebrada de Chilca*, Lima

ENOCK, C. R.
1914   *Ecuador, its ancient and modern history, topography and natural resources*, London

ERDMAN, J. A., C. L. DOUGLAS and J. W. MARR
1969   *Environment of Mesa Verde, Colorado*, United States Department of the Interior, National Park Service, Archaeological Research Series 7-B, Washington

ERNST, A.
1890   De l'emploi de la coca dans les pays septentrionaux de l'Amérique du Sud *VII International Congress of Americanists* (Berlin, 1888): *Proceedings*, 230-43

ESPINAL, L. S., and E. MONTENEGRO
1963   *Formaciones Vegetales de Colombia*, Bogotá

ESPINOSA SORIANO, W.
1967   "El primer informe etnológico sobre Cajamarca, año de 1540" *Revista Peruana de Cultura*, 11-12, 5-41

ESTETE, MIGUEL DE
1872   *Report on the expedition to Pachacamac* [1534-5], in C. R. Markham (trans. and ed.) *Reports on the Discovery of Peru*, Hakluyt Society, 47, 74-94, London

1918   *El descubrimiento y la conquista del Perú* [1534-5], ed. C.M. Larrea, Boletín de la Sociedad Ecuatoriana de Estudios Históricos Americanos, 3, Quito

ESTRADA, E.
1957a   *Los Huancavilcas: últimas civilizaciones pre-históricos de la costa del Guayas*, Publicación del Museo Víctor Estrada, 3, Guayaquil

1957b   *Prehistoria de Manabí*, Publicación del Museo Víctor Estrada, 4, Guayaquil

1962   *Arqueología de Manabí central*, Publicación del Museo Víctor Estrada, 7, Guayaquil

ESTRADA, E., and C. EVANS
1963   "Cultural development in Ecuador" in B. J. Meggers and C. Evans (eds) *Aboriginal Cultural Development in Latin America: An Interpretative Review*, Smithsonian Miscellaneous Collections, 146, Washington, 77-88

EVANARI, M., L. SHANAN, N. H. TADMOR
1958   "The ancient desert agriculture of the Negev: early beginnings" *Israel Exploration Journal*, 8, 231-68

1959   "The ancient desert agriculture of the Negev, III: chain well systems in the Wadi Arava" *Ktavim*, 9, 223-40

EVANS, C., and B. J. MEGGERS
1968   *Archaeological Investigations on the Río Napo, Eastern Ecuador*, Smithsonian Institution, Contributions to Anthropology, 6, Washington

EZELL, P. H.
1961   *The Hispanic Acculturation of the Gila River Pimas*, Memoirs of the American Anthropological Association, 90, Lancaster

FABILA, A.
1947   "Tenancingo: exploración socioeconómica" *Revista Mexicana de Sociología,* 9, 257-85

FALS-BORDA, O.
1957   *El hombre y la tierra en Boyacá,* Bogotá
1962   *Peasant Society in the Colombian Andes,* Gainesville

FARABEE, W. C.
1921   "The use of metals in prehistoric America" *The Museum Journal* (University of Pennsylvania, Philadelphia), 35-42

FARON, L. C.
1960   "The effects of the Conquest on the Araucanian Picunche during the Spanish colonization of Chile: 1536-1635" *Ethnohistory,* 7, 239-307

FEBRES CORDERO, T.
1920   *Décadas de la historia de Mérida,* Mérida and Caracas, 1935

FEJOS, P.
1944   *Archaeological explorations in the Cordillera Vilcabamba, southeastern Peru,* Viking Fund Publications in Anthropology, 3, New York

FERDON, E. N.
1950   *Studies in Ecuadorian Geography,* Monographs of the School of American Research, 15, Santa Fé
1953   *Tonolá, Mexico: an archaeological survey,* Archaeological Institute of America, School of American Research, monograph 16, Cambridge, Mass.
1959   "Agricultural potential and the development of cultures" *Southwestern Journal of Anthropology,* 15, 1-19

FERNÁNDEZ DE LARA, G. A.
1953   "Hydrology and utilization of hydraulic resources in the Arid and Semi-arid areas of Latin America" *Reviews of Research on Arid Zone Hydrology,* U.N.E.S.C.O., Paris

FERNÁNDEZ DE OVIEDO Y VALDÉS, GONZALO
1851-2   *Historia general y natural de las Indias, Islas y Tierra Firme del Mar Océano* [1535], 4 volumes, Madrid
1942   *Sumario de la Historia Natural de las Indias* [1526], Madrid
1959a   *Natural History of the West Indies* (the *Sumario*) [1526], trans. and ed. S. A. Stoudemire, University of North Carolina Studies in Romance Languages and Literatures, 32, Chapel Hill
1959b   *Historia General y Natural de las Indias* [1535], Biblioteca de Autores Españoles, 117-121, 5 volumes, Madrid

FERNÁNDEZ DE PIEDRAHITA, LUCAS
1942   *Historia General del Nuevo Reino de Granada* [1668-88], 4 volumes, Bogotá

FIELD, C.
1966a   *A Reconnaissance of Southern Andean Agricultural Terracing,* unpublished Ph.D. thesis, University of California, Los Angeles
1966b   "La agricultura de terrazas, una importante modificación en el potencial del uso de la tierra" *International Geographical Union — Conferencia Regional Latinoamericana;* Sociedad Mexicana de Geografía y Estadística, volume 2, 343-49

FIORAVANTI-MOLINIÉ, A.
1975   "Contribution à l'étude des sociétés étagées des Andes: La vallée du Yucay" *Études Rurales,* 67, 35-57

FLANNERY, K. V.
1968   "Archaeological systems theory and early Meso-america" in B. J. Meggers (ed) *Anthropological Archaeology in the Americas,* Anthropological Society of Washington, Washington, 67-87

FLANNERY, K. V., A. V. KIRKBY, M. J. KIRKBY, and A. W. WILLIAMS
1967   "Farming systems and political growth in ancient Oaxaca" *Science,* 158, 445-54

FLINT, R. F., and BRANDTNER, F.
1961   "Climatic changes since the last Interglacial" *American Journal of Science,* 259, 321-28

FLORES GARCÍA, M.
1945   "Las funciones de los andenes prehistóricos en el antiguo Perú" *Turismo,* año 10, no. 114

FLORNOY, B.
1955-6   "Exploration archéologique de l'alto Marañon" *Travaux de l'Institut Français d'Études Andines,* 5, 51-81

FLOYD, B.
1964   "Terrace agriculture in eastern Nigeria: the case of Maku" *Journal of the Geographical Association of Nigeria,* 7, 91-108

FONSECA MARTEL, C.
1972   "La economía 'vertical' y la economía de mercado en las communidades alteñas del Perú" in Iñigo Ortiz de Zúñiga *Visita de la Provincia de León de Huánuco* [1562], 2, 315-38, Universidad Nacional Hermilio Valdizán, Huánuco, Perú

FORBES, D.
1870   "On the Aymara Indians of Bolivia and Peru" *Journal of the Ethnographical Society* (London), 2, 193-305

FORDE, C. D.
1931a   "Hopi agriculture and land ownership" *Journal of the Royal Anthropological Institute of Great Britain and Ireland,* 61, 357-405
1931b   *Ethnography of the Yuma Indians,* University of California Publications in American Archaeology and Ethnology, 28, Berkeley and Los Angeles

FOSTER, G. M.
1948   *Empire's Children: the people of Tzintzuntzan,* Smithsonian Institution, Institute of Social Anthropology, 6, Washington

FOWLER, M. L.
1969   "A Preclassic water distribution system in Amalucan, Mexico" *Archaeology,* 22, 208-15

FRANCO INOJOSA, J. M., and A. GONZÁLEZ
1936   "Exploraciones arqueológicas en el Perú: Departamento de Puno" *Revista del Museo Nacional* (Lima), 5, 157-83

FRANKE, P. R., and D. WATSON
1936   "An experimental corn field in Mesa Verde National Park" in D. Brand (ed) *Symposium on prehistoric agriculture,* University of New Mexico, Bulletin 296, anthropological series 5, 35-41, Albuquerque

FUENTE, J. DE LA
1949   *Yalalag: una villa Zapoteca serrana,* Museo Nacional de Antropología, México

GADE, D. W.
1967   "The Guinea Pig in Indian Folk Culture" *Geographical Review,* 57, 213-24

1968   "Aranjuez of the New World" *Américas,* 20, 12-19

1970   "Ethnobotany of Canihua *(Chenopodium pallidicaule),* Rustic Seed Crop of the Altiplano" *Economic Botany,* 24, 55-61

1975   *Plants, Man and Land in the Vilcanota Valley of Peru,* Biogeographica 6, The Hague

GAGE, T.
1928   *The English-American. A New Survey of the West Indies, 1648,* ed. A. P. Newton, London

GAGLIANO, J. A.
1963   "The coca debate in colonial Peru" *The Americas,* 20 (1), 43-63

1968   "Coca and environmental adaptation in the high Andes: an historical analysis of attitudes" *XXXVII International Congress of Americanists* (Mar del Plata, 1966): *Proceedings,* 4, 227-39

GAIGNARD, R.
1965   "La vie humaine dans les Andes sèches: une vallée des contreforts de la Puna de Argentina" *Cahiers de l'Outre Mer,* 18, 306-12

GAMARRA DULANTO, L., and A. MALDONADO
1945   "Significado arqueológico, agrológico, y geográfico de los andenes abandonados de Santa Inés y Chosica en el valle del Rimac" *Boletín del Comité Nacional de Protección a la Naturaleza* (Lima), 2, 45-67

GAMIO, M.
1922   *La población del valle de Teotihuacán,* Secretaría de Agricultura y Fomento, Dirección de Antropología, México

GANN, T. W. F.
1926   *Ancient cities and modern tribes: exploration and adventure in Maya lands,* London

1928a   *Maya Cities,* New York

1928b   *Discoveries and adventures in Central America,* London

GARCÍA, GREGORIO
1729   *Origen de los Indios de el Nuevo Mundo, e Indias Occidentales* [1607], Madrid

GARCÍA PAYÓN, J.
1941   "La cerámica del Valle de Toluca" *Revista Mexicana de Estudios Antropológicos,* 5, 209-38

GARCÍA PIMENTEL, L. (ed)
1904   *Relación de los Obispados de Tlaxcala, Michoacán, Oaxaca y otros lugares en el siglo XVI,* México

GARCILASO DE LA VEGA
1869   *Royal Commentaries of the Incas* [1604], I, trans. and ed. C. R. Markham, Hakluyt Society, 41, London

1871   *Royal Commentaries of the Incas* [1604], II, trans. and ed. C. R. Markham, Hakluyt Society, 45, London

1966   *Royal Commentaries of the Incas* [1604], trans. and ed. H. V. Livermore, 2 volumes, Austin and London

GASPARINI, G.
1962   *La casa colonial Venezolana,* Caracas

GATTO, S.
1934   "Un granero o silo en la Quebrada de Coctaca" *XXV International Congress of Americanists* (La Plata, 1932): *Proceedings,* 2, 51-56

GEMELLI CARRERI, JUAN FRANCISCO
1955   *Viaje a la Nueva España* [1700], 2 volumes, México

GERHARD, P.
1972   *A Guide to the Historical Geography of New Spain,* Cambridge

GERSTE, A.
1909   *Notes sur la Médecine et la Botanique des Anciens Mexicains,* Roma

GIBBON, L.
1854   *Exploration of the valley of the Amazon,* Washington

GIBSON, C.
1948   *The Inca concept of sovereignty and the Spanish administration in Peru,* University of Texas, Institute of Latin American Studies, Latin American Studies 4, Austin

1952   *Tlaxcala in the sixteenth century,* New Haven

1955   "The transformation of the Indian Community in New Spain, 1500-1810" *Journal of World History,* 2, 581-607

1964   *The Aztecs under Spanish rule: a history of the Indians of the Valley of Mexico, 1519-1810,* Stanford

1966   *Spain in America,* New York

GIL-BERMEJO GARCÍA, J.
1963-5   "La geografía de Méjico en las cartas de Cortés" *Revista de Indias,* 23, 123-203, 25, 307-32

GILLIN, J.
1936   "Quichua-speaking Indians of Northern Ecuador" *American Anthropologist,* 38, 548-53

1945   *Moche: a Peruvian Coastal Community,* Smithsonian Institution, Institute of Social Anthropology, publication 3

GILSON, H. C.
1937   "The Percy Sladen Trust Expedition to Lake Titicaca" *Geographical Journal,* 91, 533-42

GOFF, C. W.
1967   "Syphilis" in D. R. Brothwell and A. T. Sandison (eds) *Diseases in Antiquity,* Springfield, 287-93

GOGGIN, J. M.
1943   "An archaeological survey of the Río Tepalcatepec Basin, Michoacán, Mexico" *American Antiquity,* 9, 44-58

GOLTE, J.
1970   "Algunas consideraciones acerca de la producción y distribución de la coca en el estado Inca" *XXXVIII International Congress of Americanists* (Stuttgart-München, 1968): *Proceedings,* 2, 471-78

GÓMEZ DE CERVANTES, GONZALO
1944   *La Vida Económica y Social de Nueva España al finalizar el siglo XVI* [1599], ed. Alberto María Carreño, Biblioteca Histórica Méxicana de Obras Ineditas, 19, México

GÓMEZ DE OROZCO, F.
1931   "Relaciones Histórico-Geográficas de Nueva España" *El México Antiguo,* 3, 43-51

GONÇALES HOLGUÍN, D.
1608   Vocabulario de la lengua general de todo el Perú, llamada lengua Qquichua o del Inca [1586], 3rd ed., Lima

GONZÁLEZ, A. R.
1963   "Cultural development in Northwestern Argentina" in B. J. Meggers and C. Evans (eds) Aboriginal Cultural Development in Latin America: An Interpretative Review, Smithsonian Miscellaneous Collections, 146, Washington, 103-18

GONZÁLEZ, A. R., and V. N. REGUEIRO
1962   "Preliminary report on archaeological research in Tafí del Valle, North West Argentina" XXXIV International Congress of Americanists (Vienna, 1960): Proceedings, 485-96

GONZÁLEZ DE AGUEROS, F. PEDRO
1791   Descripción Historial de la Provincia y Archipiélago de Chile, Madrid

GONZÁLEZ SUÁREZ, F.
1878a   Atlas arqueológico ecuatoriano, 2 volumes, Quito
1878b   Estudio histórico sobre los Cañaris, antiguos habitantes de la provincia del Azuay en la Republica del Ecuador, Quito

GORENSTEIN, S.
1971   "Archaeology, history and anthropology in the Mixteca-Puebla region of Mexico" American Antiquity, 36, 335-43

GORTARI, E. DE
1963   La Ciencia en el Historia de México, México

GOSSE, L. A.
1861   Monographie de l'Erythroxylon Coca, Mémoires couronnés et autres mémoires, publiés par l'Academie Royale de Belgique, Bruxelles

GRAÑA, F.
1940   La población del Perú a través de la historia, 3rd ed., Lima

GRANT, U. J. et al.
1963   Races of maize in Venezuela, National Academy of Sciences, National Research Council, publication 1136, Washington

GREGORY, H. E.
1913   "A geographical sketch of Titicaca, the Island of the Sun" Bulletin of the American Geographical Society, 45, 561-75

GRIFFIN, E. C.
1966   Some aspects of the alteration of hydrology by the construction of trincheras in the Pompa Basin, Sierra Madre Occidental, Mexico, unpublished MA thesis, University of Denver

GROVE, D. C.
1965   "Floating garden agriculture" The Masterkey (Southwest Museum, Los Angeles, California), 39, 23-29

GUERRA, F.
1966   "Aztec Medicine" Medical History, 10, 315-38
1969   "Aztec science and technology" History of Science, 8, 32-52

GUILLEN, V. M.
1943   "Andenes de Amoray" Revista del Instituto Americano de Arte, 1, 68-72

GUIMET, J. C.
1937   "La agricultura en el antiguo Perú" La Vida Agrícola (Lima), 14, no. 158, 3-5, 7, 9, 11, 13-16; no. 159, 115, 117-23; no. 160, 93, 195, 197, 199, 201, 203, 205-6

GUTIERREZ-NORIEGA, C.
1949   "El hábito de la coca en el Perú" America Indígena, 9, 143-54

GUTIERREZ-NORIEGA, C., and V. WOLFGANG VON HAGEN
1951   "Coca — the mainstay of an arduous native life in the Andes" Economic Botany, 5, 145-52

GUZMÁN, E.
1934   "Exploración arqueológica en la Mixteca Alta" Anales del Museo Nacional de Arqueología, Historia y Etnografía, I, 17-42, México
1939   "The art of map making among the ancient Mexicans" Imago Mundi, 3, 1-6

GUZMÁN, L. E.
1956   Farming and Farmlands in Panama, University of Chicago, Department of Geography, Research Paper, 44
1958   "The agricultural terraces of the ancient highland Maya" Annals of the Association of American Geographers, 48, 266
1962   "Las terrazas de los Antiguos Mayas Montañeses, Chiapas, México" Revista Interamericana de Ciencias Sociales, I, 398-406

HACK, J. T.
1942   The changing physical environment of the Hopi Indians of Arizona, Papers of the Peabody Museum of American Archaeology and Ethnology, 35, Cambridge, Mass.

HAHN, E.
1891   "Waren die Menschen der Urzeit zwischen der Jägerstufe und der Stufe des Ackerbaus Nomaden" ? Das Ausland, 64, 481-87

HALSETH, O. S.
1936   "Prehistoric irrigation in Salt River Valley" in D. Brand (ed) Symposium on prehistoric agriculture, University of New Mexico, Bulletin 296, anthropological series 5, 42-47, Albuquerque

HAMILTON, J. P.
1827   Travels through the interior provinces of Colombia, 2 volumes, London

HARLEM, A. D.
1964   "Cerro de Trinchera: its history and purpose" Tlalocan, 4, 339-50

HARTH-TERRE, E.
1933   "Incahuasi: ruinas incaicas del Valle de Lunahuaná" Revista del Museo Nacional (Lima), 2, 99-125

HASTENRATH, S. L.
1967   "Rainfall distribution and regime in Central America" Archiv für Meteorologie, Geophysik und Bioklimatologie, 15, 201-41
1968   "Recent climatic fluctuations in the Central American area and some geo-ecological effects" in C. Troll (ed) Geo-Ecology of the Mountainous Regions of the Tropical Americas, Bonn, 131-56

HAURY, E. W.
1953   "Some thoughts on Chibcha culture in the high plains of Colombia" *American Antiquity,* 19, 76-78
1962   "The Greater American Southwest" in R. J. Braidwood and G. R. Willey (eds) *Courses toward Urban Life,* Edinburgh

HAURY, E. W., and C. J. C. CUBILLOS
1953   *Investigaciones arqueológicas en la sabana de Bogotá: cultura Chibcha,* University of Arizona Social Science Bulletin, 22, Tucson

HAWKES, J. G.
1941   *Cytogenetic Studies on South American Potatoes,* unpublished Ph.D. thesis, Cambridge University

HELMER, M.
1951   "La vie économique au XVIe. siècle sur le haut plateau andin: Chucuito en 1567, d'après un document inédit des archives des Indes" *Travaux de l'Institut Français d'Études Andines,* 3, 115-50
1955-6 *"La visitación de los Yndios Chupachos* Inka et Encomendero, 1549" *Travaux de l'Institut Français d'Études Andines,* 5, 3-50

HENSCHEN, F.
1966   *The History of Diseases* (translated by Joan Tate), London

HENSHAW, H. W.
1887   *Perforated stones from California,* Smithsonian Institution, Bureau of American Ethnology, Bulletin 2, Washington

HERNÁNDEZ, FRANCISCO
1959   *Historia natural de Nueva España* [1571-76], 2 volumes, México

HEROLD, J.
1961   *Prehistoric settlement and physical environment in the Mesa Verde area,* University of Utah, Anthropological Papers, 53

HEROLD, L.
1965   *Trincheras and physical environment along the Río Gavilan, Chihuahua, Mexico,* University of Denver, Publications in Geography
1966   "El control del manto por medio de terrazas primitivas en la Sierra Madre Occidental de Chihuahua-Sonora, México" *International Geographical Union — Conferencia Regional Latinoamericana;* Sociedad Mexicana de Geografía y Estadística, volume 2, 350-63, México

HERRARTE, M. P.
1942   "La erosión de terrenos y la manera de prevenirla en Guatemala" *Proceedings of the Eighth American Science Congress,* 5, 191-92

HESTER, J. A.
1953-4 "Maya Agriculture" *Year Book of the Carnegie Institution,* 53, Washington

HETTNER, A.
1892   *Die Kordillere von Bogotá,* Erganzungsheft 104 zu "Petermanns Mitteilungen," Gotha

HEWETT, E. L.
1936   *Ancient Life in Mexico and Central America,* New York

HEWETT, E. L., J. HENDERSON, and W. W. ROBBINS
1913   *The physiography of the Río Grande Valley, New Mexico, in relation to Pueblo Culture,* Smithsonian Institution, Bureau of American Ethnology, Bulletin 54, Washington

HIGBEE, E. C.
1947   "The agricultural regions of Guatemala" *Geographical Review,* 37, 177-201

HILL, A. D.
1964   *The changing landscape of a Mexican municipio — Villa las Rosas, Chiapas,* University of Chicago, Department of Geography, Research Papers, 91

HILL, A. H.
1905   "Notes on a journey in Bolivia and Peru around Lake Titicaca" *Scottish Geographical Magazine,* 21, 249-59

HILL, J. N.
1966   "A prehistoric community in eastern Arizona" *Southwestern Journal of Anthropology,* 22, 9-30

HILL, S. S.
1860   *Travels in Peru and Mexico,* 2 volumes, London

HILL, W. W.
1938   *The Agricultural and Hunting Methods of the Navaho Indians,* Yale University Publications in Anthropology, 18, New Haven

HILLS, E. S., C. D. OLLIER, and C. R. TWIDALE
1966   "Geomorphology" in E. S. Hills (ed) *Arid Lands: A Geographical Appraisal,* U.N.E.S.C.O., Paris, 53-76

HIRSCH, A.
1885   *Handbook of Geographical and Historical Pathology,* 2 volumes, London

HODGE, W. H.
1947   "Coca" *Natural History,* 56, 86-93

HODGSON, R. W.
1951   "Three native tuber foods of the High Andes" *Economic Botany,* 5, 185-201

HOHENTHAL, W. D.
1957   "The concept of cultural marginality and native agriculture in South America" *Kroeber Anthropological Society Publications,* 16, 85-86

HOOKER, W. J.
1835   "Some account of the uses and properties of Coca (Erythroxylon Coca)" *Companion to the Botanical Magazine,* I, 161-70

HOOVER, J. W.
1941   "Cerros de trincheras of the Arizona Papagueria" *Geographical Review,* 31, 228-39

HOPKINS, J. W.
1968   *Prehispanic Agricultural Terraces in Mexico,* unpublished M.A. thesis, University of Chicago

HORKHEIMER, H.
1950   *El Perú prehispánico,* Lima
1958   *La alimentación en el Perú prehispánico y su interdependencia con la agricultura,* U.N.E.S.C.O., Lima
1960   *Nahrung und Nahrungsgewinnung im vorspanischen Peru,* Bibliotheca Ibero-Americana, Berlin
1962   *Arqueología del Valle Chancay,* Lima

HOVEY, E. O.
1905   "The Western Sierra Madre of the State of Chihuahua, Mexico" *Bulletin of the American Geographical Society*, 37, 531-43

HOWARD, W. A., and T. M. GRIFFITHS
1966   *Trinchera distributions in the Sierra Madre Occidental, Mexico*, University of Denver, Publications in Geography

HOWARTH, O. H.
1895   "The Western Sierra of Mexico" *Geographical Journal*, 6, 422-38

HRDLICKA, A.
1912   "The Aztec village of Xochimilco" *Smithsonian Miscellaneous Collections*, 59, Washington, 11-13

HUMBOLDT, A. VON
1966   *Political Essay on the Kingdom of New Spain*, trans. J. Black, London, 1811; facs. ed., 4 volumes, New York

HUTCHINSON, T. J.
1873   *Two years in Peru: with exploration of its antiquities*, 2 volumes, London

IBARRA GRASSO, D. E.
1958-9   "Los primeros agricultores de Bolivia" *Anales de Arqueología y Etnología* (Universidad Nacional de Cuyo, Instituto de Arqueología y Etnología), 14-15, 205-28

IMBELLONI, J.
1926   *La Esfinge Indiana*, Buenos Aires

ISBELL, W. H.
1968   "New discoveries in the Montaña of Southeastern Peru" *Archaeology*, 21, 108-14

ISHIDA, E. *et al.*
1960   *The report of the University of Tokyo Scientific Expedition to the Andes*, I, Tokyo

IVES, R. L.
1936   "A trinchera near Quitovaquita, Sonora" *American Anthropologist*, 38, 257-59

JAHN, A.
1927   *Los aborígines del occidente de Venezuela*, Caracas

JANSSENS, P.
1970   *Palaeopathology: diseases and injuries of prehistoric man*, London

JARAMILLO URIBE, J.
1964   "La población indígena de Colombia en el momento de la conquista y sus transformaciones posteriores" *Anuario Colombiano de Historia Social y de la Cultura*, 1, 239-293

JAUREGUI, E.
1968   *Mesoclima de la Región Puebla-Tlaxcala*, Instituto de Geografía, Universidad Nacional Autónoma de México

JENNY, H.
1948   "Great soil groups in the Equatorial Regions of Colombia" *Soil Science*, 66, 5-28

JIJON Y CAAMAÑO, J.
1927   *Puruhá: Contribución al conocimiento de los aborigines de la provincia del Chimborazo*, 2 volumes, Quito

1949   *Maranga: contribución al conocimiento de los aborigenes del Valle del Rimac, Perú*, Quito

JIMÉNEZ DE LA ESPADA, M. (ed)
1881-97   *Relaciones geográficas de Indias*, 4 volumes, Madrid

1965   *Relaciones geográficas de Indias — Perú*, 3 volumes, Biblioteca de Autores Españoles, 183-85, Madrid

JIMÉNEZ MORENO, W.
1966   "Mesoamerica before the Toltecs" in J. Paddock (ed) *Ancient Oaxaca*, Stanford, 1-82

JOHANNESSEN, C. L.
1963   *Savannas of interior Honduras*, Ibero Americana, 46, University of California, Berkeley

JOHNSON, A. E.
1960   *The place of the trincheras culture of Northern Sonora in Southwestern Archaeology*, unpublished M.A. thesis, University of Arizona

1963-4   "The Trincheras Culture of Northern Sonora" *American Antiquity*, 29, 174-86

1966   "Archaeology of Sonora, Mexico" in G. F. Ekholm and G. R. Willey (eds) *Handbook of Middle American Indians*, 4, Austin, 26-37

JOHNSON, G. R., and R. R. PLATT
1930   *Peru from the Air*, American Geographical Society, Special Publication, 12, New York

KAERGER, K.
1909   *Landwirtschaft und Kolonisation im Spanischen Amerika*, 2 volumes, Leipzig

KAPLAN, L.
1960   "Historical and ethnobotanical aspects of domestication in *Tagetes*," *Economic Botany*, 14, 200-202

KARSTEN, R.
1949   *The civilization of the Inca empire in ancient Peru*, Helsingfors

KASSAS, M.
1966   "Plant life in deserts" in E. S. Hills (ed) *Arid Lands: A Geographical Appraisal*, U.N.E.S.C.O., Paris, 145-79

KATZ, F.
1960   "Einige Vergleichsmomente zwischen der sozialen und wirtschaftlichen Organisation der Inka in Peru und der Azteken in Mexiko" *Estudios de Cultura Náhuatl*, 2, 1960, 59-76

1966   *Situación social y económica de los Aztecas durante los siglos XV y XVI*, México

KEDAR, Y.
1957   "Ancient agriculture at Shivta in the Negev" *Israel Exploration Journal*, 7, 178-89

1958   "Use of aerial photographs in research on physiographic conditions and anthropogeographic data in various historic periods" *Photogrammetric Engineering*, 244, 584-87

KELLEY, J. C.
1956   "Settlement patterns in North Central Mexico" in G. R. Willey (ed) *Prehistoric settlement patterns in the New World*, Viking Fund Publications in Anthropology, 23, 128-39, New York

KELLY, I.
1945   *The archaeology of the Autlán-Tuxcacuesco Area of Jalisco: I — The Autlán Zone*, Ibero Americana, 26, University of California, Berkeley

KELLY, I. *(continued)*
1947   *Excavations at Apatzingán, Michoacán,* Viking Fund
          Publications in Anthropology, 7, New York
1949   *The archaeology of the Autlán-Tuxcacuesco Area of
          Jalisco: II — The Tuxcacuesco-Zapotitlán Zone,*
          Ibero Americana, 27, University of California,
          Berkeley

KELLY, I., and A. PALERM
1952   *The Tajín Totonac: history, subsistence, shelter and
          technology,* Smithsonian Institution, Institute of So-
          cial Anthropology, publication 13, Washington

KELLY, K.
1965   "Land use regions in the central and northern por-
          tions of the Inca empire" *Annals of the Association
          of American Geographers,* 55, 327-38

KELLOGG, C. E.
1953   "Potentialities and problems of desert soils" in *Desert
          Research,* Proceedings of the International Sympo-
          sium held in Jerusalem, May 7-14, 1952: Research
          Council of Israel, Special Publication, 2, Jerusalem

KIDDER, A.
1943   *Some early sites in the northern Lake Titicaca Basin,*
          Papers of the Peabody Museum of American Archae-
          ology and Ethnology, 27
1956   "Settlement Patterns: Peru" in G. R. Willey (ed)
          Prehistoric settlement patterns in the New World,
          Viking Fund Publications in Anthropology, 23, 148-
          55, New York
1964   "South American High Cultures" in J. D. Jennings
          and E. Norbeck (eds) *Prehistoric Man in the New
          World,* Chicago, 451-88

KIDDER, A., L. LUMBRERAS, and D. B. SMITH
1963   "Cultural development in the Central Andes — Peru
          and Bolivia" in B. J. Meggers and C. Evans (eds)
          *Aboriginal Cultural Development in Latin America:
          An Interpretative Review,* Smithsonian Miscellane-
          ous Collections, 146, Washington, 89-102

KIDDER, A. V.
1962   *An introduction to the study of Southwestern archae-
          ology with a preliminary account of the excavations
          at Pecos,* originally published 1924, New Haven

KIDDER, A. V., and S. G. GUERNSEY
1919   *Archaeological explorations in Northeastern Arizona,*
          Smithsonian Institution, Bureau of American Eth-
          nology, Bulletin 65, Washington

KINZL, H.
1963   "Die altindianischen Bewässerungsanlagen in Peru
          nach der Chronik des Pedro Cieza de León (1553)"
          *Mitteilungen der Österreichischen Geographischen
          Gesellschaft* (Festschrift Hans Bobek, 2), 105, 331-39

KINZL, H., and E. SCHNEIDER
1950   *Cordillera Blanca,* Innsbruck

KIRCHHOFF, P.
1943   "Mesoamérica: sus límites geográficos, composi-
          ción étnica y caracteres culturales" *Acta Americana,*
          I, 92-107

KIRKBY, ANNE V. T.
1973   *The use of land and water resources in the past and
          present Valley of Oaxaca, Mexico,* Memoirs of the
          Museum of Anthropology, University of Michigan,
          no. 5, Ann Arbor

KLEISS, E.
1967   "The Timoto-Cuicas" *Kosmos* (Stuttgart), 63, 270-74

KOBORI, I.
1960   "Human geography of methods of irrigation in the
          Central Andes" in E. Ishida *et al. The Report of the
          University of Tokyo Scientific Expedition to the
          Andes in 1958,* I, Tokyo, 417-20
1964   "Human geography of methods of irrigation in the
          Central Andes" in *Land Use in Semi-arid Mediter-
          ranean Climates,* U.N.E.S.C.O., Paris, 135-37

KÖPPEN, W., and R. GEIGER
1930-9   *Handbuch der Klimatologie,* 5 volumes, Berlin

KOSOK, P.
1942   "The role of irrigation in ancient Peru" *Proceedings
          of the Eighth American Science Congress,* 2, 169-78
1965   *Life, Land and Water in Ancient Peru,* New York

KRAPOVICKAS, P.
1955   *El yacimiento de Tebenchique, Puna de Atacama,*
          Universidad de Buenos Aires, Publicaciones del In-
          stituto de Arqueología, 3
1958-9   "Arqueología de la Puna Argentina" *Anales de Arque-
          ología y Etnología* (Universidad Nacional de Cuyo,
          Instituto de Arqueología y Etnología), 14-15, 53-113

KRAMER, F.
1966   *Breaking Ground: notes on the distribution of some
          simple tillage tools,* Sacramento Anthropological So-
          ciety, Paper 5, Sacramento

KRICKEBERG, W.
1956   *Altmexikanische Kulturen,* Berlin

KRIEGER, H. W.
1929   "The aborigines of the ancient island of Hispaniola"
          Annual Report of the Smithsonian Institution, 473-
          506

KROEBER, A. L.
1930   *The North Coast: archaeological explorations in
          Peru: II,* Field Museum of Natural History, Anthro-
          pology Memoirs, 2, Chicago

KUBLER, G.
1942   "Population movements in Mexico, 1520-1600" *His-
          panic American Historical Review,* 22, 606-43

KUCZYNSKI GODARD, M. H.
1945   *Estudio familiar, demográfico, ecológico en estancias
          indias de la altiplanicie del Titicaca (Ichupampa),*
          Lima

LA BARRE, W.
1948   *The Aymara Indians of the Lake Titicaca Plateau,
          Bolivia,* American Anthropological Association,
          Memoir 68

LAFON, C. R.
1956-7   "Nuevos descubrimientos en El Alfarcito" *RUNA,*
          8, Universidad de Buenos Aires, 43-59

LANDA, DIEGO DE
1937 *Yucatan before and after the Conquest* [1566], trans. and ed. W. Gates, The Maya Society, Baltimore
1941 *Landa's Relación de las cosas de Yucatán* [1566], trans. and ed. A. M. Tozzer, Peabody Museum of American Archaeology and Ethnology, 18, Cambridge (Mass.)

LANDIVAR, RAFAEL
1948 *Rusticatio Mexicana* [1781], English prose translation by Graydon W. Regenos, Middle American Research Institute, Tulane University, New Orleans, publication 11, 155-314

LANGLOIS, L.
1933 "Exploration archéologique de la valle de l'Utcubamba," *Revista del Museo Nacional* (Lima), 2, 126-28

LANGMAN, IDA K.
1956 "Botanical gardens in ancient Mexico" *Missouri Botanical Garden Bulletin,* 44, 17-31

LANJOUW, J.
1936 "Studies of the vegetation of the Suriname savannahs and swamps" *Nederlandsch Kruidkundig Archief,* 46, 823-51

LANNING, E. P.
1965 "Early Man in Peru" *Scientific American,* 213, 68-76
1967 *Peru before the Incas,* Englewood Cliffs

LAPORTE, F. L. DE, COUNT DE CASTELNAU
1850-9 *Expedición en las partes centrales de la América del Sur, 1843-47,* 6 volumes, Paris

LARCO HOYLE, R.
1938 *Los Mochicas,* 2 volumes, Lima

LARES, J. I.
1952 *Etnografía del Estado Mérida,* 3rd. ed. (1st ed. 1883), Mérida

LARREA, C. M.
1965 *La cultura incasica del Ecuador,* Instituto Panamericano de Geografía e Historia, publicación 253, México

LARROUY, A.
1914 *Los indios del valle de Catamarca: estudio histórico,* Universidad de Buenos Aires, Facultad de Filosofía y Letras, Publicaciones de la Sección Antropológica 14, Buenos Aires

LAS CASAS, BARTOLEMÉ DE
1958 *Apologetica Historia* [1527-59], Biblioteca de Autores Españoles 105 and 106, Madrid

LATCHAM, R. E.
1923 *La existencia de la propiedad en el antiguo imperio de los Incas,* Santiago de Chile
1926 "La organización agraria de los antiguos indígenas de Chile" *La Información* (revista mensual, Santiago, Chile), December, 356-60
1936a *La agricultura precolombina en Chile y los países vecinos,* Santiago de Chile
1936b "Indian ruins in northern Chile" *American Anthropologist,* 38, 52-58
1936c "Atacameño archaeology" *American Anthropologist,* 38, 609-19
1938 *Arqueología de la Región Atacameña,* Universidad de Chile, Santiago

LATHRAP, D. W.
1962-3 "Los Andes Centrales y la Montaña: investigación de las relaciones culturales entre la montaña Peruana y las Altas Civilizaciones de los Andes Centrales" *Revista del Museo Nacional* (Lima), 32, 196-202
1965 "Origins of Central Andean civilization: new evidence," review of *Andes 2,* by S. Izumi and T. Sono, *Science,* 148, 796-98
1970 *The Upper Amazon,* London
1972 "Alternative models of population movements in the tropical lowlands of South America" *XXXIX International Congress of Americanists* (Lima, 1970): *Proceedings,* 4, 13-23

LATORRE Y SETIÉN, G. (ed)
1919 *Relaciones geográficas de Indias,* Centro Oficial de Estudios Americanistas de Sevilla, Biblioteca Colonial Americana, 3, Sevilla

LAUFER, B., and C. W. MEAD
1919 "Narcotics: coca and betel chewing" *American Anthropologist,* 21, 335-37

LAZARO DE ARREGUI, DOMINGO
1946 *Descripción de la Nueva Galicia* [1621], ed. F. Chevalier, Sevilla

LEICHT, H.
"Chinampas y almácigos flotantes" *Anales del Instituto de Biología* (México), 8, 375-86

LEIGHLY, J. B.
1953 "Dry Climates: their nature and distribution" in *Desert Research,* Proceedings of the International Symposium held in Jerusalem, May 7-14, 1952, Research Council of Israel, Special Publication, 2, Jerusalem

LEÓN, N.
1934 "Los indios tarascos del Lago de Pátzcuaro" *Anales del Museo Nacional de México,* I, 149-68

LEONARD, O. E.
1949 "Locality Group Structures in Bolivia" *Rural Sociology,* 14, 250-60

LEOPOLD, A. S.
1950 "Vegetation Zones of Mexico" *Ecology,* 31, 507-18

LE PAIGE, G.
1958 "Antiguas culturas Atacameñas en la Cordillera Chileña" *Anales de la Universidad Católica de Valparaiso,* 4-5, 20-77

LEWIN, B. (ed)
1958 *Descripción del Virreinato del Perú. Crónica inédita de comienzos del siglo XVII,* Instituto de Investigaciones Históricas (Colección de Textos y Documentos), Serie B, No. 1, Universidad Nacional del Litoral, Rosario, Argentina

LEWIS, O.
1949 "Plow culture and hoe culture — a study in contrasts" *Rural Sociology,* 14, 116-27

LINNÉ, S.
1937 "Hunting and fishing in the valley of Mexico in the sixteenth century" *Ethnos,* 2, 56-64
1938 *Zapotecan Antiquities,* Ethnographical Museum of Sweden, 4, Stockholm

LINNÉ, S. (continued)
1942   *Mexican Highland Cultures,* Stockholm
1948   *El Valle y la Ciudad de México en 1550. Relación histórica fundada sobre un mapa geográfico,* Ethnographical Museum of Sweden, 9, Stockholm

LIPSCHUTZ, A.
1966   "La despoblación de las Indias después de la Conquista" *América Indígena,* 26, 229-47

LIRA, J. A.
1944   *Diccionario Kkechúwa-Español,* Tucumán

LISTER, R. H.
1947-8   "Archaeology of the Middle Río Balsas Basin, Mexico" *American Antiquity,* 13, 67-77
1955   *The present status of archaeology of Western Mexico,* University of Colorado, Boulder, Series in Anthropology, 5

LIZÁRRAGA, REGINALDO DE
1968   *Descripción breve de toda la tierra del Perú, Tucumán, Río de la Plata y Chile* [c. 1600], Madrid

LLANOS, L. A.
1936   "Trabajos arqueológicos en el Departamento del Cuzco" *Revista del Museo Nacional* (Lima), 5, 123-56

LONG, R. C. E.
1942   "The payment of tribute in the Codex Mendoza" *Notes on Middle American Archaeology and Ethnology,* Carnegie Institution of Washington, 10, Washington

LONGYEAR, J. M.
1966   "Archaeological survey of El Salvador" in G. F. Ekholm and G. R. Willey (eds) *Handbook of Middle American Indians,* 4, Austin, 132-55

LÓPEZ, E.
1922   "Influencia de la desacación del Lago Texcoco sobre el clima del valle de México" *Memorias y Revista de la Sociedad Científica "Antonio Alzate,"* 40, 631-42

LÓPEZ DE GÓMARA, FRANCISCO
1954   *Historia general de las Indias* [1552], 2 volumes, Barcelona
1964   *Cortés: the life of the Conqueror by His Secretary* (from *Istoria de la Conquista de México,* 1552) translated and edited by L. B. Simpson, Berkeley and Los Angeles

LÓPEZ DE VELASCO, JUAN
1894   *Geografía y descripción de las Indias* [1571-74], Madrid

LORENZO, J. L.
1956   "Notas sobre arqueología y cambios climaticos en la cuenca de México" in F. Mooser, S. E. White, J. L. Lorenzo (eds) *La cuenca de México: consideraciones geológicas y arqueológicas,* Instituto Nacional de Antropología e Historia, Dirección de Prehistoria, publicación 2, 29-46
1958   "Una hipótesis paleoclimática para la cuenca de México" in *Miscellanea Paul Rivet octogenario dictata,* I, México, 579-84
1958-9   "Aspectos físicos del Valle de Oaxaca" *Revista Mexicana de Estudios Antropológicos,* 15, 49-63

LOTHROP, S. K.
1928   "Santiago Atitlán, Guatemala" *Indian Notes,* 5, 370-95

1933   *Atitlán,* Carnegie Institution of Washington, publication 444, Washington
1939   "The southeastern frontier of the Maya" *American Anthropologist,* 41, 42-54

LOUBAT, DUQUE DE
1900   *Codex Vaticanus A (Ríos),* Rome
1901   *Codex Fejérváry-Mayer,* Paris

LOWE, G. W.
1959   *Archaeological exploration of the Upper Grijalva River, Chiapas, Mexico,* Papers of the New World Archaeological Foundation, 2, Orinda

LOWE, G. W., and A. A. MASON
1965   "Archaeological survey of the Chiapas Coast, Highlands, and Upper Grijalva Basin" in G. R. Willey (ed) *Handbook of Middle American Indians,* 2, 195-236, Austin

LUMHOLTZ, C.
1902   *Unknown Mexico,* New York

LUNDELL, C. L.
1940   *The 1936 Michigan-Carnegie Botanical Expedition to British Honduras,* Carnegie Institution of Washington, publication 522, Washington

MCAFEE, B., and R. H. BARLOW (eds)
1945-8   "The Titles of Tetzcotzinco (Santa María Nativitas)" *Tlalocán,* 2, 110-27

MCBRIDE, G. M.
1923   *The Land Systems of Mexico,* American Geographical Society, New York

MCBRIDE, G. M., and M. A. MCBRIDE
1942   "Highland Guatemala and its Maya communities" *Geographical Review,* 32, 252-68

MCBRYDE, F. W.
1940   "Influenza in America during the sixteenth century" *Bulletin of the History of Medicine,* 8, 296-302
1945   *Cultural and Historical Geography of Southwest Guatemala,* Smithsonian Institution, Institute of Social Anthropology, publication 4, Washington

MCCABE, R. A.
1955   "The prehistoric engineer-farmers of Chihuahua" *Transactions of the Wisconsin Academy of Sciences, Arts and Letters,* 44, 75-90

MCCOWN, T. D.
1945   *Pre-Incaic Huamachuco: Survey and Excavations in the Region of Huamachuco and Cajabamba,* University of California Publications in American Archaeology and Ethnology, 39, 223-346, Berkeley and Los Angeles

MCGEE, W. J.
1895   "The beginnings of agriculture" *American Anthropologist,* 8, 350-75

MACNEISH, R. S.
1947-8   "Preliminary report on coastal Tamaulipas" *American Antiquity,* 13, 1-14
1958   *Preliminary archaeological investigations in the Sierra de Tamaulipas, Mexico,* Transactions of the American Philosophical Society, 48(6), Philadelphia

MacNeish, R. S. (continued)

1961   *Tehuacán Archaeological-Botanical Project: Report I*, R. S. Peabody Foundation for Archaeology, Andover

1962   *Second Annual Report of the Tehuacán Archaeological-Botanical Project*, R. S. Peabody Foundation for Archaeology, Andover

1964   "The food gathering and incipient agriculture stage of prehistoric Middle America" in R. C. West (ed) *Handbook of Middle American Indians*, I, Austin

1967   "An interdisciplinary approach to an archaeological problem" in D. S. Byers (ed) *The Prehistory of the Tehuacán Valley, I: Environment and Subsistence*, Austin and London, 14-24

McQuown, N. A.

1958   "The *General History of the Things of New Spain* by Bernardino de Sahagún" *Hispanic American Historical Review*, 38, 235-38

Maldonado-Koerdell, M.

1941   "Jardines botánicos de los antiguos Mexicanos" *Revista de la Sociedad Mexicana de Historia Natural*, 2, 79-84

1942   "La botánica azteca" *Boletín bibliográfico de antropología Americana*, 6, 62-74

1954-5 "La historia geohidrológica de la cuenca de México (hasta *ca.* S. XVI)" *Revista Mexicana de Estudios Antropológicos*, 24, 15-21

Maler, T.

1903   *Researches in the central portion of the Usumatsintla valley*, Memoirs of the Peabody Museum of American Archaeology and Ethnology, 2, Cambridge (Mass.)

Manglesdorf, P. C., R. S. MacNeish and G. R. Willey

1964   "Origins of agriculture in Middle America" in R. C. West (ed) *Handbook of Middle American Indians*, I, Austin, 427-45

Marcoy, P.

1873   *A journey across South America from the Pacific Ocean to the Atlantic Ocean*, 2 volumes, London

1875   *Travels in South America*, 2 volumes, London

Markham, C. R.

1856   *Cuzco: a journey to the ancient capital of Peru*, London

1862   *Travels in Peru and India*, London

1864   *Contributions towards a grammar and dictionary of Quichua*, London

1872   *Reports on the discovery of Peru*, trans. and ed. C. R. Markham, Hakluyt Society, 47, London

1880   *Peruvian Bark*, London

1908   *Vocabularies of the General Language of the Incas of Peru, or Runa Simi*, London

1912   *The Conquest of New Granada*, London

Márquez Miranda, F.

1936   "La antigua provincia de los Diaguitas" in *Historia de la Nación Argentina*, I, Buenos Aires

1939   "Cuatro viajes de estudio al mas remoto Noroeste Argentino" *Revista del Museo de la Plata: Sección Antropología*, I, 93-243

1946   "The Diaguita of Argentina" in J. H. Steward (ed) *Handbook of South American Indians*, 2, Smithsonian Institution, Bureau of American Ethnology, Bulletin 143, Washington, 637-54

1954   *Región meridional de América del Sur*, Instituto Panamericano de Geografía e Historia, Comisión de Historia, México

Martin, R. T.

1970   "The role of coca in the history, religion and medicine of South American Indians" *Economic Botany*, 24, 422-37

Martonne, E. de

1934   "The Andes of North West Argentina" *Geographical Journal*, LXXXIV, 1-16

Mason, J. A.

1925   "Archaeological researches in the region of Santa Marta, Colombia" *XXI International Congress of Americanists* (Göteborg, 1924): *Proceedings*, 2, 159-66

1931-9 *The archaeology of Santa Marta, Colombia: The Tairona Culture*, Field Museum of Natural History, Anthropology Series, 20, 3 parts, Chicago

Matheny, R. T.

1976   "Maya lowland hydraulic systems" *Science*, 193 (no. 4254), 639-46

Matienzo, Juan de

1910   *Gobierno del Perú. Obra escrita en el siglo XVI por el Licenciado Don Juan Matienzo, Oidor de la Real Audiencia de Charcas* [1567], ed. J. N. Matienzo, Universidad de Buenos Aires, Facultad de Filosofía y Letras, Publicaciones de la Sección Antropológica, Buenos Aires

Matos Mar, J.

1957   "La propiedad en la isla de Tequile (Lago Titicaca)" *Revista del Museo Nacional* (Lima), 26, 211-71

Maudslay, A. P.

1916   "The Valley of Mexico" *Geographical Journal*, XLVIII, 11-25

Maw, H. L.

1829   *Journal of a passage from the Pacific to the Atlantic, crossing the Andes in the northern provinces of Peru and descending the river Marañon or Amazon*, London

Mayer-Oakes, W. J.

1960   "A developmental concept of pre-Spanish urbanization in the Valley of Mexico" *Middle American Research Records*, 2, Tulane University, 165-76

Mayerson, P.

1960   *The Ancient Agricultural Regime of Nessana and the Central Negeb*, British School of Archaeology in Jerusalem, Jerusalem

Mead, C. W.

1916   "Prehistoric bronze in South America" *Anthropological Papers of the American Museum of Natural History*, 12, 15-52, New York

Means, P. A.

1925   "A study of ancient Andean social institutions" *Transactions of the Connecticut Academy of Arts and Sciences*, 27, 407-69

MEANS, P. A. (continued)
1931   *Ancient Civilizations of the Andes,* New York
1932   *Fall of the Inca Empire, and the Spanish Rule in Peru, 1530-1780,* London

MEGGERS, B. J.
1966   *Ecuador,* London

MEGGERS, B. J., and C. EVANS (eds)
1963   *Aboriginal Cultural Development in Latin America: An Interpretative Review,* Smithsonian Miscellaneous Collections, 146, Washington

MEIGS, P.
1953   "World distribution of arid and semi-arid homoclimates" *Reviews of Research on Arid Zone Hydrology,* U.N.E.S.C.O., Paris, 203-209
1966   *Geography of Coastal Deserts,* U.N.E.S.C.O., Paris

MENDIETA Y NÚÑEZ, L.
1940   *Los Tarascos,* Universidad Nacional Autónoma de México, Instituto de Investigaciones Sociales, México
1949   *Los Zapotecos,* Universidad Nacional Autónoma de México, Instituto de Investigaciones Sociales, México

MENDIZABAL, M. O. DE
1925   "El Jardín de Netzahualcóyotl" *Ethnos,* I, 86-95

MENZEL, D.
1959   "The Inca occupation of the South Coast of Peru" *Southwestern Journal of Anthropology,* 15, 125-42

MÉTRAUX, A.
1942   *The native tribes of East Bolivia and West Matto Grosso,* Smithsonian Institution, Bureau of American Ethnology, Bulletin 134, Washington
1946   "La civilization Guyano-Amazonienne et ses Provinces Culturelles" *Acta Americana,* 4, 130-53
1948   "Tribes of the eastern slopes of the Bolivian Andes" in J. H. Steward (ed) *Handbook of South American Indians,* 3, Smithsonian Institution, Bureau of American Ethnology, Bulletin 143, Washington, 465-506

MEYER L'EPÉE, C.
1943   "La agricultura de México en la época pre-Cortesiana" *Investigación Económica,* 2, 375-85

MIDDENDORF, E. W.
1890   *Wörterbuch des Runa Simi oder der Keshua-Sprache (Die Enheimischen Sprachen Perus,* 2), Leipzig
1891   *Die Aimara-Sprache (Die Enheimischen Sprachen Perus,* 5), Leipzig

MILES, S. W.
1957   "The sixteenth century Pokom-Maya: a documentary analysis of social structure and archaeological setting" *Transactions of the American Philosophical Society,* 47(4), 731-81

MILLON, R.
1954   "Irrigation at Teotihuacán" *American Antiquity,* 20, 177-80
1955   "Trade, tree cultivation and the development of private property in land" *American Anthropologist,* 57, 698-712
1957   "Irrigation systems in the valley of Teotihuacán" *American Antiquity,* 23, 160-66

MILLON, R., C. HALL, and M. DÍAZ
1961   "Conflict in the modern Teotihuacán irrigation system" *Comparative Studies in Society and History,* 4, 494-521

MIRANDA, F., and A. J. SHARP
1950   "Characteristics of the vegetation in certain regions of eastern Mexico" *Ecology,* 31, 313-33

MIRANDA, J.
1958   "Orígenes de la ganadería indígena en la Mixteca" in *Miscellanea Paul Rivet octogenario dictata,* 2, México, 787-96
1962   "La Pax Hispánica y los desplazamientos de los pueblos indígenas" *Cuadernos Americanos,* 125 (6), 186-90

MISHKIN, B.
1946   "The Contemporary Quechua" in J. H. Steward (ed) *Handbook of South American Indians,* 2, Smithsonian Institution, Bureau of American Ethnology, Bulletin 143, Washington, 411-70

MOLINA, ALONSO DE
1944   *Vocabulario en lengua Castellana y Mexicana* [1571], Madrid

MOLINA, JUAN IGNACIO DE
1809   *The Geographical, Natural and Civil History of Chile* [1782], trans. R. Alsop and W. Shaler, London

MOLÍNS FÁBREGA, N.
1954   "El códice Mendocino y la economía de Tenochtitlán" *Revista Mexicana de Estudios Antropológicos,* 14, 303-35

MONHEIM, F.
1956   *Beiträge zur Klimatologie und Hydrologie des Titicacabeckens,* Heidelberger Geographische Arbeiten, I

MONTES, A.
1958-9   "Cambios climáticos durante el Holoceno en las Sierras de Córdoba" *Anales de Arqueología y Etnología* (Universidad Nacional de Cuyo, Instituto de Arqueología y Etnología), 14-15, 35-52

MONTESINOS, FERNANDO
1920   *Memorias Antiguas: Historiales del Perú* [1642-4], trans. and ed. P. A. Means, Hakluyt Society, 48, London

MOODIE, D. W., and B. KAYE
1969   "The northern limit of Indian agriculture in North America" *Geographical Review,* 59, 513-29

MOORE, S. F.
1958   *Power and Property in Inca Peru,* New York

MOOSER, F., S. E. WHITE, and J. L. LORENZO
1956   *La cuenca de México: consideraciones geológicas y arqueológicas,* Instituto Nacional de Antropología e Historia, Dirección de Prehistoria, publicación 2, México

MORENO, F. P.
1901   "Notes on the anthropogeography of Argentina" *Geographical Journal,* 18, 574-89

MORIARTY, J. R.
1968   "Floating gardens *(chinampas):* agriculture in the old lakes of Mexico" *América Indígena,* 28, 461-84

MORSE, D.
1967   "Tuberculosis" in D. R. Brothwell and A. T. Sandison (eds) *Diseases in Antiquity,* Springfield, 250-58

MORTIMER, W. G.
1901   *Peru: a history of coca,* New York

MOSELEY, M. E.
1969   "Assessing the archaeological significance of *mahamaes*" *American Antiquity,* 34, 485-87

MOTA Y ESCOBAR, ALONZO DE LA
1930   *Descripción Geográfica de los Reinos de Nueva Galicia, Nueva Vizcaya y Nuevo León* [1601-3], México
1945   *Memoriales del Obispo de Tlaxcala* [1608-24], Anales del Instituto Nacional de Antropología e Historia, I, 191-306

MOTOLINÍA, TORIBIO [DE BENAVENTE]
1941   *Historia de los Indios de la Nueva España* [1541], México
1950   *History of the Indians of New Spain* [1541], trans. and ed. E. Andros Foster, Cortés Society, New York
1951   *History of the Indians of New Spain* [1541], trans. and ed. F. B. Steck, Academy of Franciscan History, Washington

MURDOCK, G. P.
1951   *Outline of South American Cultures,* New Haven

MULLER, E. F. J.
1952   "Recursos naturales del Lago de Xochimilco, del siglo X al XVI" *Boletín de la Sociedad Mexicana de Geografía y Estadística,* 73, 8-16

MURRA, J. V.
1946   "The historic tribes of Ecuador" in J. H. Steward (ed) *Handbook of South American Indians,* 2, Smithsonian Institution, Bureau of American Ethnology, Bulletin 143, Washington, 785-821
1958   "On Inca political structure" in V. F. Ray (ed) *Systems of Political Control and Bureaucracy in Human Societies,* Seattle
1960   "Rite and crop in the Inca State" in S. Diamond (ed) *Culture in History: Essays in Honor of Paul Radin,* New York, 393-407
1961   "Social structural and economic themes in Andean ethnohistory" *Anthropological Quarterly,* 34, 47-59
1962   "An archaeological 'restudy' of an Andean ethnohistorical account" *American Antiquity,* 28, 1-4
1965   "Herds and herders in the Inca State" in *Man and Animals,* American Association for the Advancement of Science, publication 78, Washington, 185-216
1967   "La visita de los chupachu como fuente etnológica" in Iñigo Ortiz de Zúñiga *Visita de la Provincia de León de Huánuco* [1562], 1, 381-406, Universidad Nacional Hermilio Valdizán, Huánuco, Perú
1968   "An Aymara Kingdom in 1567" *Ethnohistory,* 15, 115-51
1972   "El 'control vertical' de un máximo de pisos ecológicos en la economía de las sociedades andinas" in Iñigo Ortiz de Zúñiga *Visita de la Provincia de León de Huánuco* [1562], 2, 429-68, Universidad Nacional Hermilio Valdizán, Huánuco, Perú
1975   "Quelques commentaires sur 'Les sociétés étagées des Andes' de A. Fiorvanti-Molinié" *Études Rurales,* 67, 57-59

MURÚA [MORÚA], MARTÍN DE
1946   *Historia del origen y genealogía real de los Reyes Incas del Perú* [1590], Madrid
1962   *Historia General del Perú, origen y descendencia de los Incas* [1590], 2 volumes, Madrid

MYRES, J. G.
1936   "Savannah and forest vegetation of the interior Guiana Plateau" *Journal of Ecology,* 24, 162-84

NACHTIGALL, H.
1958   *Die amerikanischen Megalithkulturen,* Berlin
1961   *Alt-Kolumbien: Vorgeschichtliche Indianerkulturen,* Berlin
1966   *Indianische Fischer, Feldbauer und Viehzüchter: Beiträge zur peruanischen Völkerkunde.* Marburger Studien zur Völkerkunde, 2

NAVARRETE, C.
1960   *Archaeological explorations in the region of the Frailesca, Chiapas,* Papers of the New World Archaeological Foundation, 6, 7, Orinda

NEELY, J. A.
1967   "Organización hidráulica y sistemas de irrigación prehistóricos en el Valle de Oaxaca" *Boletín del Instituto Nacional de Antropología e Historia* (México), 27, 15-17

NETTING, R.
1968   *Hill farmers of Nigeria: cultural ecology of the Kofyar of the Jos Plateau,* American Ethnological Society, Monograph 46, Seattle

NEVEU LEMAIRE, M.
1909   *Los Lagos de los Altiplanos de la América del Sur,* La Paz

NICHOLS, H. W.
1929   "Inca relics in the Atacama Desert, Chile" *American Anthropologist,* 31, 130-35

NICHOLSON, H. B.
1967   "The efflorescence of Mesoamerican civilization: a resumé" in B. Bell (ed) *Indian Mexico Past and Present,* Latin American Center, University of California, Los Angeles, 46-71

NIKIFOROFF, C. C.
1948   "Stony soils and their classification" *Soil Science,* 66, 347-63

NILLES, J.
1942-5   "Digging-sticks, spades, hoes, axes and adzes of the Kuman people in the Bismark Mountains of East Central New Guinea" *Anthropos,* 37-40, 205-12

NOGUERA, E.
1966   "La metalurgia en Mesoamérica" *Cuadernos Americanos,* 147, 127-32

NORDENSKIÖLD, ERLAND
1906   *Investigaciones arqueológicas en la región fronteriza de Perú y Bolivia, 1904-5,* Upsala
1912   *De sydamerikanska indianernas kulturhistoria,* Stockholm

NORDENSKIÖLD, ERLAND (continued)

1913   "Urnengräber und Mounds im Bolivianischen Flach-
lande" *Baessler-archiv*, 3, 205-55

1919   *An ethnographic analysis of the material culture of
two Indian tribes in the Gran Chaco*, Comparative
Ethnographical Studies, I, Göteborg

1920   *The changes in the material culture of two Indian
tribes under the influence of new surroundings*, Comparative Ethnographical Studies, 2, Göteborg

1921   *The Copper and Bronze Ages in South America*,
Comparative Ethnographical Studies, 4, Göteborg

1924   *Forschungen und Abenteuer in Sudamerika*, Stuttgart

1929   "The American Indian as an Inventor" *Journal of
the Royal Anthropological Institute*, 59, 273-309

1931   *Origin of the Indian civilizations in South America*,
Comparative Ethnographical Studies, 9, Göteborg

NÚÑEZ DEL PRADO, O.

1949   "Chinchero, un pueblo andino del Sur" *Revista Universitaria* (Cuzco), 38, 1949, 177-230

1955   "Aspects of Andean Native Life" *Kroeber Anthropological Society Papers*, 12, 1-21

NUTTALL, Z.

1902   *Codex Nuttall*, Peabody Museum of American Archaeology and Ethnology, Cambridge, Mass.

1920   "Los jardines del antiguo México" *Memorias y Revista de la Sociedad Científica "Antonio Alzate,"* 37,
México, 193-213

1926   *Official reports of the towns of Tequizistlan, Tepech-
pan, Acolman, and San Juan Teotihuacán sent by
Francisco de Casteñeda to his Majesty, Philip II, and
the Council of the Indies in 1580*, Papers of the Peabody Museum of American Archaeology and Ethnology, 2, Cambridge, Mass.

OAKES, M.

1951   *The Two Crosses of Todos Santos: survivals of Mayan
religious ritual*, Bollingen Series, 27, New York

OBER, F. A.

1884   *Travels in Mexico and life among the Mexicans*,
Boston

O'BRYAN, D.

1952   "The abandonment of the northern pueblos in the
thirteenth century" in S. Tax (ed) *Indian Tribes of
Aboriginal America*, Chicago, 153-57

OJEA, HERNÁNDO

1897   *Libro tercero de la historia religiosa de la Provincia
de México de la Orden de Santo Domingo* [c. 1610],
México

OLIVA, GIOVANNI ANELLO

1895   *Historia del Reino y provincias del Perú, y de sus
Incas reyes, descubrimiento por los españoles* [1598],
Lima

OLSON, R. L.

1927-9   "Adze, canoe, and house types of the Northwest
Coast" *University of Washington Publications in Anthropology*, 2, 5-31

ORAMAS, L. R.

1917   "Apuntes sobre arqueología Venezolana" *Proceedings of the Second Pan American Science Congress*,
Washington, 138-45

OROZCO Y BERRA, M.

1950   *Historia antigua y de las culturas aborigenes de
México*, 2 volumes, México

ORTIZ DE ZÚÑIGA, IÑIGO

1967-72   *Visita de la Provincia de León de Huánuco* [1562], 1,
1967, 2, 1972, Universidad Nacional Hermilio Valdizán, Huánuco, Perú

ORTOLANI, M., and J. P. COLE

1963   "Tipi di sedi sulle Ande centrali" *Rivista Geografica
Italiana*, 70, 369-94

OSBORNE, D.

1943   "An archaeological reconnaissance in south eastern
Michoacán, Mexico" *American Antiquity*, 9, 59-73

OSGOOD, C. B., and G. D. HOWARD

1943   *An Archaeological Survey of Venezuela*, Yale University Publications in Anthropology, 27, New Haven

OVIEDO Y BAÑOS, JOSÉ AGUSTÍN DE

1940   *Historia de la conquista y población de la provincia
de Venezuela* [1723], New York (fascimile of 1824
ed.)

OWER, L. H.

1927   "Features of British Honduras" *Geographical Journal*, 70, 372-86

1929   *The geology of British Honduras*, Belize

PADDOCK, J.

1964   "La etnohistoria mixteca y Monte Albán" *XXXV
International Congress of Americanists* (Mexico,
1962): *Proceedings*, I, 461-78

1966a   "Oaxaca in ancient Mesoamerica" in J. Paddock (ed)
Ancient Oaxaca, Stanford, 83-241

1966b   "Mixtec ethnohistory and Monte Albán V" *ibid.*,
367-85

PADDOCK, J. (ed)

1953   *Excavations in the Mixteca Alta*, Mesoamerican
Notes, 3, Mexico

PAGE, J. L.

1930   *Climate of Mexico*, Monthly Weather Review, supplement 33, Washington

PAHISSA CAMPA, M. E., and D. G. LÓPEZ ORBEA

1967   "Uso de la tierra en el borde de la Puna" in *Contribuciones a la geografía de la Quebrada de Humahuaca*, Universidad de Buenos Aires, Facultad de
Filosofía y Letras. Centro de Estudios Geográficos,
Serie A, 25, Buenos Aires

PALACIOS, E. J.

1928   *En los confines de la Selva Lacandona*, Secretaría de
Educación Publica, Dirección de Arqueología,
México

PALERM, A.

1951   "Tecnología, formaciones socio-económicas y re-
ligión en Mesoamérica" in S. Tax (ed) *The Civilizations of Ancient America*, Chicago, 19-30

1954   "La distribución del regadío en el área central de
Mesoamérica" *Notas e Informaciones Ciencias Sociales* (México), V, 3-15, 64-74

1955   "The agricultural basis of urban civilization in Mesoamerica" in *Irrigation Civilizations: a comparative
study*, Social Science Monographs, I, Pan American
Union, Washington, 28-42

PALERM, A. (continued)
1961   "Sistemas de regadío en Teotihuacán y en el Ped-
        regal" *Revista Interamericana de Ciencias Sociales*
        (México), I, Pan American Union, Washington, 297-
        302

1967   "Agricultural systems and food patterns" in M. Nash
        (ed) *Handbook of Middle American Indians*, 6,
        Austin, 26-52

1973   *Obras hidráulicas prehispánicas en el sistema la-
        custre del valle de México*, México

PALERM, A., and E. R. WOLF
1954-5 "El desarrollo del área clave del imperio texcocano"
        Revista Mexicana de Estudios Antropológicos, 14,
        337-49

1957   "Ecological potential and cultural development in
        Mesoamerica" in *Studies in Human Ecology*, Pan
        American Union, Washington, 1-37

1961   "Agricultura de riego en el Viejo Senorio del Acol-
        huacán" *Revista Interamericana de Ciencias So-
        ciales*, I, Pan American Union, Washington, 289-96

PARDO, L. A.
1942   "Sillustani, una metrópoli Incaica" *Revista del Mu-
        seo Nacional*, (Lima), 11, 203-15

1946   "Ollantaitambo" *Revista de la sección arqueológica
        de la Universidad Nacional del Cuzco*, núm. 2, 47-73

PARK, W. Z.
1946   "Tribes of the Sierra Nevada de Santa Marta" in
        J. H. Steward (ed) *Handbook of South American
        Indians*, 2, Smithsonian Institution, Bureau of Ameri-
        can Ethnology, Bulletin 143, Washington, 865-86

PARKER, N.
1967   "A hypothesis concerning the relationship between
        Texcoco fabric-marked pottery, *tlateles* and chin-
        ampa agriculture" *American Antiquity*, 32, 515-22

PARODI, L. R.
1935   "Relaciones de la agricultura prehispánica con la
        agricultura actual — observaciones generales sobre
        la domesticación de las plantas" *Anales de la Acad-
        emia Nacional de Agronomía y Veterinaría de Buenos
        Aires*, I, 115-67

PARSONS, J. J.
1949   *Antioqueño colonization in Western Colombia*, Ibero
        Americana, 32, University of California, Berkeley

1955   "The Miskito Pine Savanna of Nicaragua and Hon-
        duras" *Annals of the Association of American Geog-
        raphers*, 45, 36-63

1969   "Ridged fields in the Río Guayas Valley, Ecuador"
        American Antiquity, 34, 76-80

PARSONS, J. J., and W. A. BOWEN
1966   "Ancient ridged fields of the San Jorge River Flood-
        plain, Colombia" *Geographical Review*, 56, 317-43

PARSONS, J. J., and W. M. DENEVAN
1967   "Pre-Columbian ridged fields" *Scientific American*,
        217, 93-100

PARSONS, J. R.
1968   "The archaeological significance of *mahamaes* cul-
        tivation on the coast of Peru" *American Antiquity*,
        33, 80-85

1970   "An archaeological evaluation of the Codice Xolotl"
        American Antiquity, 35, 431-40

PARSONS, J. R., and N. P. PSUTY
1975   "Sunken fields and prehispanic subsistence on the
        Peruvian coast" *American Antiquity*, 40, 259-82

PASO Y TRONCOSO, FRANCISCO DEL (ed)
1905-6 *Papeles de Nueva España*, 6 volumes, Madrid

1944-47 *Papeles de Nueva España: suplemento* (ed. L. Var-
        gas Rea), 2 volumes, México

PATIÑO, L. R.
1940   "Soil erosion in the central plateau of Mexico" *Pro-
        ceedings of the Sixth Pacific Science Congress*, 4,
        877-83

PATRÓN, P.
1889   *La Verruga de los Conquistadores del Perú*, Lima

PAUER, P. S.
1927   "La población indígena de Yalalag, Oaxaca" *An-
        thropos*, 22, 45-65

PAYNE, E. J.
1892-9 *History of the New World called America*, 2 volumes,
        Oxford

PAZ SOLDÁN, M.
1862   *Geografía del Perú*, Paris

1877   *Diccionario Geográfico* (Perú), Lima

PEJML, K.
1966   *Study on climatic fluctuations in the historical time
        of the western coast of South America*, Hydromet
        Ustav, Prague (in Czech with English abstract)

PEÑA, M. T. DE LA
1950   *Problemas sociales y económicos de las Mixtecas*,
        Memorias del Instituto Nacional Indigenista, 2,
        México

PEÑAFIEL, A.
1885   *Nombres Geográficos de México*, México

PENDERGAST, D. M.
1962   "Metal artifacts in prehispanic Mesoamerica" *Ameri-
        can Antiquity*, 27, 520-45

PENNINGTON, C. W.
1963   *The Tarahumar of Mexico: their environment and
        material culture*, University of Utah, Salt Lake City

1969   *The Tepehuan of Chihuahua: their material culture*,
        University of Utah, Salt Lake City

PÉREZ DE BARRADAS, J.
1951   *Pueblos indígenas de la Gran Colombia: Los Muiscas
        antes de la Conquista*, 2 volumes, Madrid

PÉREZ GARCÍA, P.
1956   *La Sierra Juarez*, 2 volumes, México

PERRY, W. J.
1916   "The geographical distribution of terraced cultiva-
        tion and irrigation" *Proceedings of the Manchester
        Literary and Philosophical Society*, 60, 1-25

PFEIFER, G.
1939   "Sinaloa und Sonora. Beiträge zur Landeskunde
        und Kulturgeographie des nordwestlichen Mexico"
        Mittleilungen der Geographischen in Hamburg, 46,
        289-460

1966   "The basin of Puebla-Tlaxcala in Mexico" *Revista
        Geográfica*, 64, 86-107

PICHARDO MOYA, F.
1956   *Los Aborigenes de las Antillas,* México

PIÑEDA, JUAN DE
1908   *Descripción de la Provincia de Guatemala: año 1594,* Colección de Libros y Documentos referentes a la Historia de América, 8, Madrid, 417-71

1925   *Descripción de la Provincia de Guatemala: año 1594,* Anales de la Sociedad Geographía e Historia de Guatemala, I, 327-63, Guatemala

PIÑEDA, V.
1888   *Historia de las sublevaciones indígenas habidas en el Estado de Chiapas,* San Cristóbal de Las Casas

PIZARRO, HERNANDO
1872   *Letter from Hernando Pizarro to the Royal Audience of Santo Domingo* [1533], in C. R. Markham (trans. and ed) *Reports of the discovery of Peru,* Hakluyt Society, 47, 113-27, London

PIZARRO, PEDRO
1921   *Relation of the Discovery and Conquest of the Kingdoms of Peru* [1572], trans. and ed. P. A. Means, Cortés Society, 2 volumes, New York

PLAFKER, G.
1963   "Observations on archaeological remains in northeastern Bolivia" *American Antiquity,* 28, 372-78

PLATT, R. S.
1942   *Latin America,* New York and London

POINDEXTER, M.
1930   *The Ayer-Incas,* 2 volumes, New York

POLO DE ONDEGARDO, JUAN
1873   *Report of the lineage of the Yncas, and how they extended their conquests* [c. 1560], trans. and ed. C. R. Markham, Hakluyt Society, 48, 151-71, London

POMA DE AYALA, FELIPE GAUMÁN
1936   *Nueva corónica y buen gobierno* [1615] — codex péruvien illustré (Renseignements sommaires par R. Pietschmann. Traduction française par M. A. Monges. Univ. de Paris. Travaux et mém. de l'Inst. d'Ethnol., 23) Facsimile, Paris

POMAR, JUAN BAUTISTA
1891   *Relación de Texcoco* [1582], ed. Joaquín García Icazbalceta in *Nueva Colección de Documentos para la Historia de México,* 3, México, 1-69 (re-issued 1941)

PONCE, ALONSO
1873   *Relación Breve y Verdadera de Algunas Cosas de las Muchas que Sucedieron al Padre Fray Alonso Ponce en las Provincias de la Nueva España* [1584-92], 2 volumes, Madrid

1932   *Fray Alonso Ponce in Yucatan, 1588,* trans. and ed. E. Noyes, Department of Middle American Research, Tulane University, Middle American Papers, New Orleans, 297-372

PORTER, P. W.
1965   "Environmental potentials and economic opportunities: a background for cultural adaptation" *American Anthropologist,* 67, 409-20

PORTIG, W. H.
1965   "Central American Rainfall" *Geographical Review,* 55, 68-90

POZAS, R.
1959   *Chamula: un pueblo Indio de los Altos de Chiapas,* Memorias del Instituto Nacional Indigenista, 8, México

PRADO, J.
1941   *Estado social del Perú durante la dominación española* [1844], Lima

PRICE, BARBARA J.
1971   "Prehispanic irrigation agriculture in Nuclear America" *Latin American Research Review,* 6, 3-60

PRICE, R.
1968   "Land use in a Maya community" *International Archives of Ethnography,* 51, 1-19

PULGAR VIDAL, J.
n.d.   *Geografía del Perú: las ocho regiones naturales del Perú,* Lima

PUTNAM, F. W.
1883   "Notes on copper implements from Mexico" *Proceedings of the American Antiquarian Society,* 2, 235-46

RADIN, P.
1920   "The sources and authenticity of the history of the ancient Mexicans" *University of California Publications in American Ethnology and Archaeology,* 17, 1-150, Berkeley and Los Angeles

RAIKES, R.
1967   *Water, weather and prehistory,* London

RAIMONDI, A.
1874   *El Perú,* Lima

1908   *Itinerario de los viajes de Raimondi en el Perú* [1864], Boletín de la Sociedad Geográfica de Lima, 24, 449-78

RAMÍREZ, BALTASAR
1936   *Description del Reyno del Piru* [1597], in H. Trimborn *Quellen zur Kulturgeschichte des präkolumbischen Amerika,* Stuttgart, 1-122

RAMOS GAVILÁN, ALONSO
1621   *Historia del célebre santuario de Nuestra Señora de Copacabana,* Lima

1886   *Historia de Copacabana,* ed. R. Sans, La Paz

RATZEL, F.
1891   *Anthropogeographie,* 2 volumes, Stuttgart

RECLUS, E.
1881   *Voyage à la Sierra Nevada de Sainte-Marthe,* Paris

REDFIELD, R., and A. VILLA
1939   *Notes on the ethnography of Tzeltal Communities of Chiapas,* Carnegie Institution of Washington, Contributions to American Anthropology and History, 28, publication 509, Washington

REED, E. K.
1964   "The Greater Southwest" in J. D. Jennings and E. Norbeck (eds) *Prehistoric Man in the New World,* Chicago, 175-92

REED, H. S.
1938   "Ixtlilxochitl II and Cempoallan: a preliminary study of a Mexican picture chronicle" *Hispanic American Historical Review,* 18, 66-75

REED, H. S. (continued)
1944   "An account of sixteenth century agriculture on the Mexican Plateau" *Journal of the Washington Academy of Sciences*, 34, 209-13

REGAL, A.
1943   "Los acueductos precolombinos de Nasca" *Revista de la Universidad Católica del Perú*, XI, 210-13

1945   "Politica hidráulica del imperio incaico" *Revista de la Universidad Católica del Perú*, XIII, 75-110

1970   *Los trabajos hidráulicas del Inca en el antiguo Perú*, Lima

REICHEL-DOLMATOFF, G.
1950   *Los Kogi*, Bogotá

1953   "Contactos y Cambios Culturales en la Sierra Nevada de Santa Marta" *Revista Colombiana de Antropología*, I, 15-122

1954a   "A preliminary study of space and time perspective in northern Colombia" *American Antiquity*, 19, 352-66

1954b   "Investigaciones arqueológicas en la Sierra Nevada de Santa Marta" *Revista Colombiana de Antropología*, 2, 154-206; 3, 141-70

1961   "The agricultural basis of the sub-Andean chiefdoms of Colombia" in J. Wilbert (ed) *The evolution of horticultural systems in native South America: causes and consequences*, Antropológica, supplement 2, Caracas, 83-100

1965   *Colombia*, London

REICHEL-DOLMATOFF, G. and A.
1951   *Investigaciones arqueológicas en el Departamento de Magdalena, Colombia, 1946-50*, Bogotá

1959   "La Mesa: un complejo arqueológico de la Sierra Nevada de Santa Marta" *Revista Colombiana de Antropología*, 8, 159-213

1961   *The people of Aritama: the cultural personality of a Colombian mestizo village*, London

REICHLEN, H.
1942   "Contribution a l'étude de la métallurgie précolombienne de la province d'Esmeraldas (Equateur)" *Journal de la Société des Americanistes de Paris*, 34, 201-28

REICHLEN, H. and P.
1950   "Recherches archéologiques dans les Andes du Haut Utcubamba" *Journal de la Société des Americanistes de Paris*, 39, 219-46

REINA, R. E.
1967   "Milpas and milperos: implications for prehistoric times" *American Anthropologist*, 69, 1-20

REMESAL, ANTONIO DE
1964-66 *Historia general de las Indias Occidentales y particular de la Gobernación de Chiapa y Guatemala* [1619], Biblioteca de autores Españoles, 175, 189, Madrid

REPARAZ, G. DE
1958   "La zone aride du Pérou" *Geografiska Annaler*, 40, 1-62

RESTREPO, V.
1895   *Las Chibchas antes de la Conquista Española*, 2 volumes, Bogotá

RESTREPO TIRADO, E.
1892a   *Ensayo etnográfico y arqueológico de la provincia de los Quimbayas en el Nuevo Reino de Granada*, Bogotá

1892b   *Estudios sobre los aborigines de Colombia*, Bogotá

RETINGER, J. H.
1928   *Tierra Mexicana: the history of land and agriculture in ancient and modern Mexico*, London

REYES, V.
1888   "Las ruinas de Tetzcutzinco" *Boletín de la Sociedad Mexicana de Geografía y Estadística*, I, 129-50

RICE, D. S.
1974   *The archaeology of British Honduras: a review and synthesis*, KATUNOB occasional publications in Mesoamerican anthropology, no. 6, University of Northern Colorado, Department of Anthropology, mimeographed

RICKETSON, O. G.
1940   "The Cuchumatanes revisited" *Scientific Monthly*, 51, 341-57

RICKETSON, O. G. and E. B.
1937   "Uaxactum, Guatemala" *Carnegie Institution of Washington*, publication 477, 2-3, 10-12

RICKETTS, C. A.
1952   "El cocaismo en el Perú" *América Indígena*, 12, 309-22

RIVERO Y USTARIZ, M. E. DE and J. J. VON TSCHUDI
1853   *Peruvian Antiquities*, New York

RIVET, P., and H. ARSANDAUX
1921   "Métallurgie mexicaine" *Journal de la Société des Americanistes de Paris*, 13, 261-80

1946   *La métallurgie en Amerique précolombienne*, Travaux et Mémoires de l'Institut d'Ethnologie, 39, Paris

ROBERTSON, D.
1959   *Mexican manuscript painting of the early Colonial Period: The Metropolitan Schools*, New Haven

RODRÍGUEZ Y FREILE, JUAN
1961   *The Conquest of New Granada* [1636], London

ROHMEDER, G.
1955   "Topoclimas y sus relaciones con relieve, vegetación y culturas en el Valle de Tafí" *Boletín de Estudios Geográficos* (Universidad Nacional de Cuyo), 2, 235-53

ROHN, A. H.
1963   "Prehistoric soil and water conservation on Chapin Mesa, South West Colorado" *American Antiquity*, 28, 441-56

ROJAS PONCE, P.
1966   "Un informe sobre las ruinas de Pajatén" *Cuadernos Americanos*, 148, 119-27

1967   "The ruins of Pajatén" *Archaeology*, 20, 9-17

ROJAS, T., R. A. STRAUSS, and J. LAMEIRAS
1974   *Nuevas noticias sobre las obras hidráulicas prehispánicas y coloniales en el Valle de México*, Instituto Nacional de Antropología e Historia, México

ROMERO, E.
1928   *Monografía del Departamento de Puno*, Lima
1929   "El aspecto económico de los antiguos andenes peruanos" *Revista Economica y Financiera* (Lima), 3-6

ROMNEY, D. H. (ed)
1959   *Land in British Honduras*, Colonial Research Publication, 24, H.M.S.O., London

RON, Z.
1966   "Agricultural terraces in the Judean Mountains" *Israel Exploration Journal*, 16, 33-49, 111-22

ROSEN, E. VON
1905   "Archaeological researches on the frontier of Argentina and Bolivia in 1901-02" *Annual Report of the Smithsonian Institution for 1904*, Washington, 573-81 (also Stockholm, 1904)
1924   *Popular account of archaeological research during the Swedish Chaco-Cordillera expedition, 1901-2*, Stockholm

ROSENBLAT, A.
1954   *La población indígena y el mestizaje en América*, 2 volumes, Buenos Aires
1967   *La población de América en 1492: viejos y nuevos cálculos*, Publicaciones del Centro de Estudios Históricos, I, México

ROSSEL CASTRO, A.
1942   "Sistema de irrigación antigua del Río Grande de Nasca" *Revista del Museo Nacional* (Lima), 11, 196-202

ROUSE, I.
1939   *Prehistory in Haiti*, Yale University Publications in Anthropology, 21, New Haven
1956   "Settlement patterns in the Caribbean Area" in G. R. Willey (ed) *Prehistoric settlement patterns in the New World*, Viking Fund Publications in Anthropology, 23, New York, 165-72

ROUSE, I., and J. M. CRUXENT
1958   *An archaeological chronology of Venezuela*, 2 volumes
1963   *Venezuelan Archaeology*, London

ROWE, J. H.
1944   *An introduction to the archaeology of Cuzco*, Papers of the Peabody Museum of American Archaeology and Ethnology, 27, Cambridge, Mass.
1946   "Inca culture at the time of the Spanish Conquest" in J. H. Steward (ed) *Handbook of South American Indians*, 2, Smithsonian Institution, Bureau of American Ethnology, Bulletin 143, Washington, 183-330
1949   "The kingdom of Chimor" *Acta Americana*, 6, 26-59
1957   "The Incas under Spanish Colonial Institutions" *Hispanic American Historical Review*, 37, 155-99
1963   "Urban settlements in ancient Peru" *Ñawpa Pacha*, I, 1-27
1966   "Diffusionism and archaeology" *American Antiquity*, 31, 334-37

ROYS, R. L.
1943   *The Indian background of Colonial Yucatan*, Carnegie Institution of Washington, publication 548, Washington

RUIZ, HIPÓLITO
1940   *Travels of Ruiz, Pavón and Dombey in Peru and Chile (1777-88)*, translated by B. E. Dahlgren, Field Museum of Natural History, Botanical Series, 21, Chicago

RYCROFT, W. S.
1946   *Indians of the High Andes*, New York

RYDÉN, S.
1944   *Contribution to the archaeology of the Río Loa Region*, Göteborg
1947   *Archaeological researches in the highlands of Bolivia*, Göteborg
1952   "Chullpa Pampa — a pre-Tiahuanaco archaeological site in the Cochabamba region, Bolivia: a preliminary report" *Ethnos*, 17, 39-50

SABOGAL WIESSE, J. R.
1961   "La comunidad indígena de Pucará" *América Indígena*, 21, 39-63

SÁENZ, M.
1933   *Sobre el Indio Peruano*, México

SÁENZ, N.
1938   *La coca*, Lima

SAFFORD, W. E.
1917   "Narcotic plants and stimulants of ancient Americans" *Annual Report of the Smithsonian Institution for 1916*, Washington, 387-424

SAHAGÚN, BERNARDINO DE
1905-7 *Historia general de las cosas de Nueva España* [c. 1570], ed. F. del Paso y Troncoso, 4 volumes, Madrid
1950-63 *Florentine Codex: General History of the Things of New Spain* [c. 1570], eds. C. E. Dibble and A. J. O. Anderson, University of Utah, Monographs of the School of American Research, 14, and the Museum of New Mexico, Santa Fé, 10 volumes (12 books)
1956   *Historia general de las cosas de Nueva España* [c. 1570], ed. A. M. Garibay, 4 volumes, México

SALAMAN, R. N.
1949   *The history and social influence of the potato*, Cambridge

SALAS, J. C.
1916   *Etnología e Historia de Tierra Firme: Venezuela y Colombia*, Madrid
1956   *Etnografía de Venezuela*, Universidad de los Andes, Mérida

SAN ANTON MUÑÓN, FRANCISCO DE [CHIMALPAHIN CAUHTLEHUANITZIN]
1965   *Relaciones originales del Chalco Amaquemecan escritas por Don Francisco de San Antón Muñón* [c. 1607], ed. and trans. from Náhuatl by S. Rendón, México and Buenos Aires

SANCHO DE LA HOZ, PEDRO
1917   *An account of the Conquest of Peru* [1535], trans. and ed. P. A. Means, Cortés Society, New York

SANDERS, W. T.
1956   "The Central Mexican Symbiotic Region: A study in prehistoric settlement patterns" in G. R. Willey (ed) *Prehistoric settlement patterns in the New World,* Viking Fund Publications in Anthropology, 23, New York, 115-27

1962   "Cultural ecology of Nuclear Mesoamerica" *American Anthropologist,* 64, 34-44

1965   *The cultural ecology of the Teotihuacán Valley: A preliminary report of the results of the Teotihuacán Valley project,* Department of Sociology and Anthropology, Pennsylvania State University, mimeographed

1968   "Hydraulic agriculture, economic symbiosis and the evolution of states in Central Mexico" in B. J. Meggers (ed) *Anthropological Archaeology in the Americas,* Anthropological Society of Washington, Washington, 88-107

1971   "Settlement patterns in central Mexico" in G. F. Ekholm and I. Bernal (eds) *Handbook of Middle American Indians,* 10, Austin, 3-44

SANDERS, W. T., and J. MARINO
1970   *New World Prehistory,* Englewood Cliffs, New Jersey

SANDERS, W. T., and B. J. PRICE
1968   *Mesoamerica: the evolution of a civilization,* New York

SANOJA, M.
1963   "Cultural development in Venezuela" in B. J. Meggers and C. Evans (eds) *Aboriginal Cultural Development in Latin America: An Interpretative Review,* Smithsonian Miscellaneous Collections, 146, Washington, 67-76

SANTA CRUZ, A. M.
1940   "Land tenure in pre-Inca Peru" *New Mexico Anthropologist,* 4, 2-10

SANTA CRUZ PACHACUTI-YAMQUI SALCAMAYHUA, JUAN DE
1873   *An account of the antiquities of Peru* [c. 1613], trans. and ed. C. R. Markham, Hakluyt Society, 48

1927   *Relación de Antiguedades deste Reyno del Pirú* [c. 1613], ed. H. H. Urteaga in *Colección de Libros y Documentos referentes a la Historia del Perú,* second series, volume 9, 127-235, Lima

SANTAMARÍA, M.
1912   *Las chinampas del Distrito Federal,* México

SANTAMARINA, E. B. DE
1945   *Notas a la antropogeografía del valle de Tafí,* Universidad de Tucumán, Instituto de Estudios Geográficos

SANTILLÁN, HERNANDO DE
1879   *Relación del orígen, descendencia, política y gobierno de los Incas* [1615-21], in M. Jiménez de la Espada (ed) *Tres relaciones de antigüedades peruanas,* Madrid, 11-133

SANTO TOMÁS, DOMINGO DE
1560   *Gramática o arte de la lengua general de los indios de los reynos del Perú,* Valladolid

SAPPER, K.
1910   "Der Feldbau mittelamerikanischer Indianer" *Globus,* 97, 8-10

1932   "Klimakunde von Mittelamerika" in W. Köppen and R. Geiger (eds) *Handbuch der Klimatologie,* 2, Teil H, Berlin

1934   "Geographie der altindianischen Landwirtschaft" *Petermann's Mitteilungen,* 80, 41-44, 80-83, 118-21

1936   *Geographie und Geschichte der indianischen Landwirtschaft,* Ibero-amerikanischer Institut, Hamburg

1938   *Beiträge zur Kenntnis der Besitzergreifung Amerikas und zur Entwicklung der altamerikanischen Landwirtschaft durch die Indianer,* Mitteilungen aus dem Museum für Volkerkunde in Hamburg, 19

SARAVIA, A. (ed)
1965   *Popol Vuh: antiguas historias de los indios Quiches de Guatemala: illustradas con dibujos de los codices mayas,* México

SARMIENTO DE GAMBOA, PEDRO
1907   *History of the Incas* [1572], trans. and ed. C. R. Markham, Hakluyt Society, 22, London

SAUER, C. O.
1933   *Aboriginal distribution of languages and tribes in Northwest Mexico,* Ibero Americana, 5, University of California, Berkeley

1935   *Aboriginal population of Northwest Mexico,* Ibero Americana, 10, University of California, Berkeley

1941   "The personality of Mexico" *Geographical Review,* 31, 353-64

1948   *Colima of New Spain in the sixteenth century,* Ibero Americana, 29, University of California, Berkeley

1950a   "Grassland climax, fire and man" *Journal of Range Management,* 3, 16-21

1950b   "Cultivated plants of South and Central America" in J. H. Steward (ed) *Handbook of South American Indians,* 6, Smithsonian Institution, Bureau of American Ethnology, Bulletin 143, Washington, 487-543

1957-8   "Man in the ecology of Tropical America" *Proceedings of the Ninth Pacific Science Congress,* 20, 105-10 (reprinted in J. Leighly, ed., *Land and Life,* 1963, 182-93)

SAUER, C. O., and D. BRAND
1931   *Prehistoric settlement of Sonora with special reference to Cerros de Trincheras,* University of California Publications in Geography, 5, Berkeley and Los Angeles

SAVILLE, M. H.
1907-10   *The Antiquities of Manabí, Ecuador,* 2 volumes, New York

SAYLES, E. B.
1936   *An archaeological survey of Chihuahua, Mexico,* Medallion Papers, 22, Globe, Arizona

SCHILLING, E.
1939   *Die "schwimmenden Gärten" von Xochimilco,* Schriften des Geographischen Instituts der Universität Kiel, 9 (3)

SCHMIDT, M.
1918   "Verhältnis zwischen Form und Gebrauchzweck bei sudamerikanischen Sachgütern, besonders den keulenförmigen Holtzgeräten" *Zeitschrift für Ethnolgie,* 50, 12-39

SCHMIDT, M. (continued)
1923a   "Los comienzos de la agricultura en la América del Sur" *Inca,* I, 960-70

1923b   *Die Materielle Wirtschaft bei den Naturvölkern,* Leipzig

1951   "Anotaciones sobre las plantas de cultivo y los metodos de la agricultura de los Indígenas Sudamericanos" *Revista do Museu Paulista,* 5, São Paulo, 239-52

SCHMIDTMEYER, P.
1824   *Travels into Chile, over the Andes, in the years 1820 and 1821,* London

SCHMIEDER, O.
1926   *The East Bolivian Andes south of the Río Grande or Guapay,* University of California Publications in Geography, 2, Berkeley and Los Angeles

1930   *The settlements of the Zapotec and the Mije Indians, State of Oaxaca, Mexico,* University of California Publications in Geography, 4, Berkeley and Los Angeles

1932   *Länderkunde Sudamerikas,* Leipzig

1934a   *Länderkunde Mittelamerikas,* Leipzig

1934b   "Der Einfluss des Agrarsystems der Tzapoteken, Azteken und Mije auf die Kulturentwicklung dieser Völker" *XXIV International Congress of Americanists* (Hamburg, 1930): *Proceedings,* 109-11

1965   *Geografía de América Latina,* México

SCHOLES, F. V., and E. B. ADAMS (eds)
1958   *Documentos para la historia del México colonial, V; Sobre el modo de tributar los indios de Nueva España a Su Majestad, 1561-1564,* México

SCHROEDER, A. H.
1966   "Pattern diffusion from Mexico into the South West after AD 600" *American Antiquity,* 31, 683-704

SCHULMAN, S.
1956   "Land tenure among the aborigines of Latin America" *The Americas,* 13, 43-67

SCHUMACHER, P.
1882   "An ancient fortification in Sonora, Mexico" *The American Antiquarian and Oriental Journal,* 4, 227-29

SEARS, P. B.
1953a   "The interdependence of archaeology and ecology, with examples from Middle America" *Transactions of the New York Academy of Sciences,* 15, 113-17

1953b   "An ecological view of land use in Middle America" *Ceiba* (Tegucigalpa), 3, 157-65

SEIFRIZ, W.
1934   "The Sierra Nevada de Santa Marta" *Geographical Review,* 24, 478-85

SELER, E.
1901   *Die Alten Ansiedelungen von Chaculá,* Berlin

1901-2   *Codex Fejérváry-Mayer,* Berlin and London

1904   *The Mexican Picture Writings of Alexander Von Humboldt in the Royal Library at Berlin,* Smithsonian Institution, Bureau of American Ethnology, Bulletin 28, Washington

1960   *Gesammelte Abhandlungen zur amerikanischen Sprach-und Alterumskunde,* 5 volumes, Graz

SHANAN, L. S., N. T. TADMOR, and M. E. EVANARI
1958   "Ancient desert agriculture in the Negev, II: utilization of runoff from small watersheds in the Abde (Ovdat) region" *Ktavim,* 9, 107-29

SHERBONDY DE TORD, J.
1969   "El regadío en el área andina central, ensayo de distribución geográfica" *Revista española de Antropología Americana,* 4, 113-43

SHETRONE, H. C.
1930   *The Mound Builders,* New York and London (republished 1964)

SHIPPEE, R.
1932a   "The Great Wall of Peru" and other aerial photographic studies by the Shippee-Johnson Peruvian expedition" *Geographical Review,* 22, 1-29

1932b   "Lost valleys of Peru: results of the Shippee-Johnson Peruvian Expedition" *Geographical Review,* 22, 562-81

SHOOK, E. M.
1952   "Lugares arqueológicos de altiplano meridional central de Guatemala" *Antropología e Historia de Guatemala,* 4, 3-40

1956   "An archaeological reconnaissance in Chiapas, Mexico" *New World Archaeological Foundation,* publication 1, 20-37, Orinda

SIEMANS, A. H., and D. E. PULESTON
1972   "Ridged fields and associated features in southern Campeche: new perspectives on the lowland Maya" *American Antiquity,* 37, 228-39

SIEVERS, W.
1887   *Reise in der Sierra Nevada de Santa Marta,* Leipzig

1914   *Reise in Peru und Ecuador,* Wissenschaftliche Veroffentlichungen der Gesellschaft für Erdkunde zu Leipzig, 8

SIMÓN, PEDRO
1882-92   *Noticias historiales de las conquistas de Tierra Firme en las Indias Occidentales* [1626], 5 volumes in 2, Bogotá

SIMPSON, L. B.
1934   *Studies in the administration of the Indians in New Spain, II: The Civil Congregation,* Ibero Americana, 7, University of California, Berkeley

1938   *Studies in the administration of the Indians in New Spain, III: The Repartimiento System of Native Labor in New Spain and Guatemala,* Ibero Americana, 13, University of California, Berkeley

1952   *Exploitation of land in Central Mexico in the sixteenth century,* Ibero Americana, 36, University of California, Berkeley

SMITH, A. L.
1955   *Archaeological reconnaissance in Central Guatemala,* Carnegie Institution of Washington, Contributions to American Anthropology and History, publication 608, Washington

SMITH, A. L., and A. V. KIDDER
1943   *Explorations in the Motagua Valley, Guatemala,* Carnegie Institution of Washington, Contributions to American Anthropology and History, publication 546, Washington, 101-82

SMITH, C. E.
1965   *Agriculture, Tehuacán Valley,* Chicago Natural History Museum, Fieldiana (Botany), 31

SMITH, C. T.
1960   "Aspects of agriculture and settlement in Peru" *Geographical Journal,* 126, 397-412

1970   "Depopulation of the central Andes in the sixteenth century" *Current Anthropology,* 11, 453-64

1971   "The central Andes" in H. Blakemore and C. T. Smith (eds) *Latin America: Geographical Perspectives,* London, 263-334

SMITH, C. T., W. M. DENEVAN, and P. HAMILTON
1968   "Ancient ridged fields in the region of Lake Titicaca" *Geographical Journal,* 134, 353-67

SMYTH, W., and F. LOWE
1836   *Narrative of a journey from Lima to Para (1834-5),* London

SOKOLOFF, V. P., and J. L. LORENZO
1953   "Modern and ancient soils at some archaeological sites in the Valley of Mexico" *American Antiquity,* 19, 50-55

SONNENFELD, J.
1962   "Interpreting the function of primitive implements" *American Antiquity,* 28, 56-65

SORIA LENS, L.
1954   "La ciencia agrícola de los antiguos Aymaras" *Boletín de la Sociedad Geográfica de La Paz,* 64, 85-101

SPENCER, J. E.
1964   "The development and spread of agricultural terracing in China" in S. G. Davis (ed) *Symposium on land use and mineral deposits in Hong Kong, Southern China and South East Asia,* Hong Kong, 105-10

SPENCER, J. E., and G. A. HALE
1961   "The origin, nature and distribution of agricultural terracing" *Pacific Viewpoint,* 2, 1-40

SPICER, E. H.
1961   "The Yaqui" in E. H. Spicer (ed) *Perspectives in American Indian Culture Change,* Chicago, 7-93

SPINDEN, H. J.
1928   "The population of ancient America" *Geographical Review,* 18, 641-60

SPORES, R.
1965   "The Zapotec and Mixtec at Spanish Contact" in G. R. Willey (ed) *Handbook of Middle American Indians,* 3, Austin, 962-87

1967   *The Mixtec Kings and their People,* Norman

1969   "Settlement, farming technology, and environment in the Nochixtlán Valley" *Science,* 166, 557-69

SQUIER, E. G.
1851   "Use of copper by the American aborigines" *Smithsonian Institution, Contributions to Knowledge,* 2, Washington, 176-87

1877   *Peru: incidents of travel and exploration in the land of the Inca,* London

STADELMAN, R.
1940   *Maize cultivation in North West Guatemala,* Carnegie Institution of Washington, Contributions to American Anthropology and History, publication 523, Washington, 83-263

STANDLEY, P. C., and J. A. STEYERMARK
1943   "The vegetation of Guatemala: a brief review" *Chronica Botanica,* 7, 315-18

STANISLAWSKI, D.
1962   "The Monchique of Southern Portugal" *Geographical Review,* 52, 37-55

STEARN, E. W. and A. E.
1945   *The effect of smallpox on the destiny of the Amerindian,* Boston

STEENSBERG, A.
1960   "Plough and Field Shape" in A. F. Wallace (ed) *Man and Cultures,* Philadelphia

STEFFEN, M.
1883   *Die Landwirtschaft bei den altamerikanischen Kulturvölkern,* Leipzig

STEIN, W. W.
1961   *Hualcan: Life in the highlands of Peru,* Cornell Studies in Anthropology, Ithaca

STEPHENS, J. L.
1963   *Incidents of Travel in Yucatan* [1843], 2 volumes, New York

STERNBERG, H. O'REILLY
1968   "Man and environmental change in South America" in E. J. Fittgau (ed) *Biogeography and Ecology in South America,* I, Monographiae Biologicae, 18, The Hague, 413-42

STEVENS, R. L.
1964   "The soils of Middle America and their relation to Indian peoples and cultures" in R. C. West (ed) *Handbook of Middle American Indians,* I, Austin, 265-315

STEWARD, J. H.
1949   "South American Cultures: an interpretative summary" in J. H. Steward (ed) *Handbook of South American Indians,* 5, Smithsonian Institution, Bureau of American Ethnology, Bulletin 143, Washington, 669-772

STEWARD, J. H., and L. C. FARON
1959   *Native Peoples of South America,* New York

STEWART, G. R.
1940   "Conservation in Pueblo Agriculture" *Scientific Monthly,* 51, 201-20, 329-40

STEWART, G. R., and M. DONNELLY
1943   "Soil and Water Economy in the Pueblo South West" *Scientific Monthly,* 56, 31-44, 134-44

STONE, D.
1957   *The archaeology of Central and Southern Honduras,* Papers of the Peabody Museum of American Archaeology and Ethnology, 49, Cambridge, Mass.

1966   "Synthesis of Lower Central American Ethnohistory" in G. F. Ekholm and G. R. Willey (eds) *Handbook of Middle American Indians,* 4, Austin, 209-33

STUMER, L. M.
1954   "Population centers of the Rimac Valley in Peru" *American Antiquity,* 22, 130-48

STURTEVANT, W. C.
1961   "Taino Agriculture" in J. Wilbert (ed) *The Evolution of Horticultural Systems in Native North America: causes and consequences,* Antropológica, supplement 2, Caracas, 69-82

SUÁREZ POLAR, M. G.
1934   "Machu Picchu" *Revista de la Universidad de Arequipa*, 7, 9-19

SUETTA, J. M.
1967   "Construcciones agrícolas prehispánicas en Coctaca, Prov. de Jujuy" *Antiquitas* (Boletín de la Asociación Amigos del Instituto de Arqueología, Universidad del Salvador, Buenos Aires), 4, 1-9

SWANSON, E.
1955   "Terrace agriculture in the Central Andes" *Davidson Journal of Anthropology*, I, 123-32

SWINSON, T.
1955   *Excavations at Yagul, I,* Mesoamerican Notes, 4, Department of Anthropology, Mexico City College

TADMOR, N. H. T., M. EVANARI, L. SHANAN, and D. H. HILLEL
1957   "Ancient agriculture of the Negev, I: gravel mounds and strips near Shivta" *Ktavim,* 7, 127-51

TAMAYO, J. L., and R. C. WEST
1964   "The hydrography of Middle America" in R. C. West (ed) *Handbook of Middle American Indians,* I, Austin, 84-121

TAPIA, ANDRÉS DE
1963   *The Chronicle of Andrés de Tapia* [1519-20], in Patricia de Fuentes (trans. and ed.) *The Conquistadors: first-person accounts of the conquest of Mexico,* London, 17-48

TAX, S. (ed)
1952   *Heritage of Conquest: The Ethnology of Middle America,* Glencoe

TAYLOR, G.
1931   "Settlement zones of the Sierra Nevada de Santa Marta, Colombia" *Geographical Review,* 21, 539-58

TEJADA JIMÉNEZ, M.
1907   "Provincia de Sandia" *Boletín de la Sociedad Geográfica de Lima,* 21, 68-85

TELLO, J. C.
1929   *Antiguo Perú: primera época,* Lima
1956   *Arqueología del valle de Casma,* Lima

TEN KATE, H. F. C.
1894   "Anthropologie des anciens habitants de la région calchaquie" *Anales del Museo de la Plata* (Buenos Aires), Sección Antropológica, I

TESSMAN, G.
1930   *Die Indianer Nordost-Perus,* Hamburg

THIERY DE MENONVILLE, N. J.
1787   *Traité de la culture du nopal et de l'éducation de la cochenille dans les colonies françaises de l'Amérique, précédé d'un voyage à Guaxaca,* Bordeaux and Paris

THOMAS, C.
1882   *A study of the manuscript Troano,* Contributions to North American Ethnology, 5, Washington

THOMPSON, D. E.
1968a   "An archaeological evaluation of ethnohistoric evidence on Inca culture" in B. J. Meggers (ed) *Anthropological Archaeology in the Americas,* Anthropological Society of Washington, Washington, 108-20

1968b   "Incaic installations at Huánuco and Pumpu" *XXXVII International Congress of Americanists* (Mar del Plata, 1966): *Proceedings,* I, 67-74

THOMPSON, J. E.
1930a   "The causeways of the Coba District, East Yucatan" *XXIII International Congress of Americanists* (New York, 1928): *Proceedings,* 181-84

1930b   *Ethnology of the Mayas of southern and central British Honduras,* Field Museum of Natural History, publication 274, Chicago

1931   "Archaeological investigations in the southern Cayo District, British Honduras" *Field Museum of Natural History, Anthropology Series,* 17, 217-337

1936   *Archaeology of South America,* Field Museum of Natural History, Anthropology Leaflet, 33, Chicago

1965   "Archaeological synthesis of the southern Maya Lowlands" in G. R. Willey (ed) *Handbook of Middle American Indians,* 2, Austin, 331-59

TOLEDO, FRANCISCO DE
1882   *Informaciones acerca del Señorio y Gobierno de los Incas hechas por mandado de Don Francisco de Toledo Virey del Perú 1570-1572* in *Colección de libros españoles raros o curiosos,* 16, 177-259, Madrid

1925   *Ordenanzas del Virrey Don Francisco de Toledo* [1572-1577], in R. Levillier (ed) *Gobernantes del Perú,* 8, Madrid

TOLSTOY, P.
1958   *Surface survey of the northern Valley of Mexico: the Classic and post-Classic Periods,* Transactions of the American Philosophical Society, 48(5)

TORQUEMADA, JUAN DE
1723   *Monarchía Indiana* [1615], 3 volumes, Madrid

TOSI, J. A.
1960   *Zonas de vida natural en el Perú,* Boletín Técnico, 5 (Zona Andina, Proyecto 39), Lima

TOWLE, M. A.
1961   *The Ethnobotany of Pre-Columbian Peru,* Viking Fund Publications in Anthropology, 30, New York

TOWNSEND, C. H. T.
1926   "Vertical life zones of northern Peru, with crop correlations" *Ecology,* 7, 440-44

TREGANZA, A. E.
1946-7   "Possibilities of an aboriginal practice of agriculture among the southern Diegueño" *American Antiquity,* 12, 169-73

TRIANA, M.
1922   *La civilización chibcha,* Bogotá

TRIMBORN, H.
1930   "Das Recht der Chibcha in Colombien" *Ethnologica,* 4, 1-55

1936   *Quellen zur Kulturgeschichte des präkolumbischen Amerika,* Stuttgart

1959   *Das Alte Amerika,* Stuttgart

TROLL, C.
1929   "An expedition to the Central Andes, 1926-8" *Geographical Review,* 19, 234-47

1930   "Die tropischen Andenländer" in O. Maull, F. Kuhn, C. Troll, W. Knoche (eds) *Süd-Amerika in Natur, Kultur und Wirtschaft,* Handbuch der geographischen Wissenschaft, Wildpark-Potsdam, 309-462

1931   "Die geographischen Grundlagen der Andinen Kulturen und des Incareiches" *Ibero-Amerikanisches Archiv,* 5, 258-94 (also in *Revista de la Universidad de Arequipa,* 9, 1935, 127-83)

1943a   "Die Frostwechselhäufigkeit in den Luft-und Boden-Klimaten der Erde" *Meteorologische Zeitschrift,* 60, 161-71

1943b   "Die stellung der Indianer-Hochkulturen im Landschaftsaufbau der tropischen Anden" *Zeitschrift der Gesellschaft für Erdkunde zu Berlin,* 93-128

1958   "Las culturas superiores andinas y el medio geográfico" *Revista del Instituto de Geografía* (Universidad Nacional Mayor de San Marcos), 5, 3-55

1968   "The Cordilleras of the Tropical Americas" in C. Troll (ed) *Geo-Ecology of the Mountainous Regions of the Tropical Americas,* Bonn, 15-56

TRUJILLO, DIEGO DE
1948   *Relación del Descubrimiento del Reyno del Perú* [1571], ed. R. Porras Berrenechea, Sevilla

TSCHIFFELY, A. F.
1933   *Southern Cross to North Pole Star,* London
1935   *Tschiffely's Ride,* London

TSCHOPIK, H.
1946a   "The Aymara" in J. H. Steward (ed) *Handbook of South American Indians,* 2, Smithsonian Institution, Bureau of American Ethnology, Bulletin 143, Washington, 501-73

1946b   *Some notes on the archaeology of the Department of Puno, Peru,* Papers of the Peabody Museum of American Archaeology and Ethnology, 27, Cambridge, Mass.

1947   *Highland communities of Central Peru: A regional survey,* Smithsonian Institution, Institute of Social Anthropology, publication 5, Washington

1951   *The Aymara of Chucuito, Peru, I: Magic,* American Museum of Natural History, Anthropology Papers, 44, New York, 137-308

TSCHUDI, J. J. VON
1844   "On the ancient Peruvians" *Journal of the Ethnological Society of London,* I, 79-85
1847   *Travels in Peru during the years 1838-42,* London
1884   *Organismus der Khetšua-Sprache,* Leipzig

TURNER, B. L. II
1974   "Prehistoric intensive agriculture in the Mayan Lowlands" *Science,* 185, 118-24
1976   "Population density in the Classic Maya Lowlands: new evidence for old approaches" *Geographical Review,* 66, 73-82

TYLOR, E. B.
1861   *Anahuac,* London

UGARTE, C. A.
1918   *Los antecedentes históricos del régimen agrario peruano,* Lima

1924   "The economic life of ancient Peru" *Inter-America,* 8, 126-38

UHLE, M.
1889-90   *Kultur und Industrie südamerikanischer Völker,* 2 volumes, Berlin
1931   *Las antiguas civilizaciones de Manta,* Quito

ULLOA-MOGOLLÓN, JUAN DE
1885   *Relación de la Provincia de Collaguas para la discrepción de la Yndias que Su Magestad manda hacer* [1586], in M. Jiménez de la Espada (ed) *Relaciones geográficas de Indias: Perú,* 2, Madrid

URICHOECHEA, E.
1871   *Gramática, vocabulario, catecismo i confesionario de la lengua Chibcha, según antiguos manuscritos anónimos e inéditos,* Collection Linguistique Américaine, 1, Paris

VALCARCEL, L. E.
1942   "La agricultura entre los antiguos peruanos" *Revista del Museo Nacional* (Lima), 12, 1-7
1959   *Etnohistoria del Perú Antiguo,* Lima

VALDEZ DE LA TORRE, C.
1921   *Evolución de las comunidades de indígenas,* Lima

VALENTINI, J. J.
1879   "Mexican copper tools" *Proceedings of the American Antiquarian Society,* 81-112

VAN DER HAMMEN, T., and E. GONZÁLEZ
1960   "Upper Pleistocene and Holocene Climate and Vegetation of the Sabana de Bogotá" *Leidse Geologische Mededelingen,* 25, 261-315

VARGAS, C.
1936   "El solanum tuberosum a través del desenvolvimiento de las actividades humanas" *Revista del Museo Nacional* (Lima), 5, 193-248

VARGAS MACHUCA, BERNARDO DE
1599   *Milicia y descripción de las Yndias,* Madrid

VÁSQUEZ DE ESPINOSA, ANTONIO
1942   *Compendio y descripción de las Indias del Perú y Nueva España* [c. 1628] (translated into English by C. U. Smith), Smithsonian Miscellaneous Collections, 102, Washington

VEGA, A. G.
1927   *Ruinas de Tizatlán,* Tlaxcala, México

VELLARD, J. A.
1963   *Civilisations des Andes: évolution des populations du haut plateau bolivien,* Paris

VERNEAU, R., and P. RIVET
1922   *Ethnographie ancienne de l'Équateur,* 2 volumes, Paris

VETANCURT, AGUSTÍN DE
1960-1   *Teatro Mexicano* [1698], 4 volumes, Madrid

VILLACORTA CALDERON, J. A.
1933   *Códices Mayas,* Guatemala

VITA-FINZI, C.
1959   "A Pluvial Age in the Puna de Atacama" *Geographical Journal,* 125, 401-3

VITANGURT, D. S.
1940   "En torno a la civilización Ccarahuarina" *Boletín de la Sociedad Geográfica de Lima,* 57, 30-37

VIVO ESCOTO, J. A.
1964   "Weather and Climate of Mexico and Central America" in R. C. West (ed) *Handbook of Middle American Indians,* 1, Austin, 187-215

VOGT, W.
1946   *The population of Venezuela and its natural resources,* Pan American Union, Washington

WACHTEL, N.
1971   *La vision des vaincus: les indiens du Pérou devant la conquête espagnole, 1530-70,* Paris

WAGNER, E.
1967a   *The prehistory and ethnohistory of the Carache Area in Western Venezuela,* Yale University Publications in Anthropology, 71, New Haven

1967b   "Arqueología andina venezolana" *Revista Colombiana de Antropología,* 13, 227-37

1969   "Problemas de arqueología y etnohistoria de los Andes Venezolanos" *XXXVIII International Congress of Americanists* (Stuttgart-München, 1968): *Proceedings,* Munich, I, 281-87

WAGNER, H. O.
1968   "Die Besiedlungsdichte Zentralamerikas vor 1492 und die Ursachen des Bevölkerungsschwundes in der frühen Kolonialzeit unter besondere Berücksichtigung der Halbinsel Yucatán" *Jahrbuch für Geschichte von Staat, Wirtschaft und Gesellschaft Lateinamerikas,* 5, 63-102

1969   "Subsistence potential and population density of the Maya on the Yucatan Peninsula and causes for the decline in population in the fifteenth century" *XXXVIII International Congress of Americanists* (Stuttgart-München, 1968): *Proceedings,* Munich, I, 179-96

WAGNER, P. L.
1962   "Natural and artificial zonation in a vegetation cover: Chiapas, Mexico" *Geographical Review,* 52, 253-74

1963   "Indian economic life in Chiapas" *Economic Geography,* 39, 156-64

1964   "Natural vegetation of Middle America" in R. C. West (ed) *Handbook of Middle American Indians,* I, Austin, 216-64

WAIBEL, L.
1946   *La Sierra Madre de Chiapas,* México

WALCOTT, F. C.
1925   "An expedition to the Laguna Colorada, Southern Bolivia" *Geographical Review,* 15, 345-66

WALGER, T.
1917   "Die Coca, ihre Geschichte, geographische verbreitung und wirtschaftliche Bedeutung" *Beihefte zum Tropenpflanzer,* 17, 1-76

WALLE, P.
1920   *Bolivia, its peoples and resources,* London

WALLÉN, C. C.
1955   "Some characteristics of precipitation in Mexico" *Geografiska Annaler,* 37, 51-85

WARD, R. DE C., and C. F. BROOKS
1934   "Climatology of the West Indies" in W. Köppen and R. Geiger (eds) *Handbuch der Klimatologie,* 2, Teil I, Berlin

WARD, R. DE C., C. F. BROOKS, and A. J. CONNOR
1938   "The climates of North America" in W. Köppen and R. Geiger (eds) *Handbuch der Klimatologie,* 2, Teil J, Berlin

WASSÉN, H.
1936   "An archaeological study of the western Colombia cordillera" *Ethnological Studies,* 2 (Göteborg), 30-67

WATTERS, R. F.
1967   "Economic backwardness in the Venezuelan Andes" *Pacific Viewpoint,* 8, 17-67

WAUCHOPE, R.
1964   "Southern Mesoamerica" in J. D. Jennings and E. Norbeck (eds) *Prehistoric Man in the New World,* Chicago

WEATHERS, K.
1946   "La agricultura de los Tzotzil de Nabenchauc, Chiapas, México" *América Indígena,* 6, 315-19

WEATHERWAX, P.
1936   "The origin of the maize plant and maize agriculture in Ancient America" in D. Brand (ed) *Symposium on Prehistoric Agriculture,* University of New Mexico, Bulletin 296, Anthropology Series, 5, 11-18, Albuquerque

WEBSTER, S. S.
1971   "Una comunidad quechua indígena en la explotación de múltiples zonas ecológicas" *Wayka,* 4-5, 55-64

WECKMANN, L.
1951   "The Middle Ages in the Conquest of America" *Speculum,* 26, 130-41

WEDDELL, H. A.
1853   *Voyage dans le Nord de la Bolivie et dans les parties voisines du Pérou,* Paris and London

WEDEL, W. R.
1964   "The Great Plains" in J. D. Jennings and E. Norbeck (eds) *Prehistoric Man in the New World,* Chicago, 193-222

WELLHAUSEN, E. J. *et. al.*
1957   *Races of maize in Central America,* National Academy of Sciences, Natural Resources Council, publication 511, Washington

WERTH, E.
1954   *Grabstock, Hacke und Pflug,* Ludwigsburg

WEST, R. C.
1935   *Geography of the Pacific Lowlands of Colombia and adjacent areas,* typescript, Department of Geography-Anthropology, Louisiana State University

1948   *Cultural geography of the modern Tarascan area,* Smithsonian Institution, Institute of Social Anthropology, publication 7, Washington

1959   "Ridge or 'era' agriculture in the Colombian Andes" *XXXIII International Congress of Americanists* (San José, 1958): *Proceedings,* I, 279-82

1964a   "Surface configuration and associated geology of Middle America" in R. C. West (ed) *Handbook of Middle American Indians,* I, Austin, 33-83

1964b   "The natural regions of Middle America" in R. C. West (ed) *Handbook of Middle American Indians,* I, Austin, 363-83

1966   "The natural vegetation of the Tabascan Lowlands, Mexico" *Revista Geográfica,* 64, 108-22

1970   "Population densities and agricultural practices in Pre-Columbian Mexico, with special emphasis on semi-terracing" *XXXVIII International Congress of Americanists* (Stuttgart-München, 1968): *Proceedings,* Munich, 2, 361-69

WEST, R. C., and P. ARMILLAS
1950   "Las chinampas de México" *Cuadernos Americanos,* 9, 165-82

WEST, R. C., and J. P. AUGELLI
1966   *Middle America: its lands and peoples,* New York

WEULE, J. K. K.
1924   *Die Urgesellschaft und ihre Lebensfürsorge,* Stuttgart

WHETTEN, N. L.
1961   *Guatemala, the land and the people,* New Haven

WICKES, D. R., and W. C. LOUDERMILK
1938   "Soil conservation in Ancient Peru" *Soil Conservation,* 4, 91-94

WIEDNER, D. L.
1959-60 "Forced Labour in Colonial Peru" *The Americas,* 16, 357-83

WIENER, C.
1880   *Pérou et Bolivie,* Paris

WILKEN, G. C.
1969   "Drained-field agriculture: an intensive farming system in Tlaxcala, Mexico" *Geographical Review,* 59, 215-41

1971   "Food-producing systems available to the ancient Maya" *American Antiquity,* 36, 432-48

WILLEY, G. R.
1955   "The prehistoric civilizations of nuclear America" *American Anthropologist,* 57, 571-93

1962   "Mesoamerica" in R. J. Braidwood and G. R. Willey (eds) *Courses toward Urban Life,* Edinburgh, 84-105

1964   "An hypothesis on the process of Mesoamerican agricultural development" in *Homenaje a Fernando Márquez Miranda,* Madrid, 378-87

1966a   *An Introduction to American Archaeology: I — Middle and North America,* Englewood Cliffs, New Jersey

1966b   "Postlude to village agriculture: the rise of towns and temples and the beginnings of the great traditions" *XXXVI International Congress of Americanists* (Sevilla, 1964): *Proceedings,* I, 267-77

WILLEY, G. R., W. R. BALLARD, J. B. GLASS, and J. C. GIFFORD
1965   *Prehistoric Maya settlements in the Belize Valley,* Papers of the Peabody Museum of Archaeology and Ethnology, 54

WILLEY, G. R., G. F. EKHOLM, and R. E. MILLON
1964   "The patterns of farming life and civilization" in R. C. West (ed) *Handbook of Middle American Indians,* I, Austin, 446-98

WOLF, E. R.
1955   "The Mexican Bajío in the eighteenth century" *Middle American Research Institute, Tulane University, publication 17,* New Orleans, 177-200

1959   *Sons of the Shaking Earth,* Chicago

WOLF, E. R., and A. PALERM
1955   "Irrigation in the old Acolhua domain, Mexico" *Southwestern Journal of Anthropology,* 11, 265-81

WOLLASTON, A. F. R.
1925   "The Sierra Nevada of Santa Marta" *Geographical Journal,* 66, 97-111

WOODBURY, R. B.
1961a   *Prehistoric agriculture at Point of Pines, Arizona,* Memoirs of the Society for American Archaeology, 17, Menasha

1961b   "A reappraisal of Hohokam irrigation" *American Anthropologist,* 63, 550-60

1962   "Systems of irrigation and water control in arid North America" *XXXIV International Congress of Americanists* (Vienna, 1960): *Proceedings,* 301-5

1966   "Prehistoric water management systems in the Tehuacán valley, Mexico" *XXXVI International Congress of Americanists* (Sevilla, 1964): *Proceedings,* I, 345-47

WOODBURY, R. B. and N. F. S.
1964   "The changing pattern of Papago land use" *XXXV International Congress of Americanists* (Mexico, 1962): *Proceedings,* 181-86

WRIGHT, A. C. S.
1962   "Some terrace systems of the western hemisphere and Pacific Islands" *Pacific Viewpoint,* 3, 97-100; comment by J. E. Spencer, 101-105

1963   "The soil process and the evolution of agriculture in Northern Chile" *Pacific Viewpoint,* 4, 65-74

WYLIE, K. H.
1942   *The agriculture of Colombia,* Bulletin of the United States Department of Agriculture, I, Washington

XÉREZ, FRANCISCO DE
1872   *Narrative of the Conquest of Peru* [1534], trans. and ed. C. R. Markham, Hakluyt Society, 47, London

YAZAWA, T.
1960   "Climatological survey of the Central Andes" in E. Ishida *et al. Andes I: the report of the University of Tokyo Scientific Expedition to the Andes in 1958,* Tokyo, 412-14

ZÁRATE, AGUSTÍN DE
1581   *The strange and delectable history of the discovery and conquest of the provinces of Peru* [1555], trans. T. Nicholas, 4 volumes in 1, London

1853   *Historia del descubrimiento y conquista de la provincia del Perú* [1555], Biblioteca de Autores Españoles, 26, Madrid, 459-574

n.d.   *Historia del descubrimiento y conquista del Perú* [1555], ed. J. M. Kermenić, Lima

ZEGARRA, J. M.
  1953   "Irrigación y técnica en el Perú precolombino" *Letras* (Lima), no. 49, 173-4

ZEVALLOS, G. D.
  1929   "Contribución al estudio geográfico-económico de los andenes Peruanos" *Revista Economía y Financiera,* 115-19

ZOHARY, D.
  1954   "Notes on ancient agriculture in the Central Negev" *Israel Exploration Journal,* 4, 17-25

ZUCCHI, A.
  1972   "Aboriginal earth structures of the western Venezuelan Llanos" *Caribbean Journal of Science,* 12, 95-99

INDEX

Abancay, 27
Abelardo San Rodríguez, 75
Abiseo, Río: valley of, 94
Acequias, 84
Achambo, 94
Achiutla, 20, 62, 65
Acolhua, Acolhuacán, 17, 20, 42
Acolman, 42
Acora, 121
Acosta, Joaquín, 88
Adams, R. M., 30, 74
Adams, R. N., 28
Adzes, 15, 124
Africa:
　Negro, 3
　Northwest, 21
　Southern, 3
　Tropical, 3
Agriculture and horticulture. *See also*
　Camellones; Draining; Fertilizers;
　Field implements; Irrigation;
　Terraces: agricultural
　Aboriginal, 1, 2, 3, 5, 22, 131, 132
　Advanced, 1, 132
　Contour ridges, 14, 29, 76, 82
　Cultivation of slopes, 2, 3, 5, 13, 20,
　　21, 25, 26, 27, 28, 29, 30, 31, 32, 34,
　　40, 42, 56, 94, 131, 133
　Cultivo de fondo, 3
　Cultivo de humedales, 56
　Distribution of, 1, 16, 20, 22, 25,
　　27, 30, 31, 36, 42, 46, 132, 133
　Dry farming, 31
　Eras, 3, 13, 88, 124
　Excavated fields. *See Hoyas*
　Extensive, 1
　Fallow, 1, 2, 13, 14, 44, 132
　Field boundaries, 28, 30, 44, 45, 73,
　　75, 76, 78, 84, 88, 105, 111
　Field or planting ridges, 3, 5, 13,
　　19, 29, 83, 88, 94, 120, 122, 131, 133
　Garden beds, 58
　Hand cultivation, 1, 3, 5, 14, 34, 133
　House gardens, 2, 48, 50, 71, 74, 76,
　　132, 133
　Intensive, 1, 57, 82, 88, 122, 132
　Mixed cropping, 1, 2, 5
　Mound fields, 3, 5, 27, 29, 131, 133
　Retreat of, 32, 36, 38, 42, 46, 52,
　　62, 63, 65, 69, 102, 120, 126, 132,
　　133
　Rotations, 1, 2, 13
　Seed beds, 19, 57

Shifting, 1, 2, 30, 71, 132
Walled fields, 20, 41
Weeding, 5, 9, 15, 16
Aguacate *(Persea americana),* 50, 71
Aguacatenango, 6, 30, 73, 74
Aguado, Pedro de, 88
Aguán, Río: valley of, 27
Aguas Calientes, 105, 108
Aguatepec, 46
Ahuitzotl, 75
Aiquina, 126
Ajayash, 75
Ajusco, 44; 45
Ajusco, Serranía de, 39, 44
Alausí, Río: valley of, 94
Alfalfa *(Medicago sativa),* 42, 50, 71,
　112
Alfarcito, 129
Alkali Ridge, 61
Alluvial deposits, 5, 26, 29, 30, 31, 32,
　39, 40, 57, 58, 61, 69, 70, 71, 76, 85,
　101, 108, 112, 114, 131, 132
Almácigos, 41, 124
Aloapaneca, Sierra, 70
Alpacas, 29
Alva Ixtlilxochitl, Fernando de, 20
Alvarado, Pedro de, 29, 76
Amantani, island of, 121
Amatenango, 30, 73
Amatitlán, 81
Amatitlán, Lake: basin of, 28, 81, 82
Amatlán, 71
Ambato, Sierra, 130
Ambrosetti, J. B., 14
Ampajango, 129
Amulucan, 35
Ancasti, 130
Ancasti, Sierra, 130
Andahua, Río: valley of, 100
Andahuaylillas, 108
Andes, 2, 9, 10, 13, 14, 22, 26, 27, 28,
　33, 34, 35, 114, 131, 133
　Central, 2, 15, 17, 19, 22, 25, 35, 37,
　　94, 132
　Northern, 5, 6, 19, 22, 25, 34, 35,
　　84, 134
　Southern, 17, 19, 32, 126
Anghiera, Pietro Martire d', 26
Animal domestication, 1
Animal husbandry, 44, 88, 132
Animal pounds, 131
Anta *(Xaquixaguana),* basin of, 20, 105
Antabamba, 100

Antabamba, Río: valley of, 100
Antilles, 6
Antofalla, Salina de, 130
Añu *(Tropaeolum tuberosum),* 13
Apartaderos, 14
Apatzingán, 56
Apenes, O., 39
Apoala, 65
Apolobamba, Nudo de, 120, 122
Apulco, Río: valley of, 53
Apurimac, Department of, 13
Apurimac, Río: valley of, 100
Aquatic insects, 28
Araranca, 122
Araucanians, 13
Archaeological sites, 15, 25, 31, 69,
　75, 76, 94, 122
Arequipa, 19, 101, 102, 108, 134
Argentina, 3, 22, 27
　Northern, 3, 15, 22, 34, 35
　Northwest, 1, 9, 10, 14, 15, 16, 19,
　　22, 25, 32, 35, 36, 119, 126, 129, 130
Arica, 126
Aricagua, 84
Arizona, 2, 61
　Northern, 61
Arma, Río: valley of, 100
Armillas, P., 31, 36, 53
Aropaya (Independencia), 124
Arrayanes, 88
Asia, South East, 16
Atacama, 15, 16
Atacama, Puna de, 126
Atacama, Salar de, 126
Atacameño (people), 13, 35
Atatlahuacá, 66
Atcor, 20
Atitlán, Lake: basin of, 28, 34, 78, 79,
　80, 81, 134
Atlixco, 50
Atoyac, Río: valley of, 69
Auche, 20
Autlán, 31
Avila, Francisco de, 21
Axes, 9
Ayacucho, 99
Ayaviri, 122
Ayllu, 133
Aymara (people), 2, 28, 119, 120, 121,
　124
Ayutla, 70
Azada, azadón, 9, 14, 16, 76
Azangaro, 122

[187]